D1528498

The Unity of
the Common Law

Philosophy, Social Theory, and the Rule of Law

General Editors
Andrew Arato, Seyla Benhabib, Ferenc Fehér, William Forbath,
Agnes Heller, Arthur Jacobson, and Michel Rosenfeld

The Unity of
the Common Law

Studies in Hegelian Jurisprudence

Alan Brudner

UNIVERSITY OF CALIFORNIA PRESS
Berkeley   Los Angeles   London

University of California Press
Berkeley and Los Angeles, California

University of California Press
London, England

Copyright © 1995 by
The Regents of the University of California

Library of Congress Cataloging-in-Publication Data
Brudner, Alan.
    The unity of the common law: studies in Hegelian jurisprudence /
Alan Brudner.
        p.   cm.—(Philosophy, social theory, and the rule of law)
    Includes bibliographical references and index.
    ISBN 0–520–08596–5 (cloth: acid-free paper)
    1. Common law.   2. Law—Philosophy.   3. Hegel, Georg Wilhelm
Friedrich, 1770–1831—Contributions in law.   I. Title.   II. Series.
K588.B78   1995
340′.1—dc20   94–37053
                                                          CIP

Printed in the United States of America

1 2 3 4 5 6 7 8 9

The paper used in this publication meets the minimum
requirements of American National Standard for Information
Sciences—Permanence of Paper for Printed Library Materials,
ANSI Z39.48–1984 ∞

In memory of my father

But that an accident as such, detached from what circumscribes it, what is bound and is actual only in its context with others, should attain an existence of its own and a separate freedom—this is the tremendous power of the negative; it is the energy of thought, of the pure I. Death, if that is what we want to call this non-actuality, is of all things the most dreadful, and to hold fast what is dead requires the greatest strength. Lacking strength, beauty hates the understanding for asking of her what it cannot do. But the life of Spirit is not the life that shrinks from death and keeps itself untouched by devastation, but rather the life that endures it and maintains itself in it. It wins its truth only when, in utter dismemberment, it finds itself. It is this power, not as something positive, which closes its eyes to the negative, as when we say of something that it is nothing or is false, and then, having done with it, turn away and pass on to something else; on the contrary, Spirit is this power only by looking the negative in the face, and tarrying with it. This tarrying with the negative is the magical power that converts it into being.

—G. W. F. HEGEL, PREFACE TO The Phenomenology of Spirit

CONTENTS

ACKNOWLEDGMENTS

Several chapters of this book have appeared elsewhere in previous versions. Chapter I contains material from "Hegel and the Crisis of Private Law," which appeared in 10 *Cardozo Law Review* (1989) and in Drucilla Cornell, Michel Rosenfeld, and David Gray Carlson, eds., *Hegel and Legal Theory* (New York: Routledge, 1991); Chapter II reworks material published in 4 *Canadian Journal of Law and Jurisprudence* (1991); Chapter III reworks and expands material published in 43 *University of Toronto Law Journal* (1993); Chapter V reworks and expands material published in Stephen Shute, John Gardner, and Jeremy Horder, eds., *Action and Value in Criminal Law* (Oxford: Clarendon Press, 1993); and Chapter VI contains material from "The Ideality of Difference: Toward Objectivity in Legal Interpretation," 11 *Cardozo Law Review* (1990). I thank the editors and publishers of these volumes for their permission to republish this material.

It is unlikely that this book would have been conceived, let alone written, without the aid of a stimulating collegial environment or without the advice and support of several very able scholars. I am particularly grateful to Bruce Chapman, who read the entire manuscript and offered invaluable criticisms and suggestions. Robert Berman, David Gray Carlson, David Dyzenhaus, John Gardner, Jeremy Horder, Robert Howse, Michel Rosenfeld, Stephen Shute, Stephen Waddams, Arnold Weinrib, Richard Dien Winfield, and Susan Zimmerman read portions of the manuscript and prompted many revisions. The students in my Hegel, Property, and Criminal Law seminars challenged me to produce as coherent a set of ideas as I possibly could.

I wish to acknowledge a special debt of thanks to Ernest Weinrib. Part of this obligation stems from his efforts in reading most of the manuscript and in patiently explaining his disagreement. The greater part, however, arises from a continuing discussion in which he, both as teacher and as colleague, has helped define for me the problems to which this book is addressed.

In writing this book, I have also incurred debts to several institutions. In particular, I wish to thank the Faculty of Law of the University of Toronto for granting me a research leave to complete the manuscript; and the Benjamin Cardozo School of Law of Yeshiva University for allowing me to test some of my fledgling ideas as a Jacob Burke Scholar-in-Residence in January and February 1990. I am also grateful to the Social Sciences and Humanities Research Council of Canada for their financial support of this project.

Tycho Manson, Thomas O'Malley, and Francine Rosenzweig helped me research the book. Diane Wheldrake performed secretarial tasks with her customary cheerfulness. Susan, Jennifer, and Avi gave my reflections on dialogic community a firm anchor in experience.

CHAPTER I

The Crisis of the Common Law

1. THE FRAGMENTATION OF THE COMMON-LAW TRADITION

The modern evolution of Anglo-American law consists in manifold expressions of a single theme. This theme is mirrored both in the body of judge-made law and in theoretical reflection on that work. In judicial practice the leitmotiv of contemporary law manifests itself in a number of transformative developments in the law of property, contracts, torts, and crime. We see it in the frequent judicial appeals to policy and the public welfare in deciding entitlements to property;[1] in the emergence of detrimental reliance as an independent and potentially exclusive basis of promissory obligation;[2] in the movement from fault to strict tort liability as a means of socializing accident costs and encouraging optimal investment in safety;[3] and in the compromise of retributive or desert-based criteria of criminal liability (such as willfulness or conscious recklessness) by the rise of ones (such as negligence) more compatible with the goal of public security.[4]

Within the domain of scholarship, the theme is even more pervasive. Here it is reflected in the impressive elaboration of a theoretical program to understand the common law as a vehicle for the maximization of wealth;[5] in the more general trend toward viewing the common law from the perspective of nonlegal disciplines that treat as surface rhetoric the discourse through which the common-law tradition explains itself;[6] and in the tendency to interpret the common law as riven by dualisms and tensions between social visions or between gender-relative ideals of moral character—dualisms that subvert the lawyer's cherished distinction between dispassionate law and morally impassioned politics.[7]

What unites these diverse phenomena into a single picture is the erosion of the autonomy of the common law. For most of its history, the common law was an ordering of human interactions independent of the political order directed to common ends. It was a system of rules ordered not to a common good but to individual rights over one's person and property conceived as existing prior to any association for a common purpose. These rules embodied—to borrow Ferdinand Tönnies's famous contrast—not a *Gemeinschaft* or natural community but an artificial society of naturally autonomous persons.[8] Because the common law's rationality lay elsewhere than in subservience to a common good, legal reasoning formed a distinctive art. It was not everyday prudence concerning ends and their most suitable means, but a special form of reasoning from principles to their endless specification in particular cases—a reasoning dependent on analogy and intuitive judgment, committed to internal coherence as its chief virtue, and needing a special intellectual training and experience. The classical view of law as an autonomous discipline is beautifully expressed in the following report of Sir Edward Coke.

> A controversy of land between parties was heard by the King, and sentence given, which was repealed for this, that it did belong to the common law: then the King said, that he thought the law was founded upon reason, and that he and others had reason, as well as the Judges: to which it was answered by me, that true it was, that God had endowed His Majesty with excellent science, and great endowments of nature; but His Majesty was not learned in the laws of his realm of England, and causes which concern the life, or inheritance, or goods, or fortunes of his subjects, are not to be decided by natural reason but by the artificial reason and judgment of law, which law is an act which requires long study and experience, before that a man can attain to the cognizance of it: that the law was the golden met-wand and measure to try the causes of the subjects; and which protected His Majesty in safety and peace: with which the King was greatly offended, and said, that then he should be under the law, which was treason to affirm, as he said; to which I said, that Bracton saith, *quod Rex non debet esse sub homine, sed sub Deo et lege.*[9]

Coke's response to the king underscores another implication of the common law's erstwhile independence of political goals. Besides grounding an autonomous intellectual discipline, this independence has traditionally operated as a normative constraint on political power expressed through legislation. If the individual's liberty and property were ends sufficiently important to organize a system of customary law, then they were worth protecting against legislative encroachments through whatever devices lay at a judge's disposal—through the strict construction of penal statutes, the interpretation of ambiguous statutory language so as to accord with the common law, and the presumption favoring compensation for public takings, to name a few. Indeed, the common law's independence of politics has been the theme of several famous controversies between lawyers and the political sovereign. It was because the moral limits on state power were thought to lie not in a general *bonum et aequum* but in a law anterior to political ends that Coke could assert a jurisdiction in common-law courts to oversee the exercise of monarchical power;[10] and that his successors in *Lochner v. New York*[11] could hold common-law rights sacrosanct even against the egalitarian will of a popularly elected assembly. More recently, the common law's normative independence has been adduced to legitimate what otherwise seems problematic in a liberal democracy: the making of law by judges unrepresentative of, and unaccountable to, the people. If the common law is unconcerned with political goals—if it deals with "principle" rather than with "policy"—then its elaboration by judges insulated from electoral preferences may be viewed as serving rather than as subverting a constitutional democracy.[12]

The classical vision of the common law as an autonomous normative order no longer commands widespread allegiance from those devoted to principle. Rather, the common law's autonomy is now under attack by a political order increasingly confident of the moral authority of its ends and increasingly skeptical of the distinctive moral concerns of lawyers. If we understand the common law (at least in its classical form) as an ordering of human interactions independent of an ordering by the common good, then the dominant theme of modern legal culture can be expressed as a crisis in the legitimacy of such an order. Doubtless no order among human beings is conceivable except in terms of something common to them. Yet the common law's discourse has traditionally sought to maintain its distinctiveness by appealing to a commonality between persons who recognize no good or end as uniformly theirs and whose interactions are therefore those of self-interested monads. Such a discourse has been called "libertarian," "individualist," or "right-based" to distinguish it from an understanding of order based on the primacy of the human good and of the duty to promote it. More important than any label, however, is the fact that the last few decades have witnessed a gradual decline of this discourse in favor of one that would shape common-law adjudication into a functionally rational instrument of the public good.

Still, to present this development as a straightforward and uncontested one would be to offer a one-sided view of recent legal history. A more balanced account would point to the considerable residue of doctrine native to the older paradigm that has stubbornly resisted the modernizing force of the new. The degree of resistance varies, of course, among the countries of the common-law world, but a pattern of mutual adjustment is discernible in all.[13] So, for example, the traditional requirement of willfulness for penal liability continues to be honored (with many exceptions) for "true crimes" but not for "public welfare" offenses;[14] the goal of loss spreading in tort is still pursued within the classical, adversarial format adapted to the task of righting wrongs committed by one person against another; the protection of reliance is superimposed on the enforcement of bargain promises involving no reliance;[15] and the mediation of property rights through the common good occurs alongside a body of doctrine that continues to speak quaintly of possession and use as sources of property anterior to civil society.

The survival of the older framework has not, however, arrested the common law's reduction from an autonomous system to an instrument of political goals; on the contrary, it has made that process more complete. A legal system coherently ordered either to the supremacy of the common good or to the primacy of the individual might lay claim to a unity authoritative against the political passion of the judge, scholar, or legal practitioner; a legal order fragmented into opposing normative systems allows such passion unlimited scope. It is precisely when the law loses (or seems to lose) its indigenous unity that it becomes vulnerable to colonization by political forces vying for control of the means of social coercion. The common law must first appear bereft of native purpose before legal scholars can urge judges to wield the law to advance the interests of particular groups or before they can debate whether the use or abandonment of rights discourse would better serve this or that cause.[16] The modern collapse of law's autonomy is the outcome not only of the crisis of the individualist paradigm of law but also of the failure of the communitarian* one decisively to replace it.

The fragmentation of the common-law tradition has spawned a corresponding crisis in the intellectual endeavor to understand and elaborate it. It now seems that there is no single theory of justice that can integrate the bewildering mass of contradictory principles and rules. Theories based on the negative right of persons against interferences with their liberty and property might have fit the common law in the nineteenth and early twentieth century; however, they are now embarrassed by a growing number of doctrines embodying positive rights to the conditions of effective autonomy and corresponding duties of concern for the welfare of others. When, for example, a court invalidates an agreement because one party has exploited its market power to extract terms harmful to the real welfare of the other, it is protecting a right unknown to the libertarian paradigm, for which benefit and harm are relative to individual desire and so irrelevant from the standpoint of a public conception of justice. In contrast,

---

*As I use it, the term "communitarian" designates the view according to which human individuals have a common good that is attained only within a political community; it does not denote the idea lately advanced by Alasdair MacIntyre that justice is relative to the parochial traditions of particular communities; see *After Virtue* (Notre Dame: University of Notre Dame Press, 1984), 181–225; *Whose Justice? Which Rationality?* (Notre Dame: University of Notre Dame Press, 1988), 389–403.

theories of justice based on a view of human welfare, while hospitable to doctrines imposing positive duties of concern, cannot stop them from submerging the common law's autonomy in the fair allocation of the costs and benefits of social cooperation. Those, for example, who would use tort law to redistribute losses caused by accidents have no reason intrinsic to their principle for shying at a general scheme of social insurance in which the right to sue in tort is abolished; while those who would use tort law to deter inefficient conduct have no compelling reason for allowing an injured plaintiff to collect the fine.[17] The dilemma confronting legal interpretation seems, accordingly, to be this: traditional libertarian theory cannot accommodate doctrines imposing a duty of concern for the welfare of others; while ostensibly the only theory receptive to these doctrines is a communitarian one that reduces courts to an arm of public administration. To the extent, therefore, that the logical momentum of the communitarian principle is contained within the doctrinal and institutional limits of the libertarian model, the law appears as a series of ad hoc compromises between antagonistic ideologies; and it seems that the only interpretive theory of law faithful to its object must be one profoundly skeptical of its coherence.

Some might say that this state of affairs is nothing to lament. The idea of a common law free of contradiction may seem too utopian to have any critical power, in which case the conflicted state of the law will appear not as a problem but as a natural, inevitable, and even welcome condition. Where no harmony of opposites is in sight, one might understandably prefer a "healthy tension" to the absolutism of a one-sided principle; and one might try to see in contradiction and strife the exhilarating new vistas that open once we have abandoned the illusions of wholeness and closure whose possibility the bad reputation of conflict presupposes. Indeed, any attempt to pose the problem of legal fragmentation must contend with a pervasive equanimity among legal scholars in the face of this predicament—an attitude one encounters at every level of theoretical endeavor. For example, much of everyday doctrinal scholarship now takes the conflict of paradigms for granted without reflecting too hard on its consequences for the possibility of law as something distinct from the dominant preference, or for the possibility of a legal scholarship that is neither revolutionary nor servile to the powers that be. Others more sensitive to the problem expend great efforts in denying its seriousness. Borrowing from Thomas Kuhn, Richard Rorty, and Richard Bernstein, they point to the requirement that judges and lawyers justify their paradigm choices in public "conversation" and with reference to "good reasons" in order to calm our fear that legal fragmentation might entail the collapse of law into masked violence.[18] Yet they neglect to tell us what makes a reason good if (as they typically contend) no neutral metalanguage exists by which to arbitrate conflicts between paradigms, leaving us to guess that a good reason is one that appeals to our (current) moral sentiments and leaving us to wonder what to say to someone who does not share these sentiments but who is nonetheless forced by the court to submit to them. While paradigm conflict may be innocuous in science, where dissenters are not compelled to submit to the dominant opinion on pain of life, liberty, or property, such conflict is disastrous in law.[19]

The disquieting implications of disunity in law have stimulated some writers to produce general theories of the common law impressive in their scope and explanatory power. Thus, Ronald Dworkin, George Fletcher, Richard Posner, and Ernest Weinrib unify vast tracts of legal doctrine around the ideas of "integrity," "reciprocity," "wealth maximization," and "corrective justice," respectively.[20] However, the imperturbability of legal scholarship in the face of paradigm conflict is apparent in these efforts as well. For even in seeking the law's thematic unity, these authors happily concede the impossibility of law's impartiality—of its elevation above the clash of ideologies—though without confronting the consequences of this admission for their reconstructive efforts. Thus, Dworkin's idea of "law as integrity" is modestly offered as one (albeit the best) of many plausible interpretations of the legal tradition, each of which imposes subjective meaning rather than discovering an immanent one;[21] Fletcher's right-based "paradigm of reciprocity" competes with a welfarist "paradigm of reasonableness" for control of tort law; Posner's once aggressive thesis that the common law has an economic logic is now tempered by the concession that "corrective justice and wealth maximization have important but limited domains of applicability" and by a rejection of any overarching concept of justice that might draw rational boundaries between them;[22] and Weinrib's belief in an "immanent rationality of law" coexists with an agnosticism as to whether human interactions are best ordered by corrective or by distributive justice (i.e., by private or by public law), which choice is for him an extralegal one.[23] So deep-rooted is the crisis of the common law that academic lawyers have either abandoned the ideal of an organically evolving order in relation to which contradiction can be perceived as a crisis; or else their attempts to revive the ideal are so shot through with concessions to disbelievers that the fragmentation of law ends up posing as the ideal itself.

Nevertheless, one loosely knit group of scholars has heightened our sense of crisis by thinking through with uncompromising rigor the implications of contradiction in the law. For the movement called Critical Legal Studies (CLS), the fact of contradiction implies the collapse of the distinction between the structured rationality of legal discourse and "open-ended disputes about the basic terms of social life, disputes that people call ideological, philosophical, or visionary."[24] Because every legal doctrine embodies some incoherent compromise between hostile normative paradigms, it can be made to support contradictory outcomes, so that appellate decisions are ultimately determined by a judge's ideological sympathies. There is, accordingly, no rule of law in the sense of a unified and gapless order capable of constraining a judge's political bias; and hence there is no prospect for the civil freedom of those subject, on pain of coercion, to judicial decisions fetched from values with which they disagree. Nor is there a rule of law in the sense of a universal norm valid for all persons. If the common law is simply the record of ideological battles won and lost, then it embodies the interests of a dominant group (class, race, or gender), whose hegemony is masked by theories depicting law as an organic elaboration of impersonal concepts or of common purposes.[25] Once this view is accepted, the only coherent theoretical approach to law is a frankly instrumental one. For if the common law is a battleground of interests, then the task for a clear-minded jurist is not to adapt himself to the law's (spurious) rationality but to manipulate doctrine to achieve his political ends. The idea of legal reform as midwifery—as the facilitation of an immanent teleology—gives way to the idea of legal change as artifice—as the embodying in law of political agendas external to it. But since any legal change wrought in this manner reflects the group interest of the artificer, it is no more legitimate than the law it replaced, and so it too is vulnerable to revision by those it in turn oppresses and excludes. From this Heraclitean view of the legal process Roberto Unger has drawn the appropriate programmatic conclusion: the most authentic legal order—the one truest to the insight into the moral instability of all legal structures—is one that maximizes opportunities for a never-ending and pointless flux.[26]

2. THE AIM OF THIS WORK

Hegel once wrote that "bifurcation is the source of the need of philosophy."[27] "When," he continued, "the power of union vanishes from the life of men and the antitheses lose their living connection and reciprocity and gain independence, the need of philosophy arises."[28] The "sole interest of philosophy," Hegel thought, is to resolve the apparently fixed dichotomies of everyday thinking into a whole of which the formerly independent extremes are constituent parts.

The motivation for this book is the contemporary bifurcation of the common law into rival doctrinal paradigms and the destructive consequences of this split for the rule of law. Its aim—simply put—is to reveal this fragmentation as a superficial appearance that conceals an underlying unity. In the following chapters I attempt to interpret the common law from a standpoint that penetrates to this unity and brings it to the foreground. The common law's unity will be shown to involve a synthesis of several interrelated dichotomies: between good-centered and right-based (or deontological) legal paradigms, between instrumental and noninstrumental conceptions of law, between externalist and internalist interpretations of the common-law system, and between communitarian and individualist foundations of law. As a synthesis of opposites, the unity I attempt to disclose poses a challenge to three sorts of interlocutors. It challenges the schools of thought that take up one or the other pole of the antinomies to the exclusion of the other; thus it argues, for example, against both good-centered and right-based theories of the common law and against both a one-sided communitarianism and a one-sided individualism. And it challenges the school of Critical Legal Studies, for which the common law is simply the jumble of armistice lines temporarily accommodating the rival camps.

While challenging these views, however, I try to avoid asserting the common law's unity *against* any of them. To do so would be to take up a dogmatic position external to rival opinions, one capable of persuading only those already predisposed to my point of view. Posner's theory of the common law is, I think, one-sided in this way, for it unifies judge-made law around a welfarist goal—economic efficiency—without subjecting to internal criticism an alternative and (at least) no less persuasive account based on mutual respect for rights of formal agency.[29] It thus gives the rights theorist no reason for abandoning his perspective, nor can it persuade someone who sees law as a patchwork of settlements between deontological and welfarist ethics. In contrast, I try to show that the unifying principle of law is already implicit in rival conceptions of law's foundation, that it comes to sight precisely when these conceptions are taken seriously—when they are pressed to their logical and self-destructive conclusion. Hence it is a unifying principle to whose thematic primacy both deontologists and welfarists can be persuaded. In the end, I oppose neither deontological nor welfarist understandings of law but only show how their logical result is an idea that embraces both as subordinate elements. Similarly, I do not so much oppose the view of CLS as show that it is partial and relative, that it mistakes the collapse of particular conceptions of law's foundation for an eternal predicament of law. CLS, I argue, is the common law's awareness of the self-contradictoriness of one-sidedly communitarian or individualist foundations of law, from which insight a new, synthetic principle emerges. Because the unifying idea I offer is already latent in the CLS insight into the interdependence of opposite principles, it is an idea to which the CLS scholar too may be persuaded.

To interpret the common law as a unified whole, one needs a philosophic standpoint capable of seeing its unity. The standpoint I adopt is, broadly speaking, Hegelian. I say "broadly speaking" because, apart from a few disparaging remarks in the *Philosophy of Right*,[30] Hegel himself made no attempt to understand the common law as it existed in his own time; and while he provided the structural outlines of a philosophy of the civil law, he did not apply this structure to a detailed elucidation of legal doctrine. Consequently, there is no fleshed-out Hegelian jurisprudence that one can simply and directly expound. There is, however, both an outline and a philosophic method by which one can interpret the common-law tradition as it has evolved to the present and with whose aid one can develop a coherent position toward the controversies and conundrums that beset current thinking about law. This is what I propose to do.

Some preliminary clarification of this project is needed to distinguish it from the scholarship to which I alluded earlier as symptoms of the contemporary crisis of law. In adopting the standpoint of Hegel's philosophy, I do not wish to add to the list of perspectives that approach law from the vantage point of academic disciplines external to it. My aim is not to present a Hegelian angle on the common law to supplement the equally partial perspectives of economics, sociology, Marxism, or feminism. These perspectives do not try to understand law as a specific system exhibiting its own rationality, for they treat law as a particular expression of an idea—for example, economic efficiency, class conflict, or patriarchy—that is exemplified in nonlegal contexts as well. Instead of surrendering to the common-law system and elucidating its own coherence, they refashion it into a vehicle for the manifestation of something else.[31] In doing so, they no doubt enrich our understanding of economic behavior, class struggle, and patriarchy; but they cannot render perspicuous the internal rationality of the common law. In contrast to these approaches, a Hegelian interpretation of the common law claims to disclose a unity indigenous to the law itself; it seeks, as Hegel put it, to "abandon itself to the life of the object or, what is the same thing, to attend to and express its inner necessity."[32]

However, this is only one side of the matter. A Hegelian understanding of the common law seeks not only to disclose its specific coherence; it seeks also to justify that coherence as possessing normative validity. It is descriptive and justificatory at once. This, however, presents an obvious difficulty. It would seem that one cannot both explain and justify the common law's internal unity unless one uncritically adopts the normative standpoint of the system. Weinrib, whose theory of tort law is unique in its internalist orientation, seems to have fallen into precisely this trap. He too wishes to make contact with law's autonomous rationality; but in seeking also to justify that coherence, he defers without reserve to the idea of the formal self as the end ordering private law.[33] For Weinrib, therefore, legal criticism can mean only the criticism of doctrine in light of the formalist foundation of the common-law system; it cannot mean criticism of the foundation itself, for such criticism must for him presuppose a normative standpoint external to the system.[34] The result is an understanding of law that comes perilously close to apologetics. In contrast, a Hegelian under-standing of the common law claims to unite two apparently contradictory theoretical stances toward its object; it claims to unite a cognitive surren-der to the law's internal standpoint as complete as any ethical positivism with a critical perspective on that standpoint as radical as any utopian ide-alism. It claims, in other words, to justify the common law's internal unity without sacrificing a normative perspective independent of the one that self-consciously informs the law.

To see how this is possible, one must have grasped Hegel's conception of the foundation of law—the reality he calls *Geist*. It is beyond my powers to set forth this idea comprehensively at the beginning, for its nature is such that it can be understood only as the result of a logical development from simpler ideas. A full explanation of Hegel's reconciliation of criti-cism and fidelity to law must therefore be left for the final chapter. Nev-ertheless, I shall try to bring the idea into view in a rudimentary way for the sole purpose of identifying those of its implications that are jurispru-dentially significant and that will form the major themes of the following chapters. I will not attempt at this point to derive these implications in a systematic way; I will simply set them forth as consequences of Hegel's foundational idea that will later be developed more fully.

3. COMMUNITY AND PRIVATE LAW:
THE PROBLEM REFORMULATED

Let us return to the picture of fragmentation I drew earlier. The common law appears broken and incoherent because its survival as a form of order distinct from the political seems incomprehensible from the standpoint of any authoritative conception of the common good. The common law's au-tonomy, it would seem, must be based on the priority of the choosing self rather than on any end supposedly choiceworthy by all. When analyzed, this premise yields a constellation of assumptions comprising the outlook of a certain form of liberalism traditionally identified with John Locke and Immanuel Kant. It implies, first of all, that human individuals, as self-conscious agents, have ultimate reality and worth in their isolation from and indifference toward one another; that justice, understood as the mu-tual respect for this worth, is thus conceivable independently of a concep-tion of the common good and so without any reliance on the possibility of a natural virtue; that private law, or the law embodying mutual respect be-tween dissociated individuals, exhausts the content of natural right and is therefore law in its paradigmatic form; and that, by contrast, public law is the outcome of political choices among contingent goods, a sphere of pos-itive and instrumental law normatively constrained by prepolitical natural rights. Because these claims are simply antithetical to those flowing from the natural authority of a common good, the coexistence of the two paradigms appears as a makeshift compromise fatal to law's coherence and hence to its power to bind.

Formulating the problem of law's incoherence as a conflict between the priority of the self and that of the good does not, of course, get us nearer a solution. However, it at least helps us see the problem as an aspect of a more familiar one. Although the common law is not coterminous with private law (criminal law straddles the border between private and public law), nevertheless the question regarding the possibility of a coherently autonomous common law is the question whether there can be a coherently autonomous *private law* once a common good is acknowledged as the end of law; or it is the question whether there can be a coherent distinction between private and public law once the latter is conceived as serving not contingent social preferences but a morally authoritative common good.

It would seem that such a distinction is possible only if private law's autonomy can be vindicated from the standpoint of the common good itself. If the good *required* a distinctive private law, then the common law might well be construable as a unified whole. The coexistence of individualist and communitarian doctrinal formations would then be logical, since individual rights, while justified by the good, would in cases of conflict have to yield to the good that legitimates them. Hegel, we shall see, provides a vindication of private law's autonomy from the standpoint of the good. Now, of course, there is no dearth of such purported vindications. One might, for example, find good utilitarian reasons for maintaining a regime of private property and contract and, in a world of fallible judgment, for insulating this regime from direct appeals to the utilitarian standard in the adjudication of disputes.[35] One might also view private law in perfectionist terms as part of the totality of communal arrangements tending to promote the realization of distinctively human capacities.[36] Yet these good-based justifications for private law are far from what Hegel has in mind; and we can attain a glimpse of Hegel's idea by contrasting it to these approaches.

However diverse in other respects, both utilitarian and perfectionist theories share the view that private law is instrumental to an end outside itself. By "outside itself" I mean outside the practice wherein private law is interpreted, applied, and extended by jurists. For the utilitarian, the end of private law is the greatest possible surplus of pleasures over pains; for the perfectionist, it is the full development of the distinctive potentialities of the human being. Because these ends are the common ends of human association, they are external to the prepolitical ends by which a distinctive private law is self-consciously organized. Consequently, to justify private law in terms of these ends is to hold that private law's true end is something other than the one apparent to those who interpret private law from within the practice of private law itself. It is to create a contrast between a philosophic understanding of private law and the jurist's understanding; and it is to privilege the former while disparaging the latter as superficial or mistaken.[37] I shall refer to the jurist's understanding of private law by various phrases: the law's self-understanding, its self-conception, its overt or manifest meaning, or law from the internal point of view; and I shall include among those who adopt the internal perspective theorists who aim to clarify the first principles of private law instinct in the practice—those who, in other words, seek to elucidate the law's self-understanding. To theories that construct private law from a standpoint external to the practice and that privilege this standpoint over the internal one, I shall apply the epithets externalist and constructionist.

There is a section of Plato's *Laws* that provides a good example of an externalist account. In book 9, the Athenian stranger turns his reformist attention to the law of delicts. This law he regards as having a conventional origin in vengeance and moral indignation, a basis that explains its urge to give like for like as well as its preoccupation with the distinction between voluntary and involuntary conduct.[38] For the Athenian, however, the true or natural end of penal law is the cure of souls ignorant of their good. Since, he argues, injustice harms the wrongdoer, and since no one willingly harms himself, the distinction between voluntary and involuntary injustice is inappropriate. A more relevant categorization would distinguish between intentional and unintentional harm—not because the two kinds of harm provoke different responses in victims and their sympathizers but because they indicate different conditions of the wrongdoer's soul and so provide a sounder basis for calibrating punishments. Thus, instead of varying penalties according to the harm inflicted, the Athenian would do so according to the therapeutic needs of the wrongdoer, although in publicly justifying the laws he would continue to employ the language of pollution and retribution of the ancient myths.[39] For the Athenian, then, the inherent nature and end of penal law is something other than the significance it has for ordinary opinion (for the slave doctors of slaves); and the problem for the legislator is to fashion laws that, while ordered to their natural purpose, make the necessary concessions to prejudice.

In his early writings on the philosophy of law, Hegel himself conceived private law in a manner consciously modeled on the Platonic.[40] Though ostensibly an autonomous system based on the supposed primacy of the individual person, private law is here understood as, in its essence, an obscure or lower-order manifestation of the primacy of community. Its natural function, therefore, is to be an infrastructural support for the maintenance of a warrior class, in which the primacy of the good is reflected as in a perfect medium. For the young Hegel as for Plato, then, the truth of private law is contrasted with the way in which private law appears to those involved in its everyday application. It appears to be independent of the priority of the good; its essential nature, however, is not this appearance but rather its subordination to the good. Moreover, this subordination is revealed decisively in war, wherein "there is the free possibility that not only certain individual things but the whole of them, as life, will be annihilated and destroyed for the Absolute itself or for the people."[41]

Now the problem with Hegel's early account of private law is the same as that which besets all contemporary externalist accounts. Its problem is that, by understanding private law in light of an external end, the theory appears from the jurist's internal perspective as an artificial construction of private law rather than as a true account of it. Private law is *reduced* to an expression of a good that is not private; hence it is justified not as private law but as an instantiation of public law. Qua private, private law is the superficial play of appearances in which something else (community, efficiency) pulsates. And because its true nature lies outside itself, its own self-understanding as an autonomous formation ordered to the atomistic person is error and illusion. Insofar, however, as the philosophy of private law contradicts the law's self-understanding, it too becomes mere opinion—a point of view—and its claim of truth an arbitrary dogmatism. The jurist, after all, has no reason to accept the philosophic view, since this view does not adapt itself to private law as it is but molds the law in accordance with a public good. Because the good-based account first reshapes what it seeks to understand, it never makes contact with private law itself, which thus remains uncomprehended. Of course, the philosopher will respond that the law's true nature lies in its reconstructed shape and that philosophy has therefore understood whatever in private law there is to understand. But for this the jurist has only the philosopher's say-so.

The constructionism of good-based accounts of private law generates an inevitable protest on behalf of private law "itself." Because good-based theories remold private law instead of adapting to it, some writers have argued that a faithful account of private law must rest on the priority not of the good but of the right, or on the normative primacy of individual personality.[42] The idea is that a faithful account must respect the law's internal standpoint, and this standpoint exalts individual agency as the principle of law rather than any substantive conception of the good. Accordingly, the fundamental opposition in contemporary legal interpretation is one between internalist accounts of private law whose internalism is based on an exclusion of the good as an explanatory principle and teleological accounts that are externalist. In this opposition, of course, each side has a right against the other. For if the nemesis of external approaches is an instrumentalism that fundamentally alters what it seeks to understand, that of right-based theory is a formalism that, while preserving private law in its account, never explains why we should be committed to it.

The tension involved here can be further explained as one between the immanence and normative force of interpretive concepts. If legal understanding, in an effort to achieve authentic contact with its object, defers to the internal standpoint of the practice, it achieves immanence at the price of an uncritical accommodation to the given norms of the tradition. It understands its object from within but fails to reveal the practice as ethically justified from a transcendent point of view. If, however, understanding attempts to construct the practice in accordance with an ideal having independent normative force, then it sacrifices immanence and becomes an external imposition, thereby disqualifying itself as an authentic understanding. Thus, for example, an understanding of contract law wholly immersed in the participants' libertarian conception of justice would perhaps be a faithful or immanent understanding; but it would fail to reveal contract law as an objectively valid normative order. As a purely positive understanding of a limited and self-enclosed normative system, interpretation would lack the connection with a transcendent norm that could confirm the normative validity of the practice. By contrast, an interpretation of contract law solely in terms of the common good would be an artificial imposition, because it would assert itself against the viewpoint of the participants whose activity it interprets. The unending controversy between good-centered and right-based accounts of the common law can be understood as a manifestation of this basic tension.

Now Hegel is significant for this controversy because he is the only philosopher to attempt a synthesis of external/good-based and internal/right-based accounts of private law. For the mature Hegel, it is not only the case that private law is justified as an obscure instantiation of community; it is also the case that private law *as thematically ordered to the primacy of the atomistic self* is so justified. That is, instead of reducing private law to a manifestation of community, Hegel argues that the independent standpoint of private law is itself required by community, which then ceases to be the dominant principle and becomes one element of a whole formed of interdependent parts. It is important to grasp the full force of the paradox involved here: a legal paradigm based on an anticommunitarian principle (that the atomistic self is an end) is said to be justified by the requirements of authentic community. By virtue of this claim, Hegel becomes the only philosopher to attempt a genuine reconciliation between good-centered and right-based accounts of justice, one that preserves the distinctiveness of both kinds of order.

But how is such a reconciliation possible? In what sense is the atomistic premise of private law necessary to the realization of genuine community? In what sense is the jurist's internal perspective needed by the philosophic account of private law as a manifestation of community? One is certainly entitled to be skeptical about this thesis, for no starker opposition can be conceived than that between the ancients' claim that community is the individual's natural end and the modern claim that the person is an end apart from community; nor between the claims that private law reflects the naturalness of community and that it reflects the worth of the atomistic self. How can both claims be right?

4. GEIST AND ITS JURIDICAL IMPLICATIONS

We can perhaps begin to understand Hegel's attempted reconciliation by thinking about the contrast between domination and friendship. Imagine a person (Crassus) who claims to possess final and absolute worth by virtue of a capacity to change his environment in accordance with an end or value that he freely originates. Such an individual might see in another person's (Spartacus's) identical independence a competitive claim contradicting his own. Crassus might therefore seek confirmation of his worth by destroying Spartacus's self-originating activity. That is, he might exploit Spartacus's fear of death to make him acknowledge Crassus's exclusive worth by working on the environment to satisfy not his own but Crassus's ends. Crassus will, however, find this mode of self-confirmation unsatisfactory; for he is now dependent for the validation of his worth on someone he holds in contempt as a "thing"—as a tool of his interests. He receives honor from someone he himself does not respect, and so the honor is worth nothing to him.[43] This experience might teach Crassus that the route to self-validation is necessarily roundabout and full of paradox. If Spartacus's recognition is to be effective in confirming Crassus's sense of worth, Crassus must support rather than seek to destroy Spartacus's independence. Instead of reducing Spartacus to a means to his realized worth, Crassus must bow to Spartacus's worth in the confident hope that Spartacus will, seeing this tribute, freely return the respect in order likewise to validate and give value to the tribute he receives. If the respect is indeed reciprocated, a relation is formed wherein each self receives satisfaction by aiming at the other's and satisfies the other for his own sake—a relation distinguished by a harmony of self-sacrifice and self-affirmation that we call friendship.[44] In friendship, accordingly, we see a kind of relationship in which apparently contradictory claims to final worth turn out to be actually complementary. The end-status* of one friend does not contradict the other's; on the contrary, it *requires* the other's for its own objective realization. Hence each fosters the other's independence for his or her own sake, and each is preserved as an end in this self-surrender by virtue of the reciprocity of respect.

*I shall be using this locution frequently throughout the book. Though somewhat awkward, its meaning is clear enough, and I could not find a commonplace noun to express the idea of being an end. Hegel's expression is being-for-self (*Fürsichsein*), which seems even less felicitous.

Now let us apply this contrast between domination and friendship to the relation between community and the individual. Given a claim by the political community that it is the natural end of the individual, how might it go about verifying this claim? One possibility is classically associated with Sparta. The community might objectify its primacy by subjugating the individual, that is, by denying his worth as an independent self and forcibly subduing him (through the collectivization of property, hard discipline, etc.) to the common life of the polity. Yet subjugation would be a self-contradictory way of verifying the end-status of community; for what is demanded is a confirmation of the *naturalness* of community, and such a proof cannot be produced through the violent imposition of unity on recalcitrant individuals. The only adequate validation of the worth of community is the individual's *free* testimony that community is his good—the basis of his essential value. And so the community must defer to the individual's spontaneity, "trusting," as Thucydides has Pericles say of Athens, "less in system and policy than to the native spirit of [its] citizens."[45] Moreover, that community is indeed the basis of the individual's worth is shown by its need for the individual's freedom to confirm its natural authority. Accordingly, each defers to the independence of the other for the sake of its own confirmation as an end.

How might someone bear witness to the naturalness of community? One might do so, clearly, by voluntarily risking one's life for the polity or by devoting oneself to public affairs. The polity might have proof of its naturalness through the individual's acknowledgment (as in Pericles's funeral oration) that his happiness lies in public deliberation and in heroic self-sacrifice for the glory of the state. Yet even this mode of confirmation seems inadequate. For in seeking the individual's recognition, the community acknowledges its dependence on the individual's freedom conceived as *absolutely other* and yet attains realization only by seeing the individual canceled as other. The individual conceived as other—the atomistic individual directed to personal ends—is submerged in community; he is excluded from citizenship, devalued as a barbarian fit only to facilitate the active citizenship of the few. However, this submersion and devaluation of the self-oriented individual is once again an act of violence just because the community needed the individual's alterity to confirm its claim of naturalness. Once community has acknowledged the individual's otherness as essential to the validation of its authority, the community cannot disdain and submerge that difference without reappearing as a violent and domineering force.[46]

This suggests that the validation of community as the individual's natural end might, as in the case of friendship, have to be achieved by indirection. Instead of demanding the immediate sacrifice of the atomistic individual, the political community might have to sacrifice *itself* to the claimed primacy of this individual, becoming a means for the protection of his or her liberty and private property. In so deferring for the sake of its own confirmed end-status to the claims of the atomistic self, community becomes the rational basis for the self's distinctive worth and so attracts a reciprocal and free recognition on the part of the individual. The sacrifice of each is then compatible with its preservation as an end because of the reciprocity of deference. Each recognizes the other as recognizing itself.

We can see how the relation of mutual recognition between community and the atomistic self might make possible a reconciliation between internalist and good-centered accounts of private law. The fundamental insight is that the common good requires a private law wherein the good's primacy is surrendered in order that it might be confirmed as the good through the free recognition of radically independent selves. The common good requires the viewpoint of the atomistic self for its own validation, just as the individual's distinctive worth presupposes the standpoint of the good from which the necessity of individualism is revealed. This means that the external account of private law in light of the good is incomplete without the internal account based on the self. The external account is no longer the privileged one, for this theory requires validation from an independent antagonist. Nor is the internal account privileged as the true one, for the relevance of the jurist's perspective is established from the standpoint of the good that needs it. Both viewpoints are mutually complementary aspects of a whole.

We can also see how the relation between community and the atomistic individual might mediate between libertarian and communitarian conceptions of the self. In contrast to the libertarian, Hegel argues that individual selfhood is established as an end not prior to or outside of community but rather as an organic requirement of community; for the latter is objectively the individual's good only insofar as it is validated out of the mouth of a self who is an *independent* end. Hence the claims of the individual self must be pursued with a moderation that reflects the embeddedness of its rights within a larger whole. In contrast to the communitarian, Hegel argues that community is authentically the individual's good only insofar as it recognizes the rebellion of the self against its primacy; hence it must leave room within itself for a sphere of asocial individualism wherein the common good is actualized with a moderation that preserves the distinctiveness of that sphere.

Hegel called the interdependence of community and the atomistic self Geist. I shall call it dialogic community.[47] The basic idea, once again, is that neither community nor the individual self actualizes itself as an end by reducing the other to a means to its own primacy. Rather each is confirmed as an end by *submitting* to the other seen as submitting to it. Each needs the other's freedom to confirm it as an end; hence each humbles itself before the worth of the other and is preserved as an end by virtue of the reciprocity of self-surrender. For Hegel, this interaction between community and individual selfhood is alone the basis for the objectively valid claim of both to respect; hence this relationship delimits the scope of both valid private rights and legitimate political authority. The mutual recognition of community and individual selfhood is for Hegel the underlying principle of law.

The implications of this principle for legal interpretation are, I think, far-reaching and profound, and they form the set of themes whose elaboration is the purpose of this book. They are: that there is a solid basis in reality for the distinction (though not the bifurcation) between private and public law, a basis impregnable against contemporary attempts to "deconstruct" this distinction; that there is thus a coherent basis for a private law of property, contract, and tort that is insulated from the demands of distributive justice and of economic regulation, though not from norms outlawing noncoercive forms of interpersonal oppression that a purely private law countenances; that the common law exhibits a coherent unity of individualist and communitarian elements, a unity that cancels the freedom of judicial choice between these polarities and so grounds a viable rule of law; that the common law's insulation from distributive concerns is logically compatible with the amenability of property and contractual rights to statutory limitation in the service of these concerns; and that the possibility exists for an interpretation of the common law that is internalist without being positivist and transcendent without being constructionist— for an interpretation that reconciles critical idealism with fidelity to law.

5. SOME REMARKS ON METHOD

Before embarking, a few more words are needed to clarify the method of argument I employ throughout this book. First, although this work is, I think, a way of studying Hegel as well as law, it is not one primarily concerned with providing an exegesis of Hegel's texts. This is because the primary object of the study is not Hegel's texts but the common-law tradition. What is normally the text of Hegel scholarship is here the medium through which another text—the common law—is understood. Still, our project will inevitably involve an interpretation of Hegel's legal philosophy as well. This interpretation will, I hope, counter what I believe are two mistaken trends in recent writing on Hegel's legal and political thought. One is the tendency to identify Hegel's legal thought with "abstract right" and so to ignore the way in which the rights of atomistic persons are qualified by subsequent legal paradigms and are ultimately situated within the context of Geist.[48] Unless an expositor of, say, Hegel's theory of contract comes to grips with the larger philosophical framework within which this theory fits, his reading will inevitably distort the theory in precisely the manner Hegel wished to avoid, and it will end up by costuming Hegel as some sort of neo-Kantian or proto-Rawlsian thinker. The other and opposite tendency is to read Hegel as a communitarian critic of the liberal's atomistic view of the self and so to downplay the significance of abstract right in Hegel's mature political philosophy.[49] We often find, for example, an exposition of abstract right that emphasizes its embeddedness within "ethical life"—but without taking seriously the partial autonomy vis-à-vis the common good that abstract right continues to possess even at the most concrete stages of freedom's development. Both readings are domestications of Hegel's legal thought, in that they reduce it to familiar ideological patterns (i.e., liberalism or communitarianism) while banishing precisely those aspects of the theory that could challenge "normal discourse."[50]

Against both of these undialectical tendencies my interpretation of Hegel's legal philosophy seeks what Emil Fackenheim called the "authentic Hegelian middle."[51] That is, it reads Hegel as a philosopher who discovered a conceptually coherent reconciliation of communitarian and atomistic foundations of law. In standard works on Hegel's thought, such an interpretation might seek assistance from Hegel's cultural milieu, might be tested against other parts of the philosopher's corpus, clarified by comparison with other philosophers, defended against contrary views, and so on. That is the method one must certainly employ if the primary object of investigation is Hegel's text. Where, however, one's object is the common law, the method of persuasion must be different. For now the criterion for the validity of our interpretation of Hegel is the same as that recognized by Hegel's philosophy itself, namely, whether it succeeds in rendering intelligible a sphere of life without doing violence to the independent point of view of its participants. To demonstrate that it does so will require abundant references to Hegel's texts, to common-law cases, and to rival interpretations of the common law but relatively few to Hegel's contemporaries or to other commentaries on Hegel's texts.

That our primary object of study is the common law accounts for another difference between this work and standard works of Hegel scholarship. Some might argue that a valuable commentary on Hegel's texts must every now and then stand back from the text and evaluate it from a viewpoint external to that of Hegel's system; for if it immerses itself in the system, it will have contributed little except perhaps to translate Hegel's thoughts into more readable language. Thus, a commentary on Hegel's philosophy might offer the suggestion that the category of Geist on which the system rests is ultimately implausible, or that it involves a bias in favor of totality at the expense of the differentiated individual (suggestions that, incidentally, I hope to show are mistaken). However, if one's thesis is that the common law can be rendered a coherent system through the lens of

Hegel's legal philosophy, one's theoretical posture is necessarily different. Immersion in the philosophy is now a virtue, for the point is precisely to test the theory for its interpretive power. It is not that we abandon the task of justification and evaluation but that the criteria of validity have altered. Within this jurisprudential enterprise, justification of the theory is not by some standard external to it but by its capacity to reveal the common law as a coherent and ethically satisfying system. Because this is the only test of validity that makes sense for our enterprise, I do not engage in external reflections about whether Hegel's philosophy is "right" (how could an external reflection prove him wrong?), nor do I attempt to justify Hegel's philosophic standpoint prior to putting it to work. Whether this standpoint is justified as an interpretive one the reader must judge at the end.

There is another reason why the justification of our interpretive standpoint must be the work of interpretation itself. Hegel's system has its own view of the nature of verification in philosophy.[52] For Hegel, an understanding of a legal system is validated when its interpretive principle—the principle of right underlying the variety of legal rules—is produced by the immanent logic of the norms by which the legal system is self-consciously organized by jurists. Stated otherwise, the justification of Hegel's thematic concept consists in depicting the logical movement of principles by which the theorists of a practice interpret it from within. This movement leads by a process I shall explain to the idea of dialogic community, of which concept the previous doctrinal formations are imperfect but progressively more adequate instances. Because this argument proceeds by way of an internal criticism of rival interpretive standpoints, it is theoretically capable of leading these perspectives to the idea that fulfills their own aspirations. It is, therefore, the method of justification I propose to follow.

Accordingly, while I avoid a preinterpretive defense of the Hegelian standpoint, this is not because I despair of the possibility of a rational defense of interpretive perspectives. I do not wish to construe the common law from a viewpoint asserted as an ideological preference; still less do I wish to rest my interpretation on the authority of a great thinker. Rather, in the chapters that follow, I try to make the best case for the Hegelian standpoint, one capable of persuading adherents of theoretical positions currently vying for dominion over the common law. However, the best case for this standpoint does not consist in any preinterpretive argument; it consists in immersing ourselves in the concepts that self-consciously inform a legal system and in showing that ours is the one to which they themselves lead.

CHAPTER II

The Unity of Property Law

1. INTRODUCTION

In this chapter I argue that the common law of property exhibits an internal unity worthy of moral respect. There are three distinct elements to this claim, each of which may be elucidated through a contrast with the view it puts in question. First, the unity we seek in property law is an internal one. This means that we seek the law's *own* unity, regarding artificial constructions as a defect of interpretation rather than as its normal product. I do not set out in advance the underlying ground for the possibility of faithful interpretations of legal practice; for that ground will emerge as the unifying theme of the common law and so must be methodically drawn from the object rather than baldly asserted beforehand. Nevertheless, we can try to indicate at the outset some of the marks by which one can distinguish a faithful interpretation of property law from ones that impose a unity foreign to it.

A faithful account of property law invokes no principle of unity that treats as dissimulating rhetoric the discourse by which the law of property presents itself.[1] The unity it discloses is intuited and corroborated rather than concealed by that discourse. This does not mean that our principle of unity is necessarily known to the participants—judges, lawyers, and doctrinal scholars—of the practice we are interpreting. These participants may indeed speak of a plurality of principles as competing for the governance of property law. Even so, our unifying idea will be faithful to law if it incorporates the principles overtly governing the practice as special cases, if it makes room for the independent rule (within limits prescribed by the theme of the whole) of those principles, and if it proves to be the unity within which alone these principles find their own coherent realization.

Were it to meet these conditions, the unity we uncover would be the law's own unity even though none of the participants had self-consciously grasped the unifying idea. For our principle would then not assert itself as the true one over against internal points of view regarded as simply false; nor (therefore) would it present itself as a mere perspective or angle, with no better claim to understanding than that of the indigenous standpoints it dogmatically opposes. Precisely this hostility to the internal discourse is the hallmark of constructionist interpretations. These accounts unify law around an end (e.g., economic efficiency or human flourishing) that is foreign to the jurist's own account of his activity and so must regard that account as either delusional or disingenuous.

An interpretation of property law that takes law's own discourse seriously must respect property law's self-conception as a branch of private law, of the law ordering interactions between persons considered to be otherwise dissociated. Concomitantly, it must do justice to those institutional features of the common law that suit it to its role as a law for atomistic individuals and that render it notoriously ill-suited as an instrument of collective action. In particular, it must make sense of an adjudicative procedure that features a passive public official relying on the private initiation and presentation of cases for legal resolution; and of a litigational format that standardly pits an individual plaintiff against an individual defendant while leaving unrepresented all those whose interests might be affected by the rule of decision. Whether an interpretation can account for these phenomena without indulging in apologetics for the status quo is an important question we shall have to address. However, no interpretation that fails to account for them can claim the virtue of fidelity.

An account of property law faithful to its private-law character will avoid interpreting it as a means to a collective goal.[2] Theories of the common law that see it as an instrument of welfare or wealth maximization are unsatisfactory both as descriptive interpretation and as prescriptive argument. As interpretations they fail because, in the absence of conscious legislative engineering, a broad conformity of property law to a collective goal is very unlikely, and whatever agreement did exist would appear fortuitous. If understanding law means disclosing its own significance rather than imposing a foreign one, then an instrumentalist approach will succeed only if legal rules embody a conscious, goal-oriented intention (as they do, for example, in an anticombines statute), for only then are the rules veritably *for* the goal: their instrumentality is their true significance. Yet a unitary intention to realize a particular goal cannot plausibly serve as a key to the common law, considering the length of its evolutionary process, the wide diffusion of decision-making authority, and the absence on the face of the record of any such uniform intention. For this reason, an instrumentalist theory of the common law must ultimately rely on a mechanistic explanation for any agreement between legal doctrine and its favored goal. If, for example, the theory is economics, it must invoke some causal mechanism (such as the strong incentive of those burdened by inefficient rules to challenge them through the appellate process) that, independently of judicial intention, tends to achieve economically efficient rules.[3] However, an instrumentalism combined with a mechanistic account of how the goal is achieved must fail as a genuine understanding, for it cannot exhibit its goal as law's own end or point, the very idea of a "point" requiring a purposive intention. Thus, no matter how numerous the instances of agreement between law and the instrumentalist's goal, identifying them will reveal nothing intrinsic about law and everything about the interests of the onlooker who is absorbed by a curious, surface feature of the object. Even were it true, for example, that there is some process tending to the unconscious selection of efficient common-law rules, this would not mean that efficiency is the common law's point or that economics is the true legal science.

If the examples of agreement between judge-made law and a collective goal appear beside the point, then the cases of disagreement will betoken no deformity in the law. A defect in law becomes visible only in the light of law's own ideal. Hence an explanatory end exhibited as law's own end will have internal moral force for legal actors; it will be a standard they can accept as distinguishing good law from bad. Ends resulting from a mechanistic chain of cause and effect will have no such force. As a positive theory of the common law, therefore, instrumentalism will possess no critical power. To acquire such a power, instrumentalist theories must renounce their interpretive pretensions and climb to a pinnacle outside the common law's internal organization, one from which to issue moral directives.[4] They must become prescriptive *rather* than positive. Thus, insofar as instrumentalism seeks to understand judge-made law, it is powerless to criticize (since it cannot exhibit its explanatory end as law's own end); insofar as it seeks to criticize, it is powerless to understand (since its moral standard is external and so not explanatory). Because, moreover, the instrumentalist's critical standpoint is external to law's own principle of coherence, his or her moral admonitions fall on deaf ears. Since the instrumentalist's favored goal is dogmatically asserted against a practice obedient to its own basic norm, moral criticism fails to produce arguments that lawyers (as lawyers) are rationally bound to accept. Accordingly, neither the interpretation nor the criticism of property law can proceed convincingly along instrumentalist lines. While a faithful account of property law must account for the subordination of private property (through taxation and eminent domain) to the ends of collective action, it cannot treat property law simply as a means to such ends.

The second component of our thesis states that an interpretation of property law faithful to its object can reveal a coherent totality. In making this claim we join issue with Critical Legal Studies, which maintains that a faithful reading of the common law can witness only fragmentation and contradiction.[5] At stake in this dispute is the possibility of an idea of law understood as a norm to which appeal may be made for an impartial settlement of conflicting claims of right. This idea requires that law form an unbroken totality, a system unified by a single theme, for otherwise there is no public reason to constrain a judge's choice among competing first principles of right, hence nothing to differentiate law from the forcible imposition of preference.[6] Our thesis is that the common law of property forms such a whole. Since this claim may initially strike some as being either trivially true or highly implausible, I shall say why I think it is neither.

The claim might seem trivial if we proposed to unify property law by abstracting from all substantive moral principles to a purely formal one (such as internal coherence) regulating how we argue whatever substantive principle we adopt. A unity of this kind would clearly be too thin to have any force against the CLS challenge. Yet our thesis is not trivial because the unity it proposes is based on a full-bloodedly substantive criterion of just law. Still, our claim would be implausible if it envisaged a unity of property law based on a singular, exclusive, or undifferentiated principle of justice; for a unity of this simple kind could be constructed only at the price of an exclusion of doctrine so massive as to render our interpretation hopelessly forced.[7] We do not, however, propose to unify property law under a singular principle. A unified body of law needs a unifying theme, but it does not require a singular principle of right; for the theme may be differently embodied in a plurality of doctrinal formations, each of which is essential to the theme's validation as the authentic ground of law. The unifying idea of property law may, in other words, incorporate its diverse manifestations in systems based on other principles and may be the idea that saves, connects, and orders these systems as parts of a whole. The law of property (and indeed the common law as a whole) may thus be a system of doctrinal systems. This, at any rate, is what I shall argue. I shall not, therefore, attempt to vindicate unity by suppressing diversity or complexity, by declaring an opposing principle to be error, or by coercing principles and counterprinciples alike into a monistic paradigm.* On the contrary, the interpretive thesis I offer has force against the critical one because it acknowledges a differentiation of principle in property law, one

---

*That the common law's unity does not declare rival *principles* as errors does not mean that it cannot distinguish between valid and invalid *decisions* or *doctrines*. On the contrary, this unity reveals as error those decisions and doctrines that flow from treating some particular principle as the exclusive foundation of law rather than as part of a whole.

that is, however, integrated within an organic and encompassing unity. The principle of this unity will generate rules both for resolving conflicts between the constituent principles and for allocating the custody of these principles to different organs of the legal system.[8]

Finally, I argue that property law's internal unity is morally justified. By this I do not mean that it is justified by a moral standard external to law; nor do I mean only that the law's internal standard is experienced as having moral force by those involved in interpreting and applying it. Rather, I wish to argue that the moral unity of property law is valid simply. With this thesis I take aim at two schools of thought that are in other respects opposed: at the positivist who maintains that, because law's nature must be understood without reference to morality, any normativity must come from a moral criterion external to law's own concept, one having prescriptive but no constitutive power;[9] and at the law-as-interpretation school, for which the interpretation of a legal tradition cannot do more than give a positive account of its changeable moral unity, since interpretation lacks a transcendent standard by which to criticize or justify the moral visions informing particular practices and traditions.[10] Both positions raise a formidable protest against the claim that the common law's internal rationality can be morally valid. The power of this challenge flows in large measure from our conviction that the norms structuring local practices are valid for those practices alone; and that, while they provide a standard for the internal criticism of particular features of a practice, they cannot criticize the practice as a whole. This conviction leads us to suspect that anyone ascribing universal validity to the moral unity of a practice is arbitrarily eternalizing that which is historically or culturally conditioned as well as ideologically excluding possibilities that the principle of the practice cannot accommodate. It may also lead us to believe that an unconditioned moral criterion, one capable of evaluating relative normative systems, must be transcendent of, or external to, all such systems.

We have already touched (in our comments on prescriptive instrumentalism) on the difficulty inherent in seeking an unconditioned moral standard outside the normative perspectives of temporal practices. Such a project seems destined to fail, because the external standpoint is itself a particular one in relation to the plurality it transcends, an ahistorical standard conditioned by the many historical ones it has fled. If the relativity of an internal norm was produced by its being alongside other normative systems, each determined as a particular system by those it excludes, then this predicament is reproduced in the relationship between the one transcendent norm and the many internal ones. Since the supposedly unconditioned norm is conditioned as monistic and ahistorical by the plurality and mutability it seeks to escape, it cannot legitimately claim a status more privileged than that of any internal principle. This conclusion seems to vindicate the historicist position of the law-as-interpretation school: that we must resign ourselves to moral contingency whether we seek to understand law from within or to criticize it from without.

Suppose, however, that the norm internal to law were not a finite or particular value (such as efficiency, solidarity, or integrity) but a philosophically rigorous conception of the unconditioned. By a conception of the unconditioned I mean a view of an end whose end-status depends on no condition that may or may not obtain. Ends (such as fame) whose worth depends on tastes, opinions, or interests one may or may not have are ends only in a conditional or relative sense. Likewise, ends (such as full employment) that are desired for the sake of something else (such as happiness) cannot be unconditionally valid, for it will make sense to pursue the subordinate end only in circumstances where it will in fact further the higher end. Neither can an end that is one among many be unconditioned, because where conflicts arise a choice must be made and so the end's validity depends on the chooser. All such ends are contingent ends; and because they are contingently valid, they cannot (as Kant taught) form the foundation of a law distinguished from a partisan interest and having binding force. An unconditioned end is one whose validity depends on no fortuity, presupposition, or particular interest. Something that depends on no fortuity is free, so that a conception of the unconditioned is also a conception of something unqualifiedly free. By a philosophically rigorous conception I mean one that does not naively ascribe unconditioned status to a value found in inclination or in a culture but that (to begin with) intentionally strives to free itself from all such given norms in order to arrive at one whose necessary validity seems assured because it is just the capacity for this self-emancipation. We shall see that the main part of property law (and of the common law generally) is organized around a view of an unconditioned end of this abstract and reflexive character.

Of course, the moral validity of property law's unity is not adequately defended by showing that this unity rests on *a* conception of an unconditioned end. Rather, it must be shown that property law is built on a conception that survives intellectual scrutiny. The conception of the unconditioned to which a morally valid common law is ordered must be an adequate conception. Let us suppose further, then, that the common law's internal rationality consists in a process wherein an abstract and negative view of the unconditioned collapses (because of its dependence on some unexamined premise or prior interest) precisely in embodying itself in a legal system, yielding to a better conception that unifies the previous one with the element it lacked. Since the downfall of the first conception is immanent to it, and since the new conception is already implied in the self-contradictory realization of the old, the process never moves outside the sphere of necessary validity. Suppose, finally, that this process produced a conception of the unconditioned that is adequate because it encompasses all previous formations as embodiments of itself (therefore being alongside none), and because it is just the rational process of its self-production (therefore being completely self-dependent). Were law's internal rationality conceived in this manner, we would not need to leap outside the common-law tradition in search of an impartial normative standpoint, for the tradition would itself generate that standpoint. Nor would we need to transcend law to criticize its foundations, because law's process would itself consist in the autocriticism and rebuilding of legal foundations; and this process we would interpretively recapitulate as yielding progressively better instances of the principle produced at the end. The self-criticism of law would take the form of a critique not only of doctrine in light of a historically regnant normative standard but also of the standard itself in light of its self-contradictory embodiment in a doctrinal system. Law's internal unity would be morally valid, because it would be the organized plurality of fallen systems of natural right, a comprehensive system itself indissoluble because it would compromise only legal principles (and the rules derived therefrom) that have been generated from an autonomous, disinterested, and lawful movement of reason.[11]

I have obviously gestured in these preliminary and doubtless cryptic remarks to the dialectical method of Hegel.[12] To defend the claim that property law's internal unity is morally valid, I shall attempt to reproduce in more detailed form the dialectical logic that structures Hegel's account of law in the *Philosophy of Right*.[13] That is to say, I shall attempt to elucidate the necessity by which an abstract conception of freedom dissolves as an unconditioned normative foundation precisely in its self-realization in a common-law paradigm, as well as the necessity by which it yields to a conception more adequate to the idea of freedom. The movement continues until the conception of freedom by which we interpret (and unify) the process is spontaneously produced by the logic of the conceptions by which jurists organize law from within. In this way, our thematic principle is not left as a hypothesis or presupposition by which we arbitrarily construct the material but is independently validated by the common law's own historical evolution.

It might seem that, in eschewing a functionalist view of property law's coherence and in affirming instead a rationality internal to its own discourse, I am atavistically defending a position commonly known as legal formalism. Were this charge justified, it would be fatal to this project, for my aim is not to meet the dogmatism of Critical Legal Studies with a one-sidedness of my own but rather to explicate the immanent unity of property law in a way that is no longer formalist (in any meaningful sense of the word) and so no longer vulnerable to the attacks to which formalism has for the most part succumbed. Accordingly, I must begin by criticizing not only functionalism but also an alternative view of property law's immanent unity, one that may properly be described as formalist.

2. CONCEPTUAL AND FUNCTIONAL APPROACHES

In its classical, nineteenth-century form, legal formalism held that the manifold doctrines making up private law could be deduced from a few basic concepts (e.g., property, license, lease, contract) and applied to particular facts so as to yield logically predictable results.[14] This was the "scientific" or "deductive" jurisprudence attacked with great energy and passion by the legal realists in the first three decades of this century. Although virtually bereft of contemporary adherents, legal formalism has shown a surprising power to rule from the grave; for it continues to shape all skeptical thought for which its deductive method is the model of an avowedly nonpartisan or apolitical rationality. For anyone who identifies the quest for a nonpartisan legal discourse with formalism, the unmasking of deductive jurisprudence as a facade for unstated value commitments will seem like the demolition of impartial legal discourse itself. In the same oblique manner, legal formalism has continued to mold our language, having turned "conceptualism"—now widely understood as a habit of thought that disguises contingent value choices as the impersonal dictates of the meaning of words—into a term of academic insult. One would think that there is no understanding of concepts except as the conventional meanings of words.

Let us try to drive a wedge between legal formalism and the quest for a nonpartisan rationality with which it is mistakenly identified. What truly distinguished legal formalism was not that it reasoned from concepts but that it reasoned from concepts understood in a certain manner. The formalist view of concepts has been well captured in the satiric metaphors of its most famous critics—in Rudolf Von Jhering's image of the "jurist's heaven of concepts"[15] and in Oliver Wendell Holmes's allusion to formalist law as "a brooding omnipresence in the sky."[16] Both metaphors express an idea of law as something autonomous vis-à-vis human subjects. For the legal formalist, law was an object externally given to the judge, something that he or she was obliged—to the extent that the application of general rules permitted it—to passively report and self-effacingly execute. The autonomous existence of law was considered the guarantee of its objectivity (hence of its status as law), of its remaining free of contamination by the moral opinions of the reporter. As the doctrinal manifold was viewed as externally given, so too were the concepts in which this manifold was abbreviated. These concepts confronted the judge as external essences or definitions having legal force independently of any connection to human purposes or values.[17] The law of property offers several examples of this reified form of conceptualism, and a consideration of one will suffice to disclose the nemesis to which it is prone.

The law of real property distinguishes between two kinds of defeasible fees simple.[18] One it calls a determinable fee and the other a fee simple with a condition subsequent. The distinction between these grants rests on the contrast between the logical categories of substance and accident. In the case of a determinable fee, the condition under which the grantee holds the estate is said to be intrinsic to the estate; whereas in the case of a fee simple with a condition subsequent, the condition is an accidental adjunct to what is in essence a fee simple. It makes an enormous difference how the grant is characterized, because the consequences of a void condition will vary drastically depending on the nature of the grant. If the grantee took a determinable fee and the condition is illegal (say, as imposing a restraint on marriage), then the grant fails entirely because the condition spoils the fee of which it is an integral element. If, however, the grantee took a fee simple with a condition subsequent, the court will excise the void condition and award the grantee a fee simple. Despite the great difference in consequences, however, the court's overt focus is never on the outcome but on the kind of estate that was created. Was the condition part of the essence of the estate, or was it external to an estate complete without it? Because the testator hardly ever reveals his or her intentions in this regard, the courts say that words such as "until," "while," or "as long as" indicate a determinable fee, while phrases like "but if" or "provided that" are the hallmark of a condition subsequent. In fact, however, discrepant judgments are reached on identical wording, and one judge has remarked that decisions on this point reflect no credit on English law.[19]

What precisely goes wrong with this way of doing law? The working premise of any attempt to interpret a branch of law is that law has a point, that it is related to an end, and that its rationality consists in this relation. To say this is to make no concession to functionalism, for something may be related to an end inwardly or essentially rather than externally and contingently: not as a tool is related to a goal of which it forms no part but as a repository of meaning (e.g., a poem) is related to the meaning it embodies. Furthermore, if property law is related to an end, then it must also be related to a subject or self; for subjectivity is the origin of a constitutive purpose—of a purpose that can be sensibly attributed to an object as its own. For example, the thing on which I sit is *for* sitting (it is a chair, *chaise*, *Stuhl*, etc.) because someone designed it with that purpose in mind. We may say that an Arctic hare's white coat is for the purpose of camouflage, but this is a figure of speech in the absence of an artificer who created the white coat for that purpose; we are here imposing rather than eliciting meaning. Accordingly, if purpose is validly ascribed to property law, it is because the latter is the work of a subject. We do not yet have to decide whether property law is related to the material interests of human subjects or to a transcendental subjectivity prior to such interests; at this point we need only remark that the rationality of property law consists in its purposefulness and that its purposefulness consists in its relation to a subject, for only a subject can be conscious of its purpose in a way that makes the realized object an embodiment thereof.[20]

Now the characteristic feature of the conceptualism exemplified above is that it makes essences *divorced* from subjectivity the premise of judgment. Concepts such as "fee simple," "determinable fee," and "condition subsequent" are defined in terms of attributes having no connection to an end one might think worthy of allegiance; and these definitions form the major premise of a syllogism whose conclusion resolves a human controversy. Formalism adheres to such "value-free" concepts because it wishes to preserve the objectivity and neutrality of law and, correlatively, the freedom of the litigant who otherwise, it is feared, would be dependent on the subjective values of the judge. The nemesis of this project occurs, however, when the poles of subject and object that are rigidly separated in theory come together in adjudicative practice. The litigant is now bound to a power that is blind and irrational, for the law is indifferent not simply to this or that human purpose but to purposiveness as such. Whether the grantee takes a fee simple or nothing depends on a formal distinction between categories that embodies no purpose whatsoever.[21] Moreover, because the categories are detached from purpose, judgment has no guide in deciding whether some concrete thing is an instance of one or the other. No rationale is available to assist in the application of the abstract concepts. In the practice of adjudication, therefore, the law's putative objectivity dissolves in the arbitrary subjectivism of a judge who conceals the real ground of his decision behind the fiat of a characterization. Thus the subject's freedom in the law becomes its bondage to the law, while the objectivity of law turns round into judicial caprice.[22]

If reified conceptualism is taken as the model of a legal science based on concepts, then the reaction against it will issue in a down-to-earth and commonsense functionalism.[23] For if concepts are divorced from subjectivity, then the reappropriation of law for the subject must involve a denial of the authority of concepts and the subordination of law to concrete human interests. Thus, from an autonomous object dominating the self, law becomes a humble servant of human goals chosen through an unfettered practical reasoning. In the law of property, this intellectual shift is epitomized by a transformation in the way property is conceived. From a premise of deductive reasoning, property becomes a conclusion of practical reasoning. The law does not protect something because it exemplifies (i.e., is capable of exclusive possession, has exchange value, is not a person) a mysterious essence called property; rather, something is property because the law protects an interest in its exclusive possession, and the law protects this interest because doing so enhances the general welfare.[24] Property is thus infinitely malleable. There are no longer any specific rights (e.g., of possession, use, and alienation) necessarily entailed by the concept of property, for property is whatever shifting combination or "bundle" of interests a court will enforce. Correspondingly, an act is a taking, not because some right essential to property has been violated, but because policy (or Pareto) decrees that the plaintiff be compensated. In sum, property is not a natural relation but a variable social construct.[25]

Viewed in relation to its conceptualist foil, the functionalist understanding of property law has an exhilarating clarity that assures it a lasting niche in the history of legal thought. Relative to the view that solutions to human conflicts are deducible from autonomous concepts, the reorientation of legal thought toward goals and interests is a progressive and emancipatory movement. Yet the limitations of that movement become apparent once we see that functionalism depends on, or is shaped by, the very conceptualism it opposes. Because it identifies the authority of concepts with that of reified concepts, functionalism rejects the rule of concepts as such. It thus indirectly allows reified concepts the very fixed reality and determining power it wants to deny them. Accordingly, once we sever that equation, the rationale for the functionalist's anticonceptualism vanishes, as do the chains that bind legal thought to the past. If functionalism is to survive this liberation, it must prove itself afresh as an independently persuasive theory of property. That is to say, it must validate itself, not through an endless polemic against formalism (as if it were the only alternative thereto), but by affirmatively showing itself to be the best understanding of property considered as a social institution interpreted by judges and lawyers independently of reflection about property.* Yet this is what it cannot do.

To show the inadequacy of functionalism as an interpretive account of property, one need only compare the functionalist view of property with the juristic conception. If property is simply a conclusion of a welfarist

---

*That this is an appropriate test can be shown by the following argument. Were it to assert itself against the discourse of property law, functionalism would contradict itself as a theory of property. This is so because functionalism purports to tell the truth about what property is. That property is a social construct or a conclusion of practical reasoning is the putative truth about property. If in making this claim functionalism opposed itself to the discourse by which the institution of property is interpreted by jurists, then the putative truth of the functionalist claim would be transformed into an arbitrary assertion. Since it could not appeal for verification to the jurist's understanding of property, functionalism would, when confronted with this understanding, appeal to its own perspective, that is, to its brute say-so. But it would thereby accord an equal standing to the say-so of its opponent and would therefore deny the possibility of the truth that it initially claimed.

calculus, then the concept of property is really superfluous; it performs no work in practical reasoning that is not fully performed by the injunction to maximize (or equalize) welfare. If a band of individuals conceives a passion for something from which I de facto exclude others, I cannot raise a right of property to defeat those appetites or even to require them to be sufficiently urgent to override the right. Rather, I discover what my "property" is only after the competing interests have been weighed; and in this balancing my interest enjoys no qualitative privilege over those of my despoilers.[26] To be sure, my possession of the thing renders my interest prima facie weightier than theirs, for confidence in secure possession is a great social boon; nevertheless, my interest carries this weight not because the thing is mine but because another criterion—the general welfare—favors it. Thus (leaving aside for the moment arguments favoring concealment of a dangerous truth) the notion of property can costlessly be dispensed with as a vestigial oddity, as an idea belonging to a conceptual scheme now superseded. To say, however, that the notion of property is redundant is to say that it refers to nothing. The consequence of the functionalist view of property, then, is that there is no such relation as property.[27] This implication is, however, directly at odds with the law of property, whose most basic postulate is that property *is*, that there exists a real relation to which the concept of property refers. Functionalism, to be sure, is not entirely without resources with which to account for this claim. If not simply a product of false, conceptualist consciousness, the claim is understandable as an exoteric doctrine needed to dissemble a truth that, if publicly acknowledged, might undermine expectations of secure possession. For the functionalist, then, the internal discourse of property law is comprehensible either as ideological self-deception or as a salutary lie. Yet to account for this discourse as meaning what functionalism means rather than what it actually says is to efface or reduce legal discourse in the very act of seeking confirmation from it. It is arbitrarily to appeal to one's own perspective under the guise of deferring to the law.

A further consequence of functionalism is that there is no essential difference between the adjudication of property disputes involving private persons and the distribution of entitlements among members of a body politic. On the functionalist view, for example, whether the Associated Press has a right to enjoin International News Services from publishing news copied from its own reports depends crucially on the likely impact of such a right on the accessibility of information to the public.[28] Hence the functionalist must weigh the need for incentives to gather news against whatever restriction on availability an injunction would entail, and he must do so whether he is a judge in a two-party dispute or a member of a legislative committee. Similarly, a functionalist will see in lease covenants, easements, and equitable servitudes nothing but a decentralized form of public land-use planning, and so he will apply to these private arrangements the same welfarist norm he would consult in interpreting a statute. Thus the judge's task becomes one of ascertaining the mix of private planning and authoritative regulation that optimally achieves the welfarist goal; and if servitude law consists of restrictions and distinctions incomprehensible from this perspective, then it is considered arcane, irrational, and obsolete.[29]

In these examples, functionalism obliterates the difference between adjudication, on the one hand, and legislation and public administration, on the other. Concomitantly, it effaces the difference between the interaction of strangers under corrective justice and the cooperative association of citizens under distributive justice. More basically, functionalism fails to take seriously the difference between private and public law. It must therefore assert the truth of its perspective over against an internal discourse for which this distinction is taken for granted. Because it reduces private to public law, functionalism has no non-question-begging account (i.e., no account that does not privilege its own public-law perspective) of the structural differences between courts and public-law bodies, for their varying job capabilities, or for the difference between the retrospective character of judicial reasoning and the forward-looking orientation of political discourse. Functionalism may be able to explain these differences; but the explanation will make the differences appear superficial, since the distinctive features of courts will be related to the same public goal sought by legislators and administrators. Now, of course, the functionalist may reply that respect for the public/private distinction is but one more example of the formalist bondage to concepts, that the distinction is historically contingent and destined to pass away. Indeed, he may point to already visible signs of change, to more candid judicial invocations of policy and to more thinly disguised manipulations of precedent. Ultimately, there is but one way to meet this argument, and that is through a nonformalist account of property law that ethically vindicates the public/private distinction and that reveals functionalism's appeal to changing legal practice as simply another appeal to itself.

3. THE STARTING POINT OF OUR ACCOUNT

The starting point of such an account must be one that overcomes the one-sidedness of both conceptualism and functionalism. Conceptualism sought to keep law pure of a subjectivity equated with individual preference; it thereby exposed law to inevitable contamination by the enemy in the process of law application. Functionalism sought to ground law in a subjectivity conceived ethically as public policy but dissolved property and private law generally in the hegemony of the collective welfare. If the defect of the former is its indifference to purpose, that of the latter is a preoccupation with material ends that ignores the formal subject of these ends. Each thus lacks an element of what the other possesses.

This leads us to the thought that an account of property law might begin from an end that is itself a concept, that transcends empirical ends as their author and possessor. Such an end is subjectivity itself, understood to begin with as the empty and purely formal point of spontaneity that we reach when we abstract from every contingent trait, preference, or purpose found in our particular makeup (34–35). The capacity for this abstraction underpins a certain dimension of freedom, a certain conception of equality, a certain conception of the public, and a certain understanding of rights. Inasmuch as these conceptions will explain key features of the common law, I shall first lay them out without criticism. Then I shall make clear the basic assumption underlying my decision to begin a justificatory account of property law with the abstract subject.

First, the capacity for detachment from all one's likes and dislikes is a capacity for freedom understood in a negative sense. The fact that I can distinguish myself from the manifold inclinations found in my consciousness means that *I* am not a nonentity pulled along by these impulses; I can always refuse to follow. And because I can refuse an impulse, any one that I yield to is a possibility I have chosen from a range of alternatives. Accordingly, the capacity for self-transcendence is a capacity for choice, understood as a purely negative power not to be absorbed in this or that appetite and hence not to be governed by the mechanistic laws according to which appetites respond to external stimuli. By virtue of this capacity, I can cease to identify myself with the empirical individual who is passively affected by desire as well as dependent on others for satisfaction; I can instead take as my essential nature the pure self abstracted from desire.[30] I cannot, of course, extricate the self from its empirical habitat; but I can (overbroadly, as it will turn out) depreciate as merely given or natural the individuated aspects of myself and regard my generic self as my true self. By thus withdrawing in thought from my empirical situation of susceptibility and dependence, I gain an intimation of freedom, for I am now dependent for my sense of solid reality on nothing outside me. To be sure, this freedom may be described pejoratively as formal (some will say insane), since the objects of choice are not yet themselves generated from the free will and reduced to an ordered system but are found as "natural" inclinations that know no bounds to their separate satisfaction (10–12). Also, it is a kind of freedom one may possess even in the most abject dependence on others for the satisfaction of one's needs or wants. Yet even if formal freedom is inadequate as freedom, still, there is no recognizable sense of freedom without its formal aspect of choice.

The capacity for abstraction is also a capacity to adopt a standpoint from which all agents may be regarded as in a certain sense equal. They are equal precisely by virtue of having abstracted from everything that distinguishes them as individuals. That is to say, their equality consists in the abstract sameness of selfhood, in which all distinctions including those of ethical merit are obliterated. Again, this kind of equality may be disparaged as formal, since it is quite compatible with extreme inequalities of welfare and because its one-sided actualization as a legal foundation results in the effacement of differences thought to be valuable (47). However, this is an indictment not against formal equality but against treating the latter as the sole ethically relevant sense of equality or as *the* foundation of law. We shall soon see that there is room within a rich and comprehensive legal system for a doctrinal paradigm governed by formal equality.

The capacity for abstraction also underlies a certain conception of public rationality. Specifically, where all values are identified with nonrational preferences, the public sphere must be conceived by abstracting from value as such to the self's bare capacity for choosing values. The public domain is constituted, accordingly, not by a common good anchored in human nature but by a free will torn loose from nature—a will hospitable by virtue of its emptiness to every conception of the good. The specific virtue of a public sphere so constituted is neutrality with respect to all values. Where all ends have the significance of natural inclination, the purity of the public domain depends on its remaining aloof from, and hence neutral toward, the private pursuit of values indiscriminately regarded as subjective.

Finally, the capacity for abstraction is a capacity for rights. This is so because the abstraction from particular interests reveals a (putatively) universal or unconditioned end behind the relativistic preferences of individuals—an end not in the sense of a supreme good one aspires to but in the sense of a self-conscious purposiveness that alone entitles one to treat one's aims as one's own and one's motion as action rather than instinctive behavior. We can call this end liberty or freedom of choice. Because it is predicable of all agents however else they may differ, liberty is an end capable of objectively binding other agents to respect it. It is not a preference that some arbitrarily impose on others. Rather, it is an end that demands respect from others precisely insofar as they assert themselves in action (and so themselves lay claim to respect) as ends; and because one's own liberty is an end valid for others, one can in turn respect their liberty without contradiction to one's equal status as an end.[31] Because, however, the universal end commanding respect is here just the formal spontaneity of the will, the rights generated by the capacity for abstraction are limited to negative rights against noninterference with liberty. No positive right to concern for one's welfare can enter here, for welfare denotes the satisfaction of natural appetite (37–38). In sum, then, the capacity for self-transcendence is a capacity for liberty and for equal rights to liberty—a capacity known to legal thought as personality.

Our account of property law thus takes as its starting point the concept of personality, conceived initially in the quite insular, decontextualized, and formal manner just described. The justification for this beginning must await the conclusion of the account, for it must await the emergence of an adequate foundational principle from which alone any initial approach to understanding law can be justified. That principle will be the true first even though it comes last in the order of argument. This means that we begin with an isolated individual not simply because property law does, nor because we wish to posit this individual as an absolute foundation in the manner of liberal political theory, but because we anticipate the idea that will accord the ethical standpoint of the atomistic individual (and of liberal theory) a partial justification. Until this idea comes forward, however, the decision to begin a justificatory account of property law with the atomistic individual involves an assumption that this individual's standpoint is worthy of respect, or that a morally justified property law must somehow include a legal formation ordered to the unconditioned as seen from this point of view.

The reason why the atomistic individual sees the unconditioned as the abstract self has already been hinted at. No value that I seek as an isolated individual can bind others to promote it, for such a value is a preference I happen to have, something simply found in my makeup and having no necessary value for others. If I am necessarily isolated from others (if there is no natural community founded on a common good), then all values have this nonrational and relative significance. Hence I can reach a basis for valid obligation only by abstracting from value per se to the pure capacity for forming values, which capacity is (supposedly) no longer relative. This is not to say that the abstract self will *remain* the only aspect of the atomistic individual to be accorded legal significance. It will not, for there is no expression of freedom except through action directed to the specific goals of concrete individuals. However, we must begin at this point, for our quest for an unconditioned end as the foundation of law must commence with the abstraction from every contingent end of the empirical individual and so from the most vacuous of concepts. Any richer or more individuated conception of the self must prove itself worthy of rights from this starting point, that is, through an immanent critique of abstract personality as the sole unconditioned end.

Accordingly, while our account of property law begins with the abstract self, it will not abide there permanently.[32] Were it to do so, it would once again be open to attack as a species of formalism, albeit one of more venerable descent. It would be vulnerable to this charge because it would have isolated and privileged as the sole essential reality a one-sidedly universal and self-related self, while correspondingly excluding from juridical recognition the well-being of the determinate and dependent individual; and it will have done so even though the abstract self presupposes, or is reflexively conditioned (as an emptiness) by, the determinate individuality from which it abstracted and on which it thus depends. Resting on this one-sided foundation, our account will perhaps succeed in encompassing the main body of property law; but it will be embarrassed by a significant number of peripheral doctrines embodying what, following Hegel, I shall call rights of intention—that is, rights against the legal power of consequences beyond one's rational control and against the legal power of interests exclusive of one's own (115–121, 132). Under this rubric I include such doctrines as proprietary estoppel, "quasi-property," contractual licenses, and certain forms of the constructive trust, all of which embody a judicial duty of concern for the effective autonomy of *individual* subjects. To the extent that it fails to accommodate these doctrines, a theory of property law will fail as an interpretive account of its object. For it will have achieved unity at the cost of repression and exclusion, thereby revealing itself as an arbitrary construction of its object rather than as a true account of it; and it will have revealed the object not as a rational whole (as it intended) but as an incoherent combination of antithetical principles.

The remainder of the chapter, then, has the following structure. We begin by deriving from self-related personality a relation of property that is independent of positive law, of societal goals, indeed even (to some extent) of the mutual adjustment of liberty in tort law. This relation will generate the doctrines that make up the legal paradigm ordered to the abstract self as unconditioned end. This paradigm we shall call formal right. We also try to show how the theory of property based on abstract personality makes sense of the common law—specifically, of the doctrines of possession, adverse possession, nuisance law, servitudes, alienability, and the criteria of property. Subsequently we show how the embodiment of abstract personality in common-law property negates rather than realizes it as the sole unconditioned end and leads to a reconceptualization of personality as self-expressive in the concrete goals of the determinate individual. With this new foundation of right we understand a legal paradigm ordered to the common good of autonomy, one whose doctrines remedy the person's self-loss in formal right and so perfect its freedom. We also understand, however, a theoretical momentum toward the dissolution of formal right in a paradigm where property is determined by considerations of distributive fairness, a momentum counteracted by the very principle of individual self-determination the new paradigm intends to realize. The resultant tension between individualistic and communal paradigms of right constitutes the modern challenge for a theory of the common law's unity. To this challenge we respond with a foundation of right already implied by the downfall of the old, one that incorporates both paradigms as subordinate aspects of a whole.

4. PROPERTY AS THE REALIZATION OF PERSONALITY

4.1 Some Puzzles

Let us begin by noting some perplexing phenomena of property law. When courts have to decide in a case of first impression whether something is amenable to protection as property, they express a variety of views as to what property is. Sometimes a judge will say that property is a conclusion rather than a premise of law, by which he means that law creates property rights rather than protecting ones antecedently established. Adopting this position, he or she may then offer the view either that the criterion of property is the general welfare or that property is secreted out of the reconciliation of liberties in tort law. So, for example, if a question arises as to whether information is property, a judge may decide the issue by weighing the social costs and benefits of legal protection or by asking whether, in taking the information, the defendant violated a confidence or breached a fiduciary duty owed the plaintiff.[33] Some judges, however, take a different view. They say (or intimate) that property is a relation existing inchoately prior to law, a relation that the law merely recognizes and perfects. Even more curiously, they say that the criteria for determining whether this relation exists are the expenditure of labor in acquiring the thing and the fact that the thing has exchange value.[34] Seldom, however, is an explanation offered for the relevance of these factors. It is certainly not self-evident that the bare fact of labor expenditure should entitle one to exclusive possession of something needed more by someone else; nor is it clear why the willingness of others to pay for the thing should determine whether it is mine. Indeed, far from helping to constitute property, this willingness seems to presuppose it.

Consider a further puzzle. An insistent theme of property law is the hostility of courts to burdens on the alienability of land and chattels. This motif is reflected in the elaborate fictions of fine and recovery that were once countenanced by courts to bar entailed estates, in common-law rules against the remote vesting of interests, and in the courts' aversion to conditions on grants involving substantial restraints on alienation.[35] Contemporary writers typically relate these rules to a social policy favoring the improvement and efficient use of property, but this rationale seems to project into antiquity an instrumentalist conception of the judicial role that is decidedly modern. The judges themselves offer more mysterious reasons for what they are doing. Perpetuities, said Lord Nottingham in 1681, "fight against God, by affecting a stability which human providence can never attain to, and are utterly against the reason and policy of the common law."[36] The policy to which Nottingham refers is, moreover, shrouded in the distant past, for "the law hath so long laboured to defeat perpetuities, that now it is become a sufficient reason of itself against any settlement to say it tends to a perpetuity."[37] As for a restraint on alienation annexed to a grant, the courts usually say not that such a condition discourages improvement but that it is repugnant to a grant of a fee simple.[38] Yet in what sense is it repugnant? If this were merely a semantic point, a point about how the concept of a fee simple is conventionally used by lawyers, there would be no real repugnance, for the grantor was obviously using the term in a nontechnical way and so was not contradicting himself. He intended to create an encumbered estate and that is what he did. The restraint on alienation is repugnant to the grant only if the right of alienation is essentially connected with property considered not as a conventional concept but as a real relation; for in that case the grantor has really done something absurd, granted something impossible to grant. But what is this connection between alienability and property?

The common law's aversion to restraints on alienating land and chattels is surpassed only by its reverse hostility to the relinquishment or sale of other sorts of entities, for example, one's liberty, one's capacity to own property, or one's life. Such transactions will be treated as void ab initio.[39] Those who view rules against restraints on alienation as serving efficient resource allocation have difficulty fitting within a single theory rules barring the alienation of life or liberty—although they have tried. For Guido Calabresi and A. Douglas Melamed, bans on alienation are economically justified when free alienability would produce significant displeasure in persons external to the transaction and when market imperfections prevent these third parties from paying the seller not to sell.[40] While this may be an economist's reason for a rule against selling oneself into slavery, one may doubt whether it is the law's reason. The common-law prohibition is categorical, whereas the economist would welcome a market in liberty if no one felt strongly enough about slavery to be willing to pay the price to stop it. Calabresi and Melamed treat the rule against alienating liberty as reflecting a "moralism"—that is, a moral preference with the same standing in the market as any other preference. But the common law is here the moralist, and rightly or wrongly no moralist regards his moral principles as moralisms in the economist's sense. We have, then, a divergence of perspective between the moralist and the economist. And since the inalienability rule is the moralist's creation, it seems sensible to seek its explanation in the moralist's mind.

Consider, finally, the ancient law of adverse possession. By this law, someone dispossessed of land or whose possession has been discontinued sees his title extinguished in favor of the squatter's if he fails to bring an action for recovery within a certain period from the time his right of action first arose. Inasmuch as time runs in favor only of someone against whom an action lies, the doctrine always rewards a wrongdoer. Once again the most common explanations for this rule are functionalist ones. The doctrine is said to have once facilitated the transfer of land by eliminating uncertainty about title and, by penalizing neglect, to have encouraged the use and improvement of land.[41] Neither of these explanations is convincing, however, because neither accounts for the cluster of rules forming the law of adverse possession. For example, if the doctrine's point is to quiet title, why require that the squatter's possession be specifically adverse, that is, inconsistent with the possession of the paper titleholder? This rule serves to exclude from the doctrine's benefit not only licensees but also trespassers making no significant use of the land. It thus introduces a requirement of substantial use that bears no clear relation to a policy of promoting certainty in the potential buyer and that may work to defeat his expectations. Even less persuasive is the rationale concerning the promotion of land use, for the doctrine encourages an owner making no use of land to oust a squatter whose use is intensive. How then are we to understand the doctrine of adverse possession?

4.2 The Formalism of Property

All of these questions inquire into the nature of the connection between property and something dimly seen by judges as required by its concept. Yet they are not questions about the essential attributes of property viewed as an autonomous concept; for property might be intelligible as the realization of a project, and its constituent elements might be derivable from that end. If we now turn to Hegel's *Philosophy of Right*, we will find a purposive account of property that vindicates and organizes common-law intuitions about the requisites and incidents of ownership.

Hegel's account of property differs from the type that predominates in the tradition of political theory. Typically, theories of property tell us why private property is useful or essential to the realization of a human goal thought desirable to attain. The goal might be virtue, the greatest happiness of the greatest number, economic efficiency, or personal autonomy, but the structure of the account in all these cases is the same: it imitates the structure of practical reasoning. With an eye to the favored goal, we show how private property is indispensable to its attainment or at least more conducive to it than any alternative.[42] Locke's theory of property departs from this model, for it is concerned not with the instrumental value of private property but with the conditions under which, and the reasons why, someone has a right to exclude others from something he or she has appropriated.[43] Yet neither instrumentalist nor Lockean theory provides a satisfactory account of the practice of private ownership; for neither suggests a plausible (let alone adequate) foundation for the participants' belief in a strong right of private property. By a strong right I mean one that has some, though not necessarily preemptive, normative weight *against* the public order. Instrumentalist theories offer notoriously weak support for such a right, for the common good that justifies private property will also justify redistributions without regard to any property right held prior to the distributive scheme. Since one's property will be defined publicly rather than by anything one does alone, there will be no property anterior to the public order that could constrain the pursuit of collective ends. By contrast, Locke takes seriously a right of private ownership but offers an extremely weak justification for it. The difficulties with the "mixing of labor" argument are too well known to require further discussion here, as are the problems with deriving a right to own things from a basic right of self-ownership.[44] To explain one relation of ownership in terms of another gets us no further in understanding ownership.

Now it would not be incorrect to say, as many do, that Hegel regards property as essential to freedom.[45] However, to offer this formulation as a description of Hegel's theory of property would be misleading, because his initial and central account of property in "Abstract Right" makes no reference to a common good. This account has at least this in common with Locke's, that it seeks a theoretical ground for the belief in the individual's sovereignty over things he has acquired in isolation. Yet it is far more sophisticated than Locke's account, for it finds a plausible conception of an absolute end that can indeed explain a belief in private property. The conception must be plausible in the sense that it must grasp an end whose validity one could reasonably think is independent of opinion or subjective interest, and that could therefore putatively ground an obligation to respect the fences one unilaterally erects around one's acquisitions. But the conception must grasp an end that is not a good, for no sovereign good can ground a property right exerting normative force against itself.

Where are we to find an unconditioned end if we cannot look among the goals that human beings strive for? One candidate for such an end that seems initially promising is independent of all opinions of the good because it is just the capacity for forming such opinions. Even if we think all goods are relative to individual desire, still, the capacity for choosing goods is necessarily given with all particular conceptions of the good; and so this capacity might be considered a background end that is universally expressed by agents as they pursue their individual goals. Accordingly, the capacity for choice offers a seemingly fixed point around which to build a system of duties. This capacity is, of course, the self or personality; and we shall now see that the centerpiece of the ethical system built around this view of the unconditioned is private property.

To begin with, the self who claims to be an absolute end conceives itself negatively, as that which is not peculiar to this or that individual. It is therefore a self stripped of all corporeal, mental, and affective characteristics. It has no concrete needs, values, or goals, no qualities of physical or moral character, no attributes of social or economic status, and no citizenship. It is simply and abstractly a person. By virtue of its abstraction from everything empirically given, the person stands opposed to a world of particular things, some forming its own natural endowment, others lying outside it. A "thing" is a being that is not a person, or that lacks the capacity for self-transcendence (42).[46] Lacking this capacity, the thing is not an unconditioned end and so offers no moral resistance (has no right) against its use and destruction by other beings. Yet while things cannot protest their subjugation to others, we do not yet see why one person must respect another's acquisition. The fact that the empirical individual needs things for biological survival cannot provide a reason for respect, for the absoluteness of abstract personality assumes the moral insignificance even of the empirical individual, who thus can claim no more right to exist than the plant or animal. Acquisition could command the respect of persons only if it were required by persons qua persons. But why should an absolute end have need of finite things?

Personality's need of things can be explained in the following way. The person claims to be an unconditioned end, and yet it is in fact conditioned as an emptiness by the very world of finite beings from which it abstracted.[47] As that which is not-finite, personality depends for its identity on the world of finite things. This dependence confers on finite things an independent reality to which personality is now juxtaposed. The juxtaposition of personality to an independent other, however, converts personality into something finite and particular. A disparity thus opens between personality's subjective conviction of absolute worth and the reality of its dependent and finite existence. Insofar, therefore, as personality remains alongside a world independent of it, it is self-contradictory as an unconditioned reality. This internal contradiction implies that personality lacks the world, whose subjugation to personality is needed to verify or make objective the person's claim of absolute worth. Because it lacks the world, personality also desires it. This is no longer an appetite for sensuous things relative to the particular individual but a universal (because conceptually generated) desire of personality for self-embodiment. The satisfaction of this desire is the cancellation of the independence of external things and their reduction to instrumentalities of the person. Because this reduction of things is to an end regarded as absolute, it is said to be constitutive of a property (39).

It is crucial to observe, however, that the necessity for this outward movement has not yet been incorporated into the notion of the self that is here regarded as an absolute end. The person regards itself as an end *prior* to its acquisitive activity, so that its objective realization in property, while inherently necessary to its end-status, is not known as such by the person through whom private ownership first becomes intelligible. We as interpreters see that the process of realization is just as essential to the unconditioned as the pure self; however, the person whose activity we are observing treats the pure self as alone essential, a view it then proceeds to refute by its own acquisitive action. This action will thus have a double significance: from the person's viewpoint, it will be the objectification of self-related personality as the sole unconditioned reality; from our viewpoint, however, it will be the manifestation in personality's freedom of the bond between self and other as the true ground of property. Later on I shall refer to this bond as dialogic community, which will come forward as the unifying theme of property law. At this point, however, we need only note the tension latent in a system of law based on the formal freedom of the isolated person. That system is intelligible as the objectification of a self that regards itself as an end independently of its concrete realization and hence independently of any relation to another. The process of realization, while necessary for the philosophic interpreter, is a matter of indifference to the conception of the unconditioned overtly governing the process. This tension ensures that the objectification of personality as the sole unconditioned reality will actually be its negation as such, for this process must involve the self's dependence on something outside it, with which its freedom is incompatible. Moreover, this result will prove the reality of a more inclusive conception of the unconditioned.

We can understand property, then, as the objectively realized claim of the person to be an absolute end. No doubt the acquisition of property is mediated by subjective needs and wants, but these can never justify a property in things, for the inclinations of one individual have no moral power to bind another. The universal and objective significance of property is that it embodies the end-status of personality (45). Because the self considers itself the sole essential reality, objects that are not selves are, from this point of view, inherently nothing in themselves, achieving their reality as instruments. Obversely, personality has a right to appropriate all things. Appropriation is thus not a violence done to things *ab extra* but is rather understood as a fulfillment of their own immanent nature (44).

From this understanding of property, we can already derive certain phenomena of the common law. First, property is here private property, because it is the embodiment of the self of the atomistic individual, external and indifferent to others. At this stage the presumed end of things is the singular self, the self of the discrete individual, a self that therefore

excludes the self of other individuals. The realization of this self as an absolute end is private property.[48] Second, the right ascribed to the person is
a liberty to appropriate, to embody its end-status in the control of things,
and legal duties are correspondingly limited to negative ones of noninterference with liberty and property. There are no juridical (i.e., coercive)
duties to bestow a benefit on anyone, for the particular advantage of one
individual cannot consistently with the equality of persons oblige others
independently of their consent, and all welfare is here understood as particularistic.[49] Since the embodiment of freedom is not yet known to be
part of freedom, there is as yet no understanding of welfare as the satisfaction of freedom's needs, hence no understanding of an individual good
that (because it is also a common good) could bind others to promote it.
Accordingly, the right of property is here independent of distributive considerations. As the abstraction from all want or need, the self has a right
qua self to appropriate but no right to any particular outcome based on
its needs as a determinate individual, for at this stage the determinate individual is invisible to right. Correlatively, the right of appropriation, while
limited by the property of others, is unlimited by any consideration of
their welfare. There is no proviso on legitimate appropriation that no one
be disadvantaged by it or even that enough be left for the subsistence of
others.

Taken together, these phenomena embody the formalism of property
law, its indifference to any dimension of selfhood other than the abstract
will and its bare capacity for choice. While this formalism will prove to be
the downfall of the system of right it organizes (insofar as that system
claims to be the totality of right), one must beware of emphasizing the
limitations of formal right at the expense of attention to its indispensable
contribution to a full content of justice. The fundamental achievement of
formal right is to grasp the individual self as an end categorically distinguished from selfless objects and equal in respect of this status to other
selves. By virtue of this status, the person cannot be forced to serve the
pleasure of another. Formal right's refusal to recognize affirmative duties
has this principle in mind; and even though this blanket refusal fails to
distinguish between particularistic and objective welfare (the ground for
this distinction having not yet appeared), still, the freedom from subjection to another's particular interests must be part of *any* conception of
what the freedom and equality of persons requires. Furthermore, one cannot be confident that respect for persons is possible without a respect for
the system of formal right itself. Critics of the meager conception of personality on which formal right is based assume that once we attain a truer,
more robust conception of the self, we can abandon the impoverished one
along with the distinctive legal system it orders. This assumption is in one
sense perfectly natural. If one takes for granted the existence of a clear di-

chotomy between truth and error, one might wonder how an erroneous conception of selfhood can retain any independent normative force so as to constitute by itself a legal paradigm. One might also deny that abandoning formal right means sacrificing any of its positive achievements, for whatever was worthy of respect in that paradigm must surely be retained under a more comprehensive and truer conception of personality.

We shall presently see that this natural way of thinking is shallow. From the fact that a conception of selfhood proves defective one may not conclude that its independent normative power is spent; for the revelation of the defect is part of the objective truth—the known truth—of the better conception, which is thus abstractly conceived without the entire critical process of which it is the organic result. Because the truer idea issues from the collapse of the inferior one, that idea contains or presupposes the imperfect form of itself; hence it cannot without cost to its own objective validity subdue that form to its one-sided imperium. Furthermore, one cannot assume that whatever is worth preserving in formal right will be honored in a system of law that subsumes formal right under a more inclusive conception of selfhood. We shall soon see that an idea of justice based exclusively on a richer, more individuated conception of personality must actualize itself by dissolving property, by treating individual rights as variable conclusions of the collective welfare, and by thus denying the end-status of individual personality. It is therefore conceptually essential to freedom that the paradigm of formal right be preserved in the transition to a better conception of justice; and the crucial question will be how these paradigms can coherently coexist so as to preserve the unity of law.

4.3 Possession

If property is the objective reality of the person's status as an end, we understand property when we understand all the conditions for the end's realization. Because these conditions will be the necessary and jointly sufficient ones of an objectively valid mastery of things, they will stand to each other not as isolated "sticks" in a "bundle" but as coessential elements of a totality.[50] That is to say, they will form what are commonly called the "incidents" of ownership—the particular rights that are involved in the notion of property. Each condition will be partly constitutive of a property in things, because each will objectify in a progressively more adequate way the person's claimed end-status vis-à-vis things. Property in the full sense will be the interconnected totality of all its partial realizations. It will be possible to distinguish, therefore, between an imperfect and a fully realized property and so between inferior and superior (or relative and absolute) titles to things; and it will be possible to parcel out for finite periods some of the constituent elements of property while keeping intact its atemporal notion, thereby making possible the ideas of a remainder and a reversion.

Let us, therefore, follow Hegel's derivation of the elements of property, relating it as we go to the common law. To begin with, the person proves itself as the end of things by physically possessing them (54–58).[51] Possession confers a (defeasible) right to exclude because it (partially) objectifies a normative claim—a claim that personality is an absolute end commanding respect. Possession is, however, the weakest form of self-validation because it leaves the thing with a semblance of positive reality. The thing is possessed, but it continues to exist independently of the self. In possession, moreover, the person's self-proving activity is hemmed in by physical constraints, for there are narrow limits to what one can manually grasp, form, or mark out. The possessive personality is thus confined by the physical world it seeks to master.

Still, the physical aspect of possession cannot imprison completely the metaphysical reality it embodies. For while initially physical, possession purports to have a conceptual significance that is independent of the contingency of sensuous possession. The conceptual significance of possession, once again, is that it objectifies the person's end-status in relation to the thing. So conceived, possession is a "property"—a right to possession—one that binds others even if physical possession is discontinued. A distinction thus arises between sensuous and juridical possession, the latter dependent on the former but striving to transcend its limitations.[52] Hence at common law a finder in physical possession of an object has a right to exclude others, subject to the right of possession of the person formerly in possession.[53] Moreover, because juridical possession is a mode of giving objective reality to the self's primacy, it comprises the two moments of this act. It requires an *animus possidendi,* an intention to master the object, for otherwise possession is not the embodiment of a self;[54] and it requires a physical occupation adequate for control and recognizable by others, for otherwise possession remains one-sidedly subjective.* Accordingly, the common-law prerequisites for the enforcement of possession are just the conditions for the person's objective realization as an end prior to en-

---

*Eads v. Brazelton, 22 Ark. R. 499 (Ark. S.C. 1861). That juridical possession must be publicly recognizable explains the importance of formalities in the common-law transfer of title. To pass title, the transferor must publicly divest himself of control of the object, while the recipient must likewise take control in public. Whether as a physical delivery of the object, as livery of seisin, or as a signed, sealed, and delivered deed, therefore, the transfer must observè a formality at which the public is theoretically present. The public is present, however, not for the evidentiary purpose of resolving disputes about title that may eventuate in the future, but for the purpose of validating the transfer of rightful possession in the present. Thus the formal requirements of delivery must be met even if they are superfluous as evidence of a firm and considered intent to alienate; and they are sufficient to constitute deliv-

forcement. In this sense the common law creates nothing new: it does not bestow property rights pursuant to some socially desired goal. Rather, it *certifies* a property already implicitly accomplished through the appropriating action of the self.

That juridical possession (the kind of possession that merits legal recognition as an objective right) is an intentional occupation sufficient for exclusive control by a person implies that objects such as air, news events, and ideas that are physically irreducible to such control cannot be the matter of common-law property.[55] It is not because these objects are plentiful that their acquisition is not regulated by common-law property rules;[56] rather, it is because they are not amenable to property that they are plentiful. Moreover, the common-law requirement that possession give public notice of itself has no need of an instrumentalist justification appealing, for example, to the utility for trading purposes of clear marks of title;[57] for notice is fully intelligible as a constituent element of property. The person's subjective claim of final worth gains no objective confirmation unless its mastery of things is recognizable by other free selves. An exclusive possession established by acts merely intended to be proprietary would subordinate liberty to someone's private aims rather than to a public standard of effective control equally restrictive of all. Because such a possession cannot be respected by a free self, it cannot confer an objective right of exclusion.

If we understand possession as an imperfect embodiment of the self's final worth, then we can further distinguish between modes of possession considered as progressively more adequate embodiments within the limitations of possession itself. Thus laying hold of a particular object would be the least satisfactory embodiment of the will, for the self seeks an intellectual or unconditionally valid dominion (a "property") and yet its control of the object is here dependent on the contingency of physical contact. Reshaping it in some way would yield a better possession, since the imprint of the self now remains even when the thing is beyond its physical grasp. Marking out or enclosing a space would be the best possession, for such an act possesses in the symbolic way most adequate to the intellectual nature of property as an embodiment or "sign" of personality (58A). With this theory of the degrees of juridical possession one can understand how the common law typically resolves disputes between claimants to possession neither of whom is an absolute owner. As between a finder of a lost object and the occupier of the space within which the object was found,

---

ery even if they fall short of providing such evidence; see Cochrane v. Moore, 25 O.B.D. 57 (1890). If we ignore the requirement of publicity, transference of the physical thing to signify a transference of the property will appear, as it did to Hume, superstitious; see David Hume, *A Treatise of Human Nature* (Oxford: Clarendon Press, 1888), 515–516.

the latter will as a rule prevail, especially if the object was found attached to or under the occupier's land.[58] To some commentators, this rule is mysterious, for the finder has the intent to possess the specific object, whereas the occupier is usually unaware of its existence. They are inclined to think, therefore, that the courts are concealing a policy preference behind a bald conclusion that the occupier was in "possession" of the object when it was found (perhaps the owner will be better able to trace the object if it remains in the hands of the occupier).[59] If, however, we understand enclosing as a possession truer than sensuous grasping to the notion of property as an inward relation between end and embodiment, then we will see why the possessor of the land has the best possession of everything attached to it. The courts' reason for preferring the occupier is thus intelligible on its own terms and stands in no need of a functionalist gloss.

It is commonly thought that first possession is the origin of title in things, that it is a self-sufficient ground of ownership legitimating all subsequent transfers. Both Immanuel Kant and Sir William Blackstone held this view, and the opinion is shared by such modern writers as Richard Epstein and Carol Rose.[69] If we take this view, however, intractable problems arise. Why should the *fact* of unilateral acquisition confer a *right* to exclude those equally desirous of the thing? Insofar as a right to exclusive possession signifies a publicly recognized claim thereto, there is as yet nothing in the act of possession that entails such a right. The possessor publicly declares his possession but neither solicits nor receives the consent of his competitors to appropriate the object for himself. Yet another problem with possession as the root of title is the one noted by Holmes, who erroneously thought that it embarrassed Hegel as well as Kant.[61] If possession is the source of ownership, then it must require an intent to possess as an owner, that is, to exclude the world. But then we are left with the puzzle as to how possessors (e.g., tenants and bailees-for-hire) who acknowledge title in someone else acquire possessory rights against the world (including the owner). Stated otherwise, if first possession confers ownership, then the right to possess must be equivalent to ownership. Someone who divested himself of the right to possess could not be an owner, while someone who acknowledged title in another would also acknowledge possession in that person and so could assert no possessory right against him. Yet tenants and bailees-for-hire have possessory rights against persons they acknowledge as owners. If possession is the root of ownership, how can juridical possession and ownership diverge?

These problems become soluble if we regard the claim that possession is the origin of ownership as mistaking the part for the whole.[62] The kernel of truth in this claim is that possession is the most primitive (and least satisfactory) mode of objectifying the self as an end; hence it confers on the possessor a title relative to all those who have yet to establish even this minimal connection with the object. Possession, in other words, is a partial or imperfect property, better than no subjugation of the thing at all. This is why the first occupier has a right to exclude all other would-be possessors, and it is why no one can defeat a possessory title (even that of a thief) by appealing to the right of the true owner.[63] Yet because possession is an imperfect property, it will be subordinate to grounds of title that represent superior realizations of personality as an end. Thus someone with the best possessory title may be distinct from the owner; while conversely, ownership that is grounded in a way fully adequate to its concept can stand independently of possession, even as possession continues to confer relative (including temporally finite) rights.[64]

That first possession is not a full or self-sufficient ground of title is attested to by the common law itself. Suppose A takes possession of an ownerless tract of land by enclosing it with a fence on which he posts signs warning off trespassers. While A takes an extended holiday, B enters the land and puts it to intensive use for ten years. If A takes no action to oust B, his title will be extinguished in favor of B's. What is the ground of B's title? Against everyone but A his title can be called a possessory one, since no one but A has established even a minimal relationship to the land. Against A, however, his title cannot be merely possessory, because there is no reason why possessory acts of B should displace those of A. On the contrary, since A's acts occurred first, they should withstand any subsequent acts of possession as those of a mere trespasser. To be sure, we say that A has been dispossessed or that his possession has been discontinued, leaving B alone in possession of the land. However, the discontinuance of A's possession is not a precondition of B's possession but a legal conclusion thereof. What we mean is that B's occupation was of such a kind as to oust A's, to deprive it of juridical force. If B had merely come onto the land and stood there for ten years, A would not have been dispossessed. Similarly, if A had made the slightest use of a portion of the fenced-in area, no acts of B would have succeeded in dispossessing him. Accordingly, A is dispossessed not because B performed acts amounting to mere possession but because he performed acts that were superior to possessory ones as objectifications of personality. What are these acts?

4.4 Use

We saw that possession fell short as an embodiment of the self because it left the thing with an appearance of independence over against the person. The negation of this independence is the thing's use for the ends of personality, a use that transforms its physical character, that consumes its use value, and that thus explicitly subdues it to the primacy of the self (59–64). Accordingly, use is a better property than possession without

use.[65] Possession is "adverse" to that of the previous occupier and sufficient to dispossess him only if it consists in public acts of use (with animus
possidendi) where the previous occupier is making no use of the land.
Thus time will not run in favor of a trespasser, because the intentional possession of the first occupier confers a title good against the world and
hence invincible against subsequent acts that are merely possessory. Yet it
will run in favor of someone whose use has the potential (needing only a
certain longevity to ripen into a mastery of the object) to override the bare
possession of the previous occupier and whose property in the thing is
thus potentially superior. The user's property is superior, however, not
because the law (pursuant to collective goals) decrees it to be so, but because use is superior to possession as an objectification of personality.
Once again, the common law merely recognizes and fulfills a preexisting
relation.[66]

That use is in itself a property explains the basic elements of nuisance
law. As part of an objectively valid mastery of things, use is inwardly circumscribed by a rule rendering it compatible with the equal user rights of
other persons. One has a property objectively binding the world (rather
than a privilege arrogated to oneself against it) only in uses capable of
being recognized without self-effacement by others. Of course, someone
may, through fear of superior force, recognize a use incompatible with his
equal right to appropriate his land to his own use; but because such a
recognition is inconsistent with the person's status as an end, it is contingent on a fear to assert this status and so cannot constitute an objectively
valid right. Such a right is established only dialogically, that is, only through
its free recognition by a self who remains an end in his self-abnegation.
But this means that a valid right to use requires the claimant's reciprocal
recognition as ends of the persons (here the totality of persons) whom the
right purports to bind.*

That a valid right to use is an equal right has two doctrinal consequences. First, one has a property right only in uses that can be the subject
matter of a universal right because they abstract from the particular desires of individuals. Accordingly, one has a property, not in idiosyncratic or
extraordinary uses based on subjective wants, but only in the uses to which
the land in its setting is ordinarily put.[67] A claim of right to a particularistic use can bind only those whose equality is otherwise embodied in the
consideration they receive for their self-abnegation. Second, no absolute
right to use is conferred simply by being there first. Even if someone has

---

*The reader will perhaps have noticed that the dialogic or intersubjective character of
property (already hinted at in the requirement of recognizable possession) contradicts the
atomistic premise of formal right. The significance of this tension will become clear in due
course.

notice of an extraordinary use (e.g., if he knowingly moves into the vicin-
ity of a socially excessive use that interferes with his ordinary use), he
could not consistently with his equal right recognize that use as valid except for consideration.[68] Thus a claim of right in rem to an extraordinarily
noxious or sensitive use cannot realize itself without subordinating one
person to the advantage of another, and it is immaterial who was there
first. Such a claim, therefore, can never obtain the recognition from a free
self needed to validate it. It is also immaterial that the benefit of the noxious use to the user exceeds the cost to the victim; for if the reasonableness of use were defined by its augmentation of welfare rather than by a
neutral custom, then one person would be forced to yield to the subjective
values of another contrary to their equal status as ends.[69] Nor does it matter that the victim is compensated for his loss so that he is no worse off for
the harm-doer's gain. If the gain results from an ordinary use (involving
no infringement of right), then a requirement of compensation forces the
defendant to submit to the particular interests of the plaintiff; if the gain
results from an extraordinary use, then allowing the interference subject
to a requirement of compensation contradicts the plaintiff's property right
(it forces a sale on him) and so also the equal end-status of persons.

That the ordinary use of a thing is in itself a property also explains what
appears to a functionalist as the irrational arcana of the law of servitudes.
Servitudes are restrictions on a landowner's or tenant's user rights for the
benefit of neighboring land. Though they may originate in a contract,
they form part of the property of the person whose land is benefited. This
means that the benefit automatically passes to a purchaser of the land,
while the burden falls on all successors to the servient land without the
need of contract. Some of these proprietary restrictions are correlative to
"natural rights" of estate ownership, such as the right to lateral support of
buildings or to the flow of riparian water. In protecting these rights, nuisance law identifies the small number of restrictions on land use that are
generally necessary to the ordinary enjoyment of neighboring land and
that are therefore always part of the neighbor's property. However, to enforce restrictions on use that facilitate the ordinary enjoyment of particular pieces of land, courts must generally rely on private agreements (or
long practice) to suggest what these restrictions are. For example, a home
owner might purchase adjoining land and sell it on condition (called a restrictive covenant) that the buyer not use it as a parking lot. A court will
elevate the home owner's contractual right into a property right (binding
the buyer's successors and running to the home owner's) provided it qualifies as property, that is, if the restriction is part of a manifest subordination of the buyer's land to the seller's reasonable use of his. To qualify as
property, then, the restrictive covenant must be recognizable (successors
must have notice of it) and must benefit the covenantee's (seller's) land

rather than some personal interest unconnected therewith.[70] Similarly, easements—property rights in the nonexclusive use of another's land (a right of way, for instance)—must serve the ordinary enjoyment of the right holder's land and be consistent with the property in ordinary use of the servient owner; otherwise they remain private agreements binding only those who specifically consent to them.

Why the requirement of a benefit to land? Why not facilitate private planning by making all servitudes binding on successors who take with notice, subject only to public policy (e.g., against bigotry) and to termination for obsolescence? Contemporary critics of servitude law typically assume that limitations on servitudes reflect a judicial aversion to restraints on alienation, one mollified only if the restraint improves other land.[71] The objection then arises that there are public interests other than land improvement that may justify burdens on alienability—interests that are best served by a more permissive enforcement of servitudes. Thus the common-law limitations appear as technical rigidities condemned by their own instrumentalist rationale.

Judicial limits on the enforceability of servitudes are, however, ill-explained by the principle of alienability. The greater or lesser attractiveness of a piece of land is a factor relevant to its price, not to its alienability per se. The deeper reason for the requirement of a benefit to land (as well as for all the limitations applicable to servitudes) lies in the person's right to enjoy his possession without regard for the particular interests of others, or in his right against being forced unilaterally to submit to such interests. Nuisance aside, the successor's liberty to appropriate his possession to his own use can be rightfully abridged without his specifically alienating it only if it encounters a preexisting reduction of an object to a will—only, that is, if the restriction has become assimilated to the prior occupation and use of another. This is so because in formal right one's right of appropriation is limited by the property of others but never by their particular advantage. Accordingly, if a restrictive covenant benefits a personal interest unconnected with the ordinary enjoyment of the covenantee's land, the successor's freedom of appropriation finds no limit in a prior incursion of personality, and so he is not bound in the absence of contract. It is immaterial that he took with notice of the covenant, for an unjustified taking of his property does not become justified through publicity. To hold him to the covenant in the absence of either a property right or privity of contract is to force him to serve the particular advantage of another. It is thus to treat him as a thing rather than as a person.* If one regards the

---

*Real covenants in a lease must be explained somewhat differently, since they are not required to benefit other land. Such covenants "run" with the land only if they "touch and concern" the land demised. The reason is that only covenants that affect the tenant's possessory

benefit-to-land requirement as an overbroad, *ex ante* control on servitudes whose utility is likely to be short-lived, then of course it must be replaced by more finely tuned, *ex post* controls less frustrating to private planning.[72] But there is no reason to view the rule as a flawed instrumentalist doctrine if it is perfectly intelligible as a sound right-based one.

If we consider together acts of possession and use as constitutive of a partial property, then we have an account of the labor theory of property frequently espoused by common-law judges.[73] It has often been observed that, considered on its face, the idea that labor expended on something confers a property in it is deeply mysterious. Even if the person is owner of his labor, it is not immediately clear why the expenditure of labor on an object entitles one to exclusive ownership of the substance of the thing rather than to the value added to it. It cannot be maintained that ownership of the thing is necessary to protect one's investment in it, for (as Epstein observes) if someone improves an object belonging to someone else, his property is adequately protected by granting him a lien on the object for the value of the improvement.[74] One may reply, of course, that the connection between labor and property is not one of logic but of policy. Labor is a ground of title because rewarding labor in this way provides incentives for its expenditure to the common benefit. The problem with this explanation, however, is that it understands labor narrowly as productive or improving labor and so fails to account for a much less discriminating common-law practice. Judges recognize title not only in someone who toils to improve something but also in someone who picks something up or who, by using a thing, makes it worse. Accordingly, if we (like Locke)[75] view labor solely as the exercise of an ability and apart from the connection it forges with the world, its role in the constitution of property will always elude us. However, if we regard labor broadly as the objectification of personality as an end, as the public reduction of things to the authority of the will, then it becomes clear why labor, specified as taking possession and using, already is a kind of property.[76]

---

and usufructuary estates define his property. If a covenant burdens his use, it must run to an assignee, since *nemo dat quod non habet*. But if a covenant is unrelated to possession or use, it does not define the tenant's estate, hence does not run with it. To bind the successor here would be to force him in the absence of contract to serve another. Real covenants in a lease may impose either negative or positive obligations, since both circumscribe the right of use (and hence the temporary property) that the landlord-tenant agreement has carved out of the landlord's estate. The positive obligation on the successor is not a duty to confer a benefit but a duty to remain within the limits of the property demised. Outside a landlord-tenant relationship, however, servitudes must be negative in order to run, for otherwise the successor is forced not simply to respect the property of another but to serve his pleasure. Thus the requirements of touch and concern, of privity of estate for positive obligations, and (conversely) of negativity in equitable servitudes (where there is no privity of estate) all serve the identical purpose of respecting the distinction between persons and things.

4.5 Alienation

It is not, however, a complete property. As so far constituted, property is defective in several respects. In possession and use, first of all, the person verifies its end-status in a self-contradictory way, for it finds itself dependent on things for the confirmation of its mastery of them. Hence the very act that cancels the object's independence also reinstates it. Second, possession and use are physical acts that claim to ground an absolute right to exclude—a right whose validity is independent of continued possession. Yet the supposedly absolute right is thus far limited by the requirement that the thing have at one time been physically possessed. While struggling to free itself from its sensuous origins, the right continues to be anchored to them. Third, we have not yet completely bridged the gulf between fact and right. Possession and use are unilateral acts that exclude other persons from control of the object. Of course, if things were not objects of competition, this de facto exclusion would be juridically unproblematic. The unilateral property established by possession and use would suffice for property, for no person would be deprived in a way that contradicts his or her equal worth. However, if someone is so deprived, then unilateral appropriation would fail as an objective property, for it could not then be freely recognized by those it excludes. Unilateral acquisition would be an assertion of power rather than the source of a right.

The ethical problem inherent in unilateral acquisition has preoccupied theorists of private property from Locke's time to the present; indeed, it is the problem that any justificatory theory of private property must overcome. Locke's own solution—lately adopted by Robert Nozick—was to attach a condition to legitimate acquisition. Because Locke and Nozick regard unilateral acquisition as potentially imposing costs on others, they limit the property so acquired with the proviso that "enough and as good" be left for others.[77] The idea behind this proviso seems to be that if acquisition is costless to others, then the arguments justifying a property through unilateral possession (e.g., the labor theory) are sufficient arguments. Accordingly, we can test whether unilateral acquisition is capable of generating a complete property by asking whether the Lockean proviso can, as a conceptual matter, ever be met.

When Locke and Nozick say that enough and as good must be left for others, they mean that appropriation is justified only if no one is made worse off in terms of want satisfaction or welfare. The standard for comparison may be the initial situation of unowned objects or it may be a person's prospects for want satisfaction in the absence of exclusive ownership; but in either case, the constraint on appropriation is that no one's level of want satisfaction be diminished. If the proviso is formulated in these welfarist terms, then (owing to the efficiencies to be gained by a property in possession and use) it is capable of being met, and unilateral acquisition is capable of generating a valid property. The difficulty, however, is that the welfarist version of the proviso is ruled out by the formalist framework of right within which private property first becomes intelligible. The person whose end-status property validates is precisely an abstraction from all particular wants and needs, which have thus been excluded from the sphere of right. Because at this stage wants and needs have the significance of particularistic appetite, they cannot consistently with personality's freedom bind others to care for them; hence they have no juridical standing. This means that the right to appropriate cannot coherently be limited by the want satisfaction of another; rather, one is entitled (within this framework) only to the level of satisfaction that accidentally materializes in the competition to appropriate. To determine, therefore, whether a unilateral acquisition can yield an objective property, we must reformulate the proviso (if indeed there is one) so as to render it consistent with the legal framework based on abstract personality.

We have seen that property originates in a contradiction between the person's certainty of being an end and the apparent independence of objects. This contradiction generates an urge of the will to cancel that independence and to validate its own primacy. Understood as a desire of the will rather than as an appetite of the body, the acquisitive project is inherently one of infinite accumulation. Personality claims a right to appropriate the totality of things and cannot in principle rest satisfied until it has done so. Furthermore, because personality is at this stage the singular and exclusive personality of the isolated individual, the presumed right of personality to infinite appropriation is the equal right of *each separate* personality to such acquisition. We have, therefore, competitive and mutually exclusive claims of right to an infinite accumulation. Under these conditions, it is conceptually impossible for any unilateral acquisition to leave enough and as good for others, for each person desires the totality. Each object is scarce in the sense that it is desired by everyone, so that any unilateral acquisition of necessity frustrates the project of another, making him worse off in terms of his self-validation as an end. Because, moreover, a unilateral act of appropriation denies the equal right of all other persons to an infinite accumulation, it fails as an objectively valid conquest of the thing.[78]

The failure of possession and use to generate by themselves a complete property naturally impels the mind to think of consent as the missing element. Thus Hugo Grotius and Samuel von Pufendorf rest property on an implied consent to individual appropriation given by the whole of humanity "in advance."[79] Among the many difficulties with this solution, one in particular concerns us most. No person could rationally, that is, consistently with his claim to be an end, consent to a unilateral and exclusive appropriation by another; for this would be to acquiesce in his permanent exclusion from the thing and hence in a permanent disparity between his self-conception and reality. We can see, then, that if property is to exist, it must come forward as the mediation of a stark contradiction. To establish my possessions as rightful property I must secure the recognition of others by reciprocally recognizing their possessions as belonging rightfully to them. Yet to recognize their right to exclusive possession is to deny my right as a person to an infinite appropriation. I cannot consistently with my right recognize the other's possession; yet I cannot consistently with my right avoid recognizing it. A complete property must therefore embody a reconciliation between the right to exclusive possession and the right to freedom of acquisition. To reformulate the Lockean proviso: a unilateral appropriation becomes property if and only if it is made consistent with the right of others to an unlimited accumulation.

To pose the problem in this way is already to bring to light its resolution. The reconciliation of property with freedom of acquisition is the institution of exchange and its supporting laws against burdens on alienability. In exchange, I recognize the other's property by awaiting his decision to alienate and by giving him an equal value in return; yet I do not thereby foreclose my opportunities for unlimited acquisition, for I recognize his right to the thing only insofar as it becomes available to me (only insofar as he ceases to be the owner), while he recognizes mine under the same proviso (72–74). Thus our final properties are not in the physical things we possess in isolation but in their metaphysical values realized in exchange. Furthermore, in alienating my possession, I resolve the contradiction between my claimed mastery of the thing and my actual dependence on it; for I now demonstrate its nothingness in relation to my will by disdainfully abandoning it. By getting rid of the thing, I show conclusively that it belongs to me rather than I to it. Yet if I abandon it as *res nullius,* I lack objective confirmation for my claim of right to dispose. If I alienate it as a gift, I obtain recognition from the donee who accepts it as such; but because the donee alienates nothing in return, he does not assert himself in the transaction as an equal end and so cannot give a satisfying confirmation of my ownership. Only in exchange am I recognized as an end by someone who, because he too reveals himself as a self-conscious end, can authoritatively validate my claim of ownership. Finally, inasmuch as my consummate property is in exchange value rather than in a material thing, I have at length attained a property adequate to its intellectual nature. When this property is established by a bare exchange of promises to trade goods in the future, its emancipation from physical possession and use is complete.[80]

The foregoing account of property reveals the intimate link between property and contract. It shows that contract is not the arbitrary transfer of a property juridically complete prior to exchange but rather the perpetually reenacted completion and legitimation of property.[81] And indeed, this is how the common law understands it. Thus de facto possession confers only a relative or "special" property, inferior to the title conferred by deed or contract. And while I have a property in the "use and beneficial enjoyment" of the sensuous thing, I have no property prior to exchange in the value of the thing or in the profit it generates, both of which may be lawfully diminished by my neighbor.[82] That is to say, my property in value does not crystallize until I alienate the sensuous thing to someone who recognizes my ownership of its value by trading an equivalent one. Furthermore, judicial dicta affirming that something is property only if it has exchange value are now comprehensible as statements that something is property only if competitive persons have recognized it as such through the institution of exchange. The court simply certifies a process of validation already accomplished by the market.[83]

Finally, that property is legitimated by exchange explains the courts' rules against restraints on alienation. These rules aim at no "policy" favoring the improvement and efficient use of land. Rather, they explicate the conditions under which someone may legitimately hold something to the exclusion of others. One may bind others to respect one's exclusive possession of something in which they have an equally valid interest only if the thing remains in principle open to their acquisition. The rules against restraints on alienation are thus deducible from the concept of property, understood as an objectively valid conquest of things. Further, the same principle (namely, that the person is an absolute end) that justifies the person's appropriation of things bars the alienation of personality itself or of the life essential to it. The basis of inalienability is the conceptual impossibility of standing back from selfhood and so of making the self into a thing. As the only entity from which one cannot abstract, the self is ineluctably subject; hence it is the condition for the possibility of owning objects. Since the conceptual basis of property cannot itself be owned, it cannot be validly alienated (66–67).[84]

5. PROPERTY, SELF-ESTRANGEMENT, AND EQUITY

5.1 The Phenomenon of the Counterprinciple

The development of property from possession to exchange reveals property as a paradox. Property was understood as the realization of the isolated person's project to confirm itself as an end. Yet the fulfillment of this project reveals the transience or nonreality of the isolated person. Property is not fully realized until the person abandons the purely self-related activity of possession and use and places itself into a relationship with another person. Not simply a solipsistic relation between a person and a thing, property turns out to be a social relation between persons as owners of exchange value. This social bond was already latent in possession and use, for even in these activities the objective reality of the self's conquest of things demanded a public act recognizable by other free selves. Thus possession had to meet an intersubjective standard of effective control, while use was restricted to customary uses acceptable without self-denial by others. In alienation by gift, the intersubjective basis of property is more explicit, for here the donor's property is confirmed by the donee (through a communicated assent to receive it as a gift) in his act of receiving it.[85] Yet the gift transaction is (as we saw) imperfectly mutual, for the donee does not assert himself as a self-conscious end and so can neither give nor receive adequate confirmation of ownership. Only in exchange does this occur. Here the intersubjective ground of property has emerged as a relation of full reciprocity, for now each person is an owner only insofar as he is recognized as such by another self-conscious end, whose property he reciprocally constitutes. Each now *receives* his status as owner from another self. By relinquishing his possession, the person makes himself a means to the other's confirmation as an end; yet this deference constitutes the property rather than the subjective depredation of the other only because the other, through a reciprocal transfer, makes himself a means to the realized end-status of the first. In recognizing the other as an end, each establishes the other's qualification to give back an objective confirmation of ownership. Property, therefore, is a dialogic bond between persons, each of whose personhood needs and confirms the free and equal personhood of the other.

Because, however, the end of property is the self-related person, its (property's) dialogic realization is simultaneously the negation of the person as an unconditioned end. Here we arrive for the first time at a Hegelian idea long familiar (because of its appropriation by Marx) to social criticism but whose possibilities for legal interpretation have yet to be fully explored. I mean the idea of self-estrangement.[86] This idea refers to a process by which the self, in giving objective reality to its claim of absolute worth, makes itself dependent for confirmation on an external will indifferent to its worth and dominating it. The reason for this inversion may be explained as follows.

If the individual self's natural condition is identified with its atomistic or presocial one, then the self can form a conception of its fundamental worth only by retreating into a pure (universal) self abstracted from the particular individual, who is seen as necessarily dependent for the satisfaction of need on other individuals indifferent to him. Since all dependence is equated with external dependence on strangers, freedom is identified with a self-relatedness excluding dependence. This means, however, that the self's objective realization as an end will inevitably involve its dependence on the very alien beings from whom it initially fled and who are all bent on their own self-aggrandizement. The person's realization in property will thus take the self-contradictory form of an alienation of self to an autonomous object indifferent to its claims of final worth.

The person's self-estrangement in property takes two basic forms: a vulnerability to other persons and subjection to a law unconcerned with this vulnerability. First, the person depends for confirmation of his final worth on external things now under the legally recognized control of the arbitrary will of another. Since he must now bargain for these things, his every need is a means by which an external will may exercise power over him, bending him to its particular advantage.[87] The reciprocity of exchange is not an inward one where each purposefully aims at the good of the other but an external one between mutually indifferent persons, each of whom uses the other's need as a means to extend a personal dominion. As a bond formed by the mutual self-renunciation of equal persons, property is an image of a dialogic community wherein independent selves recognize and sustain each other as ends; but it is the distorted image peculiar to persons who define their worth independently of all connection to others.

Furthermore, in submitting to an authority capable of enforcing the common will embodied in exchange, the person empowers against itself a framework of law that is blind and indifferent to the real relations of domination that property initially engenders. Because the basis of right is a self abstracted from particular needs, goals, or circumstances of factual inequality, the power exercised by one person over another is neither just nor unjust provided only that property and therewith the formal will are respected. Since, in other words, the worth of abstract personality entails a right to formal liberty but no right to act from self-determined goals, one person's subjection to another's one-sided advantage or caprice is so far a matter of indifference to right. Persons have a negative duty to abstain from interfering with the liberty and property of others; they have as yet no positive duty of concern for their effective autonomy—for their ability to shape their lives in accordance with self-expressive conceptions of good.

Formal right's indifference to the effective self-determination of persons can be illustrated by the distinction between law and equity as it manifests itself in property law. Suppose A invites B onto his land and looks on approvingly as B builds a house on it.[88] Later, after the house is built, A and B have a falling out and A orders B off his land. In a suit by A to eject B, A would prevail at law. The legal position is that A granted B a license to enter his land, a license revocable at will. The result would be the same had A declared an intention to give his house to B and then, without transferring possession, looked on as B made substantial improvements in reliance on A's declaration.[89] Since the gift was never completed, A remains the owner of the house and can convert B into a trespasser by revoking his license. Nevertheless, a court of equity will not permit A to do so. It will refuse to enforce his property right when doing so would frustrate projects based on expectations of nonenforcement to which A gave rise. Invoking the equitable doctrine of proprietary estoppel, a court will give B a life interest in the house or perhaps even transfer the fee simple. In either case it will take part of A's property and give it to B.

Consider next the case of a theater owner who sells a ticket to a customer, admits him to the premises, and then for no good reason tries to evict him before the performance has ended. The customer stands his ground and is bodily removed from the theater. In a suit by the customer for assault, the theater owner would win at law. The customer was a licensee and the owner could terminate the license at will, using reasonable force if the customer refused to leave. No doubt the owner was in breach of contract; but the customer's remedy is then a contractual rather than a proprietary one: he can sue for damages, but he cannot complain of assault, for he became a trespasser once his license was revoked. Again, however, the legal position is reversed by equity. A court of equity will not allow the owner to use his property right as a means of violating a contractual right. It will elevate the contractual license into an equitable property held for the duration of the performance, thereby again transferring property from one party to another.[90]

Another illustration of formal right's silence toward the use of property as an instrument of power occurs in the context of matrimonial disputes over the division of assets acquired during the union.[91] In the usual case, the wife contributes substantially to the accumulation of these assets through work in a common enterprise, or perhaps through work that frees the husband to earn a professional degree or to invest his savings in a business. If at the time of the breakup the couple's wealth lies in assets publicly registered in the husband's name alone, the wife will be entitled at common law to no share of this wealth. It will not matter that the wife acted on a reasonable belief that she was part owner of the assets or that the husband knew of this expectation. In the absence of a statute, property law will allow the husband to reap all the benefit of the wife's work and to leave her with nothing. Equity alone intercedes to prevent the husband from asserting his property so as to foil plans based on reasonable expectations that he has encouraged. It does this by deeming the wealth contributed by the wife as having been held by the husband in trust for her.

So far we have brought forward cases where property is wielded to defeat projects formed on a reasonable expectation of nonenforcement. Let us now consider the case where an owner uses his property right as a bargaining chip in negotiations with another party. We saw that the right to alienate is an intrinsic element of one's property, for alienation is the act whereby the possessor definitively manifests his mastery of the object. Because the right to alienate is essential to property, anyone wanting another's possession can rightfully acquire or use it only with the owner's consent.[92] This means that another's desire for one's possession becomes a lever by which one may exert power over his will, influencing him to satisfy one's own preferences rather than simply his own. Moreover, the stronger the buyer's need in relation to the seller's (or the greater the buyer's ignorance of his real interests), the more does this influence shade into unilateral dictation, so that at the extreme the bargain becomes an expression of one will externally imposed on the other's. To be sure, the weaker party consents to the bargain; there is no coercion of his abstract will and so no violation of the legal framework based on respect for formal personality. Nevertheless, one party has exercised a self-interested power over the other to the point where the deed, while a product of the weaker party's formal choice, nevertheless fails as a coherent *expression* of freedom because it alienates some condition (e.g., financial security, health, or the freedom to work) of effective autonomy. Since the latter concept will figure prominently in the discussion that follows, we had best pause to clarify it.

By effective autonomy (which I shall also call positive freedom and self-determination) I mean the condition of someone who acts according to a plan of life that expresses values formed on reflection and who can see in the overall pattern of his or her life the embodiment of such a plan. The antithesis of effective autonomy is not determinism but heteronomy—the condition of being a cog in another's plan, or of acting from motives simply found in one's makeup and that have not been integrated into a thought-out scheme, or of seeing one's life shaped decisively by forces beyond one's control. In acting heteronomously, one expresses one's generic capacity for choice inadequately, for one loses in the specific expression of freedom the spontaneity that the act expresses; it is in this sense that the act fails as a coherent expression of freedom. By contrast, in acting from goals chosen on reflection (from a pattern of commitments, let us say), the spontaneity revealed negatively in refusing a motive is retained in the positive choice of something specific, so that one remains self-governing throughout the transition from pure will to concrete action. Now, alienating through contract the conditions of effective autonomy is itself a case—perhaps the paradigm case—of a heteronomous act, for it accomplishes a deed that expresses no rational conception of the agent's good, having relinquished the means of achieving any plan he might conceive. The will's determination is thus not its *self*-determination, for in determining itself, the will has subjected itself to the good of another. Because the deed is beyond the range of those the weaker party would as a rational agent have affirmatively chosen for himself, it confronts him as the other's deed, as a deed in which he does not recognize himself, as one, therefore, by which he is subject to domination.

There is one type of case in which this noncoercive domination of one person by another is condemned by formal right itself. Where, for example, a person whose life is in danger cannot save himself except by means of another's property, the common law will not require him to bargain with the owner. It will accord him a "right of necessity" to help himself to the property and will correlatively enjoin the owner from withholding it.[93] A taking is justified here because, as the end of property, personality has a prior right in any true conflict between the two. In a later chapter, I will suggest that the right of necessity is actually problematic for formal right, since it involves a ranking of interests (property and life) according to their value for agency, whereas formal right treats all value as equally subjective. Here, however, I want only to consider why a bargain between the owner and the needy person is unacceptable to formal right.

It is unacceptable because the exigent circumstances have the same effect on the will as the coercion outlawed by formal right.[94] The person in need cannot rightfully renounce personality as he can renounce contingent preferences, because (as we have seen) it is impossible to stand aloof from and to make into an object personality itself. As that from which one cannot abstract, personality is an unconditioned end that cannot properly be treated as an optional value. But since the person in need cannot *validly* choose to renounce personality, any lifesaving contract would be involuntary in the eyes of the law and hence void from the outset. The situation is no different (as far as voluntariness is concerned) from one in which someone agrees to surrender his money to an armed holdup man rather than be killed. If a court cannot recognize the "choice" of the victim in this situation, neither can it do so if the threat to life originates from some impersonal source.

Cases of necessity aside, however, an owner may manipulate another's wants to his own advantage without offense to formal right. Thus a landowner may enjoin a builder from swinging a crane over his airspace until the builder pays his price;[95] or may forgo a claim in nuisance for a price that makes continuance of the activity barely worthwhile. Because formal right countenances these exercises of proprietary power, the rare cases in which courts, even in the absence of necessity, oppose them appear as excrescences wherein quixotic judges enforce an ideal of social solidarity against the common law's dominant ethic of individualism. Yet despite their marginal character, these cases exist not as mistakes do, detached from any unity of purpose, but with an acknowledged reason and force that threatens to shatter the unity of private law and to turn it into a battleground for competing ideologies.

There is the case, for example, of *Vincent v. Lake Erie Transportation Co.*[96]

There a court awarded compensation to a plaintiff whose dock was damaged when the defendant's steamship repeatedly buffeted it during a storm. The defendant had left the ship tied to the dock without the owner's consent in order to prevent it from drifting. The peculiarity of the case is that the court recognized the shipowner's right in the urgent circumstances to use the dock without the owner's consent provided he paid the dock owner for any damage the ship caused. Since neither life nor limb was endangered, the case cannot be viewed as one of necessity. In any bargaining with the dock owner (supposing it were feasible), the shipowner's will would have been free. His desire to save his ship would have been a powerful weapon in the hands of the dock owner who alone could save it, but that desire he could legitimately (according to formal right) have renounced. Had he chosen not to renounce it, the bargain would have been uncoerced in the formal sense and so unimpeachable by the standard of formal right. By permitting the shipowner to use the dock, therefore, the court was effectively protecting him from a bargaining situation of extreme inequality; and it was effectively imposing on the dock owner a duty to lend his resources to a stranger.[97]

The final example I will mention is the famous case of *International News Services v. Associated Press*.[98] In that case the Associated Press (AP) sought an injunction to restrain International News Services (INS) from using AP's published news about World War I as the basis for INS's own reports. Barred by some countries in Europe from obtaining news firsthand, INS employees read the AP reports from bulletins and newspapers published on the East Coast, rewrote them, and then sent them by telegraph to its client newspapers on the West Coast. Because telegraphic communication far outpaces the earth's rotation, INS's West Coast subscribers were able to publish news about the war contemporaneously with the member newspapers of AP. In court, AP conceded that its news reports were not protected by any copyright statute.

In one of its arguments, AP claimed it had a property right in its news based on the skill, labor, and money it had expended in gathering it and on the value that news commanded in the market. It did not succeed on this ground. Raw events cannot be reduced to exclusive possession; hence they cannot form the matter of common-law property. INS, to be sure, did not perceive the events firsthand; it learned of them from a literary source in which the data had been shaped by a form of words. Yet while the information contained in AP's reports might have been property until AP chose to alienate it, that information ceased to be property once AP published the news. At that point anyone was free to read the report and communicate its contents to a neighbor. Normally, in alienating one's possession, one can control the scope of its release, choosing this or that person as the recipient and obtaining a contractual promise limiting his or her right of disposal. Yet the same intangibility of news that makes it refractory for exclusive possession also makes it resistant to controlled dissemination. One may take steps to limit its accessibility—say, by charging admission to a room in which one communicates the news—but if one fails to thwart eavesdroppers, property law cannot erect a thicker wall, for the meaning of alienation is precisely that one abandons the thing as one's own, that one renounces rightful control over it.[99] Under formal right, therefore, there is no legal basis on which a court can restrict the alienation of something whose release the possessor could not restrict physically or contractually. Moreover, this is yet another example of the person's self-estrangement in formal right; for it is the concept of property itself that demands a surrender of control over the thing—a surrender that, in the special case of intangible goods, threatens to defeat the purpose of acquiring it in the first place.

Since the formal law of property was AP's problem, it could not be appealed to as the solution. To succeed, AP had to invoke an equitable doctrine that relieved against the formalism of property by restricting AP's alienation of its news to noncompetitors, thereby allowing it to retain a quasi-property in relation to INS. The equitable doctrine was the tort of unfair competition. Someone commits this tort who reaps the benefits of a competitor's labor without having incurred comparable costs and who thereby damages the profitability of the competitor's efforts. Because, however, the defendant's free-riding involves no infringement of a preexisting property right, the court in effect imposes an affirmative duty of concern for the success of the plaintiff's projects and an uncompensated restriction of the defendant's freedom of appropriation for the plaintiff's benefit.

The foregoing examples seem to reveal property law as deeply fragmented. On the one hand, we have a unity of doctrine based on the freedom and equality of abstract persons, a unity that embraces so much of the phenomena as to warrant our calling it the dominant paradigm. On the other hand, we have a few doctrines or cases on the periphery that disturb this unity and that cannot be dismissed as mistakes because they seem to exhibit a unity of their own. The presence of these "counterprinciples" (as they are called by the critical theorists) suggests to some the possibility of generalizing the principle on which they are based so as to subsume the dominant paradigm and therewith to revolutionize the law of property.[100] At the very least it suggests a duality of paradigms that frees judicial choice from rational constraints and that transforms litigation into political struggle. Against both of these positions, I now want to argue that the law of property is a unified whole. I will not, however, construct this unity by banishing doctrines that do not fit within the dominant paradigm. Nor will I do so by squeezing these doctrines into the dominant paradigm with an argument that their underlying principle is at bottom no different from that of formal right. It is indeed different. Rather, I will argue that there is a logical progression from the principle of formal right to that of the marginal doctrines—a progression throughout which the inferior principle is preserved (together with the paradigm it informs) as *one* part of a whole. To pursue this line of thought, however, we must first identify the principle of the equitable interventions.

5.2 A Theory of the Counterprinciple

In the discourse of property law itself, the courts' refusal to enforce property rights against someone who acted on a reasonable belief, known to the plaintiff, that they would not be asserted, embodies the principle that a court will not lend its aid to an unconscionable assertion of rights. Similarly, the right accorded the shipowner in *Vincent v. Lake Erie* embodies the principle that a court will protect someone against a bargaining situation of gross inequality, one wherein self-interested persons would produce a contract unconscionable to enforce. In the context of matrimonial disputes, the doctrine of the constructive trust is judicially explained as one preventing the unjust enrichment of one party at the other's expense; while the tort of unfair competition is explained by a principle disallowing the unfair appropriation of the fruits of a competitor's labor.

The problem with these formulations, of course, is that they fail to define the principle of equity with a precision sufficient to constrain judicial inclination. Unless we know wherein the "unconscionability," "injustice," or "unfairness" lies, the court is free to exercise a broad moral jurisdiction over a litigant's conduct, of which the other party will be a lucky beneficiary. If the equitable duty were a purely moral one of beneficence, it would imply no correlative right in the other party to enforce it for his specific benefit. Since the duty is an inward one of personal virtue, it singles out no other person as its necessary object. Hence the litigant who benefited from the court's enforcement of the obligation would enjoy a windfall from the moral censure of another. Furthermore, a moral jurisdiction in a court of equity would be inconsistent with the right enforced by a court of law. The principle of formal right, we have seen, is the free choice of the will; yet to coerce a beneficence to which there is no corresponding right in the recipient is to coerce the will in a way not justified by formal right, hence in a way that violates that standard.

Still, in all the examples noted above, the court undoubtedly transferred to one party resources that, according to formal right, belonged to another; and it thereby (it seems) enforced a positive duty of concern for the welfare of another human being. Shall we say, therefore, that the principle of these equitable doctrines is after all "altruism" or "solidarity" and admit a fundamental contradiction in the law of property?

Since the latter thesis is an interpretive one, it is adequately refuted by the availability of an alternative thesis that accounts for equity's interventions while at the same time revealing property law as a whole. In each of the foregoing examples, the uncompensated transfer of resources and the fulfillment of a duty of beneficence were by-products of the court's activity; they were not the principle thereof. The judges themselves never say they are enforcing affirmative duties of virtue, beneficence, friendship, or solidarity. Rather, they say they are preventing the use of the court to back legal rights whose assertion in the circumstances amounts to oppression.[101] In each of the examples, the court protected someone's effective autonomy against its threatened subversion by the logic of formal property. It suspended property law when the law was used or could be used as the instrument of a particular interest in a preexisting context of power and dependence, and when enforcing the law would thus negate its own universality, perverting it (as well as the court) into an external power. Now, property law can become an external power—another's good—in the following circumstances: when it confers on someone the power of advancing through contract his or her interests at the expense of some material condition of the other party's effective freedom (unconscionability); when it is used to defeat plans based on a reasonable expectation of nonenforcement that the property owner himself has raised (proprietary estoppel, the constructive trust on a spouse, the contractual license as property); and when it conceptually (through the requirement of alienation) demands the exposure of projects to hostile forces (the will of competitors) against which the owner is powerless to protect himself (quasi-property).

In the first case, the objective sense in which we understand the welfare of the protected party is crucial. The court does not suspend property rights in a case like *Vincent v. Lake Erie* merely because the benefits of a trade would be unevenly distributed or because the contract would fail to advance a favored goal of one of the parties. Were it to do so, the property owner would be forced to promote another's particular advantage, and equity would therefore contradict rather than perfect the person's freedom. It would subvert rather than reinforce and supplement the ethical achievements of formal right. Rather, the court suspends property when contractual dealing would, because of the extreme vulnerability of one of the parties, threaten that party with the loss of an objective requirement of self-determination such as the means for satisfying basic needs.[102] For in that case formal right would advance one party's good but *no reasonable definition* of the other's.* In the remaining cases, the court protects a sub-

---

* This formula might still seem to undermine formal right in the following ways. First, it seems to imply a general coercive duty to rescue someone in danger of losing some material condition of effective freedom. Second, suppose impecunious A tortiously injures wealthy B.

jective goal, but does so to prevent the exposure of investments embodying well-laid plans to a law become the hostile instrument of someone on whose whim the planner is dependent, or to an external maelstrom of forces that the concept of property itself empowers.[103]

We can thus identify the theme of the marginal cases as the protection of the agent's effective autonomy against a formal right that in the circumstances has become identified with an external (hence particular) interest. Since the court nullifies the power of law thus reduced, it guards the rule of law as well as its own integrity. It does so by attending to considerations foreign to formal right itself: to the context of power and dependence within which a legal remedy is sought; and to whether the person against whom the law of property is being enforced can in the circumstances see the law as his or her good, where good is understood rationally as the perfection of a capacity for self-determination.[104] The right vindicated in these cases is not one to the solicitude of the other party; rather, it is a right in relation to formal right itself, a right correlative to the inner necessity of the law (and of the judge as the law realized) to conform to its public character. Law is truer to this character when its universality consists, not in a precarious neutrality with respect to values indiscriminately regarded as subjective, but in its support of a universal interest in self-determination.

There is, accordingly, no contradiction between the principle of the marginal cases and the principles of freedom and equality that underlie formal right. In none of the cases is the property owner forced to serve another's particular interests; nor is he even forced to display a charitable

---

Paying damages to B will render A destitute, while leaving B to bear his loss will have little effect on his welfare. The legal result would thus be inimical to A's real welfare. No liability?

The principle we have identified implies no general legal duty to rescue. As we shall see, the right to the material conditions of effective freedom binds the community as a whole, not any individual taken singly. Since the right singles out no individual as the correlative duty-bearer, a legal duty to rescue amounts to coerced philanthropy, which is a violation of real no less than of formal freedom. In the cases where equity intervenes, it is not the right to the material conditions of freedom that is operative, at least not directly. Rather, the operative right is one against subjection to a law that embodies another's good but no reasonable definition of one's own. Since this is a right of autonomy specifically in relation to formal right, it necessarily singles out the person wishing to assert formal right as the cost-bearer. However, this does not mean that impecunious A escapes liability for his tort. Equity works to suspend formal right when it is being used as an instrument of domination and when enforcing it would thus undermine its own claim to universality. Hence there must be a relation of power and dependence anterior to the juridical relation between the parties, one to which the law threatens to become subservient. This relation may exist where a property owner induces someone to incur costs in reliance on his assurance of nonenforcement; or where someone takes advantage of the ignorance or dire need of another party to extract one-sided contractual terms. In the example of A and B, no such relation exists.

regard for the other's universal interests. Rather, his affirmative "duty" is incidental to the other's prior right to be subject to no law embodying a particular interest and whose authority would deny the person's status as an end.[105] Far from contradicting the principles of formal right, therefore, equity fulfills those principles in situations where the absolutization of formal right would effectively violate them.

We can say, therefore, that equity revokes the self's alienation in formal right—its subjection to an external power—for the sake of the self-determination of the person. Among the implications of this principle is that the person is free from subjection to a law in which he cannot recognize his good as an autonomous agent and to which he could thus not rationally assent as binding on him. Observe, however, that while the principle of the marginal cases is the *individual's* self-determination, that principle is vindicated by reinforcing the dialogic character of law as embodying the *reciprocal* recognition of persons as ends. Property itself presupposed the mutual respect of persons; but since an absolute property may become an external power, its own validity as a right requires that it be limited by a deeper reciprocity of concern for the subject's effective autonomy. From the law's internal standpoint, then, the peripheral doctrines give effect to one implication (the invalidity of law as another's interest) of the right to a subject-centered autonomy; to us they are additionally significant as manifesting a bond of mutual respect and concern *between* subjects as the ground of valid law.

In understanding the principle of the marginal doctrines as the person's autonomy in relation to law, we go some way toward vindicating the unity of property law. For the difference between the dominant and marginal patterns is now seen to rest on a distinction not between individual liberty and values opposed to individualism but between two individualistic conceptions of freedom. According to the first, freedom is the formal capacity to choose isolated from the material ends and means through which alone freedom of choice is expressed. According to the second, freedom is the capacity not only to choose ends but also to act from ends that are determinations *of* the self and to see in the sum of one's deeds only the reflection of these self-expressive ends. Clearly, the second conception of freedom does not contradict the first but rather includes it within a more comprehensive understanding of freedom that buttresses the first. Correspondingly, the marginal doctrines do not contradict the dominant paradigm but rather perfect the freedom that the dominant pattern actualizes in a self-contradictory way.[106]

Still, a number of steps remain to be traversed. We have yet to understand how equity becomes coherently fused with formal right. As long as law's foundation is formal freedom, the correctives of equity must be imposed from a position outside law and hence outside the sphere of public

reason. Where, in other words, formal right is viewed as the model of public rationality, equity must remain a matter of subjective inclination and
sympathy, located in a sovereign whose inclination is alone authoritative
and separately administered lest its sensitivity to "conscience" corrupt the
public character of law. Accordingly, we have to understand the necessity
for the transition from formal liberty to effective autonomy as the foundation of law; and we have to understand why this transition preserves and
perfects property rather than destroys it.

6. PROPERTY AS A CONDITION OF MORAL AUTONOMY

Thus far we have seen how property, while an embodiment of formal freedom, actually negates effective freedom unless suspended in appropriate
cases by equity. This outcome does not yet contradict formal freedom as
the basis of right, however, for within this framework there is no right to
effective freedom and so no conceptual embarrassment if the latter goes
unprotected. Formal freedom is refuted as a self-sufficient basis of right
only if its best embodiment as an absolute end is its own negation as such;
only, that is, if its objective realization is a *self*-contradictory one.

The objective reality of the person's mastery of things was not fully attained until the person relinquished his possession to another in return
for the other's recognition of him as an owner. Thus the person's realized
worth is grounded in a common will—a dialogic relationship—wherein
each recognizes the other and is confirmed by the other as an end. However, the person who at this stage claims to be an absolute end is not the
socially constituted person but the isolated person. The common will is
thus far the paradoxical actualization of the asocial person's claim of final
worth. This means, however, that the common will embodied in exchange
is so far subordinate to the particular will for whose sake it came into being. Like all other objects in the external world, it is a means to the embodiment of self-related personality, something that personality can use as
it pleases. That valid rights presuppose mutual respect is, accordingly, a
proposition whose truth has not yet been demonstrated to the person in
whose standpoint we are immersed. For this person, right consists in a permission to reduce the world to his or her singular self. Thus the particular
will remains free either to recognize the other or not, either to acquire the
other's possession with his consent or to take it without. Insofar as the person respects the other's ownership, it conforms to right; but because it
recognizes no binding obligation to do so, its rectitude is only the appearance or false show thereof; implicitly the will is an unrighteous will because it claims a natural right to do the wrong (81–82).

The social realization of personality's unconditioned worth thus turns
out to be its dependence on the unconstrained liberty of its self-interested

associates. This too is an instance of self-estrangement, but it is one that contradicts (never mind effective autonomy) the end-status of abstract personality that underlies formal right. The completion of property requires that the person transfer its possession to someone who claims an inherent right to break his contract if he pleases. In this way, the formal self's claim of absolute worth is confuted by the very anarchic character of the social interactions to which this view of the self gives rise. Furthermore, the person's insecurity within formal right shows that the full satisfaction of its goal involves the subjugation to its primacy not only of things but also of the persons at whose mercy it would otherwise lie. The logical outcome of the project to realize the singular person as an absolute end (the project behind formal right) is crime—the intentional violation of liberty and property. However, this outcome simultaneously contradicts the person's claim of final worth, for the absolutization of the singular person entails the unreality of liberty and property, which is to say, the unreality of the person's status as an end. Faced with this result, the person must abandon the claim that the singular self is the sole unconditioned reality. The self-destructiveness of this claim when pursued intransigently reveals the common will as a better ground for the self's objective worth and as a more coherent foundation of rights (104).

Now it might seem that absolutizing the common will as the basis of right entails no alteration in the content of right hitherto unfolded. That content comprises specifications of a duty of respect for liberty and property. This duty is a purely negative one not to interfere with the will's sovereignty over its body and possessions; it implies no positive duty of concern for another's welfare, for the basis of right was a self prior to its realization in the pursuit of individual goals. It would appear, then, that in raising the common will to a supreme normative principle, we have simply secured this content of negative rights against the absolutist claims of the isolated will, leaving the content itself unchanged.

This, however, is not the case. The very elevation of the common will from a derivative embodiment of the particular will to the principle of natural right involves an expansion in its content. This is so because the common will's normative authority implies a changed conception of what is essential to personality and a correspondingly enlarged understanding of its potential for freedom. Recall that the system of formal right was ordered to the person's abstract capacity for choice. This capacity supported a claim of right binding others to respect it only because it was thought to be the sole unconditioned end, that which one attained in abstracting from every opinion, value, and purpose relative to the particular agent. However, the logically consistent realization of this end has shown that, taken abstractly, its worth is not unconditioned after all; that it is dependent on the forbearance of persons who are all incipiently (if not actually) criminal. Moreover, this process led to a reconceptualization of the unconditioned end as a dialogic bond between persons (named law) rather than a singular person—a relation wherein each gains recognition for a right to *embodied* freedom. Accordingly, the process of embodiment that was formerly regarded as extrinsic to the free will is now known to be an essential aspect thereof.

A right to embodied freedom is, of course, ambiguous. It could mean simply a negative right against intrusions to property already acquired; or it could mean, in addition to this, a positive right to the conditions necessary for the coherent self-expression of freedom in autonomous action. That the right encompasses positive as well as negative rights is shown, I think, by the following arguments.

First, the exclusively negative form of the right to embodied freedom was linked, as we saw, to the abstract conception of freedom underlying formal right. Where the principle of right is a capacity for liberty isolated from its concrete expression in self-directed action, wrong can consist only in an interference with liberty—in coercion or in taking something without the owner's consent. Moreover, the abstract conception of freedom was in turn linked to the assumption that the atomistic self possessed a stable existence—an assumption that crime, its internal contradiction, and the resultant ascendancy of the common will has disproved. Accordingly, once the common will is freed from its dependence on the isolated will and elevated to a normative standard, there is no longer any rational basis for limiting rights of embodied freedom to those having the negative form dictated by the initial and now discredited abstraction of formal freedom. Because the common will has come forward as a superior conception of the unconditioned, it must be treated as such—which means that the right to embodied freedom must be generalized without regard to any restriction imposed by the superseded conception. But a generalized right to embodied freedom includes positive rights to effective autonomy in addition to negative rights against interference.

The foregoing argument is reinforced by a consideration of the consequences that follow if the emancipation of the common will's authority is not accompanied by an emancipation of its content. Insofar as the common will is specified in negative rights alone, it borrows its content (the laws of property and exchange) from the competitive projects for dominion of mutually isolated or self-related persons. That is to say, the common will depends for its juridical content on the atomistic will it has superseded, having no content native to itself. Because it does so, it shares the indifference to market outcomes of the formal conception of freedom that it actualizes. These outcomes are influenced by accidents of birth and endowment from which formal liberty abstracts and whose free play a conception of right based on this liberty is powerless to criticize. This means, however, that the common will is hostage to whatever relations of power and subordination are thrown up by the process of competitive accumulation. Should this process lead to a stark division between a propertied and a dependent, propertyless class, then the common will whose sole content is respect for property already acquired is perverted into an instrument of a class interest, its supposed neutrality now an ideological pretense.

This critique of "bourgeois law" will no doubt seem trite. Yet it is worth recalling that this is not an external critique launched from the standpoint of the interests of the poor. Rather, it is a critique internal to law, for it applies to private property the standard of right—mutual respect—on which property itself is now based. The normative authority of the common will implies that an institution is just only if it embodies the mutual recognition of moral agents as ends. Thus the wielding of property as an instrument of power contradicts the very standard of right on which property has finally come to rest. Considered alone, therefore, the negative right of property is inadequate to its own normative foundation, and so it becomes coherently a right only if supplemented by positive rights of autonomy that reinforce the reciprocity already inherent in property law. Accordingly, the integrity of the common will demands that its content be emancipated from that generated from the isolated will, or that it elaborate a content from itself, one adequate to its own public character. Such a content includes positive rights of self-determination by which one may criticize the natural outcomes of competitive accumulation.

That the common will's ascendancy implies a new generation of rights means that the common will informs a new legal paradigm. I shall sometimes call this paradigm equity, although equity as commonly understood really forms a subset of this framework. More often I will call it the paradigm of moral autonomy. This name is meant to convey the idea of a freedom the right to which entails duties not only of forbearance but also of affirmative concern. Let us now see what this right involves.

The positive right to self-determination is specified in the following ways. It implies, first of all, what Hegel calls a right of intention. This is a right against subjection to powers in which a rational agent could not recognize his own good or the worldly effect of his own purposes. Stated positively, it is a right to be subject only to laws to which one would assent as promoting one's interest in self-determination; and it is a right to be held legally responsible only for the immanent (because either intended or foreseeable) consequences of one's act. The right of intention is further specified in such doctrines as proprietary estoppel, the constructive trust imposed on fiduciaries and spouses, quasi-property, and the equitable portion of the law of unconscionability. The right of self-determination also implies a right of insight (132, 215, 222–224). This is a right to the procedures and practices by which the impartiality of law may be validated through the participating reason and assent of the parties. This right generates the requirements of publicity and of theoretical clarity in the law, of reasoned decisions, as well as the rules of natural justice. Finally, the right of autonomy implies a right of welfare (128–130, 230). This is a right to the material resources, the safe environment, the health care, and the education needed for an effectively autonomous life. All of these rights must be admitted by anyone who initially adopts the standpoint of formal right. For if the negative content of right was determined by an abstract conception of personality's freedom, then that content must grow in conformity with the richer conception of freedom to which the self-contradictory realization of the first logically points.

At its broadest, a positive right to self-determination is a right to the material and cultural preconditions of autonomous action. Property is one of these conditions, not only because it liberates the person for the pursuit of ends other than subsistence (and hence for the pursuit of its own ends rather than those of persons who control the means of subsistence), but also because it demarcates a moral sphere wherein the person's autonomy may find concrete expression through its exclusive use and management of things according to its own will and its own goals. In one sense property is just a very useful instrument for the realization of whatever concrete goals one might project; but more crucially its very instrumentality in relation to these goals is the realization of agency itself. At this stage, therefore, it is appropriate to speak of property as a condition of autonomy and so as a need of the human individual. Under formal right, the individual's needs were juridically insignificant, since all need signified either a natural necessity from which the free will had to abstract or a subjective desire having no normative force for other persons. At this stage, however, need is rational insofar as it refers to the objective requirements for the individuated expression of generic freedom, so that it now comes within the purview of right.

The right to the satisfaction of need does not, however, bind any individual person taken singly. It does not transform philanthropy into a coercive duty, and hence it does not alter the principle of formal right that, apart from contract, one is personally liable to another only for misfeasance. This is so because the positive right to property is a conceptual requirement of the common will's integrity and therefore binds only the legislative agent of that will. At the stage of formal right, one person's right implied a correlative duty in another, because the right was a permission to appropriate without external interference. To this negative right the paradigm of moral autonomy adds a positive right to the conditions of self-determination. This novel right was generated, however, only as an implication of the common will's authority and of the right this authority establishes to embodied freedom; and it was proved by the disintegration of the common will insofar as its content was restricted to negative rights.

Because the positive right is held against the common will as a demand of the latter's nature, it implies no affirmative duty in a *private* individual. Circumstances of necessity aside, therefore, enforcing a right to property against any single individual remains an unjustified coercion of the will.

However, once positive freedom is acknowledged as a right, the negative right of the previous paradigm cannot remain unaltered, for it is now shaped by distributive considerations as well as by the right of intention. Specifically, an owner's right against takings of property is now inwardly limited by the equal right of all persons to the material prerequisites of self-determined action. While I have no coercive duty to alleviate the poverty of another human being, I have such a duty to share the collective burden of doing so as a condition of the legitimacy of my property. Thus property may be redistributed by the public authority without violating rights, provided that the redistribution is necessary to ensure the freedom of all. Second, the right against takings is limited by the nonowner's right to be free from subjection to a property law embodying another's good. Accordingly, property can now be legitimately regulated by the state to protect the vital interests of persons (e.g., residential tenants, laborers) vulnerable to the exercise of proprietary power, or to prevent (through antidiscrimination laws) exercises of the right to alienate that deny the human equality on which property rests. In like manner, property rights can now be validly suspended by a court of *law* when their exercise would amount to oppression. Equity has thus ceased to be an external and nonlegal corrective to a right based on a nonequitable principle; it has become itself the principle of law.

Nevertheless, we have not yet succeeded in vindicating the unity of property law. Whereas earlier we confronted a law of property that seemed irreparably fragmented, we now face one whose thoroughgoing unity threatens to destroy property itself. Such a unity may be a unity of law; it is not, however, a unity of anything one can call the law of private property. Property is threatened by the new legal paradigm, because it has become a conclusion of a teleological reasoning directly oriented to a common good rather than an independent relation between thing and person worthy of respect in its own right. That one has a right to as much property as is consistent with the equal right of all to effective freedom does not necessarily imply a redistribution of wealth privately accumulated and owned. Equally consistent with this principle is a distribution for personal use and management of resources that are collectively owned. Indeed, since the right of private ownership flowed from an atomistic conception of selfhood now superseded, that right can survive the transition to the new order only if instrumentally (and so contingently) justified by the common good.

Accordingly, property rights are now viewed as having been *allocated* to private decision makers because their free bidding for scarce resources will, it is thought, alone produce socially optimal outcomes.[107] This means, however, that if in particular cases the market would fail to produce the socially desirable result, entitlements may be authoritatively reallocated without infringing property, since property rights are now defined by the exigencies of the public welfare. Whether compensation is paid depends, therefore, not on whether a taking has occurred (for a taking in the juridical sense is now impossible provided the reallocation is reasonably related to the common good), but on a separate judgment as to whether the benefits of compensation (e.g., alleviating anxiety, avoiding frustration of "investment-backed expectations") outweigh its administrative costs, or as to how far compensation is fiscally consistent with achieving the positive ends of government.[108] But then there is once again no right against the collectivity to private property except in the novel sense, peculiar to this paradigm, of a right to public benefits.[109] In allocating entitlements, moreover, one need not distribute as a unity the several rights that formerly constituted one's property in a thing; rather, one may disassemble these rights and deal with them separately, for property now refers simply to whatever bundle of entitlements one currently holds from the community.[110] Thus not only is there no right to private property; there is no real relation to which the concept of property refers. Nothing exists to anchor the concept, save perhaps a "family resemblance" among the free-floating entitlements to which the term is conventionally applied.[111]

If the thematization of individual autonomy destabilizes the old property, it also undermines the distinction between legislative and judicial roles in the determination of property rights. If a person's property derives from the common good, then a court must apply this criterion to a two-party dispute or else lose its legitimacy as an arbiter of rights. In deciding, for example, whether a company is liable to a landowner for nuisance, a court will have to "balance" the landowner's interest with those of the people whose livelihood depends on the continuance of the offending activity.[112] It will therefore abandon the notion of transitive infringements of an independently established property in favor of an idea of mutually impinging activities. Instead of aiming at a "formal" determination of rights, the court will seek a fair accommodation of interests. And it will therefore replace the rigid remedial alternatives organic to the old property with the flexible remedies of the new: compensation but no injunction, or perhaps injunction for the plaintiff with compensation for the defendant.[113] Under the previous paradigm, equity's role was confined to the suspension of property when the latter was being used as an instrument of oppression. In this marginal and ad hoc operation, equity was consistent with the concept of private property, since the subject of property was still the insular self. Under the new paradigm, however, there is no rational basis for limiting the reach of equity's principle to such interstitial qualifications of property, for private rights are now defined by the requirements of the common freedom. There is thus no sense to a private law distinct from public law, to a commutative justice distinct from distributive justice, or to a judicial determination of property rights distinct from a fair allocation of the benefits and burdens of social interaction.

The elevation of individual autonomy as the criterion of right has thus generated a theoretical momentum whose consistent conclusion is the negation of the principle. The systematic realization of the right to self-determination turns out to be the thoroughgoing submersion of a sphere of private sovereignty in the absolutism of the common will. Property reflects the centrism not of the individual self but of a common good in which the individual is effaced. Given the self-contradictoriness of this result, the principle of individual autonomy cannot coherently be pushed to its extreme conclusion. The theoretical impetus to do so is met by a countervailing theoretical pressure to reassert the formal agency of the discrete self, so that the legal order is just this restless tension between poles neither of which offers repose. On the one hand, the individual's claim of unconditioned worth finds no reality outside a common will inwardly constitutive of private rights; on the other, this very realization of the person is its dissolution. The resultant oscillation between antithetical extremes manifests itself in property law as an apparently incoherent mixture of paradigms, as the doctrines of formal right coexist with judicial innovations affirming the social basis of property and neither view is able to subdue the other.[114] This combination in turn lends force to the skeptical view that the common law reflects an irreconcilable conflict between individualistic and communitarian conceptions of personality, a conflict that dissolves the rule of law into the tyranny of ideological preference.

We now see that the vindication of property law's unity depends on our ability coherently to draw a line between the marginal corrections of formal right, on the one hand, and the wholesale subsumption of formal right under the common good, on the other. We have to show, in other words, that the system of formal right is coherently preserved as a semi-autonomous order within a totality that actualizes a positive right to self-determination. If property law is a unity, it must be one that embraces without dissolving the distinction between formal and moral right, or between private right and the common good. The systems of formal liberty and moral autonomy must be capable of limiting each other, not through a perpetual shuttling to and fro between unstable absolutes, but as tranquil parts of a whole whose thematic principle logically supports the due measure of both. At the level of public law this would mean that the agent's autonomy is guaranteed by redistributing wealth that is private property prior to redistribution; that the regulation of property is thus a taking whenever it interferes with possession,[115] or customary use,[116] or the non-oppressive exercise of the freedom to dispose;[117] that public takings (with or without compensation) are impermissible if for the particular advantage of others but permissible if for the common freedom (46R); and that public takings for the common good are compensable to ensure that the property owner is burdened only as a member of the collectivity.[118] At the level of private law, the unity-in-difference of formal and moral right would mean that formal right is subject to equitable suspension but that judicial innovations making property a conclusion of distributive policy are a mistake.

If we set aside these still isolated novelties, we find that doctrinal discourse for the most part affirms the togetherness of paradigms as the central feature of the common law. Yet in this discourse, the mutual limitation of principles appears as a pragmatic detente between values in irreconcilable tension. Because the principles are seen as both antithetical and conceptually imperialistic, their mutual accommodation appears to most commentators as an illogical though prudent syncretism, so that the dominant discourse differs from the critical one only in the insouciance with which it regards the law's disharmony. Our task, accordingly, is to provide a conceptually coherent account of what, apart from theory, appears as an incoherent albeit sensible eclecticism. We do not thereby excogitate a unity that merely ought to be but rather offer an interpretive account of one that already implicitly exists.

7. PROPERTY AS THE PASSION OF COMMUNITY

In asserting a fixed antithesis between asocial and social conceptions of personality (and the doctrinal systems they order), the skeptical interpretation of the common law unconsciously posits the same atomistic starting point that produced the antithesis in the first place. The paradigm of moral autonomy, no less than that of formal right, assumes the fixed reality of the isolated individual, for that paradigm was attained by absolutizing a common will of initially dissociated and self-aggrandizing persons. The anti-individualism of the moral paradigm is conditioned by this atomistic premise. Because individual liberty signified the lawless liberty of the isolated self, a legal foundation could be conceived only as an abstract common good opposed to spheres of private sovereignty. Yet the good's rational authority depended, we saw, on its fulfilling an individual freedom that was self-contradictory in isolation. Thus the moral paradigm's atomistic premise assured the good's hostility to the very individual liberty its authority depended on perfecting. Inevitably, this latent flaw in the conception of the good manifested itself when the good was enforced. The actualization of an abstract good meant the effacement rather than the flourishing of the individual, hence the inversion of the good into its opposite. The individual's recoiling from this outcome produced the tension as well as the indeterminacy of moral choice that the skeptic now proclaims as necessary features of law.

It now appears, however, that this indeterminacy is not an original reality but a result, not an ineluctable aspect of the human condition but the downfall of a specific conception of the good. Moreover, the collapse of this conception does not leave us destitute of normative foundations; on the contrary, it points to a new foundation, one already implied in the dissolution of the old. This is so because the principles that are opposed in property law—the negative freedom of the atomistic self and the positive freedom of the socially constituted self—are not Manichaean extremes having no connection with each other. Rather, each contains the other within itself. The common good is *individual* autonomy; and the individual self's objective worth (as the self-contradiction of crime showed) presupposes community. To the extent, therefore, that one principle sought to deny the other, it contradicted its own nature. Moreover, the self-contradictoriness of both principles when absolutized in isolation discloses a connection between them. Each needs the other for its own fulfillment. The common good cannot be the good *of* the individual unless it recognizes his or her worth as a discrete end presiding over a sphere of autonomy guarded by a peremptory right against another's advantage and by a right of compensation for justified takings. Conversely, the individual's worth is not real unless specified in negative and positive rights actualized as law by a political community. This mutual need of the polarities reveals a totality of which the public and private sides of the self are subsidiary and mutually complementary parts—a totality in which neither side claims exclusive validity.

Let us call this totality dialogic community.[119] Having intuited this idea from the downfall of the previous foundations, we must now try to clarify the nature of the connection between the poles. Having seen *that* they are connected, we must now understand *how* they are connected. First, since each needs the other for its own coherent self-identity, each must let the other be. Instead of subduing the other to its own primacy, each must respect the other's independence. This means that each must renounce its claim of primacy and lower itself to a means for the other's validation as an end. Thus the individual renounces his atomistic existence and, through voluntary public service, recognizes community as his good, thereby confirming its natural authority; likewise, the community defers to individual freedom as to something it needs to confirm it as an end, thereby becoming the ground for the objective worth of the individual. Because each submits to the other, each is preserved (and indeed validated) as an end in its self-abnegation. Each depends for confirmation on the other; yet this dependence is consonant with autonomy, for the other is no indifferent object but one that has the other's dignity for its aim (152). The interdependence of community and individual was revealed by the collapse of each when absolutized in isolation. We now comprehend this relation as a bond of mutual recognition.

Accordingly, dialogic community first comes to sight as a political life wherein individual selfhood and community recognize each other as ends. This community is no longer a stern abstraction from individual self-seeking; it is not a "state" opposed to "society," for self-seeking is no longer equated with the amoral egoism of the atomistic individual. Since the individual seeks his own good in public service, the community can, without loss of majesty, in turn submit to the distinctive worth of the individual. Within such a polity, therefore, private property is preserved, but only insofar as acquisition is acknowledged to be for the sake of public service rather than for self-glorification outside of such service. We might say that private ownership is respected because its subordination to politics is the perpetually reenacted proof of the nullity of the atomistic self and of its communitarian destiny. The true import of private property is that it reflects the primacy of community in what is distinct from community—a truth made explicit in the taxation of property to support a human elite devoted to political and military ends.[120]

Yet the realization of political community as an absolute end is simultaneously its destruction. To gain confirmation as the individual's good, the community must defer to individual choice, reciprocally recognizing the independent worth of individual selfhood. Yet the community here defers only to a self who surrenders its independence; it does not respect the one who does not. The self who renounces isolated self-seeking for public service cannot truly possess an independent worth; for it then attains its dignity as a citizen and soldier, as a reflection of the community's primacy, but not as an independent self. Hence this self lacks the qualification objectively to confirm community as an end. By contrast, the self who possesses this qualification stands outside community as an isolated atom whose worth-claim challenges community and so cannot be recognized by it. The political community is thus not yet actually the dialogic whole that it is implicitly. True, it submits for confirmation to the individual's free patriotic devotion; yet the political union is a partisan one forged through opposition to an atomistic individual, on whom the community thus depends for its self-identity. This dependence, however, contradicts the claimed end-status of community, which must therefore annul the atomistic self in order to make good its claim. The life of community—its paradigmatic activity—is just this destruction of the outsider, of the person who claims to be an end independently of any organized polity. But in destroying this person, community annuls the very independent self whom it acknowledges as essential to the confirmation of its authority as natural. Recognized by selves who surrender their independence and annihilating those who do not, the supposed natural authority of community turns round into a cataclysmic human violence.

There is, it seems, but one way in which the community and the individual can both be ends. The individual was submerged in the totalitarian community because the self-abnegation of community was not sufficiently extreme. While acknowledging its need of individual selfhood, the community respected the self only insofar as the latter sacrificed itself to the primacy of community; it disdained the self who claimed to exist on its own account. And it was the community's violence against this self that subverted its claim to be the ground of law. Accordingly, the downfall of the totalitarian community brings to light a better conception of the foundation. The ground of law must now be conceived as a whole wherein the self's *rejection* of community, its claim of absolute worth as an atomistic person, is itself respected by community in order that community may in turn be acknowledged by the independent self as its good. We have here the same relation of mutual recognition that characterized the inadequate form of community; but the relation is now more genuinely mutual because community no longer claims a one-sided primacy vis-à-vis the atomistic self. Rather, each side surrenders to the distinctive end-status of the other as to that which confirms its own worth.

Yet the foundation that has now come forward seems an impossible contradiction. How can community defer to the claimed end-status of the atomistic individual without loss to its independent authority as the good? How can the individual recognize community as its natural end without renouncing its value as an atom exclusive of others?

Let us begin again from the downfall of the totalitarian community. The self-contradictory realization of community revealed it as lacking confirmation as the good from the very atomistic person it denigrated and sought to eradicate. Obversely, the isolated person's claim of unconditioned worth presupposes community, whose dissolution as an absolute end conceptually enfranchises the self-related person (and so justifies our starting point). This means that there is a hidden relationship—a primordial interdependence—between the atomistic self and community. Their opposition is in reality a split *within* a totality that inherently embraces both poles as subordinate and mutually complementary elements. Let us reserve for this totality the name of dialogic community, understanding that, to begin with, it is only something potential, an inner bond between outwardly antagonistic extremes.

Now since the end-status of atomistic selfhood inherently presupposes the self-inadequacy of community, the self will be unstable—not fully itself—in its isolation and will seek a mediated or reflected reality through the recognition of another self. Of its own accord the self will enter into relationships that belie its claim of self-sufficiency. The result will be the sequence of legal paradigms we have already observed—paradigms in which the structure of mutual recognition is mirrored with improving clarity in the self-oriented activity of the atomistic person. That structure is thus immanent in the action of the self precisely insofar as the latter strives to realize an asocial conception of its worth. Because dialogic community is spontaneously produced by the action of the person who has spurned it, it will be possible for community to defer to that activity as to that which decisively reflects its (community's) status as the immanent end of the individual. And because community defers to legal paradigms ordered to the atomistic self, it will be possible for the self to recognize community as the ground of its truly distinctive worth.[121]

Having arrived at the idea of dialogic community, we can now look back over the course we have traveled and see that it has all along been the implicit theme of our interpretation of property law. Overtly, the systems of formal right and moral autonomy are ordered respectively to abstract personality and to the individual subject as ends; latently, however, they are manifestations of dialogic community, understood as the mutual recognition of distinctive selves. They are imprints of dialogic community in systems ordered to other principles—imprints wherein dialogic community is validated (as the ground of law) in the self-oriented action of persons who have ostensibly repudiated it. Thus property manifests dialogic community, for it gradually emerged as an intersubjective bond between persons, each of whom canceled his or her isolation for the sake of the other's confirmation as an end. Property was no doubt a weak sociality; but it was a sociality revealed in the extremity of amoral egoism, and so was the vindication of community in persons apparently the farthest from it. Equity was a clearer manifestation, for it marked the emergence of community as the self-conscious basis for the individual's worth; and it (reciprocally) made law's authority depend on its amenability to self-legislation as one's good.

That property and equity are progressively clearer traces of dialogic community does not imply that their self-conscious formative principles can be dismissed as error or delusion. To be sure, these principles are— and reveal themselves to be—false pretenders to the throne of the unconditioned. They are semblances of natural right that are unmasked in the very totalities they inform. However, because the validation of dialogic community in these totalities is essential to it, the impostors are also essential; hence they retain a distinctive normative force, though no longer an exclusive or absolute one. It is not only important, in other words, that the paradigms are imprints of dialogic community; it is equally important that they are realizations of atomistic personality, for only then is the authority of community validated dialogically—out of the mouth of personality itself.

We are now in a position to understand how dialogic community comes forward as the resolution of the tension between formal right and equity. That tension existed, recall, because each system's principle (personality and the good) obeyed a conceptual imperative to subdue an opposite it also conceptually needed. The urge to subdue the other originated in the claim of each to be the ground of law—a claim that could brook no rival. When, however, dialogic community comes forward as the ground of law, the basis for the antagonism between formal right and equity disappears. Since both paradigms are now reduced to particular manifestations of dialogic community, neither principle is subject to a hegemonic drive to extinguish the other. Each is essential to the whole, because dialogic community is objectively the ground of law only through its validation in the self-unfolding and collapse of rival conceptions of the foundation. While canceled as the absolute ground, therefore, each principle is integrated as an organic member of a totality whose logic supports both, preventing either from consuming the other.

The preservation in the whole of each superseded conception of the foundation means that the paradigms they inform are also preserved as integral systems. The fact that abstract personality yielded to a richer conception of the subject does not mean, therefore, that private property is subsumed and refashioned under the new conception; since private property too is an instance of dialogic community, it has a right to exist. Nevertheless, the right of property is no longer an absolute one, for the paradigm to which this right belongs is now part of a whole rather than the whole itself. Specifically, property is now subordinate to the system of moral autonomy, for this system realized personality in a way more adequate to its freedom and was a clearer reflection of dialogic community. That property is subordinate to, but not subsumed under, the paradigm of moral autonomy implies a certain interaction between property and the common good and so also a principle for resolving conflicts between them. Put simply, the common good overrides property but does not define what one's property is. Let us examine more closely what this formula means.

That formal right is preserved in its supersession implies that there is a right of property in possession, ordinary use, and free disposition. The ultimate basis of this right is not, as we provisionally assumed, the absolute end-status of the isolated person but rather the self-abnegation of community in favor of this person. This means that, for the sake of community, the right of property must be conceived without reference to the common good and so independently of equity. That is to say, it must be conceived *as if* the isolated person were a self-sufficient end. Translated into practice, this means that judges of property disputes (whether between private persons or between the individual and the state) should treat arguments appealing to the general welfare as irrelevant to the determination of property rights; they should instead treat possession, ordinary use, and alienation as rights of property existing prior to distributive justice or to economic regulation; and they should treat each right as an integral component of a conceptual whole rather than as an isolated stick one may remove from a bundle without destroying the bundle itself.[122]

While irreducible to the common good, however, the right of property is nevertheless subordinate to it and so subject to modification by the good *to an extent consistent with its preservation as a right.* This proviso no longer appears as an arbitrary or merely pragmatic limitation, for within the present foundation there is no longer any conceptual impetus to actualize the common good intransigently. To do so is to imply that the good is the absolute foundation, whereas now it is but a constituent element of a whole in which formal right is also maintained. Moreover, formal property is subject to modification by the good in two distinct ways: it is subject to an external (legislative) override by a distributive principle as well as to an internal (judicial) suspension for the sake of the rule of law. This division of legislative and judicial enforcements of the common good follows from the foundational status of dialogic community. If distributive regulation were internal as well as external to formal right, property would be subsumed under the good, and the latter would have arrogated to itself a supremacy belonging only to the whole. If the suspension of formal right to avoid oppression were exclusively external or legislative, judges would determine rights in accordance with a formalist paradigm regarded as absolute. The supremacy of dialogic community demands, therefore, that formal property be internally limited in appropriate cases by courts and externally redistributed by legislatures.

There is, accordingly, a coherent line to be drawn between equitable modifications of formal right and the systematic realization of equity; for the right of property, while subordinate to equity, is not a conclusion from it. There is a property prior to distributive justice, the unconsented-to appropriation of which is a transitive taking enjoinable if for private gain, compensable if for a public good legislatively enforced as an override. Compensation for a public taking is required, however, only if the owner would otherwise be singled out as a social benefactor, for only then does the redistribution amount to a forced beneficence infringing his property.[123] Taxation is not a taking, since property is rightfully subordinate to the common freedom. Furthermore, property rights are legitimately suspended without compensation by judges (or legitimately regulated without compensation by legislatures) when their exercise would amount to interpersonal oppression; but the judicial taking of property for a distributive goal is a violation of property even if compensation is paid. No compensation is required in the former case, for no property is taken if its enforcement would pervert law into a private power;[124] compensation does not save property in the latter case, for the judicial mediation of property through the common good submerges the right of property.

As an interpretive key to property law, the theme of dialogic community commends itself for the following reasons. First, it is able to unify doctrinal patterns whose principles otherwise appear mutually hostile; hence it confirms to insight the participants' intuition that property law is indeed law rather than the tyranny of moral preference. Second, the framework of dialogic community reconciles private property with nonconsensual government takings of property; and so it makes sense of a legal practice wherein it is instinctively felt that property and eminent domain coexist, though how they do so remains a mystery at this prephilosophic level. It is doubtful, moreover, whether any other conception of natural right can resolve the paradox. If natural right is formal right, then there is, as Hobbes taught, no prepolitical right of property capable of limiting the sovereign; hence there is no right to compensation for a public taking. If, however, there is a property outside of political association, then any unconsented-to taking by the state is theft with or without compensation (and a majority vote does not count as individual consent). And if the basis of right is a common good, then one's property is defined by this good and so exerts no independent normative force. Only if property and the good are progressively more adequate instances of a totality requiring both can property survive its subordination to the positive ends of government. Thus only dialogic community explains an authority to expropriate for the common good coupled with a right of compensation indefeasible by the good.

The theme of dialogic community also vindicates distinctions drawn at the level of everyday practice but that the principles of formal right and moral autonomy (taken alone) efface: those between private and public law, adjudication and legislation, and between courts and public-law agencies. Formal right supports a private law ordered to the atomistic self and structuring the relationships between otherwise dissociated persons; however, it cannot account for a differentiated public law, since it sustains only a minimal state enforcing negative or private rights. The paradigm of moral autonomy supports a developed public law directed to a common good but cannot make sense of a distinctive private law or of the structural peculiarities of adjudication: the bipolar (plaintiff-defendant) format, the judge's passive reliance on party initiation and presentation, his adherence to a model of rationality as specification of principle rather than implementation of policy, her political independence, and the typical exclusion of social interests that distributive justice makes relevant. Dialogic community, however, supports both forms of order. In drawing a stable line between permissible equitable adjustments of formal right and impermissible reductions of formal right to equity, we have preserved the distinction between private and public law without implying that they form watertight compartments. We have thereby also made sense of the structural differences between—and so of the different job capabilities of—courts and public-law bodies.

8. A CONCLUDING NOTE ON INDUSTRIAL PROPERTY

Thus far dialogic community has merely interiorized and ordered the previous paradigms, contributing no new content to property law. However, just as the transition from formal right to equity implied an expanded content of right, so does the transition to dialogic community require a new modality of property. Because personality's right to embody itself is preserved, property continues to be acquired through a process of competitive accumulation in the market. Left to itself, this process tends to the concentration of productive property in a relatively few owners on whom those without such property depend for the exercise of their labor and so for access to the material conditions of an autonomous life. The potential for oppression in this situation is externally controlled through legislation regulating remuneration, hours of labor, and safety, as well as through transfers of wealth for the support of income. These measures are generated from the paradigm of moral autonomy, where the common good is asserted against the will's formal freedom of contract. However, if these two paradigms are to be reconciled as parts of a whole, the right of self-determination thus far externally enforced by the public authority against indifferent private agents must become actualized within the private sphere itself. Such a development would be the clearest image of dialogic community yet produced; for it would signify that a common good has become the conscious aim of the person considered not simply as a citizen abstracted from his private interests but precisely as a private individual who asserts his discrete self as an end.[125] The glimmering of this development is collective bargaining and the legislative scheme that supports it, but its ultimate fruition must be worker participation in management within each workplace where a concentration of capital would otherwise leave labor in a permanent state of subjection.

There are also glimmerings, faint to be sure, of the development of such a democratic property. Its advent has been prepared by the de facto separation of ownership and control of corporate property as well as by the gradual attenuation of shareholder and legal fetters on managerial discretion;[126] for these developments permit an institutionalized responsiveness of managers to worker interests without significant impact on the real power of owners. The democratization of industrial property is reflected, moreover, in legislatively mandated occupational health and safety committees, in works councils, and more generally in the phenomenon of "codetermination" emergent in some Continental countries.[127] The idea is invoked when lawyers argue that formal property should be adjusted to the exigencies of union organizing;[128] when they advocate protection for the reliance interest of workers against the unilateral closing of plants;[129] and when they urge that managerial rights be limited by the requirement of a rational cause for dismissal.[130] These results can be reached without violence to property by extending the principle behind proprietary estoppel, constructive trusts, and *Vincent v. Lake Erie*[131] from cases of oppression as a discrete event to cases of institutional domination. Since the principle of the transfer is an equitable suspension of an alien property rather than a redistribution of valid property, no taking is involved. Moreover, since equity civilizes without abolishing the paradigm of formal property, the wider accountability of managerial power need imply no nullification of the principle that managers stand in a fiduciary relation to owners. The interests of capital could continue as the primary object of the corporation; yet these interests would yield at the point of conflict to the self-determination of those who depend on access to capital for their livelihood and self-expression.

Until now, those who have urged a limitation of property rights for the benefit of industrial laborers have felt compelled to rest their case on the supposed conclusory nature of property, on its derivation from the common good. In this way, private property in general is submerged for the sake of its modification in a special context of acute human dependence.[132] One may admire the fidelity to principle that leads one to deny the cottage owner his peremptory right to eject an intruder in order that an entire community might be protected against a sudden decision to close a plant. However, there is no conceptual need to obliterate a distinction that common sense so readily draws. The democratic management of property within the industrial workplace is the clearest embodiment of dialogic community that has yet emerged, for it signifies the good's actualization not against but in the sphere of private accumulation. So understood, it is the best expression of an idea that preserves its inferior manifestations as stages in a process through which it is objectively confirmed as the basis of just laws and institutions. Because it is the rationally connected sequence of its embodiments, dialogic community rejects all extreme actualizations of partial principles, even as it incorporates their respective contents as mutually supporting aspects of a whole.

CHAPTER III

Reconstructing Contracts

1. THE CRISIS OF CONTRACT LAW

In *The Merchant of Venice,* Shakespeare depicts the polarity between law and equity as a contrast between cities. Initially, it seems that these cities are each self-contained wholes, and that Belmont is morally elevated above Venice. Venice is the city of commerce between self-seeking strangers united only by the cold abstraction of law. The scenes there take place in drab public places: in streets, in squares, or in court. Belmont, by contrast, is the city of gentleness and charity; its scenes occur in the stately home and garden of Portia, renowned for "wondrous virtues" and the object of the world's desire. Yet the first words spoken by the characters who personify these worlds are parallel expressions of sadness. Antonio and Portia are both weary of their worlds. Portia complains that she has no freedom of choice in marriage, that her life is rigidly determined by duties of filial piety imposed independently of her will. Lacking autonomy, she feels worthless amid an abundance of good fortune. The casket whose opening wins her for a suitor reveals the truth about Belmont behind the glittering appearance: it is made of dull lead, for which, as the inscription says, the suitor "must give and hazard all he hath." Antonio's malaise, by contrast, seems to be caused by a surfeit of choice, by the fact that life in Venice is abandoned to the arbitrariness of will. Gratiano, his friend, acts from reasons difficult to find and (according to Bassanio) not worth the search; Shylock prefers his pound of flesh to the repayment of his loan because "it is my humour," and the law seems to sanction his whims. Thus our first impression that Belmont is exalted above Venice gives way to the thought that both are abstractions from a larger whole, that the virtue of each, when pursued exclusively, becomes its opposite: public justice into a tool of private malice, subjective virtue into the loss of self. That each needs the other is confirmed in the climactic scene in which the dispute between Antonio and Shylock is finally resolved. Shylock is undone not by the displacement of law by equity but by the realization of equity through the more consistent application of law. And the resolution of the conflict between Venice and Belmont is portrayed not as a conquest of one by the other but as a marriage of equals wherein each supports the distinctiveness of the other for its own sake. The significance of the action is summed up in a speech by Portia: "The nightingale, if she should sing by day, / When every goose is cackling, would be thought / No better a musician than the wren. / How many things by season season'd are / To their right praise and true perfection!"[1]

The playwright's vision of a harmony between the spheres of law and equity strikes the contemporary mind as absurdly roseate. Today, the dominant view of the common law sees it as bifurcated—split into doctrinal patterns embodying conflicting human values.[2] Though generally associated with heterodoxy, this view has lately become a commonplace of mainstream legal discourse, for which judging inevitably involves the balancing of heterogeneous concerns and competing principles of order: predictability and fairness, liberty and community, individualism and altruism, or corrective and distributive justice. The implications of this outlook are barely acknowledged by orthodox legal scholars but are openly celebrated by the heretics. If legal interpretation faces a fragmented canon, then there is strictly speaking no law to constrain the moral passion of the scholar, judge, or legal practitioner. What appears as law is really a social choice masquerading as natural necessity; and the mask can be lifted simply by revealing the opposite possibility that, while officially suppressed, inevitably insinuates itself beneath rhetorical camouflage. Once the spell is broken, legal argument may resume, but no longer with the pretense that it involves something more conceptually bounded, rational, and amenable to right answers than controversies about the best way of life or about the best social order.

The law of contracts seems especially vulnerable to this type of debunking analysis. According to the standard account, modern contract law is principally a body of doctrine that was rationalized by common-law judges during the nineteenth century in conformity with the prevailing ideology of laissez-faire liberalism.[3] The basic tenets of that outlook are familiar enough: that there is no good independent of the satisfaction of appetites and aversions; that individual choices are the most reliable manifestation of these preferences; and that the ideal agent is a rational calculator of private advantage, one who acts so as to maximize his or her satisfactions. It follows from these premises that the greatest overall social good will flow if individuals are left free to interact as they please within the minimal constraints necessary to ensure the equal liberty of all. Positive duties to others should not be imposed on individuals in the name of an independent moral law; for such a law exists only in the opinion of those who would exalt their preferences into an objective norm and inflict them on others. Rather, such duties are legitimately enforced against an individual only if he or she has chosen to bound by them. Coercion, however, is an evil and can be justified only when necessary to produce a surplus social benefit. Hence promises to serve others should be judicially enforced only in the context of bargains, where the protection of expectations is needed to generate the prosperity that flows from a refined division of labor. Even when it intervenes, moreover, the court should see its role as primarily facilitative—as giving effect to the will of the parties. Any censorial role is properly confined to scrutinizing the process of contract formation to ensure that the agreement is voluntary on both sides. Courts must not inquire into the substantive fairness of a bargain, for there is no objective criterion of a fair bargain apart from the mutual consent of self-interested parties. Nor should they impose duties of concern for the weak that deprive the strong of the rewards of their superior diligence and bargaining power. Since everyone is entitled to pursue his self-interest in the most rigorous manner consistent with the free choice of others, no one has a right to another's beneficence or candor unless such a right was paid for.

Such, according to its historians, are the essential features of the classical model of contract law. The motto of this paradigm is freedom of contract; its foundational values are individual liberty and self-reliance. Contract law is no doubt justified in terms of the collective good; but this good is understood as the sum of the satisfactions of individual preferences, so that it offers no vantage point from which to criticize voluntary bargains. Nevertheless, into this paradigm a different set of values quietly intrudes, disturbing the internal coherence of the model. This configuration lays stress on freedom from economic oppression, on the individual's responsibility for the effective autonomy (as distinct from the formal liberty) of those whom he uses for the satisfaction of his goals, and hence on his accountability to a common good independent of the satisfaction of individual preferences. To begin with, these values assert themselves surreptitiously. A concern about an oppressive bargain disguises itself as an inability to find a bargain at all,[4] as a finding of insufficient notice of terms to constitute consent,[5] or as a presumption that parties do not intend disclaimers of liability to apply to fundamental breaches of their agreement.[6] Finally, in the middle of the twentieth century, this concern becomes articulated through a full-blown doctrine of unconscionability by which courts deny the powerful the fruits of one-sided bargains voluntarily made. When this doctrine is used to invalidate clauses excluding a manufacturer's liability for product defects, the pendulum has swung from freedom of contract to the courts' imposition of compulsory warranties embodying the primacy of a common good over the free will of the parties.[7] Accordingly, writers now announce the "death of contract" as a source of social obligation independent of tort law and call for "fundamental restatements" to reorganize contract law under the new conceptual order.[8] Yet the obituary for contract turns out to have been premature. Instead of consistently subduing contract law to its social vision, the new paradigm manages only to superimpose itself on the persistent vitality of the old, with the result that contract law now appears as an amalgam of doctrines inspired by irreconcilable ideologies. Given the arrested development of the new principles, the constraining force of contract law as a coherent normative system seems to have dissipated entirely. When orthodoxy contends that "the law of contracts, like the legal system itself, involves a balance between competing sets of values,"[9] there is nothing left for heresy but to proclaim the death of law as a consequence.

The existence of rival patterns in the law of contracts is not, however, sufficient by itself to undermine completely its unity or its power to determine rationally the outcomes of particular disputes. If the freedom of contract model (as I shall temporarily call it) were internally coherent, self-enclosed, and stable, the presence of doctrines alien to that model would no doubt testify to its finitude as a normative system and so to the ideological character of its absolutist claims; but it would pose no threat to the unity of the system or to its power to generate solutions to controversies submitted to it for arbitration. Anyone who made the initial choice to be guided by its basic principle would thereafter have a law for the resolution of any dispute arising under a contract. What we call contract law would thus consist in a conflict between two mutually independent and self-contained normative systems, each capable of rationally ordering the whole field of interpersonal obligations. Contract law would be fragmented but not fundamentally unprincipled.

The truly radical challenge to the rationality of contract law depends, therefore, on a profounder claim than that which simply asserts a duality of paradigms. It rests on the claim (justified, as I will show) that the doctrinal patterns are in fact not sealed off from one another, that the principle of each contains that of the other as a necessary supplement whose rigorous actualization destroys that which it is supposed to complete. The dynamic interaction between the extremes is explained by one writer of the critical school in the following manner.[10] Freedom of contract requires a limitation on the socially irresponsible liberty one may exercise in a pure state of nature. Specifically, it requires that no one incur positive obligations as a result of fraud, duress, or the exploitation of one's nonage or mental incapacity. This means that the notion of freedom of contract already implies a judicially enforced redistribution of advantages from the strong to the weak, one that assures that the terms of the agreement will be unaffected by at least some of the unequal endowments that the parties bring to their relationship. However, once this egalitarian limitation on the state of nature is admitted, there is no principled stop short of a model of contract law wherein "formal" freedom of contract is submerged under compulsory contracts and mandatory terms protecting the effective autonomy of those too indigent or foolhardy to protect themselves. And yet this result is no more stable than the extreme libertarian point at which we began. For the principle of effective autonomy in turn requires respect for a sphere of private sovereignty wherein individuals themselves author the positive duties that will restrict their liberty, wherein they are free to buy or to forgo the security of a contractual term and so to pursue their welfare as *they* see it, and wherein the rights of persons reflect their status as discrete ends rather than as merged units of a collectivity. Relentlessly pursued, however, this supplement drives us back to the opposed model of unrestrained freedom of contract, where the circuit begins anew.

The consequence of this endless oscillation between antithetical extremes is that contract law appears structurally incoherent and thoroughly indeterminate. Because the principled actualization of each extreme leads to its self-contradiction, contract law must (it seems) consist in a series of unprincipled accommodations between the poles.* Because each antagonist fights a battle in which victory is simultaneously defeat, each must acknowledge the validity of the other even as it strives for hegemony. Thus, instead of an honorable war between self-assured opponents, we have a succession of ignoble compromises and appeasements. Furthermore, because each principle implicitly contains its antagonist, neither can rationally determine a unique set of solutions to problems submitted to it. Each leads indifferently to conclusions having a more or less libertarian or egalitarian bias, so that the choice of a position along the continuum is always unconstrained. Contract law is unprincipled (so the argument runs) not only because it requires an initial arbitrary choice between basic values but also because this choice shadows the jurist through every successive level of decision making—from choice of principle to choice of rule to choice

---

*See Jay Feinman, "Critical Approaches to Contract Law," 30 *UCLA L. Rev.* 829, 839 (1983). The mutual adjustment of the polarities is illustrated by the following phenomena of contract law: the principle of promissory estoppel is accommodated to the bargain theory by limiting its application to defensive situations involving preexisting contractual relations; see Combe v. Combe, [1951] 1 All E.R. 767; a duty of disclosure is adjusted to the doctrine of caveat emptor by limiting its application to cases of common mistake and to cases where the plaintiff knew of the defendant's error; see Solle v. Butcher, [1950] 1 K.B. 671; the courts' policing of contracts harmful to the real interests of a party is adjusted to the doctrine of freedom of contract by confining its scope to cases involving inequality of bargaining power; see Lloyds Bank Ltd. v. Bundy, [1975] 1 Q.B. 326. One of the principal aims of this chapter is to show that these apparent truce lines represent coherent boundaries.

of outcome in a particular case. Contract law is indeterminate, as the heretics like to say, all the way down.

These are the ruins from which any effort to reconstruct contract law must begin. It would be futile now to attempt a unification of contract law on the basis of either of the conflicting principles taken alone, for such a unity could maintain itself only by artificially curtailing the reach of its norm, banishing doctrines of the opposing paradigm that its own principle implicates. Any reunification must therefore invoke a thematic principle that has absorbed and so transcended the heretic's critical insight. At the same time, this principle must not assert itself dogmatically against the view that contradiction is endemic to law, for it could then claim no greater validity than the skepticism it opposes. It would not do, for example, to counter the thesis proclaiming law's incoherence with the edifying assurance that Aristotle's forms of justice are immanent in law;[11] for one assurance is as good, and therefore as barren, as another. Merely to assert the immanence of reason in the common law turns out to be self-defeating, for the effort to reclaim the law for reason then shades into (and masks) an accommodation of reason to existing law. There is, as we shall see, a unity of contract law that is indeed its very own. However, the unifying idea must not be baldly asserted against the skeptic and straightaway deployed as an interpretive tool. Rather, one must show how this idea is already implicit in the skeptic's demolition of the previous contenders; and its immanence, instead of being declared by us, must be validated in the spontaneous self-realization of that in which it is said to be immanent.

2. WHY ABSOLUTIZE THE SUPPLEMENT?

To the extent that it opposes any reconstructive project, the heretic's claim is that the incoherence and indeterminacy into which contract law has fallen is a constant feature of law, a predicament one can camouflage but never escape. The underlying dilemma is that the individual self is drawn to community as to that which actualizes its fundamental worth but is also repelled by community, which submerges its distinctive identity. The self is fragmented, torn between opposites neither of which offers repose.[12] In denying the possibility of overcoming this contradiction, the heretic is a skeptic, for he challenges not only a prevailing system of legal orthodoxy but also the possibility of any coherent system of law whatsoever. The refutation of his skepticism (but not of his heresy) comprises the following arguments: first, that it does not follow from the heretic's insight; second, that this insight already points to the principle that transcends and relativizes his skepticism.

The heretic's enduring insight is that neither individualist nor collectivist premises can succeed in unifying contract law, because each principle presupposes or needs the other for its own coherence. To the extent, therefore, that one is absolutized, it destroys the other and thereby falls into contradiction. Without any restraint in the name of equality, freedom of contract contradicts itself, for it collapses into the right of the stronger. Yet the absolutization of equality destroys freedom of contract and thereby contradicts itself as a realization of equal *autonomy.* Yet nothing in this result tells us that no unity of contract law is possible. The modern collapse of contract law as a unified system is the negation not of the possibility of unity as such but of specific conceptions of the unifying principle. To the extent, therefore, that the heretic proclaims the inevitable and fixed indeterminacy of law, he is proclaiming a nonsequitur.

But second, he is proclaiming something his own insight refutes. That each principle implicitly contains its opposite as a necessary supplement signifies that neither principle is sufficient by itself, that each needs the other for its own fulfillment. This means that each principle is one—and only one—element of the totality formed by their notional continuity or by their mutual need. The claim that contract law is necessarily incoherent rests, however, on the belief that conceptual rigor impels us to absolutize the supplement to the point where it destroys that which it is supposed to complete. The argument is that because logic requires us to universalize each pole at the expense of the other, any accommodation between the poles is illogical. But the question now arises: why absolutize the supplement? Since we now know that each principle requires the other, that it becomes the opposite of itself when generalized in isolation, we also know that neither is absolute alone. Neither, therefore, can validly claim to be the basic principle of contract law. But there is no conceptual impetus, no requirement of logic, to exalt into the principle of the whole that which we know to be a part. On the contrary, conceptual rigor demands that we grasp the *totality* as the thematic principle and that we observe limits on the jurisdiction of the partial principle to prevent its usurpation of the whole. Once we do this, all the stock-in-trade notions of the skeptic—fundamental contradiction, deep incoherence, radical indeterminacy—evaporate, or are seen to be relative to a standpoint still in thrall to the old order. Since the contradiction between the poles depended on the false claim of each to dominance, the recognition of both as mutually essential parts of a whole eliminates their mutual antagonism. There is thus no necessary contradiction between the poles of individualism and collectivism; and the assertion of such a necessity simply betrays a vestigial attachment to the old absolutes, whose sole remaining prop is the skeptic's need obliquely to affirm them in order to preserve itself.

Let us consider more closely how attention to the totality cancels the indeterminacy on which the skeptic dwells. That individual liberty and the common good entail each other implies that one is not free to embrace one or the other according to one's ideological predilections. One is constrained, rather, by the whole, which acknowledges the authority of both principles within bounds compatible with their mutual preservation. The primacy of the whole thus removes the first source of indeterminacy in contract law: the apparent opposition of paradigms. It also removes the second, for it establishes a conceptual boundary between the jurisdictions of the principles in place of the opposing continua seen by the skeptic. As there is no logical requirement to absolutize the supplement, there is nothing inherently irrational or arbitrary about the point at which we restrain its operation. To the contrary, since each pole notionally needs the other, each must respect the other's distinctiveness for the sake of its own conceptual integrity. But this means that an accommodation between the poles can be principled, for it signifies not a compromise between imperialist rivals but the mutual support of interdependent equals. Moreover, because the boundary that confines each principle also imposes a constraint on decision makers, we now have the possibility of a determinative system of law. For any contract dispute, the decision maker will have a principle for determining which paradigm to apply and how far the applicable paradigm may be modulated by doctrines emanating from the other.[13] We can see, then, that to transcend the heretic's skepticism, we need only take seriously his heresy. All that is required is that we thoughtfully grasp the whole already witnessed in his critical insight.

I have been calling this whole dialogic community. While the detailed elucidation of its structure must await further preparation, a preliminary description is possible on the basis of our experience of the downfall of the previous ordering principles. That experience taught us that neither the individual self nor the common good is an absolute end to the exclusion of the other, for each needs the other to be fully the end that it inherently is. The common good cannot be the end or good *of* the individual if it annihilates his or her distinctive identity; rather, it is the good only in being validated as such through the individual's free deference to community as to the basis of his or her independent worth. Thus the end-status of community presupposes that of the discrete self, whose spontaneous recognition it needs. Because it needs the self, the community must defer to individual liberty, making room for a distinctive sphere of individual self-realization wherein community merely "glimmers" in the legal relations formed by atomistic selves (263). Obversely, the individual's essential worth presupposes community, whose need for recognition first dignifies the self. Hence the individual must reciprocally defer to community as to the conceptual origin of its rights, acknowledging moral limits to their exercise. And because the respect between the poles is mutual, the self-abnegation of each in favor of the other is compatible with their mutual confirmation as ends.

Now the bond forged by the reciprocal deference of community and the individual self is the reality I am calling dialogic community. My thesis is that this bond is the unifying theme of contract law, the theme that knits together the libertarian and egalitarian paradigms. As we shall see, each of these paradigms is manifestly ordered to a particular conception of the absolute worth of the individual self. Though different in ways I shall explain, these conceptions are nonetheless related in that they both presuppose the fixed reality of the atomistic or asocial individual. However, if dialogic community is the ultimate basis for the self's worth, then that worth inherently presupposes the need for confirmation of another self, to whom the individual will be drawn for the validation of its claim to an absolute dignity. Hence the worth of the self (and so its right to respect) will be firmly grounded only in a dialogic relationship wherein each self receives objective worth from the self-interested deference of the other. In this way, the structure of dialogic community will be immanent in the self-realization of the atomistic individual who is at the center of the common-law paradigms. Each paradigm is a partial and imperfect manifestation of that structure, and each requires the other for its own completion. This mutual need of the paradigms reveals a dialogic unity of which each is itself a particular instance. The unity of contract law is thus a unity of distinct doctrinal formations each of which manifests this encompassing unity to the degree allowed by its self-conscious principle.

My argument for this thesis will differ somewhat from the one employed in the previous chapter on property. There I began with the abstract person as the putatively unconditioned end that grounds legal obligation in order to show how the realization of this principle leads by intelligible steps to dialogic community, whose validation as the underlying theme of the process was the point of the exercise. In this chapter I will presuppose that argument and so will explicitly deploy the notion of dialogic community from the outset. Once we have grasped this idea, we will begin to see it everywhere in the law; for, as the structure of all nonviolent order, it is the ground for the distinction between claims involving subjective impositions of will and those enforceable as an objective right. However, the fact that we possess the idea of dialogic community from the outset does not mean that we can dispense with the individualistic principles of order on which the legal paradigms are self-consciously based as if these principles were no longer essential to legal understanding. On the contrary, since community is genuinely dialogical only in submitting for confirmation of its authority to the self-seeking activity of the atomistic self, legal understanding requires that we passively observe the imprint of dialogic community in that activity. This means that we must simultaneously adopt two interpretive standpoints—the individualistic one that self-consciously orders the common-law paradigm as well as that of the philosophic observer who sees in that ordering a particular manifestation of dialogic community. In this way, understanding does not reduce the complexity of contract law to a single, repetitive theme but attends to the specific and varied patterns in which the theme expresses itself—patterns determined by the particular conception of individual freedom overtly governing the paradigm. Understanding is itself dialogical (rather than an artificial imposition) when it not only discerns the one in the many but also honors the many by respecting the diverse ways in which it spontaneously reflects the one.

Accordingly, we need to keep before our minds the individualistic principles manifestly governing the two basic doctrinal patterns discernible in the common law as well as the distinguishing features of these patterns. Since I have dealt with these matters in the previous chapter, I shall confine myself here to a synoptic restatement.

3. THE TWO COMMON-LAW PARADIGMS

The two principles by which the legal paradigms are self-consciously ordered are the formal liberty of the abstractly universal person and the concrete self-determination of the individuated human subject. By formal liberty we understand a negative capacity to transcend the manifold inclinations immediately given in one's consciousness and so a capacity to choose which of these aims to adopt and pursue. Because this capacity is revealed in the abstraction from all individual ends, it is a capacity definitive of abstract personhood, in which all individual differences are submerged (35).[14] Moreover, as an abstraction from all subjective ends, personality is a particular conception of a universal, absolute, or unconditioned end and therefore a particular conception of the foundation that supports valid rights and duties. It is logically the first such conception to which the mind is drawn, because it presupposes inclinations that are immediate or given, that have not yet been organized, channeled, or integrated in accordance with any rational scheme of life. Where all individual goals have the significance of brute, particularistic appetite, we can arrive at a public conception of right only by fastening on the bare capacity to form, pursue, and revise goals and by consigning the goals themselves to public irrelevance.

The conception of the unconditioned as abstract personality generates a legal paradigm we are calling formal right, a paradigm characterized by the following interconnected features. First, the law is indifferent to the particular projects that individuals seek to realize when they acquire, exchange, or defend property (37). Whether the individual succeeds or fails in these goals is all the same to the law, for no one may demand as a matter of right that others limit their freedom for the sake of one's particular interests. Abstracting from such interests, the law sees individuals only as abstract persons with a capacity to own things, and it is this universal capacity alone that the law seeks to vindicate. Hence someone may be entitled to a legal remedy for an infringement of rights, even though he has suffered no injury to his material interests or indeed even if he has been positively benefited; while conversely, he will be without a legal remedy no matter how great his personal suffering at the hands of another if the damage is unconnected to any infringement of personality.[15] Second, the law equates human welfare with the satisfaction of subjective values, or it is blind to any difference between welfare so conceived and welfare understood as the individual realization of a generic human capacity for autonomy. As a result, formal right is as sublimely indifferent to the latter conception of welfare as it is to the former. Because in formal right there is no such thing (except as a coincidence) as a common good, justice consists solely in the mutual respect for freedom of choice and for the embodiment of this freedom in property already acquired. Within these constraints each person is free to act in complete disregard for the interests of others—both for their particular interests and for the necessary conditions of their human well-being. Stated otherwise, there are no coercive duties independent of contract to confer a benefit, to surrender one's advantages, or to forgo one's right in order to save another from catastrophe. Similarly, there is no distinct norm of distributive justice, since no one has a right to any particular share of the things human beings want or need, nor to any minimum level of welfare.

The conception of freedom underlying formal right is obviously incomplete. It is not simply false, for no understanding of freedom can dispense with the negative idea of freedom of choice and its corollary idea of the imputability of actions to the will. However, the *identification* of freedom with the capacity to choose is erroneous, because it treats as alien or external to freedom the necessary means by which the capacity is expressed, so that freedom cannot express itself without self-contradiction. Because one is free, according to this conception, only in not being moved by this or that appetite, any realization of freedom in some concrete choice is simultaneously the loss of freedom. Because one is free only in flight from all dependence on an other, the social realization of freedom in property and contract is simultaneously one's dependence on an external will indifferent to one's own. To be coherent, therefore, the individual's freedom must be conceived more inclusively so as to reconcile the formal capacity for choice with its concrete expression in particular goals whose realization occurs within social relationships. Freedom must be understood not simply as a capacity for spontaneity revealed in the rejection of aims but also as a power to remain within the spontaneity of the self in acting from some specific aim in a context of human interdependence. So conceived, freedom is a capacity not only for choice but for self-determination as well; or it is a power to act from determinate ends that are themselves coherent expressions of freedom because they are neither adopted unreflectively nor imposed by an external will. Because this kind of freedom is a good to be achieved rather than a transcendental datum of consciousness, it yields the possibility for an objective conception of welfare as the realization in each individual of a universal human potential for inner-directedness. That is to say, the conception of freedom as self-determination fuses into a single whole the two elements—agency and welfare—that formal right kept rigidly apart. Welfare is no longer identified with the satisfaction of preferences relative to the individual, nor (therefore) is freedom identified with an abstractly generic capacity for action in which the individual disappears. Rather, freedom is now understood as the coherent actualization of agency through the specific aims, endowments, and deeds of an individuated human subject; and the real welfare of the individual is conceived in identical terms (130).

As a conception of the common good, the idea of self-determination generates a system of individual rights vis-à-vis the public order, part of which is autonomously enforced by courts as the bodies of law called equity and natural (procedural) justice and part of which consists in the legislative products of the welfare state. All the characteristic features of this paradigm flow from the rise to public significance of individual welfare once this conception of freedom is grasped. For example, while formal right remedies breaches of contract only with a monetary award in which the diversity of individual ends is obliterated, equity awards specific performance when money is inadequate, having regard to the plaintiff's purposes in entering the contract. In general, we can say that, in contrast to formal right, the system of positive rights recognizes a right to welfare conceived publicly as a realized human capacity for autonomous action. This general right is specified in three kinds of entitlements: a right of intention, or a right against subjection to forces, whether causal or legal, in which a rational agent could not recognize the embodiment of his or her goals; a right of insight, or a right to the procedures whereby the impartiality of law is validated through the participating reason of the parties; and a right to welfare properly so-called, that is, a right to the material and cultural conditions for an autonomous life. In contrast to those involved in formal right, these rights are not simply moral barriers against the interference of others with freedom of choice; rather, they are rights to the positive concern of public agencies for one's effective autonomy—rights correlative to the duty of these agencies to conform to their inherently public character. The vindication of these claims entails the result that private individuals can enforce their formal rights only within bounds consistent with regard for the human welfare of others.

These are the characteristic features of the systems in which (as I will show) dialogic community manifests itself in progressively clearer form. It cannot be emphasized too strongly that the individualistic principles overtly informing the paradigms are as essential to legal understanding as the latent, communitarian theme. If understanding simply asserted the interpretive primacy of dialogic community over against the individualistic themes by which the practice is interpreted from within, it would subvert itself as an authentic understanding; for it would then come forward as a particular perspective alongside others, with no better claim to understanding than the principles it dogmatically reduces to insignificance. Legal understanding is possible as an objective enterprise because community is—by virtue of its own dialogic nature—immanent in the self-oriented activity of the individual who claims to be an end apart from community; and the task of legal understanding is to observe the manifestations of community *in* this activity, not to impose its primacy from without.

Accordingly, the aim of what follows is to recognize the traces of dialogic community in the self-actualization of the individual self in the law of contract. Preparatory to this task, I shall try to elucidate the logical structure of dialogic community so that we will be able to recognize it in legal doctrines ordered to the primacy of the individual. Then I will show how the principal doctrines of contract law—the expectation measure of damages, offer and acceptance, the requirement of consideration—can be understood both as objectifications of the person's claim of absolute worth and as instantiations of the structure of reciprocal deference. Subsequently we turn to elements of contract law that are specifically determined by the conception of the unconditioned as abstract personality, and we observe how these doctrines render formal right both a self-contradictory realization of that conception and an imperfect instantiation of dialogic community. The argument is that the paradigm of formal right, when absolutized as a self-sufficient framework of valid obligations, contradicts the very end it purports to realize and points to equity for its own fulfillment. We then examine the contract doctrines generated by the conception of the universal end as self-determination, and we interpret them as supplements to formal right that both realize the worth of the self and reinforce formal right's dialogic structure. The argument for the unity of contract law then requires one further step. Having shown that formal right needs equity for its own completion, we then show how the absolutization of the principle of self-determination results in the negation of individual autonomy and the reinstatement of domination. That both systems are self-contradictory when absolutized in isolation reveals the genuine unconditioned as the dialogic totality of which both are subordinate and mutually complementary parts.

4. THE STRUCTURE OF DIALOGIC COMMUNITY: THE THREEFOLD MEDIATION

Since (as I maintain) legal understanding consists in recognizing the diverse iterations of dialogic community in individualistic legal doctrine, we begin by describing the generic structure of that concept. The structure of dialogic community will come into view if we observe its emergence in the famous opening paragraphs of chapter four of Hegel's *Phenomenology of Spirit*, dealing with the realization of self-consciousness.[16] Although the following discussion may seem an excursus into areas remote from contract law, this is far from the case. In the passages I shall expound, Hegel analyzes forms of social interaction that are precontractual and yet proximate to contract, so that a study of these relationships is a study of the philosophical origins of the contractual form itself.

We begin (as before) with an individual self who regards its selfhood as an absolute end outside of any association with others. The self is thus an atomistic individual who claims an unconditioned worth by virtue of its capacity to abstract from all contingent or relative aspects of its existence. This claim is initially a mere subjective opinion, however, for in grasping selfhood as an absolute end, the individual had to distinguish himself from the contingently given world, which now persists alongside the self as a challenge to its claim of primacy. Accordingly, the objective validation of the self's conviction of absolute worth requires that it reduce everything other than itself to a medium for the realization of its end-status. This it does by taking possession of things, by shaping, using, and consuming them. In canceling the apparent independence of things other than itself, the self demonstrates that they are not ends-in-themselves but only means for its own self-realization.

However, this mode of self-confirmation turns out to be inadequate for at least two reasons. First, the self desires objective confirmation for its conviction of absolute worth, and yet such a confirmation can never issue from the self's one-sided imposition of its will on other objects. The product of a unilateral assertion of will *against* objects can never be more than the subjective certainty with which the self began. Second, the very fact that the self seeks confirmation through a conquest of the not-self shows that the latter is not the nullity that the self takes it to be. Because the self needs the other to objectify its primacy, every negation of an object reproduces the lacuna in the self and gives rise to a new desire ad infinitum. This experience reveals the two conditions that must be met if the self is to gain more than an ephemeral satisfaction. First, the object whose subordination the self seeks must surrender *itself* to the primacy of the self; that is, it must surrender spontaneously, from its own side. And second, it must in the process of doing so preserve its independence from the self, so that the act of surrender can be perpetually reenacted within an abiding relationship.

There is, however, only one kind of object that can give itself up in the purely spontaneous way required for the objective confirmation of the self, and that is another self. Because only a self is an end for itself, it alone confronts another self as that which is irreducibly other, as that which is infinitely beyond the self's one-sided grasp; hence the spontaneous surrender of such an object to the self represents the definitive confirmation of the self as the natural end of the object. Only another self can deliver reality to the self; and we will soon see how the intuition of this truth underlies all of contract law. Moreover, only another self can, by virtue of its indestructible freedom, preserve its independence in its subordination to the self and thereby perpetually reenact its self-abnegation. Once an animal or an inanimate thing is reduced to the self, nothing of its independence remains; consequently, the self must leave it in search of another transitory conquest. However, the freedom of another self can never be reduced or subjugated; as an ineluctable property of self-consciousness, it endures to repeat continuously the transaction. Hence, as Hegel says, "self-consciousness achieves its satisfaction only in another self-consciousness" (*PhS*, 110).

The fact that the self is confirmed as an end only in a relationship with another self yields us our first glimpse of community within a framework overtly governed by an asocial conception of the self's ultimate worth. We must now inquire into the kind of social bond that must initially arise given that each isolated self takes itself to be an absolute end and regards everything other than itself as a nullity. Evidently, the only kind of interaction possible between persons who take this view is combat, wherein each self strives to confirm its supremacy by killing the other. The combat must be a fight to the death for the following reasons. First, each self must risk its life in order to accomplish the abstraction from contingent, individual existence by virtue of which it is authentically a self, confident of its status as an absolute end. Second, each self must risk its life in order to reveal itself to the other as a free self qualified to recognize and so objectively to confirm the other's end-status. Third, each self must aim at the other's death in order to demonstrate objectively that it is the sole unconditioned reality and that everything other than itself is devoid of intrinsic significance. Accordingly, by aiming at the death of the other, each helps the other achieve the emancipation from thinghood that qualifies it to confirm the first. In this sense there is a community even between deadly foes (*PhS*, 113–114).

Should, however, the fight for recognition actually end in the death of one of the combatants, the first condition for the self's satisfaction will have been met but not the second. In risking its life for the sake of recognition, each individual reveals himself to the other as an infinite self capable, by virtue of its radical spontaneity and independence, of objectively confirming the end-status of the other. During the fight, moreover, each recognizes the other as having risked his life, and so each gains confirmation of his worth through the respect the other pays to his courage. Yet if the fight ends in the death of one of the combatants, the victory of the other is hollow, for death is the negation of the very self-consciousness whose recognition it needed. The independence of the defeated self has been canceled, but without being preserved so as to enable it to pay continuous tribute to the victor. Moreover, since the self initially constitutes itself only by risking its life, the end of the struggle signifies for the victor a return to the mundane attachments of his individual existence and so to a loss of selfhood. For both selves, therefore, the end of the struggle means a return to thinghood (*PhS*, 114–115).

This experience teaches that the self can find satisfaction only if the recognition it received in the fight to the death can somehow be recapitulated within the framework of an ongoing relationship. This is possible only if one of the combatants, seeing that the exclusive end-status of the abstract self entails the nothingness of his specific individuality, cowers before this implication and clings to his particular life rather than risk it for the sake of a universal end in which he is submerged as an individual. In thus identifying himself with the aspect of contingent particularity or thinghood, the vanquished self regards itself as possessing no intrinsic value, while simultaneously recognizing absolute worth in the self who was prepared to die in the fight for recognition. Since he takes all value to reside in the other's self, the vanquished self is prepared to actualize that value through obedient and constant service to his will (*PhS*, 115).

We now have an ongoing social relationship in which the end-status of one self is continually recognized through the voluntary service of another but wherein the recipient of this recognition does not reciprocate the respect. Only one self is an end; the other is simply a means to the confirmation of his end-status, a selfless thing both in his own eyes and in the eyes of the victor. The relationship is one between a master and a slave. The question we must now ask is whether the master gains from the slave a satisfying confirmation of his status as an absolute end.

That he does not becomes evident when we recall the two conditions for the self's realization. The slave's recognition cannot satisfy the dominant self, for the latter needed recognition from an object that freely deferred to him, and yet the slave submitted to the master from a fear of freedom. The slave's recognition was not free, for he had not sufficiently emancipated himself from an animal attachment to life and security to have constituted himself as a free self competent to give objective reality to the selfhood of the master. Furthermore, the master required an ongoing recognition from a self who preserved himself in his sacrifice, and yet the slave has suppressed his selfhood, for he acknowledges the master's worth but denies his own. No doubt the slave continually recognizes the master; but because his recognition is not that of someone conscious of himself as an end radically independent of the self of the master, it is not the objective confirmation that the master seeks. It is not a recognition whereby the object, in the extremity of its otherness, spontaneously confirms the self (*PhS*, 116–117).

This shows that the self can gain objective confirmation for its conviction of absolute worth only if it is freely recognized as an end by a self who likewise asserts itself as an end and who is preserved as such in this recognition. But someone may be preserved as an end in submitting to the end-status of another only if the other reciprocally submits to the first. Accordingly, the self's realization as an end requires that a relationship between a master and a slave give way to one between equals, wherein each self submits to the lordship of the other in order that the other may validly confirm the first. Here we have come upon an ontological bond between independent selves, a bond we are calling dialogic community.[17]

Let us carefully analyze the process of mutual recognition, for it has a complicated structure, one that will be inscribed in every doctrine of contract law worthy of our allegiance. We can understand the process as a unity of three distinct elements, each of which logically comprises or presupposes the other two. Following Hegel, I will call this structure the threefold mediation, since each of the three elements is fully what it is only by virtue of linking or mediating itself with the others.[18] The three elements are the two selves—call them A and B—and the totality forged by their interaction and mutual dependence. These elements form a unity because each needs the other two to become completely the end that it inherently is. Consequently, each must support the end-status of the other (become a means for the other) for the sake of its own fulfillment; and because one supports the other, the other can in turn serve the first without self-loss. So, for example, A cancels itself as an isolated individual and thereby cancels its independence, making itself a means to the self-conscious end-status of B. Nevertheless, its own end-status is preserved and indeed confirmed in this self-abnegation, because B likewise cancels its isolation and defers to the end-status of A. In self-consciously appropriating the other's deference, each passively receives its objective worth from another; but this dependence is consistent with freedom, because the other is not alien or indifferent to the self but rather supports the self's worth for its own sake. Each surrenders to the end-status of the other in order that the other can, as a free self, satisfyingly confirm the first.

Accordingly, the end-status of A presupposes that of B and vice versa. This means that the end-status of both A and B presupposes the totality formed by their mutual dependence and which mediates between the iso-lated subjectivities of both. A could not be preserved as an end if it de-pended for confirmation on an isolated and egoistic B, nor could B be an end if it depended on an external and indifferent A. Rather, each is pre-served only in depending on the other seen as needing (and so as having to support) itself. A's dependence on B's will is compatible with A's free-dom because he relies on B only through the mediation of a totality in which his freedom is likewise necessary for B. The totality is thus the mid-dle term between the isolated selves, ensuring that one's dependence on the other is consistent with the autonomy of both. Moreover, this totality in turn presupposes the radically distinctive identities of the two selves, for it is intelligible only in terms of the reciprocal lack of each self for the free self of the other; and it comes into being only in the surrender of each to the other's freedom for its own sake. The totality is thus an *intersubjective* one. It is a bond between free selves that is identified with neither taken alone, nor even with an abstract equality in which their mutual difference would be submerged. The totality is a "we" rather than an abstractly uni-versal "I," a totality that embraces the distinctiveness of the selves it unites and that is a genuine totality only because it does so (*PhS*, 110). Further, because neither self is an end in isolation from the other or from the whole, it follows that the totality linking their distinctive selves is alone the foundation of the justified claim of each to respect. Since the self's claim of worth gains objective reality only within a relationship of mutual recog-nition, this relationship defines the limits of whatever rights to another's deference the self may validly claim. This means that all claims of the self to respect must be tested against the requirements of equality and reci-procity implied by the intersubjective basis of rights.

What we have described thus far is a generic process of recognition, one that abstracts from the various conceptions of the self whose realiza-tion is attained through this process. If the individual makes no claim to an unconditioned worth as an isolated and abstract self but consciously ac-cepts his or her worth as grounded in the intersubjective totality, then the process of recognition yields a relationship of love or friendship, wherein the separate existences of the selves are treated as insignificant. If, how-ever, the isolated individual claims an absolute worth on the basis of ab-stract personality, then the dialogic relation through which this claim is validated will take the form of contract. Accordingly, our task is to derive the contractual relationship from the isolated self's project to confirm it-self as an absolute end. Subsequently we will attempt to explain the basic doctrines of contract law as instantiations of dialogic community within the framework of this project. Before we begin, however, we must locate our approach to contract within the broader tradition of theories of con-tractual obligation.[19]

5. CONTRACT AS PROMISE: A CRITIQUE

The task of a theory of contractual obligation is to explain why certain nonobligatory choices of the will become binding once they are chosen.[20] Morally obligatory ends oblige us by virtue of an authority independent of our wills. Their origin is not contract but some transindividual source such as God or nature or the general will. In the social practice of contract, however, choices of the will that are in themselves morally indifferent—obtaining one's raw materials from this supplier rather than from that—become obligatory simply by virtue of an agreement of wills. This transformation is deeply puzzling because nonobligatory ends derive their sole value and moral status from the will that chooses them. These ends are not chosen because they are ends; rather, they are ends because the agent chooses them. And since their value depends entirely on the will, nonobligatory ends would seem to be always subject to revision. Nevertheless, contract binds the will to its nonobligatory choices. When I communicate an intention within the ritual framework of contract, that intention becomes binding on the very will that was originally free to form it or not. This particular expression of the will now becomes privileged in relation to all subsequent ones that vary or contradict the first, so that what would otherwise be an innocent change of mind becomes a wrong unless accompanied by steps to compensate the disappointed party. Both moral and legal discourse call these special utterances promises and distinguish them from statements of alterable intention. The problem for a theory of contractual obligation is to explain the basis of this moral distinction, to render intelligible the paradox of the free will binding itself to its own contingent preference.

The most common solution to this problem treats contractual obligation as a special case of promissory obligation.[21] On this view, the obligation to perform one's part of a bargain derives from the moral obligation to keep one's promises generally. Theories of promissory obligation typically explain the obligatoriness of otherwise morally indifferent choices by relating the performance of a promise to an end that is obligatory independently of the promise. For example, I may be obliged to keep my promises because I thereby adhere to a social practice that produces greater net benefits than the alternative and because I am independently obliged to maximize overall welfare; or because I thereby participate in an institution conducive to the common good of all and so perfect my nature as a being whose excellence consists in participation in community; or because I actualize the will's autonomy when I renounce subjective inclination in favor of a principle of promise keeping that can be coherently willed as a universal law.[22] Whatever the good that grounds it, however, all strictly promissory obligation is self-regarding. That is, the obligation is correlative not to the promisee's prior right to respect but to the authority of the promisor's ideal over his actual self.[23] The ideal self might be one that makes personal sacrifices for the collective welfare, but the reason for the sacrifice is not the right of others but the self-perfection of the moral agent. Moreover, because the obligation is one of self-fulfillment, it generates no right in the promisee to compel performance. Even though the moral duty to keep a promise is owed to the promisee, even though the failure to perform makes reproach and apologies appropriate, still, the duty lacks nothing essential if the promisee cannot enforce it, since the basis of the duty is not the promisee's right but the promisor's good. Even without state intervention on the promisee's behalf, the sanction of the duty is effective in the unhappiness or bad conscience of the agent. Indeed, one can go further. Not only is the moral duty to keep promises perfectly coherent in the absence of coercive sanctions; to the extent that the duty relies on such inducements to gain compliance, it ceases to be effective as a *moral* duty.

Inasmuch as they conceive obligation in terms of the self-fulfillment of the person obliged, theories of promissory obligation are duty-based. By contrast, the theory of contractual obligation I will be deploying to explain contract law is right-based, because it posits the person as an absolute end whose end-status requires outward confirmation through the deference paid to it by others. This theory is not part of a general theory of promissory obligation; on the contrary, it is quite content to leave to duty-based theories the task of explaining the moral obligation to keep promises. Rather, it is a theory of contractual obligation, understood not as a species of promissory obligation at all but as a species of *proprietary* obligation—that is, as an obligation correlative to *another* person's external realization as an end. The superiority I am claiming for a right-based theory of contractual obligation over a duty-based one is, to begin with, an interpretive superiority: a right-based theory will explain and integrate the phenomena of contract law far more satisfyingly than any duty-based theory can. Of course, the greater explanatory power of a right-based theory is not by itself proof of its superiority as a theory of contractual obligation, for the practice it structures may be morally inferior to one reformed in accordance with a duty-based theory. The complete argument for the superiority of the right-based theory, therefore, is that the practice it covers is ethically justified as a manifestation and necessary component of dialogic community.

That argument will, however, come later. At this point, I will begin the argument for the superiority of a right-based theory of contract by pointing out the interpretive shortcomings of its duty-based rivals. The first clue we have that a moral theory of promissory obligation cannot be the key to contract law is that the category of contract is both broader and narrower than the category of promise. First, it is broader. Although an exchange of promises will emerge as the fullest development—and therefore paradigm case—of contract, still, such an exchange is only one of two main types of contract; the other is the material exchange of possessions illustrated by the simple purchase of an item in a shop. A theory of promissory obligation cannot explain the duties arising from this kind of transaction; and so it will have to either impute fictitious promises to buyer and seller or else treat as separate kinds of phenomena what the common law views as species of the common genus of contract. As we will see, however, a right-based theory can explain the exchange of things and the exchange of promises as distinct stages of a single process involving the external realization of personality as an end.

Second, the category of contract is narrower than that of promise. Only certain kinds of promises, namely, bargains and (in limited circumstances) promises inducing reliance, are enforced by courts. Theories of promissory obligation must provide a reason for enforcing some kinds of promises but not others. Typically, they do this by appealing to the same collective good that underlies promissory obligation in general but that, in cases where confidence in promise keeping is especially important, requires an external sanction to supplement the internal one. One may argue, for example, that maximizing aggregate welfare or promoting the common good requires the protection of reasonable expectations, and expectations of performance are reasonable if something has been given or promised in exchange or if the promisor has induced the promisee to rely on the promise. The difficulty with such explanations from public policy, however, is that they leave the promisee's right to enforce the promise undetermined. The collective good will be served whether the promisee is afforded a legal right to sue on the promise or whether the state imposes a penalty for breach sufficient to deter promise breaking and to promote confidence in promising. Since the promisee has no moral right to compel performance, the sole reason for granting him a legal right is to promote reliance in order to attain the benefits of a coordinated division of labor. Accordingly, the promisee's right to sue is simply a technique for the attainment of a collective goal. There are, however, other techniques. If the penalties for theft instill the confidence in secure possession needed to encourage industry and acquisition, why should not penalties for breach of contract promote confidence in promise keeping?*

* The inability of duty-based theories of contract to determine the promisee's right to sue is illustrated in John Finnis's neo-Thomist account of contractual obligation; see *Natural Law and Natural Rights* (Oxford: Clarendon Press, 1980), 298–308. Finnis argues that, given the conduciveness of promising to the common good, I cannot take the benefits of that practice without accepting the burdens, for I then violate a duty of impartiality that the goal of my human flourishing imposes on me. Impartiality requires that I contribute to the general

Duty-based theories of contractual obligation leave not only the promisee's right to sue unexplained; they also render problematic the measurement of damages by the promisee's expectation. For we promote reliance
at minimum cost to other human goods by ensuring that the promisee has
nothing to lose by relying and everything to gain. Accordingly, if the point
of enforcing promises is to encourage reliance, then damages for breach
are appropriately measured by the reliance costs of the promisee, not by
the value of his expectation. Awarding him the value of the promise may
often be necessary to protect his reliance, for he may have forgone other
opportunities in expectation of performance. But to adopt the expectation
measure as a *principle* makes little sense from a duty-based perspective, for
this measure enforces the whole of the promisor's inward, moral obligation for the windfall benefit of the promisee. It thus involves a greater interference with human autonomy than the policy of promoting reliance
requires.

Accordingly, duty-based theories of contractual obligation fail to account for the two phenomena of contract law that set contractual obligation apart as a distinct kind of duty. The promisee's right to enforce the
promise distinguishes contractual obligation from the general duty to promote the common good; while the expectation measure of damages distinguishes contractual liability from the liability in tort to restore the plaintiff to his position prior to the wrong. These theories fail to account for
the distinctive character of contractual obligation because they rest on the
promisor's good rather than the promisee's right. Might the moral obliga-

---

practice of promising by fulfilling my obligations to discrete individuals. Finnis believes that
this reasoning explains not only the right of public authorities to demand performance but
also the right of the promisee to sue on the promise. The promisee, he writes, has a "special
locus standi," because performance "is not merely an obligation in the general . . . sense; it
also is *owed* to the other party. Given the 'general justice' of the institution of promising,
breach of promise is (presumptively) a commutative injustice" (304). Yet Finnis has here explained contractual obligation as a requirement of distributive—not of commutative—justice. The faithless person is a free-rider, taking benefits from a social practice to which others
have donated by their self-renunciation without sharing the burdens. His offense, therefore,
is primarily against a public scheme of cooperation, not against any specific individual. It is
true that the promisor's performance is owed to the promisee and that satisfying the particular beneficiary is the way to promote the common good in general. However, it does not follow from this private obligation that the promisee has a right to demand compensation for
nonperformance. If the basis for the obligation is the promisor's flourishing, then a breach
violates no independent moral right of the promisee. Hence a remedial right in the promisee would be a right to enforce the demands of virtue on the promisor, and there can be
no moral right to such meddling in another person's affairs of conscience. If the promise
breaker has violated no right of the promisee, then his only offense is against a scheme of cooperation that those responsible for the common good may enforce. They may choose to do
so through private rights of action, but nothing in Finnis's account of contractual obligation
demands this method.

tion to keep promises fare better as an account of contract if it were based on a right of the promisee?

One possibility is to argue that the obligation to keep promises is an obligation not to harm someone whom one has induced to rely on the promise and who has in fact relied on it. Breach of one's promise in these circumstances is a private wrong because the promisee has been subjected to the arbitrary will of the promisor in violation of his equal standing as a person. While several writers have advocated the reorganization of contract law under this reliance-based theory of liability, they have not persuasively shown it to be a faithful interpretive account of the law.[24] In the first place, the theory cannot account for the legal rights arising from the wholly executory exchange, where no reliance on the promise need have occurred. The fact that the common law takes the bare exchange of promises as the ideal case of contract—as the norm that determines the appropriate remedy (expectation rather than restitution) in the half-completed exchange—is incomprehensible for reliance theorists, who prefer to see the model of contract in the concrete exchange of benefits.[25] Second, the reliance theory of contractual obligation makes contract disappear into tort. There is on this view no special ground of contractual liability that would justify the promisee's right to performance (or its value) as distinct from his right to the restoration of the status quo ante. Stated otherwise, the theory attaches no special juridical significance to the promise. The basis of obligation is detrimental reliance rather than promise, so that a statement of intention, opinion, or of fact would, if uttered in the same circumstances, have the same legal consequences as a promise. Accordingly, if duty-based theories of contract explain promissory obligation at the expense of the promisee's right, the reliance theory explains the right at the expense of promise.

Charles Fried has recently attempted to improve on the reliance principle by elaborating a right-based theory of contractual liability that purports to preserve the role of promise as a source of obligation distinct from tort.[26] For Fried, the basis of contractual obligation is twofold: it rests on the impermissibility of violating another's autonomy by abusing a trust one has invited by promising; and it rests on the duty to respect the autonomy of the promisor by enforcing obligations he or she has voluntarily incurred. Fried elides these two theories of contractual obligation, but I shall deal with them separately.

When I promise, argues Fried, I invoke a convention of self-obliging that is meant to invite the trust of the promisee. Acceptance of this invitation makes the promisee vulnerable, for he is now dependent on my will. This dependence is consistent with the promisee's autonomy only if he has an enforceable right to my performance. Hence respect for the promisee's independence requires that I be obliged to keep my promise. Fried concedes that breaking a promise is on this account analogous to lying in that it exploits a trust one has invited and thus wrongfully uses another human being. But it differs from lying, he says, in that the promisor need not have been insincere when he made the promise in order to constitute his breach an abuse of trust.[27]

The trust-based account of contractual obligation explains the civil remedy that eluded duty-based theories, for it rests on the promisee's right rather than the promisor's good. However, it is questionable whether Fried has really preserved the role of promise in his trust-based account of contractual liability. His identification of the wrong involved in promise breaking bears the earmarks of tort rather than of contract. One does not deprive the promisee of a future performance that is *his*; rather, one abuses a confidence, uses another person, violates a right to autonomy that pre-exists, or that is defined independently of, the promise. Suppose I promise you something, but you, knowing that I am untrustworthy, place no confidence in my pledge. Am I bound? If so, then abuse of trust does no work in Fried's account, and we are still without an explanation for my obligation to perform. If not, then the promisee's right rests on reliance rather than on promise, and Fried's theory falls short of its objective, which was to illuminate the distinctive role of promise in contractual obligation. Indeed, while breaking a promise may be a different kind of action than lying, it nonetheless constitutes for Fried the same kind of wrong—abuse of trust—indicating that promise is playing no unique role in Fried's account of contractual obligation. Contract has again collapsed into tort.

Fried, however, deploys another theory of contractual obligation, one that undoubtedly attaches a special significance to promise. This is the so-called will theory, according to which respect for the autonomy of the *promisor* requires enforcing obligations he or she has voluntarily incurred to achieve self-chosen ends.[28] On this view, the obligation of promise is not explained by the trust of the promisee; rather, trust is explained by the obligation of promise, an obligation that arises spontaneously from the promisor's will to bind himself. However, this theory will not do either as an account of contractual obligation. The decision of the autonomous will to commit itself to a course of action cannot (without more) acquire a moral privilege over its subsequent decision to change its mind, for both decisions are particular and equally valid expressions of the free will. If respect for autonomy demands that we take seriously the choices of the self, then we must acknowledge a liberty in the self not only to adopt commitments but to abandon them as well.[29] Stated otherwise, the free will cannot simply will itself bound to a contingent choice, for it cannot will anything in contradiction to its freedom. Accordingly, if the trust argument explained contractual obligation by effacing promise, the will theory emphasizes promise at the expense of obligation. Each argument supplies what the other lacks; but since they are quite separate theories of contractual obligation, they can be joined not by conceptual fusion but only—as Fried does—by a silent elision.

The foregoing critique of theories that explain contractual liability in terms either of promissory obligation or reliance has yielded the following desideratum for a better interpretive theory. We need a right-based theory of contractual obligation that preserves the unique role of promise in defining the promisee's right and that thereby preserves the distinction between contract and tort. But this, I suggest, is what an account of contract in terms of personality's realization as an end will give us.

6. DIALOGIC COMMUNITY WITHIN THE FRAMEWORK OF FORMAL RIGHT

6.1 Contract as the Realization of Personality

In the previous chapter, I tried to show how the objective realization of personality leads from possession to use to exchange as progressively more adequate confirmations of personality's end-status and therefore as progressively superior properties. Use is superior to possession because it explicitly subjugates to the self the thing that possession leaves independent; exchange is superior to unilateral use because the self thereby renounces the thing on which use is still dependent and receives back from another self (in the form of a free transfer of equivalent value) objective recognition of ownership. Property—in the sense of an objectively valid mastery of a thing—is thus perfected in exchange. The account of contract must take up the narrative of personality's self-objectification at this point. It must first clarify the transition from use to exchange. Subsequently, it must recognize the structure of dialogic community in the exchange of possessions as well as in the law of quasi-contract that explicates the rights and duties implicit in exchange. Then it must carry the narrative further by asking what form of exchange best objectifies personality's end-status in relation to things.

Though superior to bare possession, use is still inadequate as a realization of personality. In use, first of all, the self is still self-contradictorily dependent on the sensuous thing for confirmation of its mastery of it; it seeks an unconditioned or absolute right to the thing, and yet its right is contingent on the fact of use. In use, furthermore, the self unilaterally excludes another person whose own self-realization as an end is frustrated by that exclusivity. Because formal right identifies the unconditioned end with the atomistic person, personality's right to subjugate all things is the equal right of each singular person to do so. This right, moreover, involves more than the bare permission to appropriate that formal right isolates. Because personality is self-inadequate as an end without things, it is *impelled* to objectify itself; it is not fully an end unless it does so (41). Thus any unilateral exclusion of a person from a thing denies the other's equal right to confirm itself through an infinite acquisition. Because it involves this denial, unilateral exclusion by use cannot generate an objectively valid property.

The alienation of the thing in exchange remedies the two defects inherent in use. In alienating the object, I demonstrate my capacity as a free self to withdraw myself from attachments to material things; and I thereby demonstrate to another self my qualification (as in the life-and-death struggle) to recognize or give objective reality to the end-status of another. If, however, I alienate the thing simply by abandoning it, I lack another self's recognition of my ownership and hence of my end-status in relation to the thing. If I alienate it as a gift, I gain recognition of ownership in the donee's acceptance of the thing as a gift, and he is reciprocally acknowledged as an end through my voluntary surrender of the thing to his ownership. However, the recognition received by both parties in the gift transaction is formal rather than real. Consider, first, the donee. Because the donee does not reciprocally surrender anything to me, he fails to reveal himself in the transaction as a free self capable of renouncing dependence on, and hence of owning, things; thus my recognition of him as an end is formal in the sense that I pay him a tribute he has done nothing to deserve. Equally formal is the recognition of the donor. In accepting the gift, the donee recognizes the donor's capacity to alienate the thing, to transcend particular attachments; yet because the donee has not revealed himself as a free self capable of owning, his recognition of the donor's ownership fails to validate it in a satisfying way. Thus, if the donee receives recognition for a feat he has not accomplished, the donor fails to obtain the recognition he deserves.

Exchange remedies the defects inherent in gift. In exchange, each party alienates a possession to the other, thereby demonstrating his or her qualification as a self to own and to give an effective validation of ownership. Moreover, in receiving back an equivalent value, each obtains the other's recognition of his ownership of the thing he alienates. Each self can defer to the other's ownership without a servile self-denial because each gains control of the very thing he recognizes as belonging to the other and a recognized authority over the thing he abandons. Each renounces a de facto, subjective, and hence inchoate property and receives back a de jure and perfected property (71–74).

The material exchange of possessions instantiates the threefold mediation characteristic of dialogic community. In freely relinquishing my possession to another, I cancel my atomistic isolation and make myself a means to the other's property, hence to his objective confirmation as an end. His property is no longer infected with subjectivity because it no longer involves a one-sided subjugation of the thing at my expense; rather, his property is now mediated through my free surrender of my possession to his recognized authority. But this surrender establishes his property rather than arbitrary domination only because (and to the extent that) he transfers an equal value to me, reciprocally acknowledging me as an end. The property of each is thus mediated through the parties' mutual self-surrender. Each recognizes the ownership of the other in order that the other might be qualified to give an effective recognition to the first. And because each recognizes the other, each is preserved as an end in his self-abnegation.[30] The middle term linking the isolated subjectivities of the parties—the embodiment of their union—is exchange value (77). In renouncing this particular object as well as the value it has in relation to my subjective wants, I obtain recognition of my ownership of its social value in relation to other things. This value is independent of the subjective preferences of either party, and yet it does not submerge their distinctive identities, for it embodies an intersubjective consensus, an overlap of the opinions of both. Each thus cancels his isolated subjectivity and receives back a confirmed dignity as owner within community of exchange value.

That property is completed only within an exchange of equivalent values is the idea that unifies the law of quasi-contract or restitution. According to doctrinal discourse, the law of quasi-contract imposes an obligation on someone who has been unjustly enriched at another's expense to restore or pay for the benefit he has received. Thus, if A pays money to B and fails to receive any part of what he paid for, he has a right to recover the money;[31] or if A confers a benefit on B in the mistaken belief that he is indebted to him, A has a right to a restoration of the benefit;[32] or if A partially performs services for B under a void contract, he has a right to recover from B for the services already rendered.[33] The completion of property in exchange explains the beneficiary's obligation in these cases as well as the nature of the injustice that triggers restitutionary liability. If A confers a benefit on B without intending a gift, B has an objective property in the value received only insofar as he reciprocally recognizes the end-status of A by paying him an equivalent value. Without such a reciprocal transfer, the transaction is servile; one self becomes a means to the appropriation of another without being recognized in turn as an end. But the recognition thereby accorded B does not come from a free self qualified to validate another's property, and so B has no objective right. A has a right to sue for an equivalent value, because the value in the hands of B is not *his* until he reciprocates the recognition of A.[34] B's enrichment is at the expense of A, not in the sense that it involves a diminution of A's wealth (A might be able to pass on his loss), but in the sense that it occurs within a one-sided transaction wherein B is realized as an end through the subordination of A. And the enrichment is unjust because no property—no objective confirmation of one's end-status—can emerge from such a nonreciprocal transaction.

We have now to inquire whether the material exchange of possessions (through barter or sale) adequately realizes the self as an unconditioned end. To see that it does not, we must recall the precondition for the person's self-realization. To gain confirmation of its end-status in relation to things, the self must first free itself from their hold. It cannot master the world of things as long as it is itself immersed in and dependent on it. In alienating its possession, the person partially revealed its power to withdraw itself from mundane attachments; however, in acquiring something immediately in return, the self was still driven by the particularistic appetite for things, and the rational embodiment of personality was thus still embroiled in the satisfaction of want. Furthermore, the self seeks an absolute or unconditioned worth, a worth independent of locale and time, and yet the self is thus far dependent for validation on the contingent existence here and now of an empirical exchange of possessions. These deficiencies of material exchange reveal the conditions of a complete embodiment of personality. First, to gain confirmation as the end of things, the person must reveal itself to be radically independent of them; second, the person must gain confirmation in a way that is independent of sensuous exchange—in a way that establishes a purely conceptual property abstracted from time and place.

These desiderata bring into view the executory contract, the contract that consists of an exchange not of things but of promises to exchange things in the future (78–79). Here the self decisively renounces subjective appetite as the motive force of action, for his promise signifies the subordination of alterable inclination to the rule of the abstract will. Insofar as he promises, he reveals himself as one capable of achieving this radical emancipation from the objects of momentary appetite and so as one qualified—as a self—to give objective reality to the end-status of another. Insofar as he promises *to another*, he renounces changeable inclination for the sake of the other's present property in the agreed-to value of something yet to be empirically exchanged. The value of the thing that the promisee will transfer in the future is, by virtue of the promisor's submission, his now in an intellectual present. It is his independently of whether he actually acquires the specific object pledged in return; and it is his now, not in this empirical now, but in a conceptual now in which temporality is reduced and mastered. Moreover, this conquest of temporality is the perfection of property, for it signifies a property in the purely intellectual sense that is alone adequate to the idea of an unconditioned right. But the promise accomplishes this perfect property for the promisee only insofar as the promisee reciprocally renounces impulse for the sake of the promisor, for only then is the latter preserved as an end in his self-subordination—preserved as a self qualified to give objective reality to the end-status of the other. Given this reciprocal self-surrender, the promise of each is binding, for each now has a valid confirmation of worth in the free submission of the other; and this validated claim of worth is his contractual right to the value of the promise.[35]

Accordingly, personality's objective realization as an absolute end is a dialogic relationship wherein each renounces subjective inclination for the sake of the definitive property of the other. Since we have here an exchange not of things but of promises, we have a pure relation of will to will that is free of any sensuous admixture. All the elements of the formalist paradigm of contract law are derivable from this simple relationship. To these elements we now turn.

i) The Expectation Measure of Damages. The measurement of contract damages by the value of the promisee's expectation has always puzzled contract theorists. If A reneges on a promise to B, it seems that justice requires compensating B for any benefit he has transferred to A or for any other costs he has incurred in relying on the promise, for B is thereby returned to the position he was in prior to the transaction. Yet the normal rule for contract damages puts the promisee in the position he would have enjoyed had the promise been performed. This remedy applies quite independently of any benefit the defendant has received or of any reliance costs the plaintiff has incurred, for it assumes that the promisor's obligation derives simply from the mutuality of promise. The promisee's moral boundary vis-à-vis the promisor is thus defined not by his holdings prior to their transaction but by his constructive holdings as a result of it. But why does the promisee have a right to the protection of his expectations? Morality might require the promisor to keep his pledge, but why does justice between the parties demand that the promisee gain something he did not previously possess?

There are two common explanations for the expectation measure, neither of which takes it seriously as a principle of justice between parties. Lon Fuller and William Perdue, Jr., argued that reliance costs were the only ones whose compensation was demanded by corrective justice but that the expectation measure was usually the best protector of reliance because of the promisee's lost opportunity to make an alternative bargain. Moreover, they argued, reliance was often difficult to prove, so that a remedy compensating only for reliance would be a weak deterrent to breaches of contract and hence an ineffective way of promoting reliance on promises.[36] Economists offer a different rationale. From their perspective, the expectation measure promotes an efficient allocation of resources because it provides incentives to keep promises only up to the point where a breach would be more efficient than performance.[37] If A had to compensate B only for his reliance, he would have an incentive to breach whenever a better opportunity presented itself, even if the profit he would realize would be less than B's. Requiring A to compensate B for his lost profit ensures that he will breach only when his profit from doing so exceeds the profit expected by B.

Each of these explanations has an air of plausibility when considered in isolation from the practice it is supposed to explain, but neither provides a satisfying interpretation of the practice. The account of Fuller and Perdue fails to explain why the expectation measure is applied categorically even where the promisee has lost no equivalent opportunity to bargain and where reliance costs are (as in the case of the half-completed contract) easily proven. In this account, the expectation measure begins to look like a rule that has become detached from its vivifying purpose and that is now mechanically followed whether or not its rationale applies. The theory works, therefore, more as a critique of the expectation principle than as a justification and should thus be accepted only if no theory capable of supporting the expectation measure is available. Furthermore, the argument that the expectation measure is the only effective deterrent of breach encounters the same difficulty that confronts the economist's claim that it is the only efficient deterrent. If the point of the expectation measure were to deter breaches of contract, there would be no necessity to pay anything above reliance costs *to the promisee.*[38]

An adequate account of the expectation measure must show why the promisee's present holdings are properly defined by his expectancy, so that a breach of contract infringes his property right even in the absence of reliance on the promise or of a transfer of benefit to the promisor. The foregoing account of contract in terms of the self-objectification of personality meets this requirement. The executory contract is (so far) the best embodiment of personality's absolute worth, because the exchange of promises effects the mutual recognition of ownership in a way that is independent of empirical exchange and hence of material objects. We have here an interaction of abstract wills wherein each is confirmed as an end (an owner of value) through the other's renunciation for his sake of momentary appetite. But this objectified end-status of personality through a purely intellectual (hence atemporal) union of wills is just the present right to the value of the future performance. Since each person's property is decisively confirmed through the other's promise of an equal value in exchange, each acquires a present property in the value promised. Hence a breach of contract infringes a property right irrespective of reliance or of transferred benefit; and the remedy vindicates this right by putting the promisee in the position he would have enjoyed had the promise been performed.

That the promisee's contractual right is a present property in the value of a future performance explains why compensation for damages and not specific performance is the normal remedy for a breach; and it explains the promisee's duty to mitigate his or her damages. Neither of these rules, we should note, fits within a theory of contract that sees it as a special case of the moral duty to keep promises. Were contractual obligation a species of promissory obligation, one would expect that the promisor would be required to perform his promise rather than pay damages, for otherwise the obligation would go unfulfilled in cases where the promisee suffers no monetary loss. Moreover, if the obligation were a promissory one, the fact that the promisee can mitigate his damages by returning to the market would not affect the extent of the promisor's liability; since his moral duty is to perform the promise, he can hardly demand that the promisee search out alternative bargains to lighten his burden. Holmes was therefore correct to distinguish contractual from promissory obligation and to characterize the former as an optional duty either to perform or to pay damages.[39] However, this does not mean that the law imposes a lower standard of right conduct than morality. The reason for the promisor's choice is that his legal obligation is correlative to the promisee's right; and this right, as we shall now see, is respected whether the promisor performs or compensates.

We saw that, since ownership is consummated in exchange, the self's final property is not in the thing it possesses alone but in the value the thing commands in the market. That the person's property is ultimately in exchange value rather than in a material thing is crucial to its self-validation, because the person cannot be an absolute end (an owner) if it is in thrall to material objects: exchange value thus mediates between the sensuous object and the person. Now the movement from barter to sale to the executory contract involves the progressive emancipation of the self's property in value from material exchange and hence the progressive fulfillment of property. In barter, the exchange value of one's possession is still crudely expressed in terms of some specific object. In sale, it is expressed more conceptually in terms of something—money—that abstracts from the specific character of all objects, though one's property in value is still tied to the exchange of desired objects, and the self still depends on the object it receives for proof of its mastery of objects. In the executory contract, however, the self's property is adequately realized in an exchange value divorced from all connection with material exchange, and so this property is now entirely independent of his receiving the specific thing bargained for. But if the promisee's property is in the agreed-to value of the thing he will alienate rather than in the specific thing promised in return, then he has no right to specific performance.* His property is equally respected whether the promisor fulfills his promise or compensates him for the amount by which the contract price exceeded the market price at the time (normally) of breach.

The promisee's duty to mitigate his or her damages is also explained by the proprietary nature of a contractual obligation and by the intersubjective foundation of property. Because the promisee has a right only to a certain, agreed-upon exchange value, he or she has a right to compensation only to the extent of the difference between this value and the one prevailing in the market at the time when a prudent person would have sought an alternative bargain.[40] This difference represents the middle term between the particularistic rule of the parties and thus signifies their mutual recognition. To require the promisor to compensate the promisee for losses the latter could reasonably have avoided is to subordinate the promisor to the caprice of the promisee; while to limit compensation to the difference between the contract price and the best price available between breach and judgment is to subordinate the promisee to the particular interests of the promisor. From neither of these servile relationships can an objective right emerge. Accordingly, whatever the moral obligation of the promisor to perform, his only legal obligation is to pay damages to the extent of the loss in exchange value suffered by the promisee—a loss determined intersubjectively.[41]

ii) Offer and Acceptance.   In this and the following section, I give a philosophical account of the legal elements of an enforceable contract. These are the elements that, as a matter of positive law, distinguish promises one has a coercive duty to keep from those whose obligation is an affair of private morality. We understand these elements when we see them as generated from the theory of contractual obligation set out earlier—and specifically, when we see them as instances of dialogic community.

In contract law, a promise is an offer binding on the offeror only if intended to create legal relations and only when accepted by the offeree. Moreover, the acceptance must be directed toward the offer; there is no acceptance if the offeree, unaware of the offer, makes an identical proposal that crosses the first.[42] Third, an acceptance binds the offeror only if communicated to him (though the mailbox rule is an exception). Fourth, whether a form of words or conduct constitutes an offer or acceptance de-

---

*I mean, of course, that there is no such right within the paradigm of formal right. Within this framework, money is always a good equivalent for the lost performance, since every commodity is considered in abstraction from its subjective use value to a particular individual with certain wants and goals. The possibility of a divergence between damages and adequate compensation arises only from the perspective of equity, which takes into account the motives of the parties in entering the contract.

pends on an intersubjective intention, that is, on what someone in the hearer's position would reasonably infer about the speaker's meaning. I will try to account for this cluster of rules, leaving aside for the moment the consideration requirement of a binding offer.

We can perhaps already glimpse in the rules of offer and acceptance an instantiation of dialogic community. To draw this connection more explicitly, I will describe the structure of offer and acceptance as a threefold mediation, where the legal force of each term is constituted in relation to the other and to the totality that links them.

Let us first consider the offer. An offer eligible for enforcement is distinguished from a mere statement of intention by the fact that it imports a willingness to surrender one's freedom of action for the sake of the offeree. An offer is a relational promise: it signifies a renunciation of changeable appetite for the sake of another's control of the future. Yet not all offers are candidates for enforcement. An offer directed toward the welfare of someone bound to the offeror by ties of family or friendship is not (in the usual case) legally binding, for such an offer is presumptively not in relation to the end-status of an abstract person. Because enforcement would here exalt the offeree's person above the union whose priority is the basis of family and friendship, it would contradict the essence of these relations. For contract to be possible, there must first be a self who claims absolute worth as an isolated and abstract self and whose claim the offer validates. To be potentially binding, then, the offer of self-renunciation must be in relation to the other as *person*; it must be for the sake of the objectified end-status or property of another self external to the self of the offeror. The law expresses this requirement by saying that there must be an intention to create legal relations.[43] An invitation to dinner is normally not a binding offer because it has in view the concrete individual whose company is desired rather than the abstract person and its capacity for rights. In this way the binding offer presupposes, or is mediated by, the end-status of the offeree for whose sake it is made. An offer can bind someone otherwise free to change his mind only if it signifies the objective reality of the other's status qua person as an absolute end.

Second, the bindingness of the offer depends on its acceptance by the offeree. If the promise is potentially binding only if offered for the sake of the offeree's end-status, then it becomes actually binding only when it reflects back to the offeree his end-status in relation to the value of the thing relinquished. Because the offer is obligatory only as transforming a subjective conviction of right into an objectively known right, it is binding only at the instant when the offeree self-consciously appropriates the offer, when he apprehends it as conferring on him an objective property in the value of his possession.

So far we have seen how the promise is constituted as a binding offer only in relation to the offeree's person for the sake of whose self-conscious worth it is made. But further, the offer is not binding until the acceptance is communicated to the offeror. We will understand this requirement when we consider what would follow from its absence. Were the offer binding on an unmanifested acceptance, the offeree would knowingly be master of the offeror's will, but the offeror would not knowingly be master of the offeree; and not knowing whether the offeree was bound to him, the offeror would not be self-consciously an owner of value. He could not, for example, act in reliance on the offeree's being bound. However, this asymmetry is servitude, which, because it subordinates the self of the offeror, can generate no objective right in the offeree and hence no correlative duty in the offeror.* We can see, then, that the bindingness of the offer presupposes not only the person of the offeree but also the totality formed by the parties' mutual self-surrender. The offeror is not bound except through the interaction wherein his end-status is reciprocally confirmed.

Let us now consider the acceptance. Since the bindingness of the offer presupposes acceptance in the way I have explained, acceptance is in turn a power to bind the offeror. The legal force of this power is likewise mediated both by the offer and by the interaction as a whole. First, it is mediated by the offer: the significance of the acceptance is that it is the offeree's awareness of his freedom as mirrored by another self, his seeing his end-status objectively confirmed in the self-surrender of the offeror. Hence the acceptance must be an intentional acceptance *of* the offer; it cannot be a coincidental agreement with it. Stated otherwise, the bindingness of the offer is just the objectified or known worth of the offeree. It is the normative stamp placed on an offer that succeeds in confirming *to the person* his or her end-status in relation to things. Because, however, the realized worth of the person is mediated through the offer, it depends on one's consciously apprehending the offer as made for the sake of one's property. Thus an acceptance can bind the offeror only if intentionally directed to the offer. But second, the acceptance has binding power only through the intersubjective totality wherein the offeree is reciprocally bound to the

---

* Does this mean that the "mailbox rule" stating that an acceptance by correspondence is valid when mailed rather than when received is wrong? If the acceptance were not valid until received, the positions would be reversed: the offeror, on receiving the acceptance, would knowingly bind the offeree, but the latter, not knowing if and when the offeror had received the acceptance or whether the offer had been revoked prior to receipt, would be in the dark as to whether the offeror was bound. Theoretically, then, we would need a further communication indicating that the acceptance had been received (itself not valid until received), and so on back and forth ad infinitum. The mailbox rule is an attempt to achieve symmetry in the face of the technological problem caused by noninstantaneous communication. On the one hand, a communication of acceptance is required, so that the offeree cannot bind the offeror without manifesting a reciprocal willingness to be bound to him; on the other hand, he can be sure of the offeror's being bound as soon as he mails the acceptance.

offeror. The offer does not succeed in proving the offeree's end-status unless it is the offer of a free self recognized as such by the offeree. This means that the acceptance must be communicated to the offeror in a reciprocal act of self-surrender consciously apprehended as such.

We now focus on the totality formed by the mutual dependence of offeror and offeree. Here we must show how the rules of offer and acceptance dimly reflect the intersubjective nature of dialogic community. I say "dimly" because we cannot expect a contract law ordered to the primacy of abstract personality to preserve and validate as ends the parties considered as differentiated individuals. On the contrary, the totality within which contractual rights are established is an abstract universal—a common will—wherein the parties are present only as identical. Later on, when we deal with the features of the formalist paradigm that are specifically determined by the abstract conception of personality governing this framework, we will point out how the totality comes to be hypostatized as an "objective intention" ranged against the will of the parties and negating their freedom. That is to say, we will deal with the totality under the aspect of its estrangement from the selves it is supposed to vindicate. At this point, however, our interpretive attitude is more conciliatory than critical, for we are concerned to recognize even in the formalist law of contract the lineaments of rationality.

To interpret the bond between offer and acceptance as a manifestation of dialogic community is to reveal it as a middle term between the isolated subjectivities of the parties, independent of either taken separately, yet preserving both in union with the other. The totality's independence from the isolated extremes is reflected in the legal irrelevance of a purely subjective intention.[44] The intention that is relevant in constituting a form of words or conduct an offer or acceptance is the reasonably interpreted intention—the intention as mediated through the understanding of the reasonable person in the position of the recipient. Similarly, the judge's guide for interpreting the agreement is said to be the parties' intention, but this intention is determined in accordance with a reasonable understanding of the language used. The intersubjective character of the ruling intention ensures that each party's dependence on the other is compatible with the preservation and equal confirmation of both. Were either the subjective intention of the speaker or the subjective understanding of the listener decisive of contractual rights, one party would be subordinated to the idiosyncratic will of the other. The authority of the intersubjective intention guarantees that each person remains free in surrendering to the other, for he surrenders only through the mediation of the reasonable person in whose reasonableness he participates. Moreover, while independent of the isolated subjectivity of the parties, the totality that grounds their rights and duties is nevertheless formed from an agreement of wills.

It is not a "natural law" in the sense of an externally given order imposing obligations that treat the will as a nullity; rather, it is an intersubjective law proceeding from, and ordered to, the parties' wills as ends. Hence there is no duty on the parties to enter a contract: their positive obligations have a consensual origin in a free offer and acceptance.[45] And in interpreting their agreement, the judge is not free to impose a meaning independently dictated by his sense of right reason but is constrained by the language the parties used and the context in which they used it. While independent of either will taken alone, therefore, the foundation of their rights is nonetheless a common *will*.

iii) Consideration. Although there are exceptions with which we shall presently deal, the basic rule is that a promise is not legally binding unless made under seal or unless something of value—consideration—is given in return for it. The doctrine of consideration has been greatly maligned by contract scholars. The fact that promises under seal are binding without consideration has led many to surmise that consideration must be a functional substitute for the seal.[46] If the seal's purposes are to evidence an intention to beget legal consequences, to encourage careful deliberation, and to route activity into legal channels, then the doctrine of consideration must have these purposes as well. And then it is a short step to the conclusion that many things (such as a signed writing) besides consideration may perform the evidentiary, cautionary, and channeling functions, so that the bargain requirement begins to look like a fetish if insisted on without regard to contextual features that might make it superfluous. Taken to its extreme, this reasoning issues in a proposal to redefine consideration to mean any good reason for enforcing a promise, of which the existence of a bargain is only one.[47]

The flaw in this reasoning is the assumption that consideration and the seal are interchangeable means by which to test the legal seriousness of a promise. Those who start from this premise forget that the enforcement of sealed promises in an action for debt long predates the writ of *assumpsit* from which the modern action for breach of contract derives;[48] and they forget too that promises under seal are enforceable only on delivery to the donee. These phenomena suggest that the enforcement of promises under seal rests on theoretical foundations different from that of the enforcement of promises per se.[49] In fact, promises under seal are enforced not as executory promises but as executed gifts. A gift does not pass title to the donee until delivered, but the delivery of a sealed deed of gift counts as a symbolic delivery of the object. In the same way, a promise signed, sealed, and delivered passes possessory title to the donee, and the court enforces that title.[50] Thus the seal is not an alternative to consideration in triggering the enforcement of a promise; rather, it is something that (along with delivery) transforms a promise into an executed transfer. By contrast, the element required for the enforceability of a promise *as promise* is consideration. This distinction will perhaps seem artificial to those who see only the identical act of promising in both cases. However, what matters for our understanding of deeds and contracts is not that the same raw acts of promising underlie both; what matters is the theory behind the legal enforcement of these acts. Before the law attained the sophistication of enforcing executory contracts, it enforced promises by interpreting them as symbolic transfers when accompanied by formalities signifying the crossing of a boundary between promise and "deed." But if the legal theory behind enforcement differs as between deeds and contracts, then the formalities attached to these instruments must also differ in significance, since the only meaning these formalities can have is the one that theory gives them. If promises under seal are enforced only as executed transfers of possessory title, while unsealed promises for consideration are enforced as promises, then the seal provides no hint to the meaning of consideration. The real clue to this meaning is the judges' expressed intuition that consideration for a promise is required in order to give the promisee a right to the value of his expectation. But why should consideration make the difference between a right and no right?

The theory of contractual obligation set forth earlier yields an answer. Whatever evidentiary or cautionary functions the consideration doctrine may accidentally serve, its innermost significance is that it embodies the reciprocity condition for the objectified end-status of the person that we call a contractual right. My promise signifies a surrender of my freedom of action for the sake of the realized end-status of another. But my surrender would be servile without a reciprocal act of self-surrender for my sake. It would not be the surrender of a self that likewise asserts itself as an end, that is radically other than the self of the promisee, and that is thus ontologically qualified to deliver reality to him. The promisee's end-status requires confirmation from a free self who is himself an end and whose freedom is preserved in his self-surrender. But this means that the promisee must recognize my end-status in order that my promise may succeed in objectifying his. He must reciprocally defer to me, either by performing some service for me, transferring some possession to me, or by renouncing his freedom by a promise. This, I submit, is the meaning of the doctrine of consideration. It is no mere technical requirement, as Patrick Atiyah says, having nothing to do with justice.[51] On the contrary, it is a clear manifestation of dialogic community, which, as the overcoming of one-sided relations of domination and subordination, is the very structure of whatever counts as just. It is true, of course, that the courts enforce some promises in the absence of consideration, and no interpretive theory of contract law can safely ignore these exceptions or dismiss them as mistakes. Later on we will see how (and within what limits) these exceptions are consistent with dialogic community; why they are indeed exceptions—marginalia—to the undiminished centrality of the bargain; and why there is thus no need for a "fundamental restatement" of consideration doctrine, one that would subordinate the bargain to some more general, policy-oriented theory of enforceability.*

The foregoing theory of consideration yields a solution to the controversy regarding preexisting duties. In return for A's promise, B promises A something he (B) already has a duty to give him. Is this good consideration for A's promise? If the preexisting duty arises from statute or from a contract with a third party, B's promise should be good consideration.[52] B's self-renunciation must be for the sake of A in order to give A an objective right to the value of B's performance. Since a preexisting duty arising from statute or another contract is not for the sake of A, the promise signifies a deference to A he had not previously received and is thus good consideration for A's promise. Suppose, however, the preexisting duty is a contractual one owed to A himself. In this scenario, B, reacting to an increase in the market price for his goods, extracts extra money from A by threatening to break his contract to supply the merchandise at a time when

---

* The interpretation of the consideration doctrine offered here explains the complex of rules forming the doctrine. For example, past consideration is in general no consideration for a promise; see Lampleigh v. Brathwait, 80 E.R. 255 (1615). If A, in gratitude for a previous favor from B, promises to reward him, the promise will not be enforced. The reason is that unless the favor is *for* the promise, enforcing the promise one-sidedly subordinates A to B. Enforcement thus asserts B's power over A rather than recognizing his objective right. Second, consideration must move from the promisee; see Dunlop Pneumatic Tyre Co. Ltd. v. Selfridge & Co. Ltd., [1915] A.C. 847, at 853 (H.L.). Thus, if A promises to pay B for a service to be rendered by someone independent of B, B cannot enforce A's promise. The promise is servile in respect of B, and so B has acquired no objective right. Similarly, if A promises B and C jointly to pay money to C but only B pays for the promise, C cannot sue on it because A's promise is servile in respect of him. The obverse of the rule that consideration must move from the promisee is that only a party to whom a promise is made can sue on it; unless equity intervenes, third-party beneficiaries cannot (Tweddle v. Atkinson, 121 E.R. 762 [1861]). Thus, if A pays B for a promise to benefit C, only A can sue on the promise. The reason judges give for C's disqualification is that he is a "stranger to the consideration." His problem is not that consideration did not move from him (he could not sue even if he had conferred a benefit on B) but that it did not move to him. We can perhaps now see why this circumstance should disqualify him. B's promise, being directed toward A, objectifies A's end-status alone; hence A alone acquires rights under the contract. No doubt the benefit of the promise is intended for C; but what is relevant to the crystallization of contractual rights is not the benefit to material interests (consideration need not involve such a benefit, as the example of the guarantor of a loan shows) but the objectification of personality as an end. Since B's promise was made to A, it was for the sake of his end-status alone; hence the promise establishes A's right and no one else's.

A is heavily dependent on him. Is B's promise to fulfill the contract good consideration for A's promise of a higher price?

Since A already has a right to the value of B's performance, the actual performance, while beneficial to A's interests, has no additional significance for the confirmation of his person. Hence the promise to fulfill a contractual obligation is not valid consideration for a promise to pay more money, and this is what the courts have generally held.[53] Some commentators believe the courts are here manipulating the consideration requirement in order to prevent the exploitation of unequal bargaining power. They see that the promise to fulfill what one has the power to break confers a real benefit on the promisee, and they conclude that there is here ample consideration for a promise in exchange. Their prescription, accordingly, is that the courts should enforce such bargains subject to an open scrutiny for unconscionability.[54]

There are two misconceptions at work in this reasoning. One is that a benefit to interests is sufficient for consideration; the other is that the doctrines of consideration and unconscionability rest on different ethical concerns. It is generally acknowledged by contract writers that a benefit to interests is unnecessary for consideration, that it is enough if one party restricts his freedom of action in return for a like self-restriction by the other.[55] Thus, if A promises B to pay money to C in return for B's promise to guarantee the loan, B's promise will be binding even if he derives no benefit from the arrangement.[56] Similarly, the nephew who gave up drinking and gambling in return for his uncle's promise of $5,000 gave good consideration for the promise whether or not his abstinence benefited the uncle and even though he suffered no detriment to his own interests.[57] The theory of consideration we have proposed shows why this is so. The paradigm of formal right views the parties as abstract persons seeking confirmation of their worth in property and ignores the fact that they are also determinate individuals pursuing their particular interests. Accordingly, a consideration is valid if it involves one person's self-renunciation for the sake of another's mastery of part of the world, and it makes no difference whether any special interest of the recipient is thereby advanced. But the theory that explains why a benefit to particular interests is unnecessary for consideration also shows why such a benefit cannot be sufficient. For a promise to confirm the promisee's worth (and so to be binding), the promisor must be reciprocally confirmed as an end. Hence the consideration moving from the promisee must go to the promisor as a free self and not simply as a determinate individual with particular interests. To count as consideration, an act must signify a reciprocal submission of one will to the *will* of the other. Accordingly, the mere fact that some benefit flows to the other party does not mean that consideration does. Where B, by his promise, has already confirmed A's property in the value of B's performance, no further consideration flows from B's promise to keep his promise; thus A's promise to pay more than originally agreed cannot be enforced without subjecting A to the power of B.[58]

Second, it makes no sense to castigate the courts for disguising a concern for undue pressure behind the technicalities of the consideration requirement, as if the latter embodied no ethical principle. The judges' refusal to enforce contracts in the absence of consideration rests on the same concerns about interpersonal domination that underlie the doctrine of unconscionability. To be sure, the existence of a bargain is no guarantee against domination, and this is why the framework of equity, with its expanded vision as to what constitutes domination, will give us a doctrine of unconscionability. Nevertheless, the refusal to sanction domineering relationships lies at the heart of the consideration doctrine as well. Moreover, in circumstances where the pressure exerted by the party threatening to breach is indistinguishable from the everyday commercial exploitation of want, the only "undueness" of the pressure consists precisely in the lack of consideration for the extracted promise. The absence of consideration *is* the element of domination in the relationship.[59]

iv) Formalist Excuses. The theory of contractual obligation underlying formal right generates two fundamental kinds of excusing conditions. The promisee acquires a contractual right when his end-status is objectively confirmed through the free recognition of another self. Accordingly, he fails to acquire a right either if the submission to his will is not free or if the free submission is not to his will. In either case, the promisee lacks objective reality for his claim of right, and so the promisor incurs no obligation to him. The first condition (the submission is not free) obtains in two types of situation: in those involving nonvolitional events—as when one's hand is forced to scrawl a signature on a document, an offer is altered in transmission, or assent is given by an undeveloped self-consciousness unaware of itself as a purposive agent; and in those involving coerced volition—as when a promise is extracted by threats to interests (life, bodily integrity) that personality cannot, consistently with its end-status, renounce. The second condition (the submission is not *to* the person seeking enforcement) exists if the free assent of one party issues from a mistake as to the other's identity, or as to the terms the other has proposed, or if it is directed to an impersonation—to an expression of will that masks or misrepresents its true knowledge or intention.[60]

Since all of these circumstances negate either the freedom of recognition or its relation to the person seeking to enforce a promise, their validity as excuses manifests dialogic community as the foundation of valid rights. However, I wish to focus on the excuse of mistaken terms, since we have here a manifestation that is particularly striking. We can reveal dialogic community in the excuse of mistaken terms by explicating the latter in terms of the threefold mediation.

First, A's right, his objectified end-status, is mediated by B's free self-renunciation for the sake of A's ownership of value. If B's submission is not to A's will—if, owing to a mistake about A's proposal, his promise is not in relation to the expression of A's will—then the promise fails to validate A and so A has no right. However, B is excused only if his mistake is "fundamental," only if it goes to the nature of the agreement rather than to a detail, for only then does the mistake totally negate the attornment of B's will to A's.[61]

Second, A's end-status is not objectified in B's submission unless A reciprocally submits to B and B sees his own end-status reflected in this submission. Thus, if B's acceptance is, due to a mistake about terms, not a self-conscious appropriation *of* the offer, then B is not validated and so neither is A. Hence A's right depends also on the second mediation, that of B's end-status through him. But third, A's dependence on B's knowledge confirms rather than contradicts his end-status only if he is linked to B through the mediation of an intersubjective totality that, while independent of the idiosyncrasies of both, also contains both. So whether B's mistake breaks the circuit depends neither solely on what B thinks nor on what A knows about what B thinks but on whether a reasonable person in the position of A would know of B's mistake.[62] In this way, A's right is finally mediated by the totality formed by the interdependence of the parties.

6.2 Contract as the Self-Estrangement of Personality

Thus far we have been concerned to recognize the structure of dialogic community in abstract personality's self-objectification as an end and hence in the basic principles of contract law as it appears within the framework of formal right. Now, however, we must understand the particular shape of dialogic community that is determined by the abstract and asocial conception of personality that overtly governs this paradigm. Here again we must remember that we are interpreting contract law as having both a manifest and a latent meaning. Manifestly, contract law is thematically ordered to a conception of the absolute end as the abstract self. The realization of this self, however, brings forth dialogic community—the intersubjective whole—as the authentic foundation of the person's rights and as the latent theme of private law. However, the latent meaning is not the "true" one to the exclusion of the overt theme. Rather, there is a dialogic bond between these poles as well. Intersubjectivity is validated as the authentic basis of right only through its free production by the self-related person seeking to objectify itself; while the self-related person (together with its legal productions) is reciprocally validated through the surrender of community to its free self-activity. Thus dialogic community is held to the same intersubjective test of validity that its conceptual structure demands.

There is, nevertheless, an obvious tension between the overt and latent themes of contract law, one that will explode formal right as a self-complete paradigm of justice. Because the person posits the abstract self as the sole unconditioned reality, its realization in dialogic community will be the negation rather than the validation of its end-status; for it will find itself subject to a law that is indifferent to, that excludes from relevance, the *individual* expression of generic freedom in self-determined goals. The objective reality of the self's worth will thus take the form of an external power whose authority entails the nullity of the individual self it is supposed to confirm.[63] Correspondingly, the dialogic structure of formal contract law will turn out to be imperfectly dialogic, for contract will itself become ever-susceptible to inversion into an instrument of domination, as it binds individuals independently of their concrete intentions and sanctions the subordination of one individual to the exclusive good of another. Our task now is to illustrate this downfall of the abstract person in the features of contract law that flow from its supposed primacy. The doctrines we shall focus on are the following. i) Where an agreement has been reduced to a signed writing, evidence of the parties' intention is inadmissible to vary the written terms (the parol evidence rule). ii) The existence of a bargain is a necessary condition for the enforcement of a promise; reliance by the promisee is never a sufficient reason for vindicating his expectation. iii) A court will not inquire into the adequacy of consideration. iv) In the absence of fraud, a mistake about some quality of the thing bargained for will not relieve a party from his or her obligation, even if the other party knew of the mistake or bargained under the same misapprehension.

Hitherto, our understanding of contract law has been justificatory, vindicating contract as an embodiment of dialogic community, which is the basic structure of just institutions. Now, however, the approach becomes critical, for we must now see how formal contract law is inadequate by virtue of its overt formative principle to its inherent dialogic structure and how it therefore requires supplementation to become complete.

i) The Parol Evidence Rule. Though everywhere revealing intersubjectivity as the ground of the self's reality, formal right nevertheless assumes that the atomistic individual—the individual abstracted from relation to another—has a fixed and stable existence. Given this assumption, formal right reaches the absolute end that grounds valid duties by abstracting from all concrete intentions (which are seen as mere subjective preferences) to the bare capacity for forming intentions, or to the capacity for choice. This capacity alone it deems worthy of respect. It follows that an individual is adequately respected under formal right if his or her contracting partner defers to the exercise of this formal capacity. Thus, if someone secures another's voluntary signature to an agreement, he is regarded as having respected the other's freedom in the only sense relevant within the formalist framework. The fact that the person had not read the agreement before signing it, that he was ignorant or carelessly mistaken about its content, and that the other party knew this is irrelevant to the contract's enforceability, because these facts go to the specific intention in which the person's will is expressed and not to the form of willing itself. No doubt a reasonable mistake about the terms of the agreement will excuse from contractual obligation, but not (as we have seen) because such a mistake negatives consent; rather, a reasonable mistake of terms excuses because it severs the relation of one will to another. Where, however, a party voluntarily signs an agreement in ignorance of its content, there is both formal consent and (since the reasonable person would neither exhibit nor expect such carelessness) a relation between abstract wills; hence there is no basis in formal right for relief. The result is that a rogue may persuade a trusting soul to bind himself to terms that he—known to the rogue—has not read, and (absent misrepresentation) formal right will enforce the contract.[64]

The same preoccupation with the abstract form of willing to the exclusion of its specific content produces the rule that a court will not accept "extrinsic" evidence of the parties' actual intentions to vary the import of their written agreement.[65] The written words are interpreted according to the meaning they would have to the reasonable person embedded in the parties' situation; and this meaning—called the objective intention—is enforced against the parties even though one party knew the other intended something else and even if the parties actually concurred in something else. The usual explanation for the parol evidence rule is that the writing to which the agreement has finally been reduced evidences the agreement more reliably than oral statements made during negotiations—statements that the other party may not have wished to embody in the contract.[66] However, this rationale supports at most a rebuttable presumption favoring the written agreement, not an inflexible rule of exclusion. The blanket rule is explicable only on the assumption that the parties' real intentions are ultimately irrelevant to the legal meaning of the agreement. We can see, then, how the parol evidence rule makes sense within the formalist paradigm and how it represents the self-estrangement of personality— its self-objectification in a way that negates rather than realizes it as an end. Where the sole absolute end is a self abstracted from concrete intentions, the intersubjective whole grounding the parties' rights is an abstract identity of selves (called the reasonable person) wherein all individual differences are submerged. The intersubjective intention thus takes the self-contradictory form of an "objective" intention external to the real will of the parties and purporting to bind them independently of their consent, or against their actual intersubjective intention. This result represents an inversion of the manifest aim of contract, for the latter was supposed to objectify the will as an unconditioned end, and yet the realized authority of the objective intention nullifies the will's significance.

It is important to see how the authority of the objective intention also renders formal contract law inadequate to its own implicit dialogic structure. Clearly, the rationale for the primacy of the intersubjective intention does not support the rule of the abstractly objective one. Where one party actually knows of the other's eccentric view (or ignorance) of the agreement, he is not governed by the other's private opinion if the mistake excuses, since the reasonable person *invested with his knowledge* would have no expectation—no reasonable apprehension of his end-status—to enforce. Similarly, where the parties actually concur in something other than the objective intention, enforcement of their real agreement *is* the enforcement of the intersubjective intention, since each knows that the other's intention agrees with his own, and so each has a self-conscious confirmation in the other's promise. Under formal right, however, the reasonable person is the abstractly universal person divested of the knowledge and intentions of the empirical parties and ruling them as an external power. Thus the whole in which domination is supposed to be overcome becomes itself a domineering force. The dialogic totality is imperfectly dialogic, because, as an abstract universal, it fails to preserve the radical difference between the parties. It unites by excluding difference, which it then treats as nugatory. Accordingly, in submitting to the authority of this whole, the person constitutes a power that extinguishes its autonomy.

ii) The Exclusivity of the Bargain Principle. Where abstract personality is considered the unconditioned end, the welfare of the parties is irrelevant to the determination of their contractual rights. The fact that an individual is disadvantaged as a consequence of relying on a broken promise provides no reason for enforcement, for within the formalist framework welfare means the satisfaction of subjective preferences having no moral power to bind another. We have already seen formal right's indifference to welfare in the significance attached to consideration. The meaning of consideration is not that it advantages the particular individual to whom it moves or disadvantages the individual from whom it moves; as Atiyah has shown, the cases are replete with examples of valid consideration that involves neither benefit to the promisor nor detriment to the promisee.[67] The significance of consideration is that it involves the reciprocal renunciation of one's freedom of choice for the sake of the objectified worth of another *self.* Absent this reciprocal submission, the enforcement of the other's promise is the domination of his will. Within the formalist framework, therefore, there can be no legitimate enforcement of a promise in the absence of a bargain. The fact that the promisee has relied to his detriment may be a ground for my compensating him in tort to the extent of his reliance; but it cannot justify awarding him the value of his expectation, for I cannot be rightfully subordinated to the success of his particular goals.

The exclusivity of the bargain principle becomes problematic, however, in situations where contract law is itself used by one party to subordinate another to his freedom. Suppose A and B have a contractual relationship. A gratuitously promises not to enforce his full rights under the contract knowing that B will change his position in reliance on this promise, and B does in fact rely. Subsequently, A resumes his full contractual rights to the detriment of B. Under formal right, B cannot prevent A from reasserting his rights, because there was no consideration for the promise to waive them. The effect of this doctrine is to reduce contract law to an instrument of oppression in these circumstances. Contract becomes a means whereby one person reduces another to dependency on his will and exploits this dependency to the other's disadvantage. Yet formal right is blind to this form of domination, because the latter consists not in the coercion of the will but in the abuse of a dependency in order to achieve one's own ends at the expense of another's. Since formal right attaches no significance to the will's expression in concrete projects and actions, it is not violated when the spontaneity of this expression is subverted through the power exerted by one person over another. There is no right in formal right to self-determination in the precise sense of this concept, for formal right sees freedom only in the transcendence of determinate goals, not in acting from self-expressive ones. The result in our example is that the promisee against whom the contract is unexpectedly enforced sees in contract law not his validation as an end but an external and alien power indifferent to his effective autonomy.

This result also reveals the formal law of contract as a defective embodiment of dialogic community. The bargain principle embodies the idea that no rights can emerge from a relation of domination and submission, that rights issue only from a relationship of equality and mutual recognition. But the rigorous actualization of abstract personality yields the result that contract law sanctions its own use as an instrument of domination when it allows a plaintiff to enforce a contract against someone who has reasonably relied on the plaintiff's promise to forgo his right. Thus the reciprocity condition of valid obligation that the bargain criterion embodies is violated by applying that criterion in these circumstances. Contract law under the formalist paradigm is inadequate to its latent no less than to its manifest theme and requires supplementation in order to complete it.

iii) A Court Will Not Inquire into the Adequacy of Consideration. It is a basic feature of contract law under the formalist paradigm that a court will not judge the adequacy of consideration.[68] At the extreme, this means that a court will accept nominal consideration—a peppercorn for a house—as a basis for enforcement. There are two ideas underlying this doctrine, and we will not understand the modern law of unconscionability unless we keep them distinct. The first idea is that there is no standard for the equivalence of values apart from the freely concurring wills of the parties; the second is that there is no standard for the fairness of a bargain apart from equivalence in exchange. The first proposition is part of the formalist paradigm, but is not unique to it; the second is unique to the formalist paradigm. Let us deal with them in turn.

That a court will not inquire into the adequacy of consideration does not mean (as some writers believe) that formal right is unconcerned with equivalence in the values exchanged.[69] On the contrary, equivalence is essential to a bargain's enforceability, for if one party receives more than he gives in return, then he has not recognized the other as an end in relation to the surplus. The transfer of the surplus (if not a gift) is therefore servile and so ineffective to confer on the recipient an objective right. Thus a promise to exchange $2 for $1 will not be enforced as a promise (though it will be enforced as a gift once the exchange is executed).[70] But what does it mean to say that a court will not judge the adequacy of consideration and yet that it requires equivalence in the values exchanged? Why is a peppercorn good consideration for the sale of a house, while the promise of $1 is insufficient consideration for the promise of $2?

The paradox here is only apparent. It disappears when we see that formal right's standard of equivalence can be nothing other than the mutual consent of the parties to the bargain. Once the self is posited as the sole source of value, there can be no naturally authoritative standard for comparing the value of objects except the will of the trading parties; hence there can be no objectively determined "just price" by which the fairness of a bargain could be independently judged. Not even a competitive market could provide an authoritative measure of equivalence, for the aggregated preferences of others situated in different circumstances is simply another opinion with no natural authority over the opinions freely expressed by the parties in their own circumstances.[71] The only standard of equivalence transcendent of subjective opinion and so valid for the parties is the concurrence of their wills. It follows that the parties' mutual consent is determinative of an equivalent exchange; the bargain is substantively fair if it is procedurally fair.[72] However, the consent of the parties cannot make $2 equivalent to $1, because, as the medium through which different things are expressed as equal, a unit of money involves the very same submersion of differences as the will. Contracting agents could conceivably agree to make two apples the equivalent of one apple because all apples are different in some way: that one apple equals one other apple is not necessarily true. However, that $1 equals $1 is the same tautology as I am I, since in both equations all difference is buried. Hence the value of units of money cannot be subject to the will in the way that the value of other things are.

That the self is the origin of value does not imply that all value is relative to the individual. By itself, this proposition states only that no value inheres in things independently of their relation to the self's purposes; it leaves open the possibility of an objective good derived from the concept of a genuinely self-determining agent. This possibility, however, is unknown to formal right. The conception of the self underlying formal right does indeed exclude any notion of an objective good or of a real human welfare distinguished from the gratification of subjective appetite. This is so because the positing of the abstract self as the sole unconditioned reality *presupposes* the identification of all value with subjective value. Under formal right, in other words, there is no basis for a distinction between objective welfare and welfare relative to preference, since the very abstractness of the person is conditioned by the assumption that all goods denote subjective preferences. Given this assumption, there can be no criterion besides equivalence in exchange (as determined by mutual consent to the bargain) by which a court could judge the fairness of a contract. For example, a court must be indifferent to whether a bargain favors one party more than the other—to whether the benefits of trade are equally or unequally distributed—for benefit and harm are relative to taste and want, and these are incapable of generating valid obligations in others. The significance of consideration, we have seen, is not that it benefits or harms but that it reciprocally objectifies the end-status of the person. The very promise to renounce one's freedom of action for the sake of the other's freedom accomplishes this: more or less is irrelevant. The mutuality of self-renunciation itself constitutes the fairness of the bargain. As a consequence, the parties' relative bargaining power is completely free to determine the distribution of the benefits of exchange.

Applied consistently, the rule enjoining the court from assessing the adequacy of consideration permits a party to exploit superior bargaining power to extract terms that not only favor the stronger when viewed from the standpoint of the parties' subjective ends but also embody the *exclusive* interest of the stronger because they are simply harmful to the weaker party having regard to his or her objective interests as a self-determining agent. Because formal right is blind to the distinction between subjective and objective welfare, a formalist court will refuse to judge the substantive fairness of an exchange whether someone has made an unequally advantageous bargain or has made one that is catastrophic from the standpoint of the universal interest in self-determination. In particular, it will enforce an agreement where one party has, because of ignorance of his or her real interests or because of necessitous circumstances, alienated some material condition of effective autonomy such as life savings, or the security of life and limb, or the freedom to employ one's talents as one chooses. Formal right will thus countenance the assertion of contractual rights in situations where the contract furthers one party's interests but no reasonable definition of the other's—in a situation where contract law comes forward as an instrument of domination. In doing so, formal right not only negates the worth of the self it is supposed to confirm; it also reveals itself as inadequate to the norm of reciprocity that its own equivalence condition embodies.

iv) Limited Relief for Mistaken Assumptions.   Suppose A promises B a large sum of money for a piece of land in the mistaken belief that there is oil under it. The seller, while not responsible for this misconception, knows of it but refrains from disabusing the buyer of his erroneous belief. The price on which the parties agree reflects the buyer's assumption about the land's value. Under formal right, A cannot avoid the bargain.[73] Buyer and seller are agreed on the terms of the contract: there is an offer of sale at a certain price and an acceptance intentionally related to the offer. A's mistake does not sever the relation of will to will; it simply means that he will not derive the benefit from the deal he expected. A would not have entered the deal had he known the truth, but neither A's motives nor the advantageousness of his bargain can affect obligation where the sole significance of contract is that it objectifies the end-status of personality. B had no duty to disclose the true facts to A; for to impose such a positive duty in the absence of consideration is to subordinate B to the particular interests of A, and from such a one-sided relationship no obligation can emerge. This is the rational basis for the doctrine of caveat emptor. The latter does not simply reflect a particular era's obsession with individual self-reliance; rather, it rests securely on the idea that reciprocity is the sole foundation of coercive obligations.

Can we not say, however, that there is a lack of equivalence in the values exchanged? To reach this conclusion we need not impose a standard of equivalence external to the parties' opinion, for we know that the buyer paid the price for land with oil and that the seller knew this. Indeed, we could also infer nonequivalence without imposing on the parties' relationship had the buyer's ignorance simply been obvious to any reasonable seller (say, because the truth was recondite and difficult to uncover) or had both parties thought the land was oil-rich. In analogous contexts, formal right has no difficulty in allowing a mistaken assumption to void a contract if it affects the reality of consideration. For example, if someone contracts to buy something under the mistaken belief that it exists or that it does not already belong to him, formal right will let him avoid the contract, since there is here a failure of consideration.[74] Can we not extend this reasoning to the case of the would-be oil magnate? Since there is a lack of equivalence judged by the parties' own opinions, the seller is one-sidedly enriched to the extent of the unrequited value and so has no objective right to it.

The difficulty here is that we can recognize the values as unequal only by paying attention to the motives of the parties, and formal right will not allow such an inquiry. For formal right, motives have no rational significance. They are not the material through which freedom concretely and necessarily expresses itself but are particularistic inclinations from which thought must abstract in order to arrive at a public foundation for rights. In our example, therefore, formal right brackets the parties' motives, sees only their assent to identical contractual terms, and concludes that there is an exchange of equivalents. It therefore refuses contractual relief for a mistake concerning some quality of the thing bargained for that induced someone's consent to an agreement, even if the mistake was common to both parties or was known to the party seeking enforcement.[75] And it thereby sanctions an exchange that, viewed in all the circumstances, violates its own reciprocity condition of an enforceable bargain.

7. DIALOGIC COMMUNITY WITHIN THE FRAMEWORK OF EQUITY

7.1 Self-Determination and the Critique of Formal Contract

The self-contradictory realization of the person in formal contract proves the truth of a more comprehensive notion of freedom than that which underlies the formalist paradigm. The ever-present potential for domination under formal right teaches that freedom cannot be understood simply as a self-relatedness attained through flight from particular inclinations and from dependence on another; rather, it must be conceived also as a power to remain within the interiority of the self in acting from some particular purpose in the contexts of human interdependence to which the person's quest for confirmation leads. Freedom must be understood not simply as formal choice but as concrete self-determination; and it must therefore be conceived not only as a capacity to form relative values but also as an objective good common to all human subjects. Obversely, welfare must be understood not only as the satisfaction of contingent preferences but also as the realization of the self in productive action for the sake of self-expressive ends. This is the conception of freedom, of the self, and of welfare that informs the legal paradigm called equity. Once the agent's self-determination is grasped as the common good grounding valid rights, equity sees the relations of domination that formal right sanctions as negations of right; and it generates doctrines whose effect is sometimes to supplement and sometimes to suspend formal right in circumstances where the latter acts as an external power. From one point of view, these doctrines actualize the agent's right to self-determination against an alien law and form a unity ordered by this theme; yet from another standpoint, they perfect the reciprocity or intersubjectivity already implicit in formal right. Both themes may be illustrated by the rules evolved by equity to deal with the problems just outlined.

i) Rectification.   In the parol evidence rule, the intersubjective intention that grounds contractual rights takes the form of an external, objective intention authoritative against the actual, verbally manifested intentions of the parties. Yet equity intercedes to rehabilitate the actual intention in circumstances where formal contract law would otherwise operate as a domineering power. For example, where the parties have agreed to contractual terms but have written them down inaccurately, a court of equity will accept extrinsic evidence of the parties' actual intentions and rectify the contract to accord with them.[76] Where one party is, to the other's knowledge, mistaken about the terms he has signed, the party seeking enforcement may elect either to annul the contract or to submit to rectification in accordance with the defendant's belief.[77] And where a party to an agreement has signed a document without reading or understanding it, he may avoid the contract if the other party knew of his ignorance of the terms.[78]

We can easily see the significance of these doctrines for the autonomy of the agent: since they nullify the authority of the external "intention," their effect is to reinforce the consensual basis of coercive obligations. However, these doctrines also instantiate dialogic community in a way more adequate to its intersubjective structure. It is still true that each party's right is determined not by the other's subjective opinions but by the opinion of the reasonable person who embodies the totality formed by their mutual dependence. However, the reasonable person is no longer an abstraction from the differentiated subjectivity of the parties; rather, it is now invested with their empirical knowledge and intentions. Where there is a concurring and verbally manifested intention, the reasonable person in the position of each party would have a true apprehension of his end-status in the surrender of the other; hence the actual agreement, not the erroneously transcribed one, generates authentic rights. And someone who actually knows that the other party has not read or understood the agreement has no reasonable apprehension of his end-status in the other's promise, whatever the reasonable person in the abstract might think. As a consequence of these equitable modifications, the parol evidence "rule" becomes a rebuttable presumption that the parties, as reasonable persons, intended the written agreement to be final and complete.

The doctrine of rectification provides a clear illustration of the inner continuity between formal right and equity. Here as elsewhere the aim of equity is not to subordinate "contract values" to considerations foreign to contract; it does not temper individualism with altruism or balance certainty with fairness. Rather, its aim is to fulfill the ends that formal right, left to itself, achieves in a self-contradictory way. More specifically, the doctrine of rectification revokes the self's alienation in an objective intention, thereby reasserting the self as the end of contract law. Concomitantly, it reinforces the intersubjective structure of contract law in situations where formal contract, because of its abstract foundations, undermines it.

ii) Promissory Estoppel. In *Central London Property Trust Ltd. v. High Trees House Ltd.,*[79] an English court refused to enforce a bargained-for promise against a defendant who had reasonably relied on the plaintiff's gratuitous promise not to assert its full contractual right. The case is usually regarded as seminal for the enforcement of promises on the basis of reliance alone, but the principle on which relief was granted in *High Trees* is considerably narrower than this view suggests. Lord Denning stated that the cases supporting enforcement of a gratuitous promise "have not gone so far as to give a cause of action in damages for such a promise, but they have refused to allow the party making it to act inconsistently with it."[80] Later, in *Combe v. Combe,*[81] he clarified this limitation, stating that the principle in *High Trees* "does not create new causes of action where none existed before [but] only prevents a party from insisting on his strict legal rights when it would be unjust to allow him to do so, having regard to the dealings which have taken place between the parties."[82] In the same judgment, Denning stated explicitly that, insofar as it works to enforce a promise, the doctrine of promissory estoppel applies only where there exists a prior legal relation between the parties and that it operates only to prevent a party from resuming rights he has led the other to believe he would waive.[83] The basis of the court's intervention is thus not simply reliance but reliance on a promise to forgo a legal right. The conventional metaphors are apt: promissory estoppel is not a sword by which to assert a new kind of contractual right but a shield by which to protect oneself against the oppressive enforcement of classical ones.

Limited in this way, the doctrine of promissory estoppel supplements and perfects the consideration doctrine (and the reciprocity principle it embodies) rather than overturning it or introducing principles foreign to it.* Lord Denning's formulation of the principle captures precisely equity's role in suspending formalist contract law in situations where its rigorously consistent application would lead to oppression, and where the party seeking relief sees in the law not the realization of his end-status but its negation. In applying the doctrine of promissory estoppel, the court does nothing to contradict the consideration rule, for it does not enforce a promise based on reliance alone. It does not arm the party seeking enforcement of the gratuitous promise so much as disarm the party seeking enforcement of the bargained-for one. Of course, the *effect* of disarming the plaintiff is to give the defendant the value of his expectation, the very immunity on which he relied. However, in determining whether the court's intervention is compatible with the bargain rule, we must focus on the principle of that intervention and not on its incidental effect, for only principles demand to be generalized. In principle, the court is not enforcing a contractual duty owed the relying party, for (ontologically speaking) there can be no such duty in the absence of consideration and the reciprocity it embodies. Rather, the court is conforming to its *own* duty—to the duty inherent in its nature as an agent of the intersubjective whole—to prevent the inversion of law into an external power. That there be a preexisting legal relation between the parties is thus rightly crucial to the operation of the doctrine insofar as it works to fulfill expectations rather than simply to protect reliance; for this requirement ensures that the estoppel will perfect rather than undermine the basis in reciprocity of contractual rights. In using promissory estoppel to suspend rather than to assert such rights, the court furthers the point of the consideration doctrine in a situation where enforcing it would lead to the very domination that the consideration doctrine is meant to avoid.

* Here I am concerned only to reconcile with the bargain theory of enforceability the apparent *bindingness* of some promises on the basis of reliance. I do not yet deal with the promisor's duty to compensate the promisee for his reliance costs, for this is an aspect of tort law that, so long as it makes no claim to hegemony over the field of civil obligations, poses no problem for the bargain theory of contract; see W. A. Seavey, "Reliance Upon Gratuitous Promises or Other Conduct," 64 *Harv. L. Rev.* 913, 926–927 (1951). I thus assume that the protection of reliance is perfectly valid even outside the context of a preexisting legal relationship between the parties. The hegemonic claims of the reliance principle are dealt with below.

iii) Unconscionability. We have seen that, because it has no conception of objective human interests, formal right has no criterion for a fair bargain other than equivalence between the values exchanged. And since equivalence is guaranteed in the standard case by mutual consent, formal right has no independent criterion of substantive justice by which to scrutinize procedurally fair agreements. Nevertheless, there are a few limiting cases wherein formal right has the resources to set aside an apparently consensual exchange.

Suppose A is drowning and B throws him a rope in return for a promise of a million dollars. Or suppose A is dying of thirst in the desert and B, the owner of the only available water hole, offers him a drink for an outrageous sum. Formal right must treat these bargains as void ab initio (B is entitled only to a restitutionary remedy), because the person whose life is in peril cannot consistently with personality's absolute worth (the premise of formal right) treat life as an optional value; he cannot, without making a category mistake, treat the capacity for forming values as itself one value among others. Since A could not validly renounce life as he could contingent preferences, his promise lacked the voluntariness that would have given B a right to its value.[84] The situation is identical (as far as contractual validity is concerned) with one in which someone's assent to a contract is extracted by threats of physical force. Although the person chooses to sign the agreement rather than suffer the threatened consequences, nevertheless formal right will not recognize the validity of renouncing the bodily expression of personality, and so normatively speaking there is no choice. Another limiting case involves duress of goods. If A agrees to repair B's watch for $10 but later refuses to return the watch until B pays $20, B can accede to these terms and still recover the $10 surcharge from A. By unlawfully detaining B's goods, A put B to a choice between paying $10 for what is already his or acceding to A's taking his watch. Either option required B to renounce his right as a property owner. But B cannot validly alienate the right to own, and so juridically speaking there was no choice. Hence nothing stands in the way of B's restitutionary claim for a return of the unrequited value. The same inalienability of personality allows formal right to void any bargain in which a person has surrendered a degree of control over his or her life amounting to slavery (67).[85] While consent normally guarantees an exchange of equivalents, this cannot be the case where the entity relinquished for value is the very capacity to stand back from, compare, and exchange values, for this capacity cannot itself be compared to anything; it alone has no equivalent. These examples illustrate the extent of formal right's resources to set aside as unconscionable an ostensibly consensual transaction.[86]

It is not, however, the limit of contract law as a whole. Suppose (to take the facts in *Lloyds Bank Ltd. v. Bundy*)[87] an elderly farmer mortgages his farm—his only asset—to a bank as security for debts incurred by his son's troubled business. During the course of the negotiations with the bank manager, the farmer inquires as to the state of his son's company, and the bank manager honestly informs him that he thinks the problems are deep-seated. Despite this disclosure, the farmer signs the terms of the guarantee proposed by the bank without obtaining independent advice. When a receiving order is subsequently made against the son, the bank forecloses on the mortgage, sells the farm, and seeks to evict the father from his home. Here formal right offers no relief to the unfortunate farmer. Since he was at liberty to renounce his preference for his son's well-being, his decision to act on this motive was voluntary. Procedurally, therefore, the agreement is unimpeachable. Moreover, since the farmer assented to the terms in full knowledge of what he was receiving for his promise (the bank's forbearance from demanding payment of the existing overdraft), the values exchanged were equivalent by the only standard consistent with the freedom of personality. No doubt the benefits of trade were heavily skewed in the bank's favor (the farmer purchased only a brief respite for his son); but the farmer had no right to the bank's solicitude for his particular interests. Nevertheless, an English court faced with these facts set aside the transaction. How could it do so without contradicting formal right?

The elements of domination in the transaction that are invisible to formal right become apparent once the agent's self-determination is posited as the end that grounds valid rights and duties. The decisive change is that we now have a basis for distinguishing between values that are relative to individual desire and values that are objective because universally required for the autonomous pursuit of subjective values. Armed with this distinction, we can now further distinguish between bargains that are simply tilted in one party's favor having regard to their subjective ends and bargains that are objectively inimical to one party's real welfare because they involve the alienation of some material condition of effective autonomy (in this case, the farmer's entire wealth).[88] This allows us to assess the substantive fairness of a bargain by a criterion other than equivalence and so emancipated from the procedural issue of consent. For if we can say that a bargain is objectively harmful to one party, then (unless that party still desires the bargain after thoroughly understanding its harmfulness—hence the requirement of independent advice) we can say that it furthers the exclusive interests of the other. And if contract law aligns itself with the exclusive interest of one party, then its authority negates the autonomy of the other, who now sees in the law a dominating force alien to his good. In refusing to enforce such a law, the court actualizes the defendant's right of self-determination in relation to law itself, for it holds a law valid only if the rational agent can recognize therein his real interests. But it also vindicates formal right's own mutuality condition of valid rights in a situation where the consistent application of formal right would violate it.[89]

This theory of unconscionability explains the two key elements of an unconscionable transaction identified by common-law courts. First, the bargain must be not only unevenly advantageous but "improvident," that is, harmful to the real interests of the party seeking to avoid the agreement.[90] Second, there must be inequality of bargaining power, normally identified by one party's ignorance of the transaction's full implications or by his objective human need for the commodity offered coupled with the absence of substitutes. The parties' strength must be unequal in one of these senses, for otherwise there is no nonpaternalistic basis for saying that the bargain embodies the exclusive interest of one party. Paternalistic interventions by the court are ruled out because they conflict with the principle of self-determination on which the modern law of unconscionability rests (this is also why contracts that are unconscionable by equity's standards are voidable rather than void ab initio).

Furthermore, our account of unconscionability puts this doctrine on a footing that saves everyday contractual dealings from condemnation. Inasmuch as it sees unfairness notwithstanding formal consent and equivalence, our account does not resort to the explosive fiction that unequal bargaining power vitiates consent; nor does it entail allowing other people's opinion of commodity values to override the parties' voluntary expression of their own. Moreover, our view permits us to distinguish unconscionable dealings from the everyday battle of forces involving the exploitation of want and resulting in unequal divisions of the benefits of trade. On our account, unconscionability does not consist in the exploitation of unequal bargaining power arising from want (hence take-it-or-leave-it standard form contracts are not necessarily bad). Equity no less than formal right views subjective ends as renounceable and so sees the voluptuary's bondage as self-imposed whether or not there exist competitive alternatives. Nor does unconscionability depend on an unequal—not even on a grossly unequal—distribution of the advantages of exchange. Such inequalities are not grounds for relief from obligation, for equity is as indifferent as formal right to the relative satisfaction of the parties' subjective goals. Rather, unconscionability depends on two factors: on the contract's being exclusively advantageous to one party because harmful to the real human interests of the other; and on inequality of bargaining power arising either from one party's need for a good essential to autonomy (e.g., employment or housing) or from the lack of an informed choice by the party harmed by the agreement. The factors of ignorance and need are important not as indicating immorality in the stronger party but as screening out paternalism by the court.[91]

Finally, it is important to see how equity, in reinforcing and supplementing formal right, respects the reciprocity conditions of justice generated within it. The principle of relief against unconscionable transactions is not that the stronger party owes a duty of concern for the particular advantage of the weaker. Nor is it that the stronger owes a duty of beneficence to preserve the conditions of the weaker party's objective welfare. He may be under a moral duty to do so, but the weaker party has no valid right to compel beneficence in the absence of a reciprocal submission to his benefactor, and equity preserves this insight. There are no nonmutual affirmative duties between private persons either in formal right or in equity. Rather, the principle of relief is that a *court* cannot enforce a contract harmful to a party's autonomy interest in the face of that party's objection, for it then allies the law to a particular interest. Accordingly, in striking down an oppressive bargain, a court of equity perfects rather than contradicts formal right because the duty it responds to is not the parties' but its own. If enforcing a bargain would mean law's inversion into a private power, then a court must refuse to enforce it in order to preserve itself as a court of law. Thus, insofar as the weaker party has a positive right to self-determination, that right is held not against any individual taken singly but against the agent of the intersubjective whole, as a corollary of the latter's duty to conform to the demands of its own nature.

iv) Unjust Enrichment and Mistake. We saw that formal right could not grant relief for a mistaken assumption because the disparity between the values exchanged becomes evident only when we attend to the motives of the parties, from which formal right abstracts. The result is that formal right enforces agreements that, when purposes are considered, violate its own equivalence condition of a valid bargain. Formal right abstracts from motives because it regards them as subjective inclinations with no public significance and hence with no relevance for the determination of objective rights and duties.

When, however, the agent's concrete self-determination is grasped as the end that grounds valid duties, motives are no longer devoid of rational significance. They are no longer simply purposes that matter to the individual moved by them; they are also the material in which the free will must clothe itself in order to express itself and become actual. Stated otherwise, motives cannot be equated with naturally given or arational impulses, for in acting from ends chosen on reflection, the self transforms the given into a medium for its own self-expression. Elevated to this public dignity, motives need no longer be ignored by a court in determining whether the values exchanged in a transaction are equivalent. If A promises B a sum of money for a cow that both parties mistakenly believe to be barren, the paradigm of equity will allow the seller to avoid the contract on the ground that the buyer would be unjustly enriched to the extent of the surplus value.[92] Similarly, if A sells B a house knowing that B is unaware that water will be unavailable for twelve hours of the day, B will be released from his obligations.[93] And if someone pays a premium for a hotel room offering a view of a procession that is subsequently canceled, a court will consider the parties' motives and treat the contract as "frustrated."[94] Notice, however, that these are not cases of contract values yielding to weightier or loftier considerations of equity. One party is unjustly enriched by the same standard of equivalence in exchange that informs formal right.

Here again we must emphasize how equity reinforces the dialogic structure of formal right rather than introducing principles that would subvert it. In granting relief to the mistaken party, equity does not contradict the principle of caveat emptor or limit it by opposing values. It does not enforce an altruistic duty of disclosure, for the principle of its intervention is not that the informed party owes such a duty, but that the values exchanged must be equivalent if each is to have an objective property in the value received—the very principle of reciprocity that underlies formal contract. Thus the seller who fails to reveal material facts to a prospective buyer (or vice versa) will not lose his agreement unless he is aware (or ought to have been aware) that the price agreed to reflects a fundamentally mistaken assumption about the nature or quality of the commodity, or unless he shared the buyer's misconception; for only in these cases is there a lack of equivalence judged by the parties' own opinions.[95] Absent these circumstances, a buyer who wishes to protect himself against uncertainty must still pay the price of a warranty.

7.2 The Tyranny of Equity

In the previous section, I argued that equity introduces no principles or values antithetical to those underlying formal contract—that it works to fulfill the aims of formal contract in situations where the absolutization of abstract personality contradicts them. This is so whether we understand the two paradigms from the standpoint of their overt or their latent themes. If we understand formal contract as ordered to the end-status of the individual person, then equity fulfills this end in situations where formal contract sanctions the subordination of one person to another; if we understand formal contract as an instantiation of dialogic community, then equity reinforces and perfects this structure in situations where formal contract subverts it. In deploying a richer conception of human personality and freedom than that which animates formal right, equity realizes the end-status of the person in a way more adequate to that end; and in doing so, it brings forth a superior manifestation of dialogic community.

Nevertheless, the argument for the unity of contract law is not yet complete. What we have shown is that formal right needs an equitable supplement to perfect it; we have not yet shown that equity needs formal right. Indeed, once the conception of freedom as formal choice is superseded by the better idea of self-determination, there is a natural theoretical tendency to absolutize the latter principle as the sole foundation of valid rights. Why, after all, should a defective understanding of freedom retain any independent normative power to organize a distinct legal paradigm? Moreover, since the self-determination of agents demands that laws embody the real welfare of everyone, the effect of this theoretical movement is to subsume the person-centered paradigm of formal right under the communitarian principle of equity. So, for example, once we justify promissory estoppel in terms of the effective autonomy of the agent, there seems to be no principled ground for limiting reliance-based enforcement to situations of estoppel under preexisting contractual relations. Why not protect all reasonable reliance, either with expectation or reliance damages, whichever is more effective in the circumstances?[96] And why not treat consideration as one among many modes of reliance rather than—fetishistically—as a criterion of obligation in its own right? Similarly, if a court can relieve someone from an unconscionable bargain in order to protect his or her objective goods, why can it not imply warranties of safety or habitability into consumer and tenancy contracts and invalidate clauses that try to exclude liability under them? Why can it not compel someone to enter a contract to save another's life? The logical outcome of this momentum is no doubt a unity of the law of civil obligations, but it is not a unity of anything resembling the law of contract. Since consensual obligation has been subsumed under obligations valid independently of consent, contract has been submerged in tort.

The argument for the unity of contract law thus requires a further step. If we can show that absolutizing the principle of each paradigm at the other's expense produces self-contradictory results, then we will have shown the mutual complementarity of the paradigms. We will have shown that the common good and the individual self each requires the distinctive ordering of the other for its own coherent realization. Moreover, to show the mutual complementarity of the paradigms is to show that each is a subordinate aspect of a totality that embraces both in their radical distinctiveness from the other. But this totality is nothing other than dialogic community, whose own objectifications (as the basis of valid rights) are the traces we have observed in the progressive self-realization of the atomistic self in the two paradigms. Accordingly, the unity I am arguing for is not a simple unity governed by a monistic principle but a unity of distinct unities each of which manifests the global theme within the limits imposed by its self-conscious principle. One-half of the argument for this unity has already been made, for we have already shown how the absolutization of abstract personality yields results that contradict its end-status and point to equity as a necessary supplement. It remains to make the obverse argument concerning the principle of equity.

Let us then consider what happens when we exalt the autonomy of the individual into the theme of contract law. In *Walton Stores (Interstate) Ltd. v. Maher*,[97] the plaintiff owned commercial premises that it demolished in reliance on the defendant's assurances that it would lease space in a new building. Before a contract was concluded, the defendant reconsidered its plans but failed to notify the plaintiff of its indecision even though it knew the plaintiff had commenced construction of the new building. The Australian High Court held that the defendant was estopped from retreating from its assurances because it had encouraged expectations in the plaintiff in circumstances where it was reasonable to expect that the plaintiff would act on them. The remedy awarded the plaintiff was the value of the promise. Although their judgments are ambiguous, Mason, C. J., Wilson, J., and Deane, J. seem to have regarded promissory estoppel as a basis for enforcing promises alternative to consideration. Certainly all three questioned the logic of recognizing estoppel as a shield against existing rights but not as an independent ground of promissory obligation.[98]

If we generalize the principle behind promissory estoppel, it is difficult to fault the judges' reasoning. Since the defendant induced the plaintiff to depend on its will, protection of the plaintiff's autonomy requires that the defendant be bound to conform to the reasonable expectations it raised. The case is no doubt different from *High Trees*[99] in that no promise has been made to waive a preexisting contractual right; yet from the standpoint of individual autonomy, the limitation of reliance-based enforcement to defensive situations appears incoherent, as does the continued insistence on consideration as a sine qua non of enforcement outside those contexts. Consideration may still be a relevant factor but only as indicating that the parties took the promise seriously and understood that it would be relied on.

However, when the principle of individual autonomy is absolutized in this way, equity, instead of perfecting the dialogic structure of contract law, subverts it and so reinstates domination. Assume, first of all, that the measure of damages for breach of a gratuitous promise is the value of the expectation. This means that the promisor is compelled to act for the sake of the promisee's control of the future with no reciprocal surrender to him. He is thus forced to be a means to the end-status of another without being in turn recognized as an end. The relationship is servile, and the law that enforces it is—from the standpoint of the promisor—an external power. This was not the case in *High Trees*, because there the principle of enforcement (or rather nonenforcement) was not that the promisor owed a contractual duty to the relying promisee but that the court was under a duty to prevent the inversion of a contractual right into an instrument of oppression. Thus, while the limited principle prevents domination, the generalized principle institutes it.

It will be objected, however, that the expectation measure of damages no longer fits within a theory of enforceability based on detrimental reliance. If the point of enforcement is to protect the promisee against subjection to the promisor's caprice, then this aim is achieved by compensating the promisee to the extent of his reliance. When we do this, we do not compel a one-sided subordination of the promisor to the promisee's conquest of chance; rather, we enforce a reciprocal respect for spheres of autonomy defined independently of promises. When conjoined with the reliance principle of enforcement, the expectation measure no doubt implies servitude; however, the reliance principle can be properly tested only if we assume the measure of damages congruent with it.

Let us then do so. However, we must here bear in mind precisely what principle we are testing. We are not testing the claim that reliance on a broken promise intended to induce reliance entitles the promisee to compensation for his detriment. That is certainly a valid ground of compensation in tort, one that poses no threat to the bargain principle. Rather, we are testing the proposition that reliance is the *sole* basis of promissory obligation and that consideration is relevant only as establishing reliance. This is the claim that emerges when we absolutize the reliance principle that in *High Trees* plays a subsidiary role—as a circumstance activating the court's duty as guardian of the law's intersubjectivity. When the logic of this claim is pursued to its limit, the wholly executory exchange ceases to be enforceable, consideration is no longer essential for promissory obligation, and damages for breach are normally measured by the promisee's reliance.

Yet this result is just the inversion of the principle equity is supposed to realize. The rigorous actualization of the good of individual autonomy leads to the disappearance of the institution—the wholly executory exchange—that best actualizes the person's autonomy, bringing its future into a conceptual present impregnable against the caprices of others. It leads to the disappearance of chosen obligations in favor of objective ones valid independently of choice. And it leads to the overthrow of a legal paradigm whose basic structure mirrors the dialogic pattern of interaction in which alone the equality and freedom of persons is respected. In place of this system, an absolutized equity installs an order that negates the reciprocity upheld by its limited rule, for it now appears as an external and dominating power to the individual whose distinctive end-status it submerges. This is no mere ideological critique of a collectivist regime in the name of an arbitrarily asserted value of freedom of contract. The point is not that an absolutized equity destroys something you or I might contingently value; the point is that such an equity negates *its own* principle of individual autonomy as the foundation of valid rights. Because the common good that equity enforces is the individual's self-determination, equity can hardly deny the validity of contract as an embodiment of individual autonomy and worth. But if the systematic realization of a conception of justice leads to its inversion into a particular principle *opposed* to one it must simultaneously acknowledge, then that principle cannot be the absolute that grounds valid duties; hence it cannot be thematized as the fundamental principle of contract law.

We observe the same outcome when we generalize the principle behind the equitable doctrine of unconscionability. We saw that under this doctrine the courts refuse to enforce bargains that, although procedurally unobjectionable, are substantively unfair because harmful to the real human interests of the defendant and hence exclusively advantageous to the plaintiff. The principle behind this refusal is that contract law is obligatory only if everyone to whom it applies can rationally assent to it as embodying his or her welfare. Now suppose this egalitarian principle were raised into the theme of contract law. The resultant legal order would probably exhibit some or all of the following features.

First, persons would be permitted to exploit their advantages—including informational advantages—in trading with others only when a permissive rule would promote the long-run benefit of the persons who are taken advantage of in a particular way; otherwise they would be obliged to renounce such advantages in order that the distribution of the benefits of trade might be purified of all morally arbitrary inequalities between the parties.[100] This redistribution of natural advantages would be the aim not only of tax law but of contract law itself, so that one's personal endowments would never be one's own but would belong ab initio to a common fund whose managers would deploy them for the common benefit. Second, inequalities of wealth would, like any other advantage, be justified only if conducive to the long-run benefit of the less advantaged class, and contract rules—which are justified only as serving the common benefit— would be designed to eliminate or at least to reduce inequalities that fail to meet this test.[101] So, for example, persons might be forced to enter contracts needed to improve the welfare of others; and the price terms of agreements would be authoritatively fixed or regulated with a view to preventing greater disparities in the allocation of trade benefits than can be justified by the material improvement of the less advantaged. If sellers responded by altering non-price terms in ways that frustrated the distributive goal, then these terms would likewise have to come under authoritative regulation. Third, courts and legislatures would imply nondisclaimable warranties of safety and habitability into consumer and tenancy contracts, forcing consumers and tenants to buy these warranties out of a regard for their real human interests. They would not distinguish between buyers for whom contracts without such warranties would, because of the buyers' extreme need, appear as impositions of the stronger and independent buyers who would affirmatively prefer to take their chances rather than pay the higher price for protection; for the absolute authority of the common good requires that the contract embody the real interests of the parties even if they, after careful deliberation, prefer something else.[102] Thus warranties would be nondisclaimable in order to protect the real welfare of persons not only against inequality of bargaining power but also against their own foolhardiness.[103]

The effect of this remodeling of contract law is that contractual rights and duties are now thoroughly mediated by the common good and so by distributive and paternalist principles assuring to everyone an equal share in the benefits of economic exchange and a minimum level of security. Freedom of contract is not simply subordinated to, or overridden by, the common good in situations where it produces domination. Since contractual rights are now *determined* by the common good, there is no freedom of contract to override. That is to say, there is no longer an independent or private sphere of contract wherein rights actualize the end-status of discrete persons. Instead, contractual rights embody the absolute authority of the common good and the correlative nullity of the independent self whose autonomy is nonetheless posited as the end of law. Once again, we must distinguish this critique from ones that presuppose a value external to the principle criticized. We do not say, for example, that distributive considerations in contract law are illicit because in tension with the bipolar structure of corrective justice that contract law exemplifies.[104] This argument invokes a norm of formal coherence—of coherence for its own sake—that the advocate of a distributive conception of contract law need not recognize. Rather, we say that freedom of contract is implicated or required by the very principle (i.e., individual autonomy) of distributive justice or of paternalism that destroys it, so that this principle, in attacking its complement, condemns itself as something one-sided and partial, as a principle whose supposed natural authority dissolves into violence. The argument is that the destruction of private law represents the *immanent* refutation of equity's principle as the basis of valid rights.

8. OF NIGHTINGALES AND GEESE: THE UNITY OF CONTRACT LAW

That the principle of each paradigm contradicts itself when pursued to the exclusion of the other shows that each requires the other for its own coherence. Moreover, this notional continuity of the principles implies that the foundation that supports valid rights is neither the one nor the other but the totality of which both are mutually connected elements. This totality is not simply a combination of the two systems: we do not grasp it by pragmatically accommodating one paradigm to the other or by proclaiming a commitment to pluralism where the whole is just the vague togetherness of the two previous formations.[105] Rather, we apprehend the totality through a fundamental reconceiving of law's foundation—one that is already implied in the mutual need of the previous conceptions but that is nonetheless independent of both. This rethinking grasps the structure of intersubjectivity—of the reciprocal dependence of the collective and the particular self—implied in the downfall of the previous conceptions and thematizes this dialogic interaction as the authentic ground of law. We may apprehend this structure through the following steps.

The principle of each paradigm implicitly contained that of the other: the end-status of the individual self is objective only in community with another self, while the common good is the autonomy or realized end-status *of* the individual. Because each principle implicitly contains the other, each is self-contradictory alone; hence each needs the other to fulfill it as an end. Lacking the other, each desires the other's free recognition that it is essential to the other's good, and the need of each for the acknowledgment of the other is the objective confirmation of both as possessing essential worth. Thus the common good is validated in the individual's free submission to its authority as to the basis of his or her dignity, while the individual is likewise confirmed as an end through the community's reciprocal deference to its freedom as to that which is needed to confirm itself. This dialogic structure is itself genuinely intersubjective, however, only insofar as its own authority (as the basis of valid rights) is validated through the spontaneous action of the atomistic self seeking its own radically individualistic worth. Hence dialogic community must defer to the independent agency of the self for the sake of its own confirmation, making room for legal paradigms in which its own presence is veiled, latent, and imperfectly manifested. Conversely, the individual is ultimately confirmed through its free recognition of the totality that requires and acknowledges its independent selfhood. It is just this dialogic relation between self and other whose manifestations we have discerned in the previous paradigms and whose thematic primacy binds these formations together as mutually essential parts of a whole.

Accordingly, the paradigms of formal right and equity gain their ultimate justification in terms of a thematic principle that transcends both. Both are justified as embodiments of intersubjectivity proceeding from the freedom of the individual self and as stages in the objective realization of intersubjectivity as the genuine foundation of law. They are thus ultimately grounded in the self-developing whole that is independent of either and yet that contains both as instantiations of itself. The relationship between formal right, equity, and the totality exhibits the threefold mediation characteristic of dialogic community. Equity respects the independent existence of formal right even as it brings the latter back to its own immanent fulfillment; conversely, formal right defers to equity for the sake of its own self-realization. But both poles are preserved in recognizing the other because each defers only through the mediation of the intersubjective whole that, while independent of both, also contains both as essential stages of its own development.

That law's foundation is the totality we call dialogic community implies that the principles of formal right and equity are valid only within definite and rational limits. Because formal right and equity are both instantiations of the genuine ground of law, each must be actualized with a moderation that reflects this subordinate status and that preserves the distinctive identity of the other. Courts practice such restraint when they limit the consideration doctrine by promissory estoppel but use the latter only as a shield; when they allow relief for mistaken assumptions but only in cases of common or known mistake; and when they scrutinize free exchanges for substantive fairness but set aside improvident bargains only if the parties' strength is unequal. What to the skeptic appear as irrational truce lines are in fact principled boundaries.

By now it is clear that a court's duty of restraint in applying the paradigms has nothing to do with balancing one value against competing ones according to one's political commitments; rather, the duty is to observe borders rationally drawn by the theme of the whole, borders whose respect ensures the coherent self-realization of each paradigm. How this duty of restraint translates into doctrine has been well enough worked out in the case of formal right: the equitable doctrines we have examined limit the application of the formalist paradigm when the latter generates or sanctions the domineering relationships its own dialogic structure proscribes. The matter is not as clear, however, in the case of equity, for the movement to universalize equity's principle has not yet run its course. I shall conclude, therefore, by suggesting a general principle for distinguishing between valid and invalid judicial protections of autonomy.

I believe that the relevant distinction is between what Hegel calls rights of intention and rights of welfare. Stated positively, a right of intention is a right to the coherent realization of one's generic agency in subjective goals one can affirm as one's own and in deeds one can recognize as the embodiment of these goals. Stated negatively, it is a right against subjection to powers in which one cannot recognize one's own interests and one's own deeds. The right of intention is specified, among other ways, as a right against subordination to a purported law that embodies the exclusive good of another (107, 120, 132). A right of welfare is a right to the material and cultural conditions that allow one to act from self-determined goals rather than from natural necessities or from the projects of those who control access to the means of satisfying these needs. Both kinds of rights are concretizations of the general right to self-determination, but the *judicial* vindication of only one of them is consistent with the preservation of formal right.

In actualizing a right of intention, a court enforces formal right only when the party against whom it is being enforced can, as a rational agent, see it as embodying his good. The court thus acts defensively (as in *High Trees* and *Lloyds Bank*), disempowering formal right in situations where it comes forward as an external and alien power. This mode of actualizing individual autonomy is consistent with the preservation of formal right as a distinctive paradigm because the court acts interstitially—indeed in an ad hoc manner—suspending a principle whose rule in ordinary circumstances is still respected. Were a court, however, to actualize the right of welfare, it would explicitly elevate into a principle of contract law a conception of distributive justice in which formal contract law would disappear. Contract rights would be directly determined through a common good rather than being overridden by it, so that the person-centered paradigm of formal right would dissolve. Accordingly, the limits of equity are observed when courts actualize the right of intention as a modification of formal right, while legislatures actualize a right of welfare through taxation—that is, through redistributions of property originally allocated through free exchanges unrestricted by distributive considerations.[106] To regard contract law as properly governed by distributive justice is to assert a claim as falsely hegemonic as the opposing claim that it is unified under formal liberty.

Of course, the distinction we have drawn between kinds of rights that are both specifications of the right to autonomy will seem arbitrary to someone who wishes to absolutize the principle of individual autonomy, or who believes that we must thematize *either* formal liberty *or* the right to self-determination as the principle of contract law. From the standpoint of such a critic, the introduction into contract law of just so much of the common good that is consistent with the preservation of the libertarian paradigm will seem like so much ad hocery. Yet the apparent arbitrariness of the limit disappears once we grasp dialogic community as the genuine foundation of law; for in light of this theme, both paradigms are valid as particular embodiments, each limiting and fulfilling the other. The expansionary tendency that each exhibits in isolation is tamed when each is seen to be self-consistent only as part of a more comprehensive whole. The limits the autonomy principle places on formal right may be ad hoc in the sense that a court of equity responds to specific situations in which the enforcement of formal right would contradict the latter's own end.

However, the confinement of the autonomy principle within this role is conceptually required, for it is determined by the concept of dialogic community, whose objective realization as the ground of law is the self-unfolding and crisis of *both* paradigms, and in which both are therefore preserved as developmental phases. It is this concept, then, that makes rational the boundaries between the two systems, that determines the appropriate allocation of autonomy-promoting roles to courts and legislatures, and that governs the extent to which each paradigm may modify the other, that each may attain, in the playwright's words, its "right praise and true perfection."

CHAPTER IV

The Case for Tort Law

1. THE TRANSFORMATION OF TORT LAW
AND ITS CRITICS

In previous chapters we observed the logical impetus toward the submersion of private in public law once positive freedom displaces formal liberty as the end of law. While every branch of private law bears traces of this theoretical movement, the law of torts has succumbed the most. In the laws of property and contract, the apparent stalemate between rival paradigms makes the central theoretical issue whether the law can be grasped as a coherent whole. In the law of torts, the issue is whether the whole that is currently evolving is the tort law we should have.

The original common-law understanding of tort evinced a primitive simplicity. A tort (or wrong) was a trespass against the body, land, or chattels of a person. A trespass was an act inconsistent with the plaintiff's exclusive authority over his body or external possessions; and the remedy consisted in compelling the wrongdoer to acknowledge this authority by restoring the plaintiff to his position prior to the trespass.[1] The property right vindicated by this process envisaged individuals unrelated to each other except through the exchange of commodities; for the right was unmediated by any conception of societal welfare or by any notion of distributive justice. One had an exclusive right valid against the world in whatever one originally possessed, acquired through adverse possession, or received in a consensual exchange. An act was tortious not because it jeopardized a goal thought desirable by the community, nor because it upset a just pattern of holdings, but because it violated an individual right held prior to any human association for a common end. Obversely, the point of the remedy was not to further a communal goal but to actualize the right. I shall call the original understanding of tort by various names: the right-based model, the private-law model, the formalist model, and the classical model. These names all refer to a tort law conceived as a regime for vindicating individual rights of liberty and property against acts disrespectful of these rights.

The right-based model of tort law held uncontested sway throughout the common-law world until the middle of the twentieth century. The fruition of negligence law in the nineteenth century was a development within this framework (although one that, as we shall see, simultaneously burst it); for despite the economic explanations standardly proffered for fault-based liability,[2] and notwithstanding Learned Hand's economic formula for the standard of care,[3] the gist of negligence is the defendant's infringement of the plaintiff's right to security against harm from impositions of extraordinary risk. In the last half-century, however, the right-based model of tort law has steadily yielded ground to a welfarist or social insurance model.[4] Under this regime, tort law becomes transformed into "accident law," the principal aim of which is to compensate accident victims from public sources regardless of the occurrence of wrongdoing. In Commonwealth jurisdictions, the right-based system remains dominant, although the social insurance model is plainly visible in relaxations of the plaintiff's burden of proof in cases of manufacturers' and medical negligence,[5] in judicial extensions of the vicarious liability of employers and car owners,[6] and in the sub rosa influence of liability insurance on the application (and sometimes definition)[7] of the traditional criteria of fault. In the United States, however, the same incremental changes have culminated in a revolutionary transformation of tort law. In 1948, Fleming James, one of the intellectual fathers of the revolution, described the new order he saw arising as follows:

> Human failures in a machine age cause a large and fairly regular—though probably reducible—toll of life, limb, and property. As a class the victims of these accidents can ill afford the loss they entail. The problem of decreasing this toll can best be solved through the pressure of safety regulations with penal and licensing sanctions. . . . But when all is said and done, human losses remain. It is the principal job of tort law today to deal with these losses. The best and most efficient way to do this is to assure accident victims of compensation, and to distribute the losses involved over society as a whole or some very large segment of it. Such a basis for administering losses may be called social insurance.
>
> This at once brings in an important new element. For while no social good may come from the mere shifting of a loss, society does benefit from the wide and regular distribution of losses. . . . If a certain type of loss is the more or less inevitable by-product of a desirable but dangerous form of activity, it may well be just to distribute such losses among all the beneficiaries

of the activity though it would be unjust to visit them severally upon those individuals who happened to be the faultless instruments causing them.[8]

Several points in this passage deserve emphasis. First, the new tort law (now a misnomer) deals not with wrongs but with losses. Second, it concerns itself not with losses relative to individual want but with "human" losses of "life, limb, and property"—losses measured against a common standard of human well-being. Third, the aim of the new tort law is to shift the monetary burden of these losses from those who can ill afford them to all members of society or to as many as possible. Fourth, the rationale for shifting human losses in this manner invokes a principle of distributive justice: the accident costs produced by otherwise desirable activity should be shared by all who benefit from that activity rather than allocated by chance to a few. Fifth, the tort law thus reconceived is justified as an instrument for promoting a "social good."

The new tort law imagined by James in the 1940s has become a palpable reality in the America of the 1990s. Beginning with California's in 1963,[9] the appellate courts of most states have instituted a model of tort law conceived no longer as a regime for vindicating individual rights to liberty and property but as an instrument for the attainment of collective goals. The goals of American "tort" law are the social diffusion of losses created by risky but beneficial activity and the attainment of an economically efficient level of accident avoidance. The doctrinal innovation that centrally reflects this conceptual revolution is the strict liability (or liability without fault) of enterprises for accident losses caused by defective products.[10] The point of this doctrine is to shift losses from those on whom they would fall with ruinous impact onto firms that can insure against civil liability and spread the cost thinly (through the price of their products) over the mass of consumers who benefit from their activity. In addition, the internalization of accident costs to the activities that generate them will, it is thought, encourage firms to find cost-justified ways of making their products safer (and consumers to choose safer products).[11]

The internal transformation of tort law from a system for remedying private wrongs to one for promoting public goals is, however, merely a way station on the path to more radical change. Once it is decided that a principal aim of accident law is the wide social distribution of accident costs, it is a short step to the conclusion that the traditional doctrines of tort law, evolved in accordance with an individualistic legal paradigm, are hopelessly unsuited to this objective; that they are, in James's phrase, "horse and buggy rules in an age of machinery."[12] Since the defendant firm is now simply a means of access to an insurance fund, it makes sense from a compensation perspective to bypass this conduit, to dispense with the costly and unfairly discriminatory requirement of proof of causation, and to compensate all disabled persons directly from a public fund. Moreover, in areas other than product defects where defendants are ill-situated to distribute losses and where liability is still based on negligence, compensation for accident victims depends on the chance that the defendant was at fault and has the resources to satisfy a judgment. Even if the plaintiff's claim is successful, years may pass between the time of injury and the time of compensation as the procedures adapted to the protection of individual rights are punctiliously observed and often exploited. In the majority of cases, it seems, the prospect of delay as well as the uncertainty attending proof of fault encourage settlements that, because of the negotiating pressures on the claimant, tend seriously to undercompensate precisely when the victim's need is greatest.[13] Accordingly, the rationale of loss distribution leads to a scheme of no-fault social insurance administered by a quasi-judicial tribunal. Such schemes are common throughout the industrialized world for workplace accidents and are becoming increasingly employed for automobile mishaps. The common feature of these plans is that accident victims surrender their right to sue in tort for full compensation (including pain and suffering) in return for guaranteed compensation for pecuniary losses. The logical extreme of this development has been realized in New Zealand, where pecuniary losses from all types of accident are compensated from a fund supported by levies on risk-creating activities and where the right to sue in tort for personal injury has been abolished.[14]

The revolution in tort law has produced its inevitable counterrevolutionary theorists. In particular, Richard Epstein, George Fletcher, and Ernest Weinrib have sought to buttress the right-based or private-law model of tort law by elaborating theories of civil liability that make no reference to public goals. Epstein would turn the clock back to the period before the maturation of negligence law when trespass was the paradigmatic tort and the defendant was strictly liable for all injuries consequential on an invasion of person or property.[15] Fletcher has attempted to unify all of tort law under the idea of nonreciprocal risk,[16] while Weinrib has essayed a similar integration under a theory that combines Aristotle's idea of corrective justice with a Kantian theory of personality and rights.[17] In this chapter, I too shall present an argument for the retention or restoration of a private-law conception of tort law as well as for the preservation of tort law alongside legislative schemes for social insurance. Before doing so, however, I want to show why the arguments of Epstein, Fletcher, and Weinrib are inadequate to the task of saving classical tort law from oblivion.

1.1 Fletcher and Nonreciprocal Risk

George Fletcher's "Fairness and Utility in Tort Theory"[18] was the first significant protest against the movement to refashion tort law into an instrument of public policy. Fletcher saw the fundamental conflict in modern tort theory as one between two models of liability, which he called the paradigm of reciprocity and the paradigm of reasonableness. Under the former, the basic issue in any tort dispute—whether the plaintiff has a right to recover his losses from the defendant—is decided by attending solely to the transaction between the parties and by asking whether in that transaction the defendant wronged the plaintiff without excuse. In this inquiry, the impact of the defendant's activity on the general welfare is irrelevant, as are the broad welfare implications of the court's rule of decision. The defendant wronged the plaintiff if he took more liberties with the latter's safety than those to which he was exposed in return; and this principle of liability is justified not by its tendency to promote a social goal but by its fair allocation of losses as between plaintiff and defendant.

Under the model of reasonableness, by contrast, a social calculus replaces a narrow focus on private rights. Within this paradigm, liability depends on whether the defendant's conduct was reasonable from the standpoint of social utility—whether it took the care that was cost-justified in the circumstances—and the rule of decision is evaluated for its tendency to promote an optimal level of investment in safety. Here conduct is negligent if it incurs accident costs greater than the costs of avoiding them, and the point of the damage award is to deter such wasteful conduct. Because the reasonableness model sees tort law as a tool of social policy, Fletcher calls its reasoning "instrumentalist" and contrasts it to the noninstrumentalist orientation of the reciprocity model, for which the point of tort law is corrective justice rather than the maximization of welfare. I shall henceforward borrow this idiom, although we should note that Fletcher equates instrumentalism in tort theory with utilitarianism, a simplification I shall presently criticize. At one level, Fletcher's aim is merely to set forth the two paradigms as an aid to understanding the tensions in the body of tort law. Yet the description of the reciprocity model has a polemical point. By presenting a unified theory of tort law that is both noninstrumental and normatively cogent, Fletcher erected a breakwater against the tide of instrumentalist theory, whose success had hitherto owed as much to the absence of an alternative moral theory of tort as to the force of its own vision.

For Fletcher, the idea that integrates tort law in noninstrumental terms is liability for the imposition of nonreciprocal risk. This idea, he argues, explains not only negligence law but also the enclaves of strict liability that survived the transition to negligence as well as the intentional torts. Cases of strict liability (e.g., crashing airplanes, straying cattle, and ultrahazardous activities) are those in which the defendant imposes risks on the plaintiff that are nonreciprocal, not because of the manner in which the activity is performed, but because of the unusually risky nature of the activity itself. Negligence consists in the imposition of nonreciprocal risk by performing a common activity (such as driving or sport) involving reciprocal risks in an unusually risky way. Intentional torts involve a "rapid acceleration of risk" toward a specific victim that sets the danger apart from the quotidien risks that people impose on each other and expect to incur. Fletcher presents the idea of reciprocal risk as a principle of fairness, for it states that each individual has a right to as much liberty to impose risks on others as is consistent with the equal security of all. Tort law under the principle of reciprocity is thus a coherent totality worthy of respect.

There are two points I wish to make about Fletcher's theory of tort. I will pass over certain problematic details of the theory, in particular, the extension to tort law of a criminal law theory of excuses and the resulting severance of the plaintiff's right to compensation from the defendant's duty to pay.[19] I will instead focus on two fundamental shortcomings of Fletcher's theory as a means of identifying the desiderata of an improved one. The first concerns the general polemical strategy Fletcher employs; the second concerns the principle of nonreciprocal risk.

Fletcher's strategy against the reasonableness paradigm is to exhibit an alternative model of tort that can plausibly claim to unify the field and that has normative power. As noted earlier, such an argument is not without force, for it prevents a victory of instrumentalism by default. As long as the only alternative to an instrumentalist conception of negligence was thought to be a primitive and amoral regime of strict liability, instrumentalism faced no serious challenge.[20] In place of this lopsided dichotomy Fletcher sets up a contest between moral Titans and shows that a victory for instrumentalism must be at the cost of an ethico-legal system of stature. The problem, however, is that the instrumentalist paradigm can also persuasively claim to cover the field (particularly the American one); and it too lays claim to normative power, since it aims, after all, at a fair social distribution of losses, at the prevention of poverty, and at optimal investment in accident prevention. We are thus left with a conflict of paradigms and are offered no powerful reason to prefer the paradigm of reciprocity. Fletcher's only argument of substance against the instrumentalist model is that, by immunizing from liability all activity that is welfare maximizing, it sacrifices injured plaintiffs on the altar of social utility.[21] Yet this argument applies only against a utilitarian version of instrumentalism. It has no force against an instrumentalism concerned with protecting against calamity the basic conditions of human autonomy—life, limb, and property; and, in particular, it is powerless against strict enterprise liability, under which plaintiffs are never sacrificed and defendants are simply conveyor belts for accident costs.[22] An advocate of an instrumental tort law might justifiably protest that Fletcher has substituted one oversimple dichotomy for another: in lieu of the supposed antagonism between moral negligence and amoral strict liability, he has posited the equally simplistic opposition between a noninstrumental tort law protective of individual autonomy and an instrumentalism concerned only with aggregate welfare. The result is that Fletcher has no argument against the *autonomy-driven* ideology that has lately reduced tort law to an instrument of social insurance and of optimal accident prevention.[23]

The second basic weakness of Fletcher's theory is the principle of nonreciprocal risk itself. Fletcher's discovery of nonreciprocity as the criterion of wrong marked a watershed in tort theory, and the synthesis of tort law I shall presently offer will only build on this discovery.[24] There are, however, a number of problems with Fletcher's formulation of the idea. First, by identifying civil wrongdoing with the ex ante imposition of nonreciprocal risk, Fletcher's theory would allow a plaintiff a right of action (for an award compensating him for self-protective measures) whether or not the risk materializes in damage. The theory thus fails to account for the rule of negligence law that the defendant's activity must have caused harm to the plaintiff. Of course, Fletcher might respond that the common law is mistaken to insist on actual harm. Yet the harm requirement seems to be one of those well-settled features of negligence law that a theory of tort must accommodate if it does not wish to seem arbitrary. Certainly, a theory that explained this requirement would be preferable, ceteris paribus, to one that banished it.

Second, Fletcher's principle of wrong is insufficiently general. By speaking only of nonreciprocal *risk*, Fletcher equates the principle of negligence with the principle of tort as a whole. It is implausible to suggest, however, that battery, unlawful entry on another's land, and the conversion or detention of another's goods are cases of nonreciprocal risk.[25] In the vocabulary of the common law, risk denotes potential harm. If actual harm is irrelevant to a particular wrong, then a fortiori the potential for harm must also be insignificant. But battery, trespass to land, and the conversion of chattels are actionable as violations of person and property even if the plaintiff is not harmed and even if he has benefited from the wrong. A physician, for example, who injects an unwilling patient with a riskless and lifesaving drug is guilty of a battery. Fletcher might reply that he meant to identify nonreciprocal impositions in general as wrongful and that nonreciprocal risk is only an example of this. However, it is not clear that a harmless trespass to person or property involves a nonreciprocal imposition of any sort, for it does not consist in crossing a threshold of socially normal (i.e., reciprocal) invasions. The common-law position is that any unconsented-to touching, entry, or taking is wrongful, even if part of the ordinary irritations of human interaction.

Fletcher's principle is also insufficiently diversified. One may grant that an account of tort law that simply described the multiple grounds of liability thrown up by history would not qualify as a theory of tort law. A theory, we think, must explain the multiplicity immediately presented to the observer by comprehending the many particulars as instances of a general idea. However, a unifying principle of tort law must not only unify; it must do so in a way that respects the internal differentiation of the subject matter. We recognize Thales's declaration that "all is water" as a primitive theory of nature because it both identifies a particular object with the universal principle of all objects and because it submerges the lush diversity of nature into an undifferentiated substance, affording no specific understanding of anything. Likewise, the theme of nonreciprocal risk effaces the differences between trespass, nuisance, and negligence and so fails to comprehend tort law as it exists in its own right.[26] This theme not only obliterates harmless trespass; it also blurs the difference between nuisance (a proprietary tort enjoinable regardless of care) and negligence (a failure to take due care for another's welfare remediable only by damages). The unity Fletcher produces is thus not a unity *of* tort law but an artificial reduction of differences to an external monism. Yet his failure in this regard instructs us. It shows that an adequate theory of tort law must somehow reconcile the extremes of monism and pluralism into which defective theories fall. It must grasp a general principle of wrong without doing violence to the diversity of torts; obversely, it must pay respect to pluralism and to the historical evolution of tort law without losing sight of the single idea progressively instantiated in both.

1.2 Epstein's Theory of Strict Liability

Like Fletcher, Richard Epstein has sought to counter the move toward an instrumentalist organization of tort law by developing a normative theory of tort that explicates commonsense beliefs about the requirements of fairness in two-party interactions. Yet whereas Fletcher saw the enemy in a particular, economic interpretation of negligence, Epstein (or so it seems) regards negligence law as inherently geared to economic efficiency. This view stems from his assumption that negligence law must be a repository either of ordinary intuitions about moral responsibility or of economic insights.[27] Since the legal concept of negligence ignores the individual's capacity to conform to the standard of care (insanity, for example, is generally no excuse for negligence),[28] it cannot, he argues, be explained morally. This leaves only the economic interpretation of negligence as a failure to take cost-justified precautions. Because Epstein accepts the economic interpretation of negligence, his elaboration of a noninstrumental theory of tort becomes a matter of rehabilitating strict liability—the faultless causing of harm to another—as a general basis of civil responsibility.

Epstein justifies strict liability not as a means of loss distribution or of efficient resource allocation but as a principle that justly assigns responsibility for harm inflicted on others. His basic argument is that we should be answerable for the harm we cause others whether or not we intend or negligently produce the harm, for we have no right to impose the costs of our self-interested activity on others. We must confront and bear those costs just as we would have if they had originally fallen on us.[29] This is an extremely broad principle of civil liability, one that Epstein subsequently limits but never entirely abandons. We can call it a principle of personal responsibility for the consequences of one's voluntary acts. The losses caused by our volitional activity are inherently *our* losses—they are imputable to us as moral agents—and strict liability works to ensure that we do not succeed in shifting them onto others.

Epstein's theory of tort has attracted much attention over the years, and we need not rehearse here all the criticisms to which it may be vulnerable.[30] Our sole interest lies in understanding the inadequacy of the theory as a defense of a private-law conception of tort law. The argument I shall make is that Epstein's theory of tort accounts for an exceedingly narrow segment of what we know as tort law, namely, that part dealing with trespassory interferences with proprietary sovereignty. It provides no satisfactory account of the wrongdoing that consists in the infliction of harm to fundamental human interests and so abandons this ground entirely to policies of loss spreading and of optimal deterrence.

Epstein declares that "the defendant must bear the costs of those injuries that he inflicts upon others as though they were injuries that he suffered himself."[31] Yet it soon becomes clear that Epstein has a rather lax version of strict liability. To hold the agent answerable for all effects in the causal chain leading out indefinitely from his act would offend a common-sense understanding of responsibility. Since the traditional but-for test of causation (but for the defendant's act would the injury have occurred?) makes the defendant's act a cause of the plaintiff's injury no matter how remote its connection therewith, the test, says Epstein, can be dispensed with along with that of reasonable foreseeability by which the absurd results of the but-for test are corrected. In place of these traditional causal criteria, Epstein constructs four "paradigm cases" of causation that he claims "respond to ordinary views on individual blame and accountability"[32] and that can be applied to determine whether a defendant can fairly be held liable for the plaintiff's loss. The cases are A hit B; A frightened B; A compelled B to hit C; and A created a dangerous condition that resulted in harm to B. A fact pattern conforming to any of these paradigms raises a prima facie case of liability, rebuttable by proof of facts (e.g., that B trespassed on A's land) undermining the causal priority of what A did to B.

Once we decide that the defendant cannot justly be held responsible to the plaintiff for all the injurious effects of his act, we need a principle for distinguishing those losses for which he must compensate the plaintiff from those which must lie where they fall. Although Epstein sometimes delivers himself of formulations suggesting a belief that legal responsibility is coextensive with moral imputability, this is not his considered view. An entrepreneur who drives a competitor out of business by selling more cheaply is responsible in a moral sense for the harm he causes (the harm is attributable to him), but Epstein would not hold this person legally accountable for the competitor's losses. Rather, he would hold someone legally responsible only for those hurts caused by acts that fit one of the paradigm cases: hit, frighten, compel, and so on. These cases thus already implicitly embody a distinction between those hurts caused by the defendant for which the plaintiff has a right to compensation and those for which he does not. A theory of tort must formulate the principle of this distinction. Yet in the article in which he first introduced his theory of strict liability, Epstein never makes explicit the criterion of compensable harms. Instead, he makes the concept of causation do the work of a substantive criterion of legal responsibility. We are responsible to our neighbor, according to Epstein, whenever we "cause" him harm. Causation, however, cannot do this work alone, for as an empirical notion it encompasses remote consequences of an act and so would counterintuitively hold the agent responsible for unforeseeable effects; and as a moral notion it embraces indifferently foreseeable harms that involve an infringement of rights and foreseeable harms (e.g., to commercial or amorous interests) that do not. Causation may be a necessary condition of civil liability; but it has too broad a compass to be a sufficient one.

Epstein deals with this difficulty by autocratically stipulating the meaning of cause. The paradigm cases, he decrees, are cases of causation; cases where we would not hold the agent legally responsible for harm are not such cases. Thus A causes B harm if he creates a dangerous condition that results in harm to B, whereas he does not cause B harm if he creates a "mere" condition that leads to injury.[33] Yet nothing in the bare concept of a cause selects a dangerous condition over other necessary conditions of an injury as the sole cause of the injury. Moreover, the paradigm cases of causation identify the bearer of legal responsibility only because Epstein arbitrarily excludes troubling examples from the paradigm. Consider the paradigm, A frightened B. This seems to be equivalent to the locution, A caused B to be frightened. Suppose, however (to take Epstein's example), that an ultranervous B is frightened when A raises his arm to mop his brow fifty feet away. This situation, Epstein tells us, does not come within the paradigm, because B has induced his own fright.[34] It seems, then, that A frightens B when Epstein thinks he should be legally responsible for the consequence, whereas he does not frighten B when Epstein believes he should not be responsible. But the tail is now wagging the dog, for the paradigms were supposed to determine when the defendant is responsible, and yet Epstein's preconceptions about responsibility are in reality determining what counts as an instance of the paradigm. The arbitrariness of this procedure is all the while concealed behind the pretense that the paradigm case is dispositive.

The concept of causation cannot alone tell us when we are legally answerable for another's losses. We need a theory of individual rights to tell us when our causal impingements on another have wronged him by contradicting those rights.[35] Such a theory will also tell us whether liability must be strict or fault-based, for to know how a right is constituted is also to know the kind of conduct to which it is vulnerable. Epstein does not offer a developed theory of rights, but throughout his writings he assumes that individuals have natural property rights in their bodies, in the things they are first to possess, and in the things they acquire through consensual transfers. He has also argued that the concept of ownership itself entails a regime of strict liability for infringements of property.[36] This is so, he contends, because ownership rights are absolute; they are not mediated or limited by any accommodation to the liberty of other persons. If you make an unwanted entry on my land, you are a trespasser and the court will award me nominal damages without inquiring into whether you were at fault; if you take my car, you must return it or an equivalent value even if you reasonably believed the car was yours; and if you are a surgeon about to operate on me in the reasonable but mistaken belief that I have consented, I should be able to get an injunction to stop you. Epstein believes that this property-based argument for strict liability is an argument for a general regime of strict liability applicable not only to battery, entry on land, and the taking of chattels but also to the creation of dangerous conditions causing personal injury or damage to property. He believes this because at bottom he believes that causing harm to the body or to items of property is equivalent to violating rights of ownership.[37] But this belief, as I shall now argue, is mistaken.

The property right that entails strict liability for trespass is the will's exclusive sovereignty over its body and possessions. Any unwanted touching or entry involves an interference with that sovereignty and so contradicts the right whether or not harm ensues and irrespective of the intention or negligence of the defendant.* The fact that the defendant reasonably believed he had a right to enter the plaintiff's land or to take his goods cannot negate the trespass, since his very belief challenges the owner's rightful control. Furthermore, the will's exclusive sovereignty over its body and possessions is quintessentially a private right, because it entails a

---

*The argument for strict liability for interference with property is made more fully below. As we shall see, fault is irrelevant only to liability for the invasion of sovereignty (and hence for purposes of nominal damages, restitution, or injunctive relief); it is, I shall argue, essential to liability for any *harm* caused by the invasion.

correlative obligation in other discrete individuals not to interfere with that sovereignty and to restore it if they do. Thus, if A takes something belonging to B, only A can restore B to his rightful position, for only the person who has arrogated an authority belonging to someone else can reinstate the victim's right. A civil remedy is required here because the defendant has wrongfully claimed or acquired what the plaintiff has wrongfully lost. Accordingly, the plaintiff not only must recover his loss; he must recover it from the person who inflicted it.

Now Epstein's property-based argument for a generalized strict liability depends on the claim that all inflictions of harm on the body or on material possessions involve interferences with the will's sovereignty with respect to these things. This claim, however, is surely erroneous. If A leaves open a manhole in a public street and B falls in, A has not contradicted B's exclusive right to control his body. B was free to avoid the hole; he was not pushed or compelled to jump. Similarly, if A spills an inflammable substance into a harbor and B's ship is damaged as a consequence, A has done nothing to interfere with or usurp B's proprietary sovereignty; B is still undisputed owner of the ship, however much transformed by the damage.[38] True, A has in both cases put a danger in B's path that compromises B's control over what *befalls* his body or possession; but A would do this by any risky act performed in proximity to B without contradicting B's ownership. Thus, however much A has harmed B, he has done nothing to depose B from exclusive command over his physical motion or possession.

To explain A's wrong in these cases, then, we need a nonproprietary conception of a right. That is, we need a conception of B's right that refers not to his exclusive sovereignty over his body or possession but to his right to security against harm to interests essential to human welfare—to the interest in life, in health, and in the physical integrity of one's possessions. Later on I shall have something to say about the conceptual genesis of such a right. Whatever its derivation, however, a right to security cannot entail strict liability for its breach, for an absolute right to security against harm (the counterpart of strict liability) is incompatible with the right of others to act, all action involving a risk of harm. The plaintiff's right to security must be reconciled with the defendant's freedom of action; and fault is the notion that, by delimiting a threshold wherein agents may inflict harm free of liability, achieves the reconciliation.[39]

The fault requirement for liability for harm will be discussed more fully below. More important for our present purposes is a feature of a right against harm that, at least at first blush, distinguishes it from a right of ownership. A right to security against harm does not self-evidently entail a correlative obligation in discrete individuals to repair the loss they have inflicted. My right to proprietary sovereignty necessarily means that if you usurp it, you must relinquish it to me whether by returning the thing you have taken or by paying me nominal damages for an entry; only you can repair my loss for you have claimed an authority that is mine. However, if I am harmed by your activity without contradiction to my proprietary sovereignty, it is not so obvious that my loss is your correlative gain.[40] You may have gained nothing from accidentally harming me, and in any case you have gained nothing *of mine.* Consequently, one is entitled to doubt whether *you* must repair my loss and so whether there is any inherent necessity in a common-law practice that allocates the compensatory burden for harm to harm-doers. It seems possible to vindicate my right to basic security by imposing on the community a duty to insure me against accident or illness (whether through enterprise liability or public insurance) and to deter negligent conduct through regulatory sanctions. Nothing in Epstein's theory of tort shows us why this path would, if taken to the exclusion of a civil remedy, be the wrong one to choose.

We can summarize the foregoing argument as follows. Epstein's theory of strict liability rests at bottom on an idea of proprietary sovereignty to which the right to security against harm is assimilated. The conflation of the right to security with that of ownership has these consequences: first, Epstein illicitly extends the liability regime appropriate to protecting rights of ownership to the vindication of rights to security against harm; second, he gives us no independent account of how the right to security against harm entails a correlative obligation in discrete persons to repair the losses they inflict on others. Without such an account, Epstein's theory of tort logically reserves for private law only the enforcement of the will's right to proprietary and bodily sovereignty through nominal damages, restitution, or injunctive relief. It leaves the entire realm of harms to health, bodily integrity, and material possessions (by far the major part of tort law) open to exclusive appropriation by public-law mechanisms for loss distribution and deterrence.

1.3 Weinrib, Abstract Right, and Coherence

In a series of recent works,[41] Ernest Weinrib has sought to ground a private-law model of tort law on a Kantian theory of justice that explains not only the tort of trespass but also that of negligently causing harm. While these works bear witness to the intimate link between great originality and great humility before a philosophic tradition, they also exemplify the pitfalls of eliding the differences within a tradition. Kant's theory of justice is basically identical to the legal paradigm that Hegel calls abstract right and that we have all along been calling formal right. This identity between Kant's *Rechtslehre* and Hegel's philosophy of abstract right has apparently led Weinrib to believe that Kant's theory of justice is in all essential respects the same as Hegel's and that his own theory of tort finds as much support in one as in the other.[42] This, however, is an unfortunate error. Hegel's understanding of abstract right may be identical to Kant's philosophy of law; but whereas Hegel views abstract right as a finite and particular manifestation of a more comprehensive idea of right, Kant identifies it with right as such. For Kant, the foundation of formal right is the absolute foundation of law; hence there are for him no coercive duties beyond the negative ones that formal right generates. For Hegel, however, the foundation of formal right is a transitory conception of law's foundation, one that requires justification through a more complex normative idea. This idea incorporates formal right within an ethical system wherein it (formal right) is limited and modified. Weinrib's conflation of Kant's and Hegel's philosophy of law is more than an error of philosophical scholarship; it is an error with serious consequences for tort theory, for its effect is to assimilate a strong foundation for a noninstrumental tort law into a weaker one, thereby depriving classical tort law of what is perhaps its firmest theoretical support.[43]

The feature of Kant's philosophy of right that prima facie qualifies it to support a noninstrumental model of tort law is its postulate that the right is prior to the good.[44] This means that rights attach to personhood considered as a capacity to form and revise relative conceptions of happiness, and that because personality is prior to, or more fundamental than, these conceptions, its rights of liberty impose constraints on the political pursuit of what is conventionally regarded as desirable. Because individual rights are for Kant established independently of the exigencies of the general welfare, they can form the foundation of a tort law intelligible without reference to collective goals; and because these rights are more fundamental than goals, they can (it seems) form the basis of a tort law resistant to immersion in public policy.

Since Weinrib rests his defense of a noninstrumental model of tort law on the foundation of formal right, his defense can only be as strong as that foundation. Yet, as we have seen in previous chapters, the foundation of formal right will not stand still. Formal right cannot possibly ground on its own a noninstrumental model of tort law because its fate is precisely to pass over into a paradigm of law governed by a common good. Formal right thus necessarily *leads* to an instrumentalist conception of law, and the contemporary crisis of classical tort law is just a reflection of the inherent instability of the formalist paradigm. I have tried to pinpoint the cause of this instability in earlier chapters, but I shall try now to put the argument in a somewhat different way.

The foundation of formal right is, as Weinrib sees, the free will abstracted from all particular interests, goals, or conceptions of welfare. Because every content of the will is thought to involve a subjective judgment of value, formal right can reach an absolute normative foundation only by a negative act of self-transcendence toward the formal capacity for freely choosing and revising values. In formal right, only this capacity is normatively significant; particular choices are important only in a negative sense—as indicating what the free will is not identical with or bound to. Thus, even though all action involves an expression of the generic capacity for choice in the choice of something specific, formal right identifies the ground of normativity exclusively with the generic capacity.[45] As Weinrib points out, "the status of the free will *as a universal* is the ground of the actor's obligations in abstract right."[46] These obligations are negative ones of noninterference with the will's formal spontaneity. As the absolute end presupposed in the choice of all relative ends, the formally free will is an end valid for all persons, obliging every agent to respect beings with a capacity for freedom as existing for themselves rather than simply as a means for others. Yet, although the free will is an end, it is not a goal. To have a goal is to desire some yet-to-be state of affairs, but the will as here conceived is the abstraction from all desire as well as from temporality. The will is an end not in the sense of a goal to be achieved or a potentiality to be realized but in the sense of a transcendental purposiveness that necessarily underlies all goal-seeking action. Now it is just the self's transcendence of all concrete goals that Weinrib sees as the ontological basis for a noninstrumental model of tort law. Since the foundation of private law is not a goal but the a priori condition of goal-oriented action, there is nothing that tort law could be conceived as furthering or promoting.

The fly in this ointment, however, is that the abstract will is unstable in its abstractness. As Weinrib readily admits, the will cannot remain aloof from concrete action; it must embody its freedom externally.[47] This is so because a will that is an absolute end only for itself is self-contradictory. The will is authentically an end only insofar as it actually subdues will-less entities to itself in socially recognized property. The movement toward self-embodiment is thus necessary to the will's notion as an absolute end, *but this necessity was not taken account of in the initial conception of the ground of normativity as an abstract will generating only negative obligations.* The necessity for self-embodiment means that the free will is in reality a unity of distinct phases—the formal will and its expression in goal-seeking action—but abstract right (and Weinrib) privileges one pole of this unity (viz., the formal will) and calls it alone the absolute end that grounds valid obligation. Since formal right must nevertheless acknowledge the necessity of the will's embodiment, it becomes tangled in a web of equivocation wherein it affirms now the abstract will and now its interest in self-realization but never unites these two elements in a single idea. On the one hand, it posits as the sole unconditioned reality the pure will as such; on the other, it treats assaults on the body and takings of property as violations *of* personality, thereby acknowledging that property and physical integrity are essential to freedom and that the pure will by itself is *not* absolute. On the one hand, it treats all interests as subjective and only the pure will as universal; on the other, it recognizes the interest in property and physical integrity as universal and objective but does not allow this insight to force a revision of its initial idea of the foundation as a will prior to interests, one that grounds only negative rights.[48]

The equivocation of formal right is thus made possible by a selective amnesia ensuring that one side of the truth is forgotten when the other is present. In affirming the pure will as the foundation of right, formal right forgets its acknowledgment of universal interests essential to the will's status as an end; and in acknowledging these interests, it forgets that its conception of the foundation as a pure will presupposed the subjectivity and normative insignificance of all interests. Legal thought can remain within the framework of formal right only as long as it persists in this self-deception—only as long as it does not synthesize the formal will and its embodiment in a new conception of the foundation. Once it does so, the framework of formal right is transcended. A new paradigm of law unfolds from the idea of the self-*determination* of the will—from the idea that the self is an end not in flight from all interests but in transforming reality in accordance with freely chosen projects. Freedom is now understood not simply as a negative capacity always to have done otherwise but also as a positive power to act from self-expressive goals. But since this kind of freedom depends on material conditions as well as on personal cultivation, it is no longer an abstraction from every conception of the good; it is rather itself such a conception. And once the foundation of right is conceived as a common good, the way is open to viewing law as an instrument for promoting it.

Perhaps because he understands the unsteadiness of the abstract will as a basis for a noninstrumental model of law, Weinrib offers an alternative exposition of his theory of tort law.[49] In this version, there is no mention of personality, the free will, or abstract right. Instead, the idea that integrates tort law in noninstrumental terms is the correlativity of doing and suffering harm and of plaintiff's right and defendant's obligation in corrective justice. A basic feature of classical tort law is that the tortfeasor is obligated to pay compensation to the plaintiff, and the plaintiff is entitled to receive exactly what the defendant is obligated to pay. There is thus a nexus between plaintiff and defendant that is instantiated in all valid institutional and doctrinal features of tort law, for example, in the bipolar format of the lawsuit and in the various conditions of liability (the defendant's action must have caused harm to a plaintiff and must have breached a duty owed specifically to the plaintiff rather than to the public at large). Understanding tort law in light of this nexus is superior to instrumentalist interpretations, argues Weinrib, because it alone reproduces tort law as a coherent whole wherein each of its procedural and doctrinal elements is notionally contained in every other. Instrumentalist theories, by contrast, reproduce tort law as an incoherent hodgepodge of conflicting aims, for they explain each side of the plaintiff-defendant relation by a different goal that irrationally limits the conceptual thrust of competing ones. So, for example, the goal of optimal deterrence explains the defendant's obligation to pay but logically requires that he pay whether or not his negligence happened to harm a plaintiff, and fails to explain why the plaintiff receives the payment or why the amount paid is measured by the plaintiff's loss rather than by the amount needed to deter. Conversely, loss distribution justifies compensating the plaintiff but fails to explain why the defendant pays and makes irrelevant the fact that the defendant caused the harm or took all cost-justified precautions. Thus features that in tort law are indissolubly linked become decomposed through an instrumentalist rendering, as the receipt and payment of compensation are each ordered to a purpose alien to that of the other.

While these arguments have considerable force against forms of instrumentalism (e.g., economic analysis) that purport to understand tort law as it is, they are powerless against the instrumentalism whose aim is to transform tort law into a mechanism for compensating accident victims. From the perspective of this (Jamesian) antagonist, Weinrib's arguments merely capitalize on the fact that the internal coherence of tort law rests on a model of rights that this instrumentalism has rejected but whose native institutions it now wishes to turn to its own purposes. The nexus between plaintiff and defendant reflects a paradigm for which the foundation of law is the atomistic self, whose rights of proprietary sovereignty entail correlative obligations in other selves not to interfere. Since in formal right all legal obligations mirror prior rights of exclusion, no one can commit a legal wrong unless he invades another's right, and no one can vindicate his right except by securing its recognition from the person who violated it. The reform-minded instrumentalist, however, holds that the ground of law is a common good rather than a proprietary self; and he believes that individuals have rights vis-à-vis the community to the basic conditions of an autonomous life. Despairing, however, of a legal revolution that would see his communitarian vision coherently realized, the instrumentalist wishes to adapt the historically existing, bipolar framework of tort law to the new conceptual order. Because the rationality of this framework depends on individualist premises, the process of adaptation will inevitably produce the logical tensions that Weinrib dissects. But the instrumentalist will reply that the elevation of coherence to an evaluative criterion is mere fetishism, that (provided no substantive injustice is done) a partial realization of the true ground of law is better than a systematic realization of a false one. The instrumentalist will admit that his revamped tort law is no work of art;

but he will argue that aesthetic values must be subordinated to ethical ones and that a second-best strategy must be adopted when the best is impracticable.[50] In ascribing evaluative force to coherence (or "intrinsic ordering") as such, Weinrib's argument amounts to a disguised absolutization of a legal paradigm whose justness the instrumentalist contests and whose natural necessity he denies. Furthermore (as Weinrib admits), the argument from coherence obviously has no force against the coherent actualization of the common good through the abolition of tort law in a scheme of social insurance.

Accordingly, in thematizing now coherence and now the abstract will, Weinrib oscillates between a foundation without normative force and a conception of normativity without solid foundation. Nevertheless, Weinrib's failure adequately to defend a noninstrumental model of tort law illuminates the path we must take. It teaches us that a cogent defense of this model must first face up to the transience of the formalist legal paradigm to which the private-law model of tort essentially belongs. To persuade the instrumentalist, one must first side with him, so that one may persuade him from a standpoint that has absorbed and so fortified itself against his critique of private law. This does not mean that we must seek to justify classical tort law directly in light of some conception of the good. Since (as Weinrib has shown) classical tort law derives its internal coherence from the formalist foundation, it would be the merest chance if it could be justified independently of that foundation. We are faced, therefore, with the following dilemma: a noninstrumental tort law cannot rest securely on the formalist foundation and probably cannot rest on anything other than the formalist foundation. The abstract self that alone supports a private law of tort is an unstable ground of law.

Formulating the problem in this way, however, suggests a promising approach to a solution. If a private law of tort is to be justified, it must be justified on a normative foundation that reinstates and encompasses formal right as a necessary condition of its own validity. A cogent defense of classical tort law must thus combine self-criticism with justification. It must show that the private-law model of tort rests on an untenable conception of the ground of law but that this conception (along with the paradigm it orders) is nevertheless necessary to a totality that embodies an adequate conception.

That the formalist legal paradigm is both transitory and normatively valid is, of course, the paradox that Hegel teaches in his philosophy of law. Hegel, however, did not try to develop this thesis in detailed jurisprudential studies; his account of tort in the *Philosophy of Right* is extremely cursory and general and is based on a tradition that antedates the development of negligence law. There is thus no full-blown theory of tort that one can simply extract from Hegel's writings through exegesis. Nevertheless, there is a philosophical method that one may apply to the tradition of tort law as it currently stands in order to produce a theory of tort that, if not Hegel's, is at least Hegelian. This is what I shall endeavor to do. More specifically, I shall try to give a theoretical account of the contemporary crisis of tort law that—in the spirit of Hegel—assigns to the classical model a continued, though subordinate, role in a mature legal system.

2. TORT LAW IN FORMAL RIGHT

2.1 The General Form of the Argument

A theory of tort consists of three main elements: a theory of rights, a theory of wrong, and a theory of remedies. The theory of rights is the principal part of a theory of tort, for once we understand how a right is established we shall also understand what kinds of events contradict it and what must be done to actualize the right in the face of these events. This means that the foundations for a theory of tort have already been laid, for Chapter II dealt with the preconditions of a legally recognizable right of ownership, breach of which is a tort. In that chapter, I argued that a property right is the legal certificate bestowed on a process whereby personality's claim to be an absolute end has acquired objective reality. This process comprised three distinct stages—possession, use, and exchange—representing progressively more adequate objectifications of the person's end-status in relation to things. Because the stages are modes of objectifying personality as an absolute end, each confers a right that other persons must (according to the paradigm of formal right) respect. Now, since a tort is, in Blackstone's phrase, "a privation of right,"[51] an understanding of tort requires that we traverse the stages of property again, this time with a view to deriving the elements of the wrong correlative to the right conferred at each stage. To each modality of property there will correspond a distinctive way of infringing the right, and this will give us an account of the elements of civil wrong that respects the diversity of common-law torts.

Before I begin, however, I want to outline in advance the general form of the argument to follow. My aim is to present a case for the validity of a noninstrumental model of tort law that is persuasive to one who holds that human welfare is the end of law. To that end I begin with a critique of the model of tort law that asserts the normative insignificance of welfare. This critique lays bare the basic tension in formalist tort law—that between the law's overt indifference to considerations of welfare and its covert attention to such matters, a tension focally exemplified in the ancient distinction between trespass and the action on the case. We have already observed this contradiction at various points in our analysis thus far. In the chapter on property, we noted the tension within formal right between the abstract conception of the end overtly governing the paradigm and the necessity for this end's objective realization. Formal right rests on a view of the absolute end as a self abstracted from interests indiscriminately regarded as subjective; at the same time it acknowledges that the self must embody its end-status in control of its body and in external property. On the one hand, welfare is equated with preference satisfaction and so excluded from the public ground of law; on the other hand, certain interests are admitted to be essential to personality's freedom, so that the notion of welfare has a public meaning. This is the latent contradiction of the formalist paradigm, and the development of this model consists in a movement toward its resolution—one that, however, bursts the limits of the framework.

The tension is implicitly overcome when the action on the case moves from the periphery of tort law to the center—when negligence displaces trespass as the central case of civil wrongdoing. The wrong of negligence consists in a breach of a duty of affirmative care for the conditions of another's effective freedom and is complete regardless of whether proprietary sovereignty is infringed. Negligence law thus recognizes a right to a certain level of security from harm to interests essential to human welfare. Once this right is self-consciously grasped, the idea of a formal liberty abstracted from interests and indifferent to welfare can no longer endure as the ground of law. It yields to the idea of effective autonomy (or positive freedom) as the proper goal of legal institutions; and this reformulation of law's foundation creates a theoretical drive to revolutionize tort law in its image, first through enterprise liability and ultimately through an explicit scheme of social insurance exclusive of tort law.

We shall see that the movement of negligence from periphery to center can be grasped in conceptual terms. The ascendancy of fault-based liability in the nineteenth century was not a historical accident, nor is it adequately understood as a reflection of the prevailing ideology of laissez-faire[52] or as a judicial subsidization of industrial growth.[53] Whatever the motives that induced historical actors to generalize fault-based liability, the movement from trespass to negligence has its own inner rationality, consisting in a development toward an end. The development involves the progressive self-validation of the person in possession, use, and contract— a process through which personality learns by stages the intersubjective basis of its worth. As property rights gradually come to be understood as emerging from a relation of mutual recognition, the wrong correlative to the right (trespass to possession, nuisance to use) is pari passu conceived as a transgression of limits more and more intersubjectively defined. Finally, the realization of personality's end-status in the contractual relation leads to the grasping of negligence as the paradigm of wrongdoing; for negligence law is (as we shall see) nothing but the structure of mutual benefaction underlying contract but emancipated from the consensual form and asserted as an independently authoritative normative standard. Negligence law is implicit in contract law, and the idea of social insurance is implicit in negligence law. There is thus an unbroken conceptual path from trespass to negligence to social insurance. The full realization of the end of formalist tort law itself leads to tort law's demise.

The exhibition of this development is the argument for the transience of the formalist model of tort law and for the validity of social insurance. It is also a philosophical account of the modern crisis of classical tort law. The argument for tort law's continuing validity as part of a whole consists in showing (a) that the absolutization of positive freedom as the end of law contradicts rather than realizes the end-status of the person; (b) that the self-contradictoriness of both positive freedom and formal liberty when absolutized to the exclusion of the other reveals the genuine ground of law as dialogic community—the mutual recognition as ends of community and individual selfhood; (c) that this relationship is latently and progressively embodied in each of the stages of personality's self-realization; and (d) that these stages are therefore preserved as phases of dialogic community's self-realization as the authentic ground of law.

2.2 The Attributes of Formal Tort Law

We have seen that the distinctive quality of the formalist foundation of law is its abstractness. The end that alone commands respect is a self emptied of all interests and judgments of value, a self conceived solely as a capacity for choice. Since, moreover, welfare denotes the satisfaction of interests, the normative insignificance of interests means that an individual's welfare need be of no concern to others. Whether an act promotes or damages a person's welfare is considered irrelevant to whether a wrong has occurred, for welfare is identified with the gratification of subjective wants having no moral power to bind others.[54] The abstractness of the formalist foundation is reflected in the three basic features of classical tort law: the disjunction between wronging and harming, the rule excluding liability for nonfeasance, and the correlativity of right and obligation.

In formal tort law, one can wrong a person without harming him and one can harm him without committing a wrong. That one can wrong without harming is shown by our earlier example of the physician who injects someone with a riskless and lifesaving drug against the will of the recipient. Such an act is unquestionably a battery. That one can harm without wronging is illustrated by the case of *Fountainebleu Hotel Corp. v. Forty-Five-Twenty-Five, Inc.*[55] There the defendant planned to construct a fourteen-story addition to his resort hotel that would have cast a shadow over the swimming pool and sunbathing area of the plaintiff's neighboring hotel. There was evidence that construction of the tower would result in serious injury to the plaintiff's interests. The trial judge granted the plaintiff an injunction on the sole ground that "no one has a right to use his property to the injury of another." However, the appellate court reversed the decision, pointing out that the maxim *sic utere tuo ut alienum non laedas* meant "only that one must use his property so as not to injure the lawful *rights* of another."[56] Since the plaintiff had no right to the unobstructed flow of sunlight over adjoining land, the defendant had done him no actionable wrong; and the fact that the plaintiff would suffer serious harm from the defendant's action was irrelevant.

The contrast drawn by the court between injury to interests and injury to rights is intelligible in terms of the distinction between abstract personality and its determinate interests. Because in formal right all interests have the significance of subjective preferences, welfare denotes nothing but the satisfaction of such preferences, and doing harm to another means diminishing his level of satisfaction. Since there can be no right (absent contract) to a person's solicitude for one's pleasure, there is no wrong in harming per se. Rather, one has a right only to the other's respect for one's person as an end, so that only those actions are wrongs which infringe one's property or interfere with one's freedom of movement. Since the actions of the defendant in building on his own land violated no property right of the plaintiff, the latter had no basis for legal complaint.[57]

The abstractness of the formalist foundation is further reflected in the general rule of tort law that one owes another no coercive duty to save him from harm. Within the formalist model, legal duties are exclusively negative duties not to encroach on another's sovereignty with respect to his or her body or external possessions; there is in general no liability for failing to act even when action could save a life or limb at no risk to oneself.[58] As we have seen in earlier chapters, the rule excluding liability for nonfeasance might be valid even were formal right not the final word about rights; for even if one acknowledges a right to welfare objectively conceived, the duty-bearer must be the community rather than any single individual. However, such considerations play no role within formal right itself. Here liability for nonfeasance is excluded, not because the duty to protect real welfare lies with the community, but because no distinction is recognized between real and subjective welfare. All interests are regarded as particular interests, and there is no compellable duty on a free self gratuitously to serve the pleasure of another.[59]

That the ground of obligation in formal tort law is the abstract self is also reflected in the correlative structure of tort law's rights and duties. Since the fundamental end is conceived as a capacity for choice, the person's right consists solely in a liberty to act as he or she pleases within a zone that others must respect and that is consistent with their equal right. Thus a right in one person implies a negative obligation in another not to interfere, and conversely, all obligations presuppose exclusionary rights in others. This correlative structure of rights and duties, where one person's right is *another's* duty, can be contrasted with a structure of complementarity, where one's rights (e.g., to state benefits) presuppose one's own positive obligations to others and where one's positive obligations are binding only insofar as one has reciprocal rights to another's affirmative concern.[60] Here, in other words, a right in one person implies a duty not only in another but also in the right-bearer, and a duty presupposes a right not only in another but also in the person obliged. For rights and duties to coalesce in one person, however, there must be a right to the positive action of others, and yet such a right is inconceivable within a paradigm founded on the abstract self.

2.3 The Latent Contradiction

Although the abstract self is in theory the foundation of classical tort law, the latter in its practice constantly confesses the untenability of this ground. It does so, first of all, by protecting the *embodiments* of freedom in control of one's body and of external possessions, recognizing that the will is free only in exercising exclusive authority over these things. The protection of sovereignty with respect to body and property is already inconsistent with the claim that the pure self is an absolute end, for it testifies that the self is an absolute end only as embodied. But second, the necessity for embodiment further implies that the self cannot be indifferent either to the well-being of its body or to the quantity or condition of its property, since both are needed for the actualization of its freedom. Yet because the explicit foundation of classical tort law excludes from normative significance all concrete interests of personality, the inescapable relevance of *some* interests is acknowledged only tacitly and without allowing this admission to penetrate the citadel of abstraction. The result is a pattern of dissemblance revealed in the following phenomena of classical tort law.

First, a victim of a trespass is entitled to recover from the defendant not only nominal or restitutionary damages for an infringement of his property right but also real damages for any harm caused to his body or property as a result of the trespass. On the one hand, the formalist paradigm views the person's end-status as realized in a purely intellectual ownership abstracted from sensuous interests; on the other, it compensates the plaintiff not only for conceptual contradictions of title but also for physical damage to the res.[61] On the one hand, wrongdoing is intelligible wholly apart from doing harm, so that it is possible to suffer a wrong without suffering damage; on the other, personal injury and property damage are regarded as part of the wrong suffered by the plaintiff, but this admission is not allowed to confront the initial absolutization of the abstract self (nor, correlatively, the belief in the subjectivity of all interests) underlying the disjunction between wronging and harming as well as the exclusion of positive obligations.

Second, we have the fundamental distinction within formalist tort law between trespass and case. Within a legal formation ordered to abstract personality and its proprietary embodiment, wrongdoing *is* trespass, for the latter is just the interference with one's exclusive authority over one's body and possessions. Initially, therefore, the only writs available in the King's Court were those alleging that the defendant had, with force and arms, imprisoned or assaulted the plaintiff or had broken the plaintiff's close or had carried off his goods, all variants of the writ of trespass. Anyone who suffered harm as a result of nontrespassory conduct had suffered no recognizable wrong. In the thirteenth or (perhaps) fourteenth century,[62] however, there emerged a writ initially called "trespass on the case" (i.e., suited to the particular facts of the plaintiff's case) and later nicknamed the "action on the case" or simply "case." The original understanding of case saw it as involving wrongful harm but without the use of force that was initially considered the hallmark of trespass. In later centuries, however, this view underwent revision. Ignoring the original connection (reflected in the technical phrase *vi et armis*) of trespass with forcible usurpations of proprietary sovereignty, judges in the eighteenth century began to distinguish case from trespass by focusing on the consequential character of the damage recoverable in case and contrasting this with the direct damage recoverable in trespass.[63] Thus (to take the usual example), if A drops a beam on B's head, he causes direct damage, and B must sue in trespass; but if A drops a beam in the street and B subsequently trips over it, any damage is indirect and B's action lies in case. However, since a trespasser was liable for all consequential damage resulting from his trespass, the distinction between direct and indirect damage never truly corresponded to that between trespass and case and only served to conceal the latter's real significance.

The crucial feature of case was not that damage was indirect but that damages for harm to the body or to items of property were recoverable (on the basis of negligence) even though the damage was unconnected to any interference with liberty or proprietary sovereignty. That is to say, the most important fact about the action on the case was that it gave a remedy for a wrong that was *not* a trespass. The person who negligently dropped a beam in the street had neither invaded anyone's property nor interfered with anyone's freedom of choice; nevertheless, he was obliged to repair the injuries suffered by anyone who faultlessly tripped over the beam. Evidently, the action on the case protected a right to a certain degree of security from harm to essential interests rather than a proprietary right in the strict sense, and so took to its logical conclusion the recoverability in trespass itself for real (as opposed to nominal) damages. But the legal protection of essential interests—of the existing condition of one's body and possessions—is entirely inconsistent with the abstract foundation of formalist tort law; and so until the nineteenth century the action on the case occupies a kind of conceptual hinterland ancillary to trespass, with no attempt (beyond the pretense that case was a modification of trespass distinguished only by the indirectness of the damage) being made to integrate the two ideas into a unified theory of wrong.

Third, we have in classical tort law the defense of necessity by which someone can overcome the injunctive bar to a taking of property if his life is threatened and provided he compensates the property owner afterward.[64] That this defense is problematic for formalist tort law becomes clear when we set it alongside the rule against liability for nonfeasance. No one owes a legal duty to offer succor to a needy person, but there is, it seems, a legal duty not to withhold one's goods from such a person if he has already laid hold of them. Thus, in *Depue v. Flateau*,[65] the plaintiff had come by horse-drawn carriage to the defendant's farmhouse on a winter evening to discuss business. While there, he fell ill and asked his host if he could spend the night. The defendant refused, and the plaintiff was found the next day lying on the roadside suffering from exposure. The court held the defendant liable for turning the plaintiff out in his condition, although it conceded that the defendant would have owed no duty to invite a freezing traveler into his home. The rule against liability for failing to offer one's resources assumes that all interests are subjective and so can generate no coercive duties in others; the rule against resisting a necessary taking of one's resources assumes an objective ranking of the interests in property and life according to their value for freedom and permits a taking of property when necessary to preserve the person that justifies property in the first place. The defense of necessity is thus radically at odds with the premises of the formalist paradigm; and perhaps for this reason it has traditionally led a shadowy existence on the periphery of tort law, one that judges are reluctant to acknowledge and that scholars continually puzzle over.[66]

In all these phenomena, then, we see the tension between formal tort law's constitutive indifference to considerations of welfare and its tacit acknowledgment of certain interests as essential to the freedom it exalts as an end. This tension is itself constitutive of formalist tort law; it can be resolved only in a conception of law's foundation that synthesizes freedom and welfare and that thus takes us beyond the formalist paradigm. Let us now see how the internal development of the formalist principle itself leads to this synthesis.

3. FROM SELF-RELATION TO DIALOGIC COMMUNITY

3.1 Possession, Trespass, and Strict Liability

We must return to the beginning of personality's quest for self-validation as an end. We have seen that the person's objective realization draws it by stages into association with another self, but that this social foundation of the person's worth is not fully explicit until the stage of contract. The pre-contractual modes of personality's self-realization assume that the person is an end in atomistic isolation, and this assumption will shape the law's understanding of the nature of wrong. Specifically, if the person has a right to exclusive control of its body and possessions that is established independently of the will of others, then it is wronged by any interference with its will in respect of those things regardless of whether the interference is intentional or unintentional, negligent or unavoidable—in short, regardless of fault. This is so because a requirement of fault implies that the plaintiff's right not to be imposed on is mediated by the defendant's right to act freely within certain bounds; the plaintiff's right is not absolute but is limited by the area within which the defendant can act free of responsibility to the plaintiff. A requirement of fault, in other words, implies a fully intersubjective definition of rights. Where, however, rights are understood asocially, no accommodation will be made to the defendant's liberty in defining the plaintiff's right. Thus the counterpart in tort law to an asocial or self-related conception of the person's right is strict liability.

The most asocial embodiment of personality's end-status is the control it exercises over its body. The person is not an end unless it is the end of its own action, of which the body is a necessary instrument.[67] Divorced from purposive action, the person is the end of nothing and therefore no end at all. Because the person is not an end apart from its expression in purposive motion, its absolute end-status entails a right to control its body. This means that the right to self-possession is established a priori and so independently of any relationship with another. But since the corporal boundary of one's sovereignty is defined asocially, it presupposes no deference to other wills; hence the right of self-possession is not limited by any qualified freedom of others to use one's body. As far as other individuals are concerned, the right to self-possession is absolute.[68]

Furthermore, the right to self-possession is not conditional on the person's having done anything to reduce or discipline the body to its will.[69] In contrast to the situation with respect to external things, the person need not have taken the body into its possession through physical education to acquire an exclusive right to control its motion; it has such a right even if it has always neglected its body. The reason, once again, is that the person's end-status cannot be conceived except in relation to a body of whose motion it is an end. Because the connection between the person's worth and its right to self-possession is a priori, the right is independent of any particular action of the person. By contrast, it makes no sense to say that the person is an end of anything external to it unless it has actually reduced the thing to its possession.

The failure to respect the end-status of personality as manifested in the control it exercises over its body is the tort of trespass to the person, specified as assault, battery, and forcible confinement. The essence of the tort is the displacement of the victim's will by the tortfeasor's as master of his or her body whether by destroying it as an organism, maiming it, confining it, or by touching it without the victim's consent. The wrong here does not consist in personal injury resulting from the transgression of a moral boundary reconciling liberties. Such a conception of wrongdoing assumes a social understanding of rights that has not yet made its appearance. At this stage the person's right is not to a certain intersubjectively defined level of security against harm; rather, it is a purely individualistic or self-related right to control one's body. Because the wrong correlative to this right consists in an interference with self-possession rather than an infliction of harm, it is actionable without proof of damage.

Now since the right of self-possession is established prior to any social interaction, any voluntary interference with self-possession is wrong and it makes no difference whether the defendant acted reasonably or unreasonably, with fault or without. If A strikes B accidentally and nonnegligently, he has committed a trespass against B because B did not want to be struck.[70] If a natural force moves A's arm so that it strikes B, there is no wrong, for there is here no usurpation of B's will by A's, hence no event that contradicts B's exclusive sovereignty over his body. Accordingly, infringement of the right to self-possession requires a voluntary act, but that is all. If A touches a nonconsenting B, A has committed a trespass against B even if he thought B was consenting and even if the belief was reasonable in the circumstances, for B's control over her body has certainly been interfered with; she did not want the contact and yet she was made to suffer it. However, liability is strict only for interference with self-possession and hence only for nominal damages or for purposes of an injunction, assuming (a fanciful hypothesis, to be sure) that such a remedy were feasible. Liability for physical injury presupposes a right to security against harm, and because such a right is (as we will see) determined intersubjectively, the wrong of inflicting harm is not committed without fault.

It may be thought that this account of trespass is at odds with the common law. The story usually told of the evolution of tort law is that strict liability for trespass is ancient law, that in the late nineteenth century strict liability came (albeit with certain exceptions) to be replaced by fault-based liability, and that trespass now refers only to intentional harms.[71] However, this story is too simple. The historical evolution of tort law has not been from strict liability to fault but from an undifferentiated liability regime toward one of increasing subtlety and refinement.[72] Ancient law imposed strict liability for trespass and did not distinguish in this regard between nominal and real damages or between damages and injunction: strict liability held no matter what the plaintiff's remedy. Ancient law did not bother with these distinctions because its formalist foundation in the abstract self could not coherently accommodate the infliction of harm as a possible wrong distinct from the wrongs of interference with self-possession and proprietary sovereignty. The latter were the paradigm cases of wrong-doing, and so if you suffered harm as a result of a trespass you obtained damages on the same no-fault basis that governed trespass per se.[73] The transformation wrought in the nineteenth century consisted not in the overthrow of strict liability but in making fault the basis of all liability for *personal injury and damage to property*—that is, for harm.[74] This development, however, left untouched strict liability for interference with self-possession. Strict liability for trespass has never disappeared; it has simply fallen from its status as the liability regime of tort law to a more subordinate and minor position. It is now the liability regime of a particular aspect of tort law—that which specifically vindicates (through nominal damages, restitution, and injunctions) the rights to self-possession and proprietary sovereignty.[75]

The end-status of the person is not adequately objectified in control of its body, since the person remains confronted by external objects apparently independent of it. Thus the objective realization of personality as an end further requires the reduction of external things to its will. Since this reduction is an actualization of the person's end-status in relation to the thing, it confers a right to exclusive possession valid against the world. This right has more of a social dimension than the right to self-possession, because the right requires some external act of taking control of which others must have notice if they are to be capable of respecting it. Hence possession must, to confer a right, satisfy an intersubjective standard of control: the claimant must have exercised the control of which the thing is capable and that a prudent owner would have sought.[76] However, this social dimension is merely embryonic, for the right to exclusive possession is held to depend on a unilateral acquisition requiring no leave from (and hence no reciprocal accommodation to) any other will.[77] In formal right, one has a right to whatever one possesses first, and there are no limits besides another's property to the right of accumulation.

It follows from this asocial conception of the right to exclusive possession that liability for interference is once again strict.[78] If A takes something out of B's possession, he must return it or pay B an equivalent value even if he reasonably believed the thing was his own. If A enters land previously occupied by B, B can eject A even if A reasonably believed his occupation was first, and B can get nominal damages for a trespass.[79] The right to exclusive possession is established independently of any other will, and so (vis-à-vis other individuals) the right is held absolutely. Moreover, where unilateral possession is taken to be the paradigm of property rather than an imperfect modality thereof, liability will be strict not only for interference with proprietary sovereignty but also for damages resulting from such interference. Some of the enclaves of strict liability in tort law—those involving crop damage by straying domestic animals, for example—are probably best understood as holdovers from this privileging of asocial possession as the model of the person's rights against others. However, as better and more social embodiments of personality's end-status are achieved, distinctions are drawn between usurpations of proprietary sovereignty and harms to welfare interests and between the strict liability regime connected to the former and the fault principle appropriate to the latter.[80]

3.2 Use and Nuisance

The social constitution of property that is incipient at the stage of possession becomes more explicit at the stage of use, though the latter still presupposes atomistic and self-related persons. We have seen that use confers a property superior to that established by bare possession, because use signifies a more thoroughgoing reduction of the thing to one's will and so a better objectification of the will as an end. The basis of the right to use is thus still the unilateral and asocial reduction of the thing to the will. However, whereas at the stage of possession the intersubjective ground of property showed itself only in a requirement of publicity and so in the need for the recognizability of rights established outside of society, here at the stage of use the right is itself defined intersubjectively. One does not have a property in whatever uses one desires for one's land or in whatever uses one stakes out first; for this would mean that someone who wished to use his land in ways incompatible with a neighbor's desired use must unilaterally renounce his interests for the sake of the neighbor's pleasure contrary to his equal status as an end. Rather, one has a property only in "ordinary" uses—that is, only in uses in which every person has a like property, for then the deference of one person to another is matched by the other's equal and reciprocal deference to him.[81] One has a right only to that use which another self can recognize without compromising his equal status as a self.

Not only is property in use mediated through the concept of ordinary use; the concept of "ordinary" is itself socially mediated, in that one's property in uses is internally limited by the other's freedom to use his land for purposes that are ordinary in a given social environment. "A dweller in towns," wrote Lord Halsbury, "cannot expect to have as pure air, as free from smoke, smell, and noise as if he lived in the country."[82] The locally relative definition of ordinary use again ensures that one person's deference to another is compatible with the equal end-status (and so property right) of both. No one is compelled to sacrifice the ordinary use of his land for the sake of a neighbor's comfort or convenience; rather, each is free to interfere with the other's use as long as he keeps within the locally customary uses with which others may likewise interfere with him. Conversely, each person's use is vulnerable to interference from the other to the same extent as the other's use is vulnerable to him. Each pays to others the same degree of respect as they pay in return.[83]

Inasmuch as property in use reflects an accommodation between dissociated users of land, it occupies a middle ground between an asocial and a fully intersubjective establishment of rights. This in-between status is reflected in the nature of the wrong correlative to property in use. To the extent that user rights are intersubjectively defined, they can be violated only by a breach of reciprocity in the exercise of the liberty to use one's land. One does not commit a nuisance as one commits a trespass—by the invasion of a boundary established in one's absence. Thus the mere physical emission of noises, fumes, smells, or vibrations onto another's land does not by itself amount to a nuisance; nor does the simple interference with an already established use of the plaintiff: "first in time is first in right" is a maxim applicable to possession but not to use.[84] Rather, one commits a nuisance only through a socially extraordinary use of one's land that interferes with the ordinary use of another's. Such a use is wrongful because it arrogates to oneself a degree of liberty to interfere with another greater than that to which one submits in return. It thus claims a right of action with respect to another that the other cannot, consistently with his equal end-status, recognize as valid.

The asocial character of use as an embodiment of personality is likewise reflected in the nature of the wrong correlative to property in use. Specifically, it is reflected in the irrelevance of fault to liability for nuisance. If one's exceptional use interferes with another's ordinary use, then one has wronged the other even if the interference could not have been avoided by the exercise of reasonable care. This is so because one's property in use is socially mediated only up to a point. A user right is limited by the neighbor's equal right to the ordinary use of his own *land*, but it is absolute in relation to the neighbor's freedom to pursue *extra-proprietary ends* that impose risks of harm on others. Property in use is absolute in relation to such freedom because it is established outside of social interaction. One acquires a property in use simply by using. The right is not *received* from another self whose freedom one would then have to reciprocally accommodate in order to preserve his qualification (as a free self) to give a satisfying recognition. Since the framework of formal right presupposes dissociated and mutually indifferent property holders, the intersubjective foundation of their worth as persons appears here only as an abstract ordinariness of the uses to which they separately put their land. The situation is analogous to the commodity fetishism analyzed by Marx in the first volume of *Capital*.[85] Just as atomistic producers are related only through the equivalent values of the commodities they exchange, so atomistic users of land are related only vicariously through the sameness of ordinary use. There is not yet a real interaction and mutual exchange where one receives one's end-status from the deference of another provided one reciprocally acknowledges his liberty to act self-interestedly within bounds consistent with equal security. Since fault is just the imposition of risk above this threshold, it assumes a fully intersubjective foundation of rights that has yet to emerge.

This interpretation of nuisance helps us understand the famous case of *Rylands v. Fletcher*.[86] There the plaintiff's coal mines were flooded when water from his neighbor's reservoir escaped and seeped through an abandoned mine that led into the plaintiff's. The case stated to the House of Lords included a finding that the defendant had not been negligent in constructing the reservoir. The Court nevertheless held for the plaintiff. Lord Cairns stated that, while the defendant would have been immune from liability had he kept within the "natural user" of his land, once he overstepped that use he became liable for the resulting damage to his neighbor no matter how much care he took to avoid it. The case has traditionally been viewed as an exceptional pocket of strict liability within a tort law based generally on fault and, indeed, as the progenitor of a whole class of exceptions gathered under the rubric of "ultrahazardous activities."[87] However, this turns out to be a misconception. *Rylands v. Fletcher* is not an exception to a general rule of fault, because there is no such general rule. As we shall see, fault-based wrong is only the most developed conception of wrong corresponding to a fully intersubjective understanding of rights. As such, it exists alongside less developed conceptions correlative to more or less asocially constituted rights and that are essential to the truth—to the known validity—of the consummate idea. *Rylands v. Fletcher* does not stand at odds with the fault rule for tort; rather, it conforms to the strict liability rule for nuisance.*

3.3 The Relation Between Contract and Negligence Law

In possession and use, rights over things are established through unilateral action by dissociated persons, and the intersubjective ground of rights

---

*We can now draw together our accounts of strict liability in tort law as follows. 1.) Strict liability for trespass reflects an asocial constitution of possessory rights. 2.) Strict liability for harms consequential on trespass (e.g., grazing cattle) are relics of a period when trespass is the paradigmatic tort, and there is as yet no developed theory of liability for harms to fundamental interests. Such instances of strict liability are without rational support. 3.) Strict liability for nuisance reflects an asocial constitution of user rights. *Rylands v. Fletcher* is a case of strict liability for nuisance. 4.) Strict liability for ultrahazardous activities is really liability for activities that are negligent regardless of care because the product of risk × harm is so great that no feasible precautions can reduce it to the ordinary.

shows through only dimly in a requirement of publicity in the former case and in a social definition of ordinary use in the latter. In both of these modalities, however, property is imperfect, because the person seeks an objective confirmation of its final worth and yet such a confirmation is lacking as long as the person is self-related and isolated from others. The perfection of property, we have seen, occurs in contract. Here we have a real interaction between persons wherein each is confirmed as an end through the other's self-abnegation for the sake of its ownership of value. Contractual rights are socially mediated through and through: my right to the value of the other's performance depends on his promissory self-renunciation in my favor, on my reciprocal submission to him, and on the understandings of the "reasonable person" who embodies our connection. Here my right is not established through solitary action and then held to the exclusion of a faceless world; rather, it is a right in relation to a specific person with whom I enter into a relationship of mutual deference. Each does something positive for the other in return for a like affirmative action. In contract, the intersubjective foundation of rights is fully explicit.

If the process by which personality is confirmed as an end culminated in contract, the content of justice would be exhausted by the laws protecting possession, use, and contractual rights. There would be no natural rights or obligations beyond proprietary ones, for the person would be satisfied in the confirmation of ownership received through contractual exchange. However, personality is not satisfied in contract, and so justice encompasses more than proprietary rights. We will understand the origin of a more expansive body of rights if we understand the instability of contract as a resting place for personality.

The instability of contract is a product of two factors: the implicit recognition in contract of duties of affirmative action and the limitation of these duties to those to which the parties consent. First, the realization of personality in contract discloses the necessity to freedom of another self's positive deference—a necessity that, however, is only partially satisfied in contract itself. Prior to contract, the person's right was simply a negative right against interference with its sovereignty over its proprietary embodiments; hence wrongdoing consisted in a misfeasance, never in a nonfeasance. We have already understood this exclusive focus on negative rights: it follows from privileging the formal will as the absolute end, disregarding its need for realization. Yet in contract the identification of rights with negative rights is implicitly overcome, as is the dichotomy between misfeasance and nonfeasance. In contract the person's right is established by another's positive action for the sake of its objectively realized freedom. Correlatively, wrongdoing here consists in the breach of an affirmative obligation. In the relationship of mutual service between free selves, therefore, we have a foundation for a right to positive freedom. Breach of contract no doubt infringes a preexisting property right; however, it does so not by usurping another's sovereignty over possessions unilaterally acquired but by reneging on a positive commitment to another's mastery of chance. Accordingly, the realization of abstract personality in contract incipiently bursts the framework of negative rights over which the abstract person presides.[88]

We say "incipiently," because the right to another's positive action is so far limited by the consent of the person obliged. In contract, the intersubjective ground of rights has become explicit, but it is still dependent for its authority on the will of the atomistic parties.[89] This limitation is inherently unstable, however, for it implies that the normative force of the intersubjective will is underdeveloped. As a creature of the parties' will, the intersubjective will does not yet have an autonomous reality that could be realized against all assertions of individual will inconsistent with the equal end-status of persons; consequently, the absolute worth of personality still lacks objective reality. To be sure, the contract, once completed, has a life of its own that can be enforced against subjective intentions as well as against breaches of contractual obligations. However, inasmuch as it originates in consent, the intersubjective will remains subservient to the very atomistic will whose claim of self-sufficiency it disproves and whose claim to supremacy now appears as the gravamen of wrong. This subservience is reflected in the fact that the intersubjective will remains dependent on the isolated will for the specific obligations it imposes, having no content of its own to realize in the world.

Now if we emancipate the structure of mutual benefaction from the consensual form it assumes in contract; if we grasp it as the universal foundation of the person's worth and elevate it to a norm generally authoritative against all acts inconsistent with its demands; that is to say, *if persons are subject independently of their consent to a mutual duty of care,* we have, of course, the germ of the entire growth of negligence law. The person's end-status is now objective in the care taken for the embodiments of his freedom by someone whose own end-status is preserved by virtue of the other's reciprocal care for him. The confirmation of the person's worth through this relation of mutual care generates for the first time a coherent right to security against harm to essential interests; and so the discovery of this relation makes possible a rational reorganization of tort law. As long as trespass was viewed as the essence of wrong, the wrongdoing that consists in the negligent infliction of harm stood outside the conceptual unity of tort law. The recognition of such a wrong was therefore tacit only, and it fragmented tort law into inconsistent conceptions of wrongdoing. This fragmentation gave rise to the anomaly that losses consequential on trespasses were actionable without fault, while those resulting from nontrespassory conduct were recoverable only if the defendant failed to exercise due care.[90]

When, however, the relation of mutual care is grasped as the foundation of the person's objective worth, the positions of trespass and negligence are reversed. Negligence now becomes the paradigm of wrongdoing, while the ancient action for trespass (understood as a purely proprietary tort) recedes to a developmental stage on the road to a fault-based theory of wrong. This reshuffling makes possible a unified approach to recovery for harm. Since the right to security against harm is now known to be grounded in a relationship of mutual care between free and equal persons, damage to fundamental interests becomes actionable only on the basis of a failure, whether intentional or negligent, to take due care.[91] Strict liability remains the tort regime only for interferences with liberty, possession, and ordinary use.

Furthermore, the grasping of mutual care as the ground of the person's objective worth implies a corresponding rethinking of the nature of wrong. Wrongdoing is not exhausted by interferences with personal sovereignty over one's body and external possessions; that is now understood as a special case of a more general idea of wrong. The general nature of wrong—the "common ground . . . of all liability in tort"[92]—is the transgression of limits that reconcile the liberty of each with the equal *objective* freedom of all—the claiming of a right to more liberty in relation to the other than is consistent with the equal security of both in the conditions of effective freedom. Trespass, nuisance, and negligence all instantiate this idea of wrong as a breach of mutual recognition, but they do so with progressive degrees of clarity. In trespass, the idea shows forth in the voluntariness requirement, signifying that a person suffers a wrong as distinct from a misfortune only if the invasion of his sphere of control is the usurpation of another *person*. Yet in trespass the idea is dimmest, for wrongdoing here consists in the crossing of a boundary established with minimal accommodation to the claims to final worth of others: it is enough that the possessor is recognizably in control. In nuisance law, the idea is clearer, for now the boundary itself reflects the equal freedom of persons. Here we encounter for the first time a conception of wrong as the exceeding of a threshold of legitimate because reciprocal interferences, though wrong still consists only in an infringement of property. In negligence law, the idea is reflected adequately, for it is now generalized to embrace all harms to essential interests. Here we see a clear awareness that rights to security are intersubjectively defined; that persons are free to act selfishly up to a limit consistent with their equal security in the material conditions of effective freedom; that wrong thus consists in causing harm through the imposition of socially abnormal risk.

That the law of negligence merely frees the intersubjective foundation of valid rights from the consensual form of contract can be seen in the historical origins of modern negligence law. Everyone agrees that the decisive step in the evolution of the modern law of negligence was the breaking of the privity barrier. The doctrine of privity stated that where a contract governed the relation between two parties, no one outside the contractual relationship could sue a party for injuries resulting from the negligent performance of the contract. Thus, in *Winterbottom v. Wright*,[93] a mail-coach driver sued the manufacturer of a defective coach for injuries suffered when the coach broke down. Because the manufacturer was contractually responsible to the postmaster-general for the safe condition of the coach, the Court of Exchequer held that the driver, as a stranger to the contract, could not sue the manufacturer. While Lord Abinger and Baron Alderson were content to raise the specter of unlimited liability if the privity restriction were overthrown, Baron Rolfe saw the point. The manufacturer's duty to take care for the safe condition of the coach, he said, arose "solely from the contract."[94] As an affirmative obligation, it could arise only if the manufacturer had voluntarily incurred it in return for payment. Since the duty arose only through contract, it was a duty owed to the postmaster-general, who alone had given value for it. To hold the manufacturer responsible to the coachman would be to force the manufacturer to have regard for the coachman's interests without any reciprocal duty on the part of the coachman. And from such a one-sided relationship no rights can emerge.

The privity barrier was breached when common-law courts discovered a principle that satisfied the reciprocity condition of rights to affirmative action independently of the consideration requirement.* The right to another's solicitude is emancipated from the specific form it has in contract when the neighbor principle is installed as a surrogate for the bargain principle in establishing a duty to take care for another. I owe a duty of care to "persons who are so closely and directly affected by my act that I ought reasonably to have them in contemplation as being so affected when I am directing my mind to the acts or omissions which are called in question."[95] In place of a contractual relationship dependent on will we now have a notional relationship between persons so situated in relation to each other that they are, as rational agents, deemed to have the other in mind as likely to be affected by their acts or omissions. As between such

---

*The connection between contract and negligence law is vividly demonstrated by the law of occupier's liability, where the duty of care is just emerging from the womb of contract but is not yet fully independent. The occupier owes no positive duty of care to the trespasser or to the licensee who enters for his own benefit (he is liable only for misfeasance). He owes a duty of care only to an invitee who enters for the landowner's benefit; see F. Bohlen, "The Basis of Affirmative Obligations in the Law of Tort," 44 *Amer. Law Reg.* 209, 220–234 (1905). Thus the duty of care is independent of consent, and yet it requires consideration. Only when a principle is discovered to substitute for consideration does negligence law assert its full independence of contract.

persons, the duty of care of one to the other is consistent with the end-status of both, since the duty is reciprocal and of equal scope. The mutual care of "neighbors" is thus freed from their contingent consent and imposed on them as an independently authoritative basis of their rights.[96]

4. DIALOGIC COMMUNITY IN THE LAW OF NEGLIGENCE

We have been calling the relationship of mutual recognition between free and equal selves dialogic community. Since the conscious grasp of this relation as the source of individual rights underlies the law of negligence, we can resume the interpretive method we employed in the chapter on contract. That is to say, we shall understand negligence law by recognizing in its central doctrines the intersubjective structure characteristic of dialogic community. Let us first briefly recall the elements of this structure.

An individual right begins as a claim of absolute worth by the person. This claim must be objectively validated, and the right enforced by law is the outcome of the process of validation—the legal recognition of a claim that has gained implicit confirmation prior to enforcement. The person's claim of absolute worth is satisfyingly validated only through the submission to its freedom of another self, for only another self has the requisite alterity and independence to confirm objectively the end-status of another. In contract, the submission of one self to another is centrally effected through promise; apart from contract, it consists in the care exercised by one self for the human welfare of the other. To give an effective or satisfying recognition (i.e., to constitute the other's right to care), however, the self must preserve its independence in its submission, and this is possible only if the other self reciprocally submits to the end-status of the first. In contract, where affirmative duties are narrowly circumscribed by the will of the parties, this reciprocal act of submission can take the relatively simple form of a promise or the performance of some discrete service. However, to gain a right to the generalized care of another, a more complicated exchange must occur if the other's end-status is to be preserved in its submission. In particular, the self can retain its independence in generally caring for another's welfare only if the following two conditions are fulfilled: first, the self must reserve (and gain recognition for) a space for self-oriented action, that is, a space where it can act for its own ends free of any requirement to defer to the other's interests; second, the object (O) of the self's (S) care must reciprocally defer to S's welfare to the same degree as S defers to O. We can call the first condition of a valid right to care the requirement of equal respect; we can call the second the requirement of equal concern.[97]

Accordingly, the self's worth is objective only within a relationship of mutual regard between selves who are conscious of themselves as ends;

and so legally recognizable rights to another's care are grounded in such a relationship. This means that a right to another's care is the product of a threefold mediation. The self's worth is mediated, first of all, through another self's respect for its liberty to pursue its self-interest as well as through the other's concern for the well-being of the necessary instruments of its doing so; second, it is mediated through the self's reciprocal respect and concern for the other; third, it is mediated through the connection formed by each self's need for the other's freedom—a connection ensuring that the dependence of each on the other's will is compatible with their mutual preservation as ends. Our task now is to interpret the basic doctrines of negligence law as embodiments of this structure.

4.1 The Standard of Care

According to the rule in *Vaughan v. Menlove*,[98] one must compensate another for injuries caused by one's failure to take the care that an ordinarily prudent person would have taken in the circumstances. A full comprehension of this rule requires an understanding of its three components. First, one is liable to compensate a person one has injured only if one was at fault, and fault is understood as a failure to take reasonable care. Second, the standard for determining whether the care one took was reasonable is an objective one; what matters is not whether the agent acted to the best of his judgment but whether he acted as a reasonable person of ordinary prudence would have acted. Third, one must understand the formula for determining how much care the reasonable person would have taken. Here there is controversy in the law, and the approach we take can suggest a solution.

First, the fault requirement. Earlier we saw that liability for trespass to the person and to property is independent of fault. Because possessory rights are established by unilateral action, they presuppose no, or (in the case of nonbodily things) only the barest, reciprocal accommodation to the liberty or welfare of others. Strict liability for trespass means that one has *no* liberty to touch another or to take his goods without consent; there is no sphere of privileged invasions. However, negligence law protects not a property right strictly understood—not an exclusionary right of sovereignty over one's body and possessions—but a right to another's affirmative care for the material conditions of one's freedom, for one's health, bodily integrity, and possessions. Thus damage or harm is essential to an action for negligence but not to an action for trespass. Moreover, the right to another's affirmative care emerges only from a complex reciprocity of respect and concern between independent selves. My worth is objective in the care exercised by another self for my sake. Yet this submission is effective to validate my worth only if it is the submission of a free self who regards himself as an end and who preserves himself as such in the relationship. Hence my worth is also mediated by my reciprocal respect for the other. To respect someone as an end, however, is to acknowledge a moral space wherein he is free to act for his own ends and to prefer these ends to mine. Hence my right to another's care presupposes my recognition of his claim to a limited sphere wherein he may act *without* care for my interests.

Now a regime of strict liability for harm implies the absence of such a sphere of self-regarding liberty. Under strict liability, one has no right to act in ways that happen to injure another. Since, however, all action carries the risk of such injury, strict liability means that I have a right that you be governed in all your actions by concern for my welfare, and you have the same right over me. No doubt there is a mutuality of care here; but it is the mutual care of extreme altruists who, because they claim no worth as independent selves, can neither give nor receive effective confirmation of worth and hence can acquire no valid right to care. By contrast, a fault requirement establishes a reciprocity of care between *selves*. Such a requirement signifies that each person acknowledges the other's liberty to act for his own ends and careless of the other within bounds compatible with their equal security against harm. Each is liable to compensate the other only if he oversteps these bounds.

So far we have understood why fault—understood as the exceeding of a threshold of reasonable indifference to the other's welfare—is the correct principle of interpersonal liability for causing harm. We have now to consider the specific issue raised in *Vaughan v. Menlove*—whether the reasonableness of risk-imposing conduct should be determined by the best judgment of which the defendant is capable or by that of the ordinarily prudent person. We will understand the law's decision in favor of the objective standard when we see it as required by the structure of dialogic community.

It will help to recall the facts in *Vaughan v. Menlove*. The defendant built a hayrick on the edge of his field close to the wood and thatch buildings of his neighbor. He was warned that hayricks are prone to spontaneous combustion and that they posed a danger to the surrounding area. Nevertheless, the defendant decided to "chance it." Sure enough, the hayrick burst into flames and destroyed the neighboring buildings. The trial judge instructed the jury to find for the plaintiff if they thought that the defendant failed to exercise the care of the ordinarily prudent person. The defendant appealed against this instruction, arguing that he had done enough if he had acted to the best of his judgment and that "he ought not to be responsible for the misfortune of not possessing the highest order of intelligence."[99]

The application of our usual analysis will show that the objective standard is the only one supportive of a valid right to care. We have said that the person's end-status is confirmed through the care exercised on its behalf by another self. Yet this dependence on another's will would contradict rather than confirm the absolute worth of the person if it were a dependence on an arbitrary will external and indifferent to its own. The person is dependent on an external will if it is dependent on another's subjective opinion as to whether the care he or she exercised was reasonable. Hence if the plaintiff's right to care depended on the intelligence or other idiosyncratic capacities of the defendant, it would be no right at all. By contrast, the person's dependence on another for self-confirmation is compatible with its absolute worth (and so with a right to care) if it is dependent only through the mediator of a common will ensuring that dependence on another is consonant with autonomy. The idea of the reasonable person of ordinary prudence is this mediator. Each person is dependent for self-confirmation on an exercise of care judged sufficient not by the opinion of the other but by a reason common to both.[100]

Finally, we have to understand the formula the court applies to determine the standard of ordinary prudence. Here the American and Commonwealth traditions are at odds. Following Judge Learned Hand's test in *United States v. Carroll Towing*,[101] American courts determine whether conduct is negligent by comparing the present cost of a potential accident with the cost to the defendant of avoiding it. The present cost of the accident is calculated by multiplying the expected cost by the probability of the accident's occurrence. Thus, if the expected cost of an accident is L, the probability P, and the cost of avoidance B, the defendant is negligent if he failed to take precautions when $B < L \times P$. If the cost of avoidance is greater than the present cost of the potential accident, no liability is incurred by failing to take the necessary precautions.

The English test, by contrast, takes the cost of avoidance into account only in limited circumstances. In *Bolton v. Stone*,[102] Lord Reid stated that one had a duty to avoid imposing "substantial" risk on one's neighbor. By a substantial risk he meant a risk in excess of that ordinarily adjunct to social interaction in "the crowded conditions of modern life." The magnitude of the risk was a product of the seriousness of the expected harm and the probability of its occurring. If the product of these factors is substantial in the sense of extraordinary, then one must avoid the risk whatever the cost to oneself. In *Wagon Mound, No. 2*,[103] Lord Reid amplified this rule, stating that one must also avoid a risk falling within the range of the ordinary if one can do so at no disadvantage to oneself. For Lord Reid, therefore, the cost of avoidance becomes relevant only within the range of reciprocal risks, and it works only to enlarge the sphere of duty, never to contract it. Which test—the English or the American—is the proper one?

In the discussion of the fault requirement, we saw that a right to care is generated only from a relationship wherein each self recognizes the other's right to prefer its own interests within bounds compatible with the equal security of both. On the one hand, the relationship must be one between persons who are mutually caring; but on the other, it must be one between mutually caring *persons*. The substantial cost test of *Bolton v. Stone* reflects such a relationship: as long as the present cost of the accident (i.e., risk times seriousness) falls within the range each imposes on the other as an incident of everyday social interaction, each may pursue his ends without thought for the safety of others. Only a nonreciprocal cost must be avoided. The amplification in *Wagon Mound* does not disturb the relationship as one between mutually caring egos, for one must take thought for the other within the range of the ordinary only if doing so involves no cost to oneself; so the principle of self-preference within the range of the ordinary still holds (although one may question whether avoidance is ever costless).

The Learned Hand formula, by contrast, reflects a relationship that either lacks mutuality of care or is not a relation between persons. Since the agent is always permitted to prefer his own interests if the cost of avoidance exceeds the present cost of the accident, the formula permits self-preference even if the risk exceeds the ordinary and so allows scope for liberty greater than that consistent with the equal security of both. Since no person could recognize such a liberty in another without compromising himself as an end (and hence without disqualifying himself as one capable of giving an effective recognition), there can be no right to a liberty of that scope. At the same time, the Learned Hand formula disallows self-preference in some cases within the range of ordinary risks, for it requires one to prefer the other's interest whenever the cost of avoidance is lower than the present cost of the accident. In requiring greater altruism than is necessary for the equal security of both, the formula envisages beings who do not assert themselves as ends and who can thus acquire no validation for their worth from the relationship. On either count, the formula generates no valid right to care.

4.2 To Whom Is a Duty Owed?

In *Palsgraf v. Long Island Railroad Co.*,[104] a guard stationed on a railway platform helped push a passenger into a train after it had begun moving and when the passenger was in danger of falling. In the process, a package containing fireworks dropped from the passenger's grasp and exploded. The force of the explosion knocked down a scale at the far end of the platform, and the scale struck Palsgraf, causing her injuries. Palsgraf sued the railroad. Justice Cardozo, speaking for a majority of the New York Court of Appeals, argued that the guard's conduct, while perhaps negligent in relation to the holder of the package, did not wrong Mrs. Palsgraf. The guard may have failed to exercise due care, but negligence in the abstract is not a tort, for the plaintiff must show that she in particular had a right to the defendant's care for her physical security. She could not do this, argued Cardozo, because "[n]othing in the situation gave notice that the falling package had in it the potency of peril to persons thus removed."[105]

Justice Andrews thought otherwise. He argued that a failure to take reasonable care for the security of others was in itself wrongful, because "[e]veryone owes to the world at large the duty of refraining from those acts that may unreasonably threaten the safety of others."[106] Someone who violated this public duty was legally responsible to anyone whom he injured whether or not the person injured was someone he could reasonably contemplate as standing within the ambit of the risk.

Andrews's conclusion is surely a non sequitur. From the fact that one has committed an offense against the public welfare it follows that one must pay the penalty for the offense; it does not follow that one has a duty to compensate an injured person. The latter duty follows only from a civil duty of care correlative to the injured person's right to one's solicitude *for her*. Cardozo believed that a plaintiff had a personal right to the defendant's concern only if she was "within the range of apprehension" as someone likely to be injured by the defendant's act. He did not say why this should be the criterion of the plaintiff's right, but we can perhaps supply the missing reasoning.

We have seen that a right to another's care is the product of a relationship of mutual concern and respect. My worth is objective in the self-abnegation for my sake of someone whose selfhood I reciprocally confirm by my respect for his liberty and by my concern within limits for his welfare. This relationship may arise contingently through contract, or it may be grasped in thought as a necessary symmetry between relations of deference. In the latter case, my right to another's care is mediated through a concept wherein the parties are so identical that the duty of care of one for the other is simultaneously the other's duty of care for the first. This is the neighbor principle according to which someone whom a reasonably circumspect person would contemplate as likely to be injured by his activity has a right to the exercise of care on his behalf. The reasonably circumspect person merges all individuals into one; hence the duty of each is matched by a reciprocal duty of all. Given this reciprocity of concern, the neighbor principle generates an authentic right to care.

Justice Andrews's principle, by contrast, fails to ensure mutuality in the parties' relationship. To compel an agent to compensate anyone who happens to be injured by his negligence is to compel his solicitude for a stranger under a rule that fails to impose necessarily reciprocal duties. Whereas plaintiff and defendant are identical in the idea of the reasonably circumspect person, they remain discrete in the sight of the Andrews principle, for the latter provides no homogenizing standpoint from which the parties' duties toward each other (however asymmetrical in fact) may be regarded as one and the same. The Andrews principle generates one-sided relationships of deference from which, as we have seen, no right can emerge.[107]

4.3 Remoteness

The same analysis helps us understand the rule governing the extent of damages for which a negligent defendant is responsible. In this regard, William Prosser once posed an interesting hypothetical:

> The defendant, delivering a parcel, drives his truck up a private driveway to the back door of a home. On the way up he notices at the side of the driveway a large paper box or carton, open and visibly empty. Two minutes later, coming down the driveway, he negligently runs over the box. Negligently, because he knows it is there, it may be owned by someone, and it has some small value. In the meantime a two-year-old child, whose presence could not reasonably be anticipated, has concealed himself in the box. Is the defendant liable for the death of the child?[108]

Prosser thought he was. He was supported at the time by the leading English case of *In Re Polemis*,[109] where it was stated that once a defendant had failed to exercise due care for the plaintiff, he was liable for all harm "directly" caused by his negligent act even if the damage was unrelated to the foreseeable harm he was obliged ex ante to prevent. However, the *Polemis* case was overruled by the Judicial Committee of the Privy Council in a case known as *The Wagon Mound, No. 1*.[110] There Viscount Simonds stated that one is liable to a plaintiff whom one has negligently injured only for the type of harm that a reasonable person would foresee as likely to result from one's failure to take care. Under the rule in *Wagon Mound*, the truck driver in Prosser's hypothetical would be liable for damage to the box but not for the death of the child.

Our analysis supports the rule in *Wagon Mound*. It is not enough to ask whether the plaintiff has a right to the defendant's care on his behalf. One must further inquire as to the kinds of harm the plaintiff may compel the defendant to avoid for his sake. The plaintiff has a right only to as much exertion for his benefit as is consistent with the equal worth of the defendant, for (as we saw) only another end can give the objective confirmation of one's worth that we call a right. Yet in the absence of a contract, liability for all chance harm would one-sidedly subordinate the defendant to the plaintiff, for the defendant would be compelled to submit to the plaintiff under a rule that fails to ensure the plaintiff's matching duty to him. By contrast, a rule limiting recovery to reasonably foreseeable harms merges the parties in the concept of the reasonably circumspect person and imposes a duty on one that is identical in all respects to that owed by the other.

4.4 Causing Harm

Suppose A breaches a duty of care owed B but the negligence does not materialize in any harm to B. Or suppose A breaches a duty of care owed B and B is harmed but not as a result of A's breach of duty; he would have suffered the same harm even had A not acted negligently. In either case, A has failed to take the care to which B has a right, but by chance the breach of duty has occasioned no harm. Why is B not entitled to nominal damages from A? Why is B not entitled to an injunction against A's negligent conduct?

One might argue that the causing-harm requirement singles out the plaintiff from the public at large as the one to whom a civil remedy is owed.[111] He is, after all, the one in whom the unreasonable risk of harm created by the defendant has materialized. But this is not an adequate answer. The neighbor principle already singles out the plaintiff as someone to whom a duty of care is owed. Why is wrongdoing not complete with the breach of this duty? There are certainly ways of enforcing a civil duty of care besides requiring the defendant to compensate for injuries caused. One could, for example, require the defendant to pay a token remedy to any foreseeable and unharmed plaintiff who brought suit; or one could allow the plaintiff to recover from the defendant the cost of any reasonable measures he took to guard against the risk.[112]

Perhaps the causation requirement singles out the *defendant* from the world at large as the person responsible for the plaintiff's injury.[113] If the defendant did not cause the injury, there is no link between him and the plaintiff's misfortune and so no more reason to lay the burden of compensation on him than on anyone else. Yet this answer assumes what must be explained. If wrongdoing is not complete until harm is caused, then of course the defendant is a wrongdoer only if *he* caused the harm. But why is the chance causing of harm necessary to wrongdoing? Why is not the defendant who has breached a duty of care owed the plaintiff already a wrongdoer? Can our theory of the foundations of a right to care support the requirement of causing harm as a necessary element of negligent wrongdoing?

The harm requirement was already implicit in the transition from a trespass theory of wrongdoing to a negligence theory. Each of these theories, we saw, presupposes a certain conception of individual rights. Since a wrong is the infringement of a right, the elements of wrongdoing are determined by the manner in which rights are defined. Now in formal right, the person's rights are proprietary only; they are rights against interference with the sovereignty of one's will over its body and possessions. Such interference is trespass, and the latter is complete even in the absence of harm to the things to which one's dominion extends, for one's sovereignty over a thing may be contradicted whether or not the thing is damaged. The rights generated by formal right are exclusively proprietary because of the abstract foundations of formal right. Where all interests are regarded as subjective, rights will attach only to the end-status of the formal will as embodied in proprietary sovereignty; there will be no explicit recognition of a right against harm to essential interests. Such a right, however, is implied in the will's need for embodiment, and so as long as formal right remains the dominant paradigm, this right will exist somewhat as a bastard child—theoretically disowned but practically acknowledged.

In negligence law, however, all this formalism and dissemblance are superseded. As a result of contract law, the person's absolute worth is known to be real in the mutual submission of independent persons, and this relationship grounds a right to the positive realization of freedom. This positive right is foundational for negligence law. The right underlying negligence law is not simply a right to do as one pleases with one's body or possessions; the plaintiff is compensated for damage even if no challenge to his proprietary sovereignty has occurred. Rather, the right vindicated by negligence law is a right to the *well-being* of the will's embodiments, a right against harm to interests essential to the objective realization of freedom. The precise scope of this right is no doubt determined in accordance with the concepts of duty, remoteness, and fault reflecting the intersubjective basis of rights. However, these concepts have no status apart from their role in framing the limits of the person's right to compel a stranger to take heed for his welfare. They do not themselves create rights but only structure a right vis-à-vis others to security against harm. Since, however, the underlying right of negligence law is a circumscribed right against harm, there is no wrong until harm is caused.

4.5 Corrective Justice

So far we have dealt with concepts—fault, duty, remoteness, harm—that define the contours of a right to another's care. We have seen that such a right is established only within a dialogic relationship reconciling selfishness and altruism. Each cares for the other's safety up to a point that allows space for their equal liberty to prefer their own ends; and each respects the other's liberty to pursue his ends within bounds consistent with their equal concern. Since a person has a right to care only within the parameters defined by this reciprocity of concern and respect, it follows that he is wronged only when indifference to his safety breaches the condition of reciprocity—that is, flows from an exercise of liberty greater than that consistent with their equal respect and concern. Such an exercise of liberty is wrong because it asserts one's end-status at the expense of another's and so claims a right to liberty in excess of that capable of being validated through the process of mutual recognition.

With this understanding of the nature of wrong we shall be able to understand the way in which the common law remedies negligent wrongdoing. The remedy takes the form of a payment by defendant to plaintiff of a sum of money sufficient to restore the plaintiff (as far as money can do so) to the level of welfare he or she enjoyed prior to the wrongful transaction. This remedy is supposed to accomplish two things at once: it is supposed to annul the defendant's wrong and to vindicate the plaintiff's right. An adequate explanation of this secondary transaction must resolve the problem we noticed in our critique of Epstein. There we observed that vindication of a victim's right requires a remedy moving from the tortfeasor (i.e., a private-law remedy) only if the victim's loss and the tortfeasor's gain are correlative. Loss and gain are correlative if one person's gain implies another's symmetrical loss and vice versa. An image might help to clarify this relation.

Imagine a teeter-totter on which two riders are sitting at opposite ends of the board. They are initially balancing the board so that each rider is equidistant from the ground. Any upward movement of one rider will necessarily involve a downward movement of the other of an equal number of degrees. The lower rider cannot return to the position of balance unless the upper rider is lowered to that position—that is, unless the upper rider yields to the lower each degree by which his position exceeds the one of balance. Only if the tortfeasor's wrongful gain and the victim's wrongful loss are related in this way does the satisfaction of the victim require that the tortfeasor surrender his gain to him; for only then can we say that the victim's loss *is* the tortfeasor's gain and vice versa.[114] Moreover, the correlativity condition must obtain if the same payment of damages is to annul the wrong and vindicate the right, for only in that case does the gain surrendered by the wrongdoer equal the deficit recovered by the victim. If plaintiff's wrongful loss and defendant's wrongful gain are not correlative, then the defendant's surrender of his gain to the plaintiff either overcompensates or undercompensates the plaintiff, and conversely the compensation of the plaintiff either leaves the defendant with some of his wrongful gains or takes these gains and then some. A perfect match would be a mere coincidence.

The problem, however, is that, while the correlativity of gain and loss is evident in wrongs involving infringements of property, it is not so evident in wrongs involving negligent inflictions of harm. In the former case, the defendant claims an authority over something that rightfully belongs to the plaintiff. The plaintiff's right can be vindicated only by the defendant's relinquishing to him the authority he wrongfully claimed, either by paying nominal damages or by returning a value equivalent to the one he took. However, where the wrong consists in an infliction of harm without an usurpation of proprietary sovereignty, we could not earlier see the correlativity between plaintiff's loss and defendant's gain. At first sight, the defendant's gain from the transaction equals the wealth he saved by forgoing the required precautions, and this amount bears no necessary connection to the loss suffered by the plaintiff. In view of this asymmetry, one might be attracted to a system of remedial justice that required wrongdoers to disgorge their wrongful gains to a public fund from which reparations would be made to victims of wrongdoing.[115] Why does the common law assume that the same sum of money annuls the defendant's wrong and vindicates the plaintiff's right? Why does it assume that remedial justice requires that the negligent tortfeasor compensate the victim?

Having come this far, we can now see that in the case of negligent wrongdoing too, there is a correlativity between plaintiff's loss and defendant's gain. Negligence consists in an infringement of a right to security against harm through an exercise of liberty greater than that which the other can, consistently with his equal end-status, recognize as valid. Just as in trespass, therefore, the wrong involves an assertion of one's end-status at the expense of another's. This means that the wrong suffered by the victim and the wrong committed by the tortfeasor are strictly correlative. The wrong suffered is a debasement of self that presupposes the self-elevation of the wrongdoer; and the self-elevation of the wrongdoer entails the debasement of the victim. The defendant's wrongful gain is not the savings realized in forgoing precautions (he would have been a wrongdoer even had the precautions cost nothing); rather, it is the preeminence vis-à-vis the plaintiff signified by his act, and this preeminence is correlative to the wrongful humbling of the plaintiff. The correlativity of wronging and being wronged means that there can be no satisfaction for the victim unless the wrongdoer gives it and no atonement for the wrongdoer unless he atones to the victim. It means that the victim's right to redress is a right exclusively in relation to the one who wronged him and that the wrongdoer's duty to make amends is a duty specifically to the person he wronged.[116]

That the victim's remedial right and the wrongdoer's remedial duty are exclusively in relation to each other explains the importance in classical tort law of a causal nexus between plaintiff's injury and defendant's negligent conduct.[117] Correspondingly, it explains the availability of defenses (such as contributory negligence) involving the claim that, while the plaintiff has been wrongfully injured and the defendant has been negligent in relation to him, nevertheless the defendant is not bound to repair the injury because his negligent conduct did not cause it. The requirement of a causal link between plaintiff's injury and defendant's negligent conduct serves to pair the persons whose wrongful gains and losses are correlative. It excludes from liability to the plaintiff all those whose wrongdoing is not at the plaintiff's expense; and it denies a right of recovery from the defendant to all those whose loss is not obversely related to the defendant's gain.

So far we have explained why the victim's remedy must move from the tortfeasor and why the tortfeasor's amends must be made to the victim. We have now to explain the specific form the remedy takes—a sum of money that compensates the victim for his or her loss of welfare.

The remedy that simultaneously annuls the defendant's wrongful gain and actualizes the plaintiff's right is one that restores the reciprocity of respect and concern as between plaintiff and defendant. Since this reciprocity was disturbed by the wrongdoer's self-exaltation at the plaintiff's expense, it can be restored only through the wrongdoer's unilateral self-humbling before the plaintiff, one just sufficient to relinquish the preeminence acquired by the tort and so to raise the plaintiff to the antecedent position of equality. The payment of damages to the plaintiff is this act of deference. Because the defendant's wrongful gain consisted in his arrogation of an unrealizable self-worth rather than in material profit, one and the same act of deference can yield up the defendant's wrongful gain and repair the plaintiff's wrongful loss.

One might object, however, that this account of corrective justice does not explain the damage award. We can see why the plaintiff's remedy must consist in the wrongdoer's unilateral submission to him. But why must this act take the form of a reparation of the plaintiff's loss of welfare? It would seem that the tortfeasor's amends could as easily take the form of an apology or a payment of token damages for an affront to a dignitary interest.

That the tortfeasor must compensate the victim for his loss of welfare follows from the concrete conception of personal dignity that underlies negligence law. The latter is based on an explicit awareness that the person's end-status is real only in a recognized right to security for the embodiments of freedom; that the claim of personal dignity is objective not only in a mutuality of respect for liberty (as in trespass and nuisance) but also in a mutuality of concern for welfare. Hence the deference required of the tortfeasor is not simply a submission to the victim's formal self; such a remedy would imply that the person's dignity is radically independent of its worldly circumstances—an implication of formal right that negligence law has forsworn. Rather, the act of deference called for is one that acknowledges what the tort denied, namely, the victim's right to as much concern for his human welfare as is consistent with the equal liberty and security of both. The tortfeasor acknowledges this right by restoring the victim to the level of welfare he enjoyed prior to the transaction that wrongfully set him back.

5. THE COMMUNITARIAN ASSAULT
ON THE PRIVATE-LAW MODEL

In the law of negligence the paradigm of formal right is already implicitly superseded. Negligence law protects a right to security against harm to essential interests and so imposes a duty of affirmative care for the conditions of another's effective autonomy. Gone, therefore, is the disjunction between wronging and harming: in negligence law there is no wrong without damage. Gone too is the hard-and-fast dichotomy between misfeasance and nonfeasance: wrong now consists not only in an invasion of spheres of private sovereignty but also in a failure to exercise care for another's welfare when a duty of care is owed. Thus, in addition to negative rights of exclusive ownership one has positive rights to concern. Superseded as well is the correlative structure of right and duty where each inheres separately in different persons. In formal right, one person's right is *another* person's duty not to interfere; in negligence law, each has rights to respect and care just insofar as he has reciprocal duties, and each owes duties just insofar as these duties are reciprocated as rights. In place of the simple correlativity of rights and duties we have a more complex structure, wherein rights presuppose duties not only in another but also in the right holder and wherein duties to others presuppose rights in the person obliged.

However, while negligence law bursts the framework of formal right, it does so in a seemingly halfhearted way. Although it recognizes a right to security against wrongful harm to essential interests, its conception of these interests is at first arbitrarily limited to those protected under formal right because linked to sovereignty interests, namely, to the interests in physical integrity and in the preservation of one's tangible possessions. Only gradually and haltingly is protection extended to other interests essential to effective autonomy—to the interest in emotional well-being and in the preservation of nontangible wealth.[118] Further, while negligence law affirms a right independent of contract to mutual care, it actualizes this right only in the limited context of transactions between atomistic persons. That is to say, negligence law grasps a bond of mutual care between free agents as the basis of their realized worth; yet instead of radically transforming rights and duties in light of this communitarian idea, it enforces rights to care only within limits consistent with formal right's view of individuals as dissociated atoms presiding over inviolable spheres of sovereignty. So, for example, one has a right *against* a person's infliction of wrongful harm but not *to* his assistance as a fellow citizen when one's life or health is in peril and when he could help at little cost to himself. In this way, formal right's dichotomy between misfeasance and nonfeasance, though implicitly transcended in negligence law, continues to limit the right to care. This constraint is illogical, however, because the communal basis of individual worth belies the self-sufficiency of the abstract self on which the distinction between misfeasance and nonfeasance rests.

The rigorous actualization of the idea of community nascent in negligence law leads to the overthrow of negligence law by social insurance.[119] The revolution begins with a matricide. Sprung from the womb of contract, modern tort law now turns against it. The right in community to concern for one's welfare destroys the freedom to define one's positive obligations by mutual agreement. More specifically, an absolute communal right to concern entails the invalidity of contractual agreements to exclude a loss spreader's liability for product defects whether the product satisfies an individual fancy or a human need (and so regardless of unequal bargaining power) and whether or not the consumer desires the bargain. Obversely, it means the firm's answerability to judicially imposed warranties holding it strictly liable for injuries caused by its products even to persons outside the contract.[120] The collapse of private law into social insurance is also reflected in a systematic assault by courts and legislatures on those features of tort law that distinguish it as a regime for remedying private wrongs between atomistic selves and that differentiate it from a public scheme for the fair distribution of the costs of desirable activity. These features are fault-based liability and the requirement of a causal link between defendant's act and plaintiff's injury.

Generalizing the communitarian idea implicit in negligence law leads to strict liability for the purpose of socializing losses and encouraging optimal investment in safety. We need not dwell long on the erosion of the fault requirement in American tort law, for it is a well-known story.[121] Our sole concern is to exhibit this development as the elaboration of a principle already germinally present in negligence law. We have already seen that negligence law grasps a relationship of mutual care between free selves as the ground of rights and that it thus embodies the insight that the individual self has objective worth only in community. However, in actualizing the right to care only against wrongdoing, negligence law remains confined by the formalist model of rights it has implicitly superseded; for it presupposes the general validity of the distinction between misfeasance and nonfeasance, or it assumes that one actualizes rights by remedying infringements but not by commanding the conferral of benefits. Yet negligence law itself affirms a duty in community of affirmative care, and nothing in the idea of this duty limits it to a negative one not to overstep a threshold of permissible risk creation. To be sure, the right to a benefit does not imply a correlative duty in any discrete individual to confer it in the way that a right to redress implies a correlative duty in the

wrongdoer to give it. However, to deny the right because there is no individual on whom the correlative obligation uniquely falls is once again to
be constrained by the atomistic mind-set of formal right that negligence
law has already transcended. If one's right to care is grounded in community, then it is a right in relation to community; and this right is equally a
duty to share the communal burden of actualizing positive rights to care.

Now to realize this communitarian idea as the basis of individual rights
is to swamp the formalist model of tort law, for the latter is ordered to the
end-status of the atomistic self. Moreover, it seems logically imperative to
carry the communitarian idea through to this extreme conclusion. After
all, the culmination in community of the self's quest for objective confirmation shows that the initial atomistic postulate was mistaken. Hence the
legal edifice built on that postulate can, it seems, be bulldozed and the
ground rebuilt in light of the new communitarian understanding of rights.
Accordingly, we must say not only that there is a right to security against
harm to basic welfare interests whether or not the harm results from
wrongdoing; we must also say that this right is exclusive, that it supplants
the right to have one's claim adjudicated as a claim of redress for wrongdoing. We must also (it would appear) evaluate solely from the standpoint
of communal goals the tort law that has historically come down to us;
which is to say, we must assess it as an instrument of compensation, deterrence, and public admonition.[122] Naturally, we will find it hopelessly deficient in these respects; indeed, since its coherence is grounded independently of these considerations, any other result would be miraculous.
Viewed as a mechanism for compensating accident victims, tort law appears as a "forensic lottery,"[123] while any advantage it might claim as a deterrent to carelessness is wiped out by the prevalence of liability insurance.
Viewed as a method of public admonition, tort law appears both inefficient and unjust: inefficient, because it punishes careless conduct only if
an accident results; unjust, because (given the objective standard of fault)
liability is unconnected to moral blame and the penalties exacted bear no
relation to whatever degree of moral fault may exist.[124] Others may object
that it is senseless to criticize tort law from the standpoint of collective
goals, for it has its own rationality, one based on individual rights and the
rectification of wrongs.[125] Yet we can perhaps now see the sense of a critique that impugns tort law for performing poorly tasks it never set for itself.[126] The individualistic paradigm on which tort law rests has yielded by
the force of its own internal logic to the communitarian one, which now
seems to possess exclusive normative force. Thus, if tort law cannot be justified by communal goals, then it cannot—it seems—be justified at all. It
must be replaced by a regime that imposes liability without fault on defendants who cause the injury and who are capable of spreading the costs
over the community through the price of their products.[127]

Who *causes* the injury? We will recall that the requirement of a causal nexus between plaintiff's injury and defendant's conduct reflected the correlativity of tortious gains and losses. Since the victim's subordination is obverse to the wrongdoer's self-elevation, his remedy must proceed from the one who wrongfully harmed him. However, if the individual's communal right to security against harm is exclusive, then wrongdoing is irrelevant, and the victim's claim is in reality against the community, not against the person who harmed him. The defendant in the action for damages serves merely as a conduit to an insurance fund and as a conveyor of costs to the public, and for these purposes any large enterprise will do. Thus, if loss spreading were the only goal of accident law, no causal connection between plaintiff's injury and defendant's activity would be necessary. There is, however, the matter of efficient deterrence, which requires that enterprises face the costs of their activity and which thus demands an allocation of costs to their source.[128] Yet the internalization of costs for deterrence purposes does not require the kind of ex post, historical, and particularistic inquiry into causal origins that classical tort law needs to ensure that this plaintiff and this defendant are properly paired. It requires only that enterprises calculate the present cost to them of the accidents their existing methods will probably cause over a certain period of time. Determining which accidents they have actually caused is one way of forming a statistical base from which to predict future costs, but it is not the only way; general studies investigating statistical links between activities and the incidence of injuries or disease are often a cheaper alternative.[129] Moreover, because of evidential uncertainties (due to long latency periods, the contribution of underlying predispositions, etc.) making proof of factual causation unfeasible where the harm suffered is a disease, insistence on the traditional "balance of probabilities" standard of proof would frustrate the goals of compensation and loss spreading and would lead to underinvestment in safety.

Accordingly, the coherent actualization of the communitarian idea involves a steady erosion of the requirement of factual causation. The first step is to shift the burden of proof to the defendant when one of two actors caused the injury but no one knows which one.[130] Here the 50 percent chance that the defendant caused the injury is thought sufficient to justify saddling him with the whole loss, although the traditional standard of proof requires a probability substantially in excess of that ratio. The court's focus is still on factual causation, but the plaintiff's standard of proof has been lowered. The next step is to make the probability of causation, no matter how low, itself the measure of the defendant's liability. Thus, if a plaintiff cannot determine which of many drug manufacturers produced the pills that caused her cancer, why not allocate liability among all defendants in proportion to the chance that they caused the illness, a chance measured by their share of the market?[131] And if a plaintiff cannot prove an actual link between the defendant's toxic emission and his illness, why not pin liability on the defendant in proportion to the percentage by which its conduct increased the incidence of that illness among a given population?[132] At this extreme, it is no longer important whether the defendant actually caused the plaintiff's injury; the court is openly apportioning liability in the service of loss spreading and efficient deterrence.[133]

Once the requirement of factual causation is abandoned, the last thread tying protection of social security rights to the atomistic premises of formal right has been cut. Protection of the right need no longer be limited to compensating injuries suffered through interactions with other persons; any disabling injury or illness, no matter how caused, can be compensable. We can, moreover, do away with the adversarial adjudicative model connected to the correlativity of wronging and being wronged and that drains resources away from compensation. We can replace this model with an administrative one that promptly compensates for all injuries from a public fund regardless of wrongdoing. Compensation need not be total, for only corrective justice requires restoration of the victim to the status quo ante, and corrective justice has been submerged in the aim of fairly distributing the social costs of enterprise. The measure of compensation can now be limited by a social decision about what is affordable and what is required to preserve incentives to take care. In this calculation, the traditional award for pain and suffering will be particularly vulnerable, for compensation now aims to secure the conditions of autonomy for the future, not to remove every trace of a deficit wrongfully suffered in the past. Other features of the traditional damage award are similarly dispensable. That compensation has an insurance rather than a rectificatory aim implies that compensation need not be tailored to the particular plight of the victim nor awarded in a lump sum; it can be administered more cheaply according to a tariff schedule for various classes of injury, and it can be paid in installments to ensure a steady stream of income for the recipient. Finally, because the communal right is (under the new paradigm) the only right that exists, the remedies afforded by this scheme can be exclusive; the individual's right to sue in tort for full compensation for *his* injuries can be abolished.[134] The rigorous actualization of the principle of negligence law implies the disappearance of tort law.

6. THE CASE FOR TORT LAW

The case for tort law is an argument for two kinds of legal change. It is an argument, first of all, for a noninstrumental or private-law model of tort law and so for an end to loss-spreading and deterrence justifications of the common-law tort system. Second, it is an argument for the retention (for those who wish to use it) of this model of tort law alongside administrative schemes for no-fault social insurance. I shall not argue for any particular plan combining social insurance and tort law but only for the principle of such a dual system.[135]

The argument will be a conceptual one. While many pragmatic considerations could be adduced to support a dual system, I shall forgo whatever uncertain advantage such arguments may yield.[136] My claim, rather, is that a dual system is the *logical completion*—the immanent goal—of the development hitherto traced from trespass to negligence to social insurance. This view challenges the customary one, which sees a mixed system as a political compromise between antagonistic theories of accident law and, indeed, between irreconcilable principles of social organization. The argument presented here aims to reveal a mixed system as logically coherent.

The conceptual case for tort law not only must shun arguments from expediency; it must also avoid any unmediated reliance on the abstract self that has been superseded in social insurance. That principle is no longer available to us as a supreme normative foundation, and so we must take care not to presuppose its autonomous validity. We may retrieve it, to be sure; however, we must do so not by smuggling it in as contraband but by openly vindicating it from the standpoint of the communitarian shore already reached. This means that the case for tort law must proceed by way of an immanent critique of social insurance. This critique will show that the submersion of the standpoint of the abstract self contradicts social insurance's *own* end and that social insurance thus requires the superseded standpoint for its own self-consistency.

A few words more about the kinds of argument I shall avoid. In opposing instrumentalist justifications of the common-law tort system, I shall not rely in the first instance on arguments about the institutional competence of courts or about the need for political accountability for the levying of taxes. It is true, of course, that the bipolar format of the classical model is ill-suited to the wide-ranging distributive tasks that the social insurance model imposes on courts; and it is true that a loss-spreading rationale for tort doctrine amounts to the imposition by (mostly) nonelected judges of a consumer tax on products. However, these arguments lead as easily to tort law's submersion in a pure administrative model as they do to the retention of the classical one, and so they are incomplete. Their true force will become evident later—after we have provided a teleological argument for a dual system and when the dysfunctions these arguments point to will appear as symptoms of a legal system's underdevelopment. Nor shall I rely on an argument about the incoherence of loss-spreading and deterrence rationales for tort law. Undoubtedly, these goals are in tension with the traditional doctrines and institutions of tort law: deterrence is weakened by penalizing only those who cause harm to a plaintiff, while loss spreading is arbitrarily limited by the requirement that compensable harm be caused by a defendant. However, this argument is likewise impotent against a pure administrative model supplemented by criminal and regulatory sanctions and is not even effective against a social insurance orientation for tort law. The advocate of enterprise liability will respond that the features of tort law at odds with his goals indicate an obsolete system destined to disappear in an ideal world, but to which the reformer must in the meantime adapt. Those who think that the argument from incoherence is an argument against enterprise liability and not against classical tort law must be assuming that the classical model has a fixed and eternal validity. However, given the inbuilt tendency of the classical model to pass over into social insurance, such an assumption is, in the absence of argument, simply a prejudice for the status quo.

Accordingly, we must now supply the argument. The conceptual case for tort law begins by showing that social insurance, when absolutized as the exclusive basis of individual rights to care, contradicts *itself,* or accomplishes the opposite of what it intends. It intends to actualize the end-status of persons by guaranteeing the material conditions of effective freedom. The individual person's worth is thus social insurance's own end. Yet, when pushed to its logical extreme, social insurance reveals itself as indifferent to the worth of persons, for it permits acts inconsistent therewith to go unchallenged. The wronged individual may be insured (whether by strict liability or by administrative compensation) against the loss of welfare he has suffered from the wrong; however, he is deprived of the institutional means by which to redress the wrong qua wrong and so to vindicate his self-worth against acts that contradict it. More specifically, he is deprived of an authoritative determination that the disrespect shown for his person is an infringement of his right; and he is likewise deprived of a remedy for another's debasement of his person, one that would require the *wrongdoer* to annul *all* the losses connected with his wrong. The full realization of the person's end-status is thus a legal order in which negations of that status are allowed to stand, or in which that status *lacks* objective confirmation.

The indifference of social insurance to acts inconsistent with personality's worth also alters the significance of the benefits it affords. Social insurance came forward as the realization of human personality. Persons had a right in community to security of welfare because they were objectively ends only insofar as the material conditions of their autonomy were mutually guaranteed. In the theory of social insurance, accordingly, welfare is normatively significant not as the gratification of appetite but as the satisfaction of the conditions for the realization of freedom. However, in submerging the tort action (or the fault requirement of civil liability), social insurance implies that welfare is desirable independently of its connection to freedom, for once the wronged individual's loss has been socially compensated, it declares that he has no further claim of public importance. Social insurance, it turns out, regards welfare as publicly significant but not the vindication of the person whose welfare it insures. Indeed, so great is its disdain for the vindication of personality that social insurance sees in tort law only another (inefficient) system of compensation made redundant by itself, regarding as nugatory tort law's self-conception as a vehicle of corrective justice. When, however, the vindication of personality is depreciated by community, then the welfare it guarantees becomes detached from the end that gave welfare its human significance. The welfare at which social insurance aims is no longer the welfare *of* persons; it is the contentment of purely sentient creatures. The rigorous actualization in social insurance of personality's worth is the depersonalization of the human individual.

That the hegemony of social insurance implies the nullification of the person it meant to actualize does not complete the argument for tort law. The self-contradictoriness of social insurance leaves us with the result that neither atomistic selfhood nor community provides a stable foundation for the person's worth. On the one hand, the realization of the atomistic self impelled it to a community in which the self's independent worth was canceled; on the other, the actualization of community destroys the individual it was supposed to fulfill and so contradicts itself as the common good of individuals. Accordingly, in actualizing itself without regard for the other, each ceases to be itself. This shows that each pole of the antithesis implicitly contains its opposite: the individual's end-status presupposes a community in which it is recognized and given effective legal force; the end-status of community presupposes the independent worth of the individual whose end it purports to be. Since each pole notionally contains the other, each needs the other's independence to be self-consistent; hence each pole must preserve the other for its own sake. Yet as long as each claims to be the absolute ground of rights, each must preserve the other *against* the logical momentum of its principle, so that the peace between them appears as an unstable truce rather than as a genuine reconciliation. Instead of a unity of opposites we have a deadlock between ambivalent foes, each of which seeks simultaneously to deny and to affirm the other. Thus the instability on their own of both tort law and social insurance points to the need for a dual system but does not yet reveal that system as logically coherent.

The next step in the argument, therefore, is to lay hold of the unity disclosed by the mutual need of the extremes. The antagonism between community and individual selfhood results from the claim of each to be the absolute ground of rights. Yet that each needs the other for its own coherence belies this claim and reveals the true ground of right as a unity of which both are constituent and mutually complementary elements. Once the unity of the extremes is intuited, it remains to conceptualize this unity, or to formulate a theory of the relationship between the polarities that makes sense of their revealed interdependence. The relationship between the poles is one of mutual recognition. Each defers (becomes a means) to the end-status of the other for the sake of its own confirmation as an end. Thus the community defers to the independent self-existence of the individual, for it is objectively an end only insofar as it is spontaneously produced by the atomistic self seeking confirmation of its own worth; likewise, the individual self defers to community as to that whose need for confirmation first establishes its (the individual's) independence as an objective right. But this bond of mutual recognition is dialogic community, whose progressively clear manifestations we have observed in the various stages of personality's self-realization. The argument that dialogic community is the true ground of right is just the entire preceding development from trespass to negligence to social insurance to the latter's self-disclosure as a one-sided (external, violent) subjugation of an individual its own concept needs. This means that dialogic community is *demonstrably* the foundation of law only as the result of this development. But then each phase of the process is necessary to the known validity of dialogic community, and so each is preserved as a subordinate element of a complex whole.

Here we must be careful not to elide an important step in the argument. The case for tort law is not even complete once dialogic community emerges as the ground of law from the self-discordance of each of the conceptions leading to it. A further argument is needed to show why the ground of law is not simply the *result* of the developmental process but the result together with the entire process of achieving it. If the final structure of mutual recognition (of communal and individual selves) were alone the ground of law, then the atomistic self's claim to worth could not, after all, be taken seriously; and neither, therefore, could a private law of tort. The atomistic self would be important only as spontaneously revealing its transient character—only as passing over into a community that perpetually devoured it. Yet this result would be a self-contradictory realization of dialogic community, for the latter would then submerge the very individual it avowedly requires for self-confirmation and would thus show itself to be again one-sided and violent. Accordingly, dialogic community is alone a ground of *law* when it truly conforms to its dialogic nature; and it does so when it encompasses within itself the entire process whereby it is spontaneously validated through the self-interested action of the atomistic self. This self is now important not simply as a perpetual witness to its own nullity in a communitarian destiny but as a positive and enduring element of an intersubjective whole. The preservation in dialogic community of the process of attaining it completes the case for tort law.

The conclusion of our argument is that there is a conceptual basis for a pluralistic law dealing with human losses. Once dialogic community comes forward as the ground of law, the logical impetus of each putative ground to dominate the other ceases. As one element of an organic whole, each minds its own business and leaves the others to mind theirs. Neither strict liability nor fault seeks to engulf the law of torts, nor does social insurance seek to displace the law of negligence. Rather, each rules within limits consistent with the preservation of the others' distinctive existence—limits made coherent by the primacy of the whole with respect to its constituent parts. Thus strict liability remains the regime appropriate for invasions of proprietary sovereignty and for interference with use, while negligence is the basis of liability for the infliction of harm to human interests. Further, there is a rational basis for a tort law unresponsive to communal goals of loss spreading and deterrence—for a tort law ordered exclusively to personality's vindication against acts inconsistent with its worth. Finally, the goals of loss spreading and deterrence are the business of an independent regime of social insurance combined with regulatory sanctions—a regime that preserves the individual's option to sue a wrongdoer in tort.

The foregoing argument sought to vindicate the individual's right to a tort action in the face of the development of social insurance. It remains only to understand how conflicts between a civil right of action and social insurance are to be resolved. Is the right to a tort action an absolute right, one indefeasible by the common good? If not absolute, what are the considerations of policy that override it? What policy considerations does it resist?

That the right to a tort action is not absolute is implied by the argument that established it. Since tort law was vindicated as a necessary phase in the development of dialogic community, it is subordinate to phases that represent superior embodiments of that idea. This means that while the right to a tort action cannot be extinguished by social insurance, that right must nonetheless yield to the extent necessary to insure a basic level of welfare for all members of the community. Thus, if the retention of a tort action would render economically unfeasible the guarantee of a basic minimum of human welfare, then statutory limitations on the right to sue would be legitimate if they were needed to achieve the welfare objective. However, in a contest between the right to vindicate self-worth and guaranteed levels of welfare above this minimum, the former must prevail, since personality is more fundamental than any of its contingent goals. Accordingly, the state cannot legitimately curtail the right to a tort action for the sake of a gilt-edged compensation scheme. Only the individual can surrender it.[137]

Once a dual system is seen as the goal of tort law's development, the distortions occasioned by the failure of this system to materialize can be understood for what they are: symptoms of the contradiction between tort law's existing condition and its inherent potential. Thus the failure to

develop an independent scheme of social insurance leads to the continuing attempt by judges to pursue social insurance objectives within the tort
system itself. At the extreme, this involves a judicial appropriation of administrative power that both strains the court's competence and threatens
the constitutional division of powers. It also produces a sphinxlike mixture
of social insurance doctrine and tort remedies: full, individually tailored
compensation regardless of fault at a cost that includes the legal expenses
of plaintiff and defendant incurred during protracted litigation or negotiations. This is the most extravagant, inefficient, and capricious system of
social insurance conceivable, one financed through a hidden consumer
tax imposed by the judiciary.[138] The resultant "liability crisis" engenders
legislation placing ceilings on damage awards for noneconomic losses, but
these are then applied indiscriminately to claimants suing in strict liability
and to those suing for wrongdoing.[139] The mirror image of this disorder
occurs when an independent scheme of social insurance abolishes the
right to sue in tort. Now someone wronged by another is undercompen-
sated by the scheme, for he can recover only for pecuniary losses fixed in
advance by an impersonal schedule, and the wrongdoer is never brought
to court. These anomalies have long been evident to tort lawyers, and they
have led some to propose and in a few cases to institute a dual system as
the most sensible practical solution.[140] I have argued that, appearances
notwithstanding, it is also a conceptually demanded solution.

CHAPTER V

Agency and Welfare in
the Penal Law

1. INTRODUCTION: THE PROBLEM OF HARM

In his monumental work on the moral limits of the criminal law, Joel Feinberg makes the concept of harm—understood as a setback to interests—central to the definition of crime. The "common element," he writes, in willful homicide, rape, aggravated assault, battery, burglary, and grand larceny "is the direct production of serious harm to individual persons and groups."[1] Other acts somewhat farther removed from the core of uncontroversial crimes sound variations on the theme of harm. Thus counterfeiting, smuggling, income tax evasion, contempt of court, and the violation of zoning and antipollution ordinances are offenses because, while seldom harming specific persons or groups, they nevertheless cause harm to "the public," "society," "the general ambience of neighbourhoods, the economy, the climate, or the environment."[2] Generalizing from these clear cases of permissible criminalization, Feinberg concludes that penal restrictions on individual liberty are morally justified when they prevent harm or the unreasonable risk of harm to parties other than the person whose liberty is curtailed.[3]

No sooner, however, does Feinberg begin to define the harm principle than the principle slips away. Clearly, not all cases of harming are crimes, for individuals have interests—commercial or amorous—that often conflict with those of others, and the satisfaction of one person will often mean the thwarting of a competitor. We thus need a criterion of seriousness to distinguish harming that is wrong from harming that is permissible. For Feinberg, serious harms are those that invade "welfare interests," by which he means interests in the possession of goods everyone needs in order to attain his or her personal goals.[4] Obvious examples are the

211

interest in life, physical health, financial security, and liberty. Yet this formulation soon runs up against the depressive who has no interest in life
(because no goal seems worthwhile to him), the vagabond who has no interest in property, the ascetic who has no interest in bodily health, or the
multimillionaire for whom the theft of a dollar threatens no basic interest
in security. Since he does not wish to deny that killing the depressive, maiming the ascetic, and so on, are wrong, Feinberg must postulate a "standard
person" who has normal interests and whom legislators must have in view
when they formulate general laws.[5] Yet this device places Feinberg on the
horns of a dilemma. The standard person is standard either in a statistical
or in an ideal sense. If the standard person has interests that *most* people
have, then killing the depressive who has no interest in living is not wrong,
though the law may punish it to forestall a defense (harmless killing) that
may tempt the unscrupulous and give too worrisome a discretion to authorities. If the standard person has interests that the rational agent has,
then killing the depressive is wrong though no interest *of his* is set back, in
which case the harm principle as Feinberg conceives it does no work in
defining crime.

The disjunction of wronging and harming illustrated by the examples
of the depressive and the millionaire is well known to the law of torts and
crimes.[6] A *damnum absque injuria* is not actionable, whereas an *injuria* is
often actionable without proof of damage. A trespass to land may incidentally benefit the landowner's interest and yet nonetheless be a proscribable wrong.[7] Feinberg explains such "hard examples" by arguing that the
trespass is a harm to a proprietary interest, although one that is possibly
outweighed by other benefits. But why, if the prevention of harm is the
theme of the least controversial criminal laws, do we punish if the invasion
of the proprietary interest works a net increase of benefits for the property
owner? The fact that the trespass is "to some extent" a harm ceases to have
explanatory power if we can punish even though the harm is more trivial
than some we do not proscribe (e.g., the harms from economic competition) and even if the trespass produces an overall benefit.

The idea to which Feinberg continually returns to rationalize these
cases of apparently harmless wrongdoing is that of freedom of choice.[8]
Stealing a dollar from a millionaire, killing a suicidal depressive, or tres-
passing on another's property deprives someone of the freedom to decide
what to do with his or her life or wealth; and since everyone (we can assume) has a strong interest in such a liberty, these actions too are harmful.
However, the idea that is hurried in to rescue the harm principle in these
problematic cases actually supplants it. This becomes evident when we jux-
tapose the following two examples.

Suppose V is suffering great pain from a disease that is curable by drugs.
The disease is so debilitating that V is unable to perform any but the sim-

plest of life-preserving functions. Nevertheless, V obstinately refuses treatment. He refuses not from any religious or moral convictions but from an ungrounded fear that the treatment will produce side effects worse than his illness. One day D forcibly injects V with the appropriate medication, and V recovers to lead a normal and productive life. D is here unquestionably guilty of an assault, and the fact that his act was of untold benefit to V is irrelevant to his culpability. Contrast this situation with one in which V is rendered a lifelong quadriplegic by D in a sporting match of which V is a willing participant. Here D is innocent of wrongdoing if his act imposed a risk within the range to which V consented.

Some may be inclined to explain these cases by attributing to the interest in freedom of choice a preponderant weight, one that tips the welfare scales in its favor when measured against other interests. Thus, in the example of the timorous patient, one might say that injecting people against their will in this kind of situation would produce harms exceeding the benefits to be gained from medication, and that is why D's act is wrong. But this explanation is surely unconvincing. Few would doubt that the person who refuses treatment because of a gross misperception of its likely effects on his welfare (and who would thus accept treatment were he not blind to the true state of the facts) is on balance better rather than worse off for the assault; and no one will say that absolving D in the second case enhances V's welfare by giving effect to his choices, as if choice were the one thing needful for a life valuable to the agent. What these examples show, on the contrary, is that the criminal law does not weigh violations of freedom in the same scales with setbacks to welfare interests. Instead, it assigns freedom a privilege or absolute value such that disrespect thereof is a crime *regardless* of the benefits it confers on the victim (and regardless of whether the victim subjectively values freedom) and such that respect for a person's freedom of choice absolves a defendant regardless of the magnitude of harm inflicted on him.* This means, however, that disrespect for another's freedom performs the thematic role that Feinberg wished to assign to the harm principle. It and not the infliction of harm is the gravamen of crime.

If we pursue this suggestion, other features of the criminal law that are unintelligible from the standpoint of the harm principle begin to cohere. For example, it is no excuse to an intentional homicide that society has been rid of someone who is a source of far greater suffering in the world than good. It is as wrong to kill an unreconstructed Scrooge as it is to kill a Tiny Tim. Nor is it an excuse to theft that the accused redistributed wealth

*The fact that the victim's consent is no defense to murder is not a counterexample to this proposition but rather its limiting case. It is because liberty is the foundational principle for the criminal law that one cannot effectively alienate it.

from those for whom the loss was barely felt to those for whom the gain meant the difference between misery and contentment. Disrespect for freedom is wrong no matter how great the consequential benefits to society.[9] Conversely, the excuses recognized by the criminal law appear perverse from the standpoint of preventing harm to others. An involuntary agent is excused even though someone is seriously harmed by his physical movements and even though he is thereby freed perhaps to inflict harm again. Taking someone's property in the belief that the object is one's own is not a crime, nor is an assault in the mistaken belief that the victim consented to contact. In all these cases someone is harmed—perhaps seriously—but the accused has shown no disrespect for the victim's freedom of choice.

Regarded as a whole, these phenomena support a thesis that is the antithesis of Feinberg's: that the criminal law—or at least that part of it with a common-law origin—systematically excludes considerations of harm and benefit from the concept of criminal wrongdoing. This exclusion is masked by the fact that most cases of wronging are also cases of harming, but the independence of wrongdoing from harm is revealed by thought experiments in which one alternately isolates setbacks to interests and violations of freedom. Moreover, the repulsion of harm from the notion of wrongdoing is the obverse of a rigorously exclusive focus on personality, agency, or free will as the concept that gives thematic unity to the criminal law. Thus, the *actus reus* (guilty act) of crime is the subjugation to oneself of the body or external property that demarcates another's sphere of inviolable liberty; the *mens rea* (guilty mind) of crime is the intentional or reckless disdain for the liberty of another self; penal justice consists in the connection between punishment and the free choice of the criminal; and the paradigmatic form of punishment is imprisonment, which may or may not disadvantage the prisoner (he may be a vagrant who prefers the security of prison) but which certainly deprives him of liberty and of the dignity based thereon.

Having drawn this stark picture, however, we must now point out its one-sidedness. The thoroughgoing exclusion of considerations of harm from the concept of crime applies only to wrongs that one person may commit against another in a context abstracted from any human association for a common end. That is to say, it applies only to wrongs that one may commit in a prepolitical state of nature and that are of common-law origin—to interferences with freedom of movement and with personal sovereignty over one's body and possessions. This means that the exclusion applies to a very narrow segment of the penal law of the modern, regulatory state. Beyond this segment, the welfare of individuals is undeniably the aim of the penal law. For example, the promotion of welfare is the point of laws controlling the use and sale of narcotics and liquors, of laws regulating the production and marketing of food, of laws protecting the environment, and of laws promoting road, air, and industrial safety. Under these laws, one may incur penalties for acts that do not dominate the free will of others, either because (as in the case of a breach of a safety regulation) they involve no transaction with another person or because (as in the case of trafficking in narcotics) the transaction is consensual.* Judges often refer to acts that violate these laws as "public welfare offenses" to distinguish them from "true crimes," and they typically require standards of fault for a conviction that fall short of the willfulness required for criminal liability.[10]

Ultimately, then, the problem with Feinberg's harm principle is not that it fails to capture intuitions about wrongdoing embedded in the penal law but that it obliterates a distinction within the penal law between two paradigms of wrongdoing. I shall call these paradigms the pure (or formal) agency paradigm and the welfarist paradigm, and I shall use the term "criminal law" to designate that part of the penal law governed by principles unique to the framework of pure agency. The questions I want to discuss in this chapter emerge from the puzzling coexistence of these two normative frameworks within the penal law. First, what assumptions about the nature of personality and freedom underlie the pure agency paradigm, and is this view of freedom internally coherent? Second, is the conception of freedom underlying the welfarist paradigm a superior understanding of freedom, and if so, why has it not succeeded in establishing its hegemony over the whole domain of the penal law? Is its failure to do so a matter of historical inertia, or is there a conceptual basis for a differentiation of paradigms within the penal law, each with its characteristic aim, standard of fault, and criterion of penal justice? Can these paradigms be grasped as interconnected parts of a totality that requires both?

I shall try to respond to these questions by developing the consequences for the penal law of the thesis defended in the previous chapter on tort. The thesis is that the pure agency paradigm of the common law rests on an untenable conception of freedom but that it is nevertheless essential to a whole that embodies an adequate conception. The paradigm of formal agency errs insofar as it claims to contain the whole content of penal justice; but it is preserved as a subordinate sector of a totality that also includes the welfarist framework. Similarly, the conception of freedom underlying the welfarist paradigm, while superior to its predecessor, nevertheless cannot do without a legal paradigm autonomously ordered to the abstract self.

This thesis will yield implications across a broad front of controversy in

---

*The correspondence of the criminal/regulatory distinction with that between transactional and nontransactional conduct is only a rough one, as the cases of attempt and victimless reckless driving show. I make the appropriate refinements in my discussion of the actus reus of crimes.

the theory and practice of penal law. The principal source of strife within contemporary penal law is the apparent hostility between the two paradigms. As long as it appears that the two frameworks exist independently of each other, there will be a theoretical imperative to absolutize the normative principle of one or the other. The frameworks will thus be antagonistic, and any modus vivendi achieved between them will appear as an intellectually disreputable compromise. Principled adherents of each paradigm will seek to extend its dominion over the entire penal law, while moderate pluralists will seem bereft of principle as well as unclear about the boundaries of the frameworks. So, for example, an advocate of the subjective standard of fault in the criminal law will insist on its application to welfare offenses as well;[11] while the welfarist who favors a negligence standard will urge its extension to all crimes, which he will reinterpret as harms.[12] Similarly, those for whom criminal justice consists in meting out punishment to the deserving will want to make desert the criterion of just punishment throughout the penal law;[13] while those who see the irrelevance of desert in a paradigm ordered to the prevention of harm will want to eliminate it entirely (as part of an outmoded retributivism) in favor of a welfare-justified constraint of respect for autonomy.[14] In the absence of a principle for demarcating the paradigms, those dissatisfied with the consequences of either extreme position will tend to mix agency and welfarist doctrines throughout, preferring the untidiness of a salutary policy to the coherence of a destructive logic. And the resultant patchwork of accommodations will be fertile ground for skepticism about law, for it will leave legal discourse vulnerable to a critique exposing its structured modes of reasoning from underlying principles as a cloak for political advocacy.[15]

Suppose, however, that the two paradigms were internally connected as subordinate and mutually complementary aspects of a whole. In that case, their differentiated and mutually tolerant existence would have a solid conceptual foundation. We would not have to choose between an imperialism of principle and an unprincipled pluralism, for there would be support for pluralism and moderation in the realm of principles. We would coherently have a system of criminal law ordered to respect for agency abstracted from embodiment in determinate values and a system of welfare law aimed at the promotion of good. The choice between frameworks would not be open-ended, for each would apply to a distinctive category of offenses whose (otherwise elusive) boundary would be stabilized by the primacy of the whole over its constituent parts. Moreover, each paradigm would have the features necessitated by its thematic principle. In the pure agency paradigm, the standard of fault would be the willful disrespect of freedom, and the point of punishment would be the vindication of mutual respect as the sole coherent foundation of the person's worth. In the welfarist paradigm, the point of sanctions would be the prevention of harm, and the standard of fault would be negligence. Each paradigm would thus be liberated from the tyranny of the other; and the quarrel between subjectivists and objectivists, retributivists and consequentialists would be pacified, for each would hold sway within its respective sphere.

The aim of this chapter, then, is to disclose the conceptual ground for the reconciliation of the pure agency and welfarist paradigms in the penal law. I begin by describing the internal coherence of the pure agency model, relating its basic features to the abstract conception of freedom that informs it. I then try to show how the limitations of this conception are revealed within the pure agency paradigm itself, notably in the concessions the law must make to considerations of welfare in differentiating crimes according to seriousness and in dealing with conflicts between property and the right to self-preservation. I then set out the welfarist paradigm and show how the absolutization of this model negates the autonomy of the self it means to actualize. The self-contradictoriness of each principle when absolutized to the exclusion of the other reveals the genuine ground of law as the totality that includes both as subordinate moments. This totality is dialogic community, whose structure of mutual recognition is the latent theme of both paradigms.

A final introductory word about the method of argument employed in this chapter: Because I shall be partly concerned with describing the internal coherence of paradigms, my theoretical attitude will be one of immersion in the standpoint of each of the paradigms in turn. As a result, it may sometimes be unclear whether I am stating positions I mean to endorse. To avoid this problem, I shall state at the outset my theoretical stance toward the legal principles and doctrines generated by the models. Since my thesis is that penal justice consists in the unity of the paradigms, I mean to endorse all the principles and doctrines derived from the foundational norm of a paradigm insofar as that norm keeps within bounds consistent with a recognition that the paradigm is merely part of a whole. I will, however, criticize those implications of the model that flow from treating its norm as the whole itself. What these implications are will become clear in due course.

2. SOME CASES

It will help make concrete the discussion that follows if we consider some actual cases in which the fundamental problems of penal law theory crystallize. The cases illustrate three perennially troubling issues in the penal law: What is the appropriate level of fault for criminal negligence? What is the appropriate test for the actus reus of attempts? What is the proper scope of the rule that ignorance of the law is no excuse for an offense? These issues in turn raise more basic problems: What is the role of mens rea in the criminal law? What is the significance of the act requirement? What is the criterion—if any exists—for the distinction between crimes

and public welfare offenses, and what implications does this distinction
have for the structuring of excuses?

2.1 R. v. Tutton and Tutton[16]

Mr. and Mrs. Tutton were parents of a five-year-old son. The son was a
diabetic who required regular injections of insulin to survive. His parents
had been well informed of the boy's need of insulin, but on two occasions
they withheld the drug because they believed the child had been healed
by the power of the Holy Spirit. On the first of these occasions, the boy fell
seriously ill and was taken to the hospital, where he recovered on being
given the appropriate medication. At that time doctors told the parents
never to discontinue the insulin injections and warned them of the dire
consequences of doing so. On the second occasion (a year later), the boy
died.

The parents were charged with criminal negligence causing death. Under the Canadian Criminal Code, someone is criminally negligent "who in
doing anything, or omitting to do anything that is his duty to do, shows
wanton or reckless disregard for the lives or safety of other persons."[17] The
"wanton or reckless disregard" formula codifies the common-law requirement of recklessness for manslaughter (or causing bodily harm) by criminal negligence. The parents' defense was that they honestly believed the
boy had been miraculously cured, that they were thus unaware of the grave
risk to which they were exposing him, and that they had therefore shown
no wanton or reckless disregard for his life.

The Tuttons' fate depended on the meaning of "wanton or reckless
disregard." On this question, there are two opposing views. One holds that
the test for recklessness is objective, that wanton or reckless disregard consists in a marked and obvious departure from the standard of care of the
ordinary prudent person.[18] Recklessness, in other words, is egregious negligence, where the aggravating factor is not any mental state of the accused but simply the greater disparity (considering the magnitude of the
risk and the seriousness of the potential harm) between the accused's conduct and that of the reasonable person. If the accused's conduct manifests
this degree of negligence, he is open to criminal prosecution regardless of
whether he subjectively foresaw the danger to which he was exposing the
victim. Those who advocate this test usually also favor a modification originally proposed by H. L. A. Hart, one that would allow a jury to consider
any physical or mental characteristics of the accused that might have inca-
pacitated him from conforming to the standard of care.[19] What exonerates,
however, is not the accused's obliviousness to the danger but his incapacity
to take the care of the ordinary prudent person.

The other view holds that recklessness differs from civil negligence not
in degree but in kind. On this view, recklessness is *advertent* negligence,

which means that the jury must be able to infer from all the evidence that the accused directed his mind to the excessive risk he was imposing on the victim and resolved to proceed despite the risk.[20] Usually an obvious danger will permit this conclusion, but the accused may introduce evidence (such as his religious beliefs) that rebuts an otherwise natural inference of advertence. According to this subjectivist view of criminal negligence, the latter need not involve egregious negligence, nor is gross negligence sufficient; for the crucial factor (once a breach of the standard of care is proved) is the mental state of the accused. For the subjectivist, criminally negligent conduct is any negligent conduct performed with a consciousness of the unreasonableness of the risk. Obviously, it matters a great deal how we resolve this controversy. On the objective test, the Tuttons are guilty of manslaughter and liable to imprisonment for life; on the subjective test (if we believe their story), they are innocent.

The Supreme Court of Canada split evenly on the test for criminal negligence, sending the case back for retrial without giving the trial judge any guidance on how to instruct the jury. I will not go into the judges' reasons, for on neither side do they give the best defense of the position. Instead, I will set out an argument widely viewed as having presented an invincible case for the (modified) objective test of criminal negligence and that has greatly influenced courts and legislatures toward accepting negligence as a basis for criminal liability.

The argument is H. L. A. Hart's.[21] Hart advanced his argument in a critique of a famous essay by J. W. C. Turner in which Turner equated criminal liability for gross negligence with absolute liability or liability without fault.[22] Hart's main argument begins as follows:

> At the root of Dr. Turner's arguments there lie, I think, certain unexamined assumptions as to what the mind is and why its "states" are relevant to responsibility. Dr. Turner obviously thinks that unless a man "has in his mind the idea of harm to someone" it is not only bad law, but morally objectionable, as a recourse to strict or absolute liability, to punish him. But here we should ask why, in or out of law courts, we should attach this crucial importance to foresight of consequences, to the "having of an idea in the mind of harm to someone." On what theory of responsibility is it that the presence of this particular item of mental furniture is taken to be something which makes it perfectly satisfactory to hold that the agent is responsible for what he did? And why should we necessarily conclude that in its absence an agent cannot be decently held responsible?
> . . . [T]here is nothing to compel us to say "He could not have helped it" in *all* cases where a man omits to think about or examine the situation in which he acts and harm results which he has not foreseen.[23]

So far Hart's argument deals with the conditions of responsibility or of validly attributing harmful consequences to an agent. Advertence to an unreasonable risk of harm, he says, is not the sole basis on which we can justly hold an agent responsible for the harm he causes; for if the agent could have attended to such a risk, he is responsible for having failed to do so. Hence punishing the agent for this failure does not amount to imposing absolute liability.

Taken alone, this argument does not take us very far in justifying punishment for gross negligence. From the fact that someone is responsible for a wrongful act or consequence it does not follow that punishing him is justified. If I voluntarily take something that belongs to another, I am responsible for the other's deprivation and must make good his loss; however, it does not follow that I can also be punished, for I may have sensibly thought that the thing was my own. It is certainly reasonable to think that responsibility for a wrongful act is a necessary condition of just punishment. However, it is not sufficient, for nothing in the idea of responsibility for a wrong entails punishment as the appropriate response. Moral censure as well as a civil action for damages are eligible alternatives both of which also presuppose an act imputable to the agent. Accordingly, we need a further argument to bridge the gap between the idea of responsibility and the idea of punishment, or at least to show why it would not be unjust to punish actors whose responsibility lay only in their negligence. Hart supplies such an argument.

> The reason why . . . strict liability is odious . . . is not merely because it amounts, as it does, to punishing those who did not at the time of acting "have in their minds" the elements of foresight or desire for muscular movement. These psychological elements are not *in themselves* crucial though they are important as aspects of responsibility. What is crucial is that those whom we punish should have had, when they acted, the normal capacities, physical and mental, for doing what the law requires and abstaining from what it forbids, and a fair opportunity to exercise these capacities. Where these capacities and opportunities are absent, as they are in different ways in the varied cases of accident, mistake, paralysis, reflex action, coercion, insanity, etc., the moral protest is that it is morally wrong to punish because "he could not have helped it" or . . . "he had no real choice." But . . . there is no reason . . . *always* to make this protest when someone who "just didn't think" is punished for carelessness. For in some cases at least we may say "he could have thought about what he was doing" with just as much rational confidence as one can say of any intentional wrongdoing "he could have done otherwise."[24]

The bridging argument is thus a comprehensive theory of excuses from criminal liability. According to this theory, it is just to punish someone only if he had a "fair opportunity" to conform his activity to the law. In another essay, Hart explained why this opportunity was so crucial to just punishment.[25] Only if the agent could have avoided the sanction is the punishment not a blind fate imposed on him ab extra but something over which he can exercise control. The requirement of a fair opportunity to comply with the law thus embodies respect for the agent's autonomy, a value Hart thought worth preserving even if (as he believed) the justifying rationale of punishment were instrumentalist or goal-oriented rather than retributive or desert-based. The reason why mistake, automatism, insanity, and duress excuse from crime, argues Hart, is that under these conditions the agent has no opportunity to avoid breaking the law; to punish him would thus be to subject him to an uncontrollable necessity and so to subordinate him to a policy in which he cannot see respect for his freedom. But, continues Hart, failure to advert to a risk does not necessarily mean that the agent could not have avoided it. In the absence of incapacitating conditions, an agent has an opportunity to inform himself of the dangers attending his action, and so punishing him for failure to do so is consistent with the underlying rationale for excuses.

We can see that in this argument the fair opportunity to avoid criminal sanctions operates as a constraint on punishment; it does not tell us what justifies punishment in the first place. Hart believed that punishment is justified by the public good it serves through its deterrent and reformative effects.[26] The argument against Turner, therefore, only cleared away a moral obstacle to punishment for negligence; it did not present a positive case for it. For Hart, the positive case could come only from empirical evidence showing that punishment for negligence would produce an increment of social benefit worth its cost.

This is indeed a powerful argument for regarding advertence as irrelevant to liability for criminal negligence. The only difficulty that initially leaps to view is that Hart's argument provides no reason for limiting criminal liability to *gross* negligence; it would also permit criminal sanctions for any breach of the standard of care. Yet there is nothing obviously wrong with this, provided that the moral difference between gross and "ordinary" negligence were reflected in the penalties attached to them. So Hart's case does indeed seem invincible. Nevertheless, my argument in this chapter will yield the conclusion that negligence, gross or otherwise, has no place in the criminal law and that the Tuttons are therefore innocent of criminal (though not necessarily of all) wrongdoing. The argument, moreover, will be one that someone who adopts Hart's standpoint could accept. For I will try to show that punishing someone as a criminal for negligence does indeed violate Hart's constraint of agent autonomy; and second, I will argue that Hart's error lies not in having misconceived the rationale for excuses but in having extended a legal paradigm to which this rationale belongs over a domain in which it is an alien intruder.

2.2 Campbell and Bradley v. Ward[27]

On approaching his parked car, Eastwick noticed McCallion, a stranger, exiting the car from the front seat. Eastwick began chasing McCallion, who hurried into another car that had been standing nearby, motor running, with Bradley at the wheel. Eastwick jumped onto the car's running board and managed to drag McCallion from his seat as Bradley sped away. Eastwick then took McCallion to a nearby hotel where he handed his captive over to the police.

When Bradley was later apprehended, he told the police that he, McCallion, and Campbell had been driving along when their car's headlights began to fail. They decided to steal a battery as well as any other equipment they could get their hands on (Campbell needed a car radio). McCallion then tried unsuccessfully to enter a number of cars before he found Eastwick's. When he saw Eastwick approaching, McCallion fled the car empty-handed. McCallion, Bradley, and Campbell were subsequently charged with attempting to steal a battery from a motor vehicle. All three were convicted by a magistrate, and Campbell and Bradley appealed.

The central issue on appeal was whether the accused had gone far enough toward achieving their aim to be guilty of a criminal attempt. Like that of most common-law jurisdictions, New Zealand's law of attempts distinguishes between acts that are mere preparation for the commission of an offense (and hence too remote from completion to be a crime) and acts sufficiently proximate to the completed purpose to constitute an attempt. This verbal distinction cannot decide cases, however, until some principle is found to guide the mind in determining whether an act is or is not too remote. At the time of the appeal, Adams, J. felt himself bound by the test enunciated in a minority judgment by Salmond, J. in *R. v. Barker*.[28] According to Salmond, J., an act is an attempt if it manifests on its face a criminal intent, or if it cannot reasonably be interpreted otherwise than as embodying a criminal purpose.[29] This has become known as the unequivocality test of attempts; and it is a crucial part of this test that in deciding whether the act unequivocally manifests a criminal intent, a judge is required to ignore all evidence of intent—for example, from a confession—extrinsic to the act itself. The point of this exclusion is to preserve the act requirement as something distinct from the requirement of intent. In demanding an act unambiguously manifesting a criminal purpose, the judge is not seeking in the acts of the accused evidence of intent in order to satisfy himself that the accused had the requisite mens rea. Rather, he is insisting that the accused have outwardly *embodied* his intent, and he determines this by asking whether the act in itself *signifies* a criminal purpose. Obviously, he could never receive an answer to this question if he allowed evidence of intent from external sources to color his judgment about the meaning of the act.

In applying the unequivocality test to the facts in *Campbell and Bradley*, Adams, J. held Bradley's confession to be inadmissible on the question of remoteness. He then asked himself whether the accused's acts taken by themselves unequivocally manifested an intent to steal a battery (for that, recall, was the charge against them). He naturally concluded that they did not. The most natural inference from the acts, he said, was that the accused had intended to steal the car, but attempted theft of a vehicle was a more serious offense for which the accused lacked the requisite intent. Since their acts were consistent with an attempt to steal any number of different objects, and since the judge could not resort to the confession to resolve the ambiguity, Adams, J. quashed the convictions. "In these circumstances," he said, "though the Court knows full well . . . that it was theft that was contemplated, it is impossible to convict them of attempted theft. Accordingly, the convictions for the attempt cannot stand. If this be regarded as unsatisfactory, the remedying of it seems to rest with the Legislature."[30]

The New Zealand Legislature accepted this invitation and overruled the unequivocality test by statute.[31] The test has also been trenchantly criticized by Glanville Williams, who argues that no acts falling short of a completed criminal purpose will unequivocally manifest a specific criminal intent.[32] The example he gives is that of a masked man discovered in someone's backyard at night. Unless we take into account what we know of his intention from other sources, we shall never be able to conclude whether the man intended burglary or arson or any other offense. Thanks largely to Williams's critique and to cases like *Campbell and Bradley,* the unequivocality test has been almost universally abandoned in the common-law world. In some cases, it has been replaced by locutions like "substantial step" or "relative proximity" that add nothing to the preparation/attempt distinction and leave judicial discretion untrammeled.[33] In other cases, it has been supplanted by tests designed to catch "dangerous" persons and that ask whether the accused would likely have carried out his plan if not interrupted.[34] In still others, the unequivocality test has yielded to one that effectively eliminates the act requirement by asking whether the act yields evidence of purpose that, when considered together with evidence from all other sources, conclusively proves a specific criminal intent.[35] Despite the uniformly low regard in which Salmond's unequivocality test is currently held in the common-law world, I shall argue that, properly understood, it is the correct one and that McCallion and his friends are guilty under it.

2.3 R. v. Campbell and Mlynarchuk[36]

Ms. Campbell was convicted under the Canadian Criminal Code for taking part in an immoral performance. She had danced nude before an audience in an Edmonton nightclub after having been assured by her employer that "bottomless dancing" was legally permissible. In fact, a trial judge of the Supreme Court of Alberta had recently ruled that dancing nude in a public place was within community standards of tolerance, and the employer informed Ms. Campbell of this ruling. It was only on being assured that nude dancing was permissible that Ms. Campbell agreed to perform as she did.

Ms. Campbell appealed her conviction. However, by the time her appeal was heard, the trial decision on which she had relied had been reversed on appeal. The Alberta Court of Appeal had held that nude dancing was indeed an immoral performance, and the district court judge in Ms. Campbell's case was naturally bound by that decision. The question, then, was whether Ms. Campbell could be excused because, having relied on a declaration of law by a Supreme Court judge, she reasonably believed her performance was lawful. The district court judge rejected this argument. Ms. Campbell's mistake was one of law rather than fact, and the Criminal Code states unambiguously that ignorance of the law is no excuse for an offense.[37] The judge acknowledged that the effect of this rule was to require Ms. Campbell to know the law better than a Supreme Court judge but expressed the Holmesian view that the rationale for the rule lay not in justice but in policy: allowing ignorance of the law to excuse would reward the ignorant, whereas the law wishes to promote knowledge of its commands.[38] Nevertheless, the judge saw a way out of his dilemma. Though Ms. Campbell was guilty as charged, the judge's sentencing discretion allowed him to rectify the injustice of the rule. This he did by granting Ms. Campbell an absolute discharge. As fate would have it, the trial decision on which Ms. Campbell originally relied was later reinstated by the Supreme Court of Canada.[39]

That ignorance of the law is no excuse is a common-law principle of ancient origin. Sir Matthew Hale, writing in 1680, articulated the assumption behind the rule. "Every person of the age of discretion and *compos mentis*," he wrote, "is bound to know the law, and presumed so to do."[40] This means that a plea of ignorance or mistake of law will be heard from an adult accused only within the context of a plea of insanity. Many have observed that the presumption of legal knowledge, while sensible in the case of serious crimes, is out of place in the context of the regulatory state with its myriad obscure statutes, regulations, ordinances, and by-laws. In the United States, accordingly, the rule has been greatly relaxed to the point where ignorance of the law will excuse if there was nothing to alert the accused to the possibility of a violation or if he took reasonable steps to ascertain the law.[41] In Commonwealth countries, however, the ignorance rule is applied more rigidly. While exceptions are made for unpublished regulations as well as for reasonable reliance on erroneous official representations (the trial judge's statement on which Ms. Campbell relied was presumably not erroneous but correct at the time he made it), Commonwealth courts have balked at recognizing a general defense of reasonable mistake of law.[42] This is all the more puzzling when we consider that they have had no difficulty in accepting a plea of reasonable mistake of fact. Thus, if Ms. Campbell had reasonably believed she was wearing a covering (it having dropped off during the performance), she would have had a valid excuse to the charge; yet a reasonable belief that dancing nude was lawful afforded her no defense.

The law's traditional refusal to acknowledge ignorance of law as an excuse has had an importance transcending the confines of the rule itself. Specifically, it has played a crucial role in interpretive debates about whether guilt at common law is a matter of conscious defiance of law or of negligently failing to conform to it. Those who argue that negligence is a proper ground of criminal liability point to the rule about ignorance to buttress their position, for the rule apparently allows the punishment of someone who did not know his act was unlawful but should have. Holmes, for example, argued that the rule exemplifies the criminal law's tendency to judge persons by an external standard of average competence, one that ignores the actual capacities, knowledge, or innocent intent of the accused. The sole aim of the criminal law, he thought, was to induce persons to conform their actions to a certain standard, and this aim would be subverted if the accused's ignorance of the standard could nullify its force.[43] Fletcher has also taunted the subjectivists with the rule about mistakes of law. There is no sound basis, he argues, on which a subjectivist can distinguish between mistakes of fact and those of law, since in neither case does the accused make a conscious choice to break the law. The subjectivist is thus committed to allowing even a negligent mistake of law to excuse, a position endorsed by no Western legal system and offensive to "basic sensibilities of justice."[44] Obversely, Fletcher argues, the fact that intuition rejects negligent mistake of law as an excuse shows that criminal liability cannot be explained by a theory equating culpability with the conscious choice to do wrong.

The interpretation of the penal law that follows will generate two propositions regarding the rule concerning ignorance of the law: first, that insofar as the rule applies to "true crimes," it is fully in harmony with the requirement of subjective fault and so provides no comfort to advocates of an objective or negligence standard of criminal liability; second, that insofar as the rule applies (as in *Campbell and Mlynarchuk*) without appropriate qualification to public welfare offenses, it involves an expansion of the pure agency paradigm of the penal law into a territory over which that model has no valid authority. In contrast, therefore, to those who see the blanket ignorance rule as supporting an objective theory of criminal culpability, I view it as embodying the obverse error. Whereas the objective theory involves the imperialist extension of the welfarist paradigm, the blanket ignorance rule manifests the hegemonic impulse of the pure agency model.

It will perhaps already be evident that almost all of the doctrinal criticisms and prescriptions I will offer turn on the judicial distinction between true crimes and public welfare offenses. The validity of this distinction will not, of course, be taken for granted. On the contrary, the theory of the penal law I offer will vindicate the distinction and suggest a criterion for it. It will also show the origin of the currently widespread skepticism regarding the distinction in the imperialism of the welfarist model; and it will show why this expansionism is wrong on the model's own terms.

3. THE PARADIGM OF PURE AGENCY

3.1 Mutual Recognition as the Basis of Rights

The requisites of criminal culpability—and hence the variety of exculpatory factors—are generated from a theory of criminal wrongdoing. The theory I will deploy for interpretive purposes is the one that Hegel sets forth in the *Philosophy of Right*.[45] The justification for adopting this theory lies partly in its interpretive power and decisively in its validation through the best conception of the ground of law. Since the best conception of law's foundation is the one to which rival conceptions (when pursued intransigently) themselves lead, the justification for adopting Hegel's theory of criminal wrong must be the end-result of our interpretation rather than a matter for preliminaries. Furthermore, the theory of criminal wrong I shall deploy builds on the understanding of rights developed in previous chapters and implies a certain conception of the difference between tort and crime. Let us therefore briefly recapitulate the theory of rights and of civil wrong elaborated thus far.

We have seen that a legal paradigm is ordered by a particular conception of the end that grounds valid duties. Because a legal order seeks to differentiate itself categorically from a condition of violence, its conception of a foundational end must be a philosophically plausible (though not necessarily adequate) conception of an absolute end, of one that is necessarily valid for all agents. The connection between law and an absolute end was taught to the modern world by Kant.[46] No value that is relative to the desire of a particular agent can ground a duty in another to respect or promote it, for the particular good of one individual (or group) provides no sufficient reason for another's renouncing his own. Subjective values can hold sway over others only by compulsion—that is, only by an appeal to fear and self-interest incompatible with the idea of an unconditionally valid obligation. Binding duties are possible only if there is an end that transcends the objects of particularistic appetite and that necessarily commands the respect of all agents.

There are, of course, various ways in which one might conceive such an end. One might, for example, conceive it as thinkers of antiquity did—as a good common to all agents by virtue of their rational natures, a good consisting in the full development of the civic and intellectual potentialities inherent in that nature. On this understanding of the foundational end, penal law appears primarily as an instrument of moral education, one whose function is to inculcate, through the creation of appropriate incentives, the habits and attitudes necessary to the full development of one's humanity.[47] Yet, whatever one might think of the classical conception of law's foundation as a philosophical idea, it is quite clearly not the conception of the absolute end that informs the common law. Here thought repudiates the assumption of an immutable human nature given independently of the will and to whose ethical prescriptions the will must conform; and because it identifies the idea of a common good with a good rooted in such a nature, legal thought repudiates the common good as such, treating all value as relative to individual desire.[48] Given this identification of value with preference, thought can reach an absolute end only by rigorously abstracting from all determinate values to the agent's bare capacity spontaneously to form, pursue, and revise values, that is to say, to the capacity for freedom. This capacity legal thought calls personality. The person is an absolute end not in the sense of an excellence of human nature to be attained through cultivation but in the sense of a self-conscious purposiveness necessarily given with all goal-oriented action, the background end to which all purposive activity is ultimately directed. Moreover, as the end that is universally and necessarily posited in the pursuit of all relative ends, the abstract person or self is the unconditioned end that supports valid obligation—or so the agency paradigm assumes.

At the outset of this chapter we adduced several examples indicating (contrary to what we might initially surmise) that the infliction of harm is irrelevant to criminal liability at common law. We can now see why this is so. If all human interests are identified with subjective preferences, then benefit and harm are relative to a particular individual's appetites and aversions. They signify not an enhancement of, or subtraction from, a well-being grounded objectively in human nature but an increase or diminution of happiness, here understood as a feeling accompanying the satisfaction of want. When conceived in this way, however, benefit and harm must be excluded from any public conception of right. There can be no coercive duty to abstain from harming others, for (unless part of a bargain) such a duty would be a servile one to cater to the pleasure of others—an ideological mask for interpersonal domination. Rather, the only duty generated by the framework of pure agency is one to respect personality, both in oneself and in another, as an absolute end (36). To respect personality in oneself is to refuse to acknowledge any duty to subordinate oneself unilaterally to the particular interests of another; to respect personality in another is to abstain from one-sidedly subordinating the other to one's will. The exclusively negative character of the duty toward others is determined by the formal conception of freedom regnant within the pure agency paradigm. Where freedom is understood reflexively (from causal determination) as a capacity for choice without regard to whether the ends chosen are authentically one's own or externally imposed, the duty to respect personality is simply a duty not to interfere with choices that are compatible with a like liberty for oneself.

At the foundation of the pure agency paradigm, then, is a claim about the absolute worth of individual personality, considered as a formal capacity for choice. By virtue of this capacity, persons are fundamentally distinguished from "things," which are seen as naturally instrumental to persons. To begin with, however, personality's claim to be an absolute end is a subjective one, challenged by the apparent independence of things in the external world. An end that is absolute only for itself is self-contradictory, and so personality is subject to a conceptual imperative to act in order to objectify itself as an end or to verify its claim of absolute worth (39). Here, of course, we advance no empirical hypothesis about the psychological dispositions or behavior of actual individuals; rather, we are describing the ideal conception or theory of the person that organizes a legal paradigm as well as the model of action to which this person is understood to be necessarily impelled. The action of the person consists in the subjugation of things to its will. Thus the person confirms itself as an absolute end by reducing its body to an obedient instrument of its purposes (but see p. 178); and its end-status is validated in the legally enforced respect each shows for the other's exclusive authority over his or her body. The person also takes possession of and uses external things; and its dignity gains objective reality in the recognition it receives for its rights of use and enjoyment as well as for its ownership of the value of things it alienates to others. The pure agency paradigm of law is thus best understood as the objective realization of the self's claim of primacy over the world of things; and this objectively validated claim of primacy is what a right of personality is.

The conceptual demand that the end-status of personality acquire objective reality draws the person into relationships with others. Within the pure agency paradigm, the social bond takes the form not of a cooperative association of individuals for a common good but of an external connection between putatively self-sufficient selves, each of whom claims to be an absolute end in isolation from others and yet paradoxically requires others to validate its worth. The need for the other arises because one's property in a thing is decisively established as an objective reality (as distinct from a subjective claim) only when it is freely recognized by a being radically independent of oneself—which is to say, by a being who, by virtue of a like capacity for freedom, also claims to be an absolute end. However, a person may recognize the absolute end-status of another without compromising his own (and so without disqualifying himself as one competent to deliver objective reality to another) only if the other reciprocally recognizes the first. The end-status of personality is thus real only within a relationship of mutual recognition of worth between free and equal persons; and so this relationship marks the bounds of whatever rights to the forbearance of others a person may validly assert (71).[49]

In previous chapters, I tried to vindicate the structure of mutual recognition as the ground of individual rights by showing how this structure's normative force is extensively corroborated in the prephilosophic discourse of private law. We have seen, for example, that one's property in uses of land is never determined simply by one's desires. This would imply a duty in neighboring owners to defer to one's pleasure without any reciprocal deference to them. Reciprocity is ensured by defining one's property in terms of a social standard of "ordinary use" to which all are equally entitled and by requiring anyone who wishes protection for an exceptional use to bargain for it.[50] Similarly, the right to impose risks on others is limited to those ordinarily concomitant with action in society and that the self-respecting agent would thus consent to suffer as being consistent with an equal liberty for himself.[51] And the right to compel someone to make good the value of his promise standardly depends on a reciprocal self-submission to his will. Accordingly, the person's end-status exists objectively only within an intersubjective exchange of respect that I am calling dialogic community.

3.2 The Nature of Criminal Wrong

Having established the intersubjective matrix within which alone the right of the person exists, we are now in a position to understand the nature of criminal wrong as conceived within the pure agency paradigm. This nature will come into view if we first recall the generic meaning of wrong discussed in the previous chapter. A wrong, we said, is an exercise of freedom wherein the self claims a right of action vis-à-vis another that the other cannot consistently with his equal end-status recognize as valid; or wherein the will makes claims for its worth in excess of those objectively validated through the framework of mutual recognition. Inasmuch as the wrongdoer's right-claim implies the subordination of the very independent self needed to confirm it, the claim is doomed to remain a fantasy. This is why Hegel calls wrong a show (Schein) or a pretense. In wrong, what inherently lacks reality and cannot possibly obtain it makes a show of reality (82).

Now an agent may engage in this pretense in two different ways.[52] He may do so, first of all, in the mistaken belief that he is acting within limits consistent with the equal end-status of the other. He may, for example, take something out of another's possession believing it to be his own; or he may injure someone as a consequence of imposing a risk greater than that ordinarily incidental to the equal freedom of both, believing the risk to be within these limits. In these cases, one agent wrongs another because he asserts a freedom of action in relation to the other that the other cannot recognize without subordinating himself to the preeminence of the first, hence without disqualifying himself as an absolute end capable of objectively confirming the worth of another self. The fact that the defendant acts in good faith cannot nullify the wrong, for otherwise the defendant's subjective beliefs would unilaterally determine the plaintiff's rights contrary to their equal status as ends. The rights of persons are determined intersubjectively; hence the ubiquitous standard of the reasonable person in private law. Nevertheless, the unintentional character of the wrong is not insignificant. Insofar as the wrongdoer oversteps the bounds of rightful liberty unwittingly, he does not deny the intersubjective foundation of his rights. He does not deny, in other words, that his rightful liberty is confined within bounds consistent with the other's equal right to be master of his body and possessions. On the contrary, he acknowledges this limitation but errs as to what the standard of equal freedom permits, or as to where the boundaries of his freedom lie (85). Consequently, the actualization of intersubjectivity as the standard of right takes the form not of a subjugation of a contrary principle but of an adjustment of the relation between plaintiff and defendant in accordance with its requirements. Thus the remedy for a civil wrong consists in the tortfeasor's unilateral deferral to his victim's person to the degree necessary to redress the asymmetry produced by his earlier action. By compensating the plaintiff for the damage caused by his excess, the tortfeasor relinquishes the preeminence his action implied; by receiving compensation, the victim gains recognition for the dignity previously offended. Both are thus returned to the normative position of equality and mutual respect.

Suppose, however, that the wrongdoer *knowingly* exercises a degree of freedom inconsistent with the equal freedom of the other, say, by knowingly taking another's property, or by having his way with another's body in defiance of the other's refusal of consent, or by knowingly imposing an excessive degree of risk and injuring someone as a consequence. In these cases, the wrongdoer not only transgresses the moral boundary reconciling his freedom with another's; he challenges the intersubjective foundation of valid claims to respect, claiming an absolute worth for his isolated self and denying worth to the other. When I unintentionally wrong a person, I do not deny that he is a right-bearing person worthy of respect but merely err as to the scope of his rights or as to the things to which they extend. However, when I intentionally wrong him, I deny his right to respect and therewith set up my isolated self—the self outside of social reciprocity—as an absolute end, in effect claiming a right to an unbridled liberty. I thus not only infringe *this* person's right; I challenge the existence or validity of rights as such (95).[53] This denial of the validity of rights in general marks the specific difference of criminal wrong, that which distinguishes it from tort; and it explains why the public prosecutor, as agent of the legal order, carries the criminal action in its own name and not simply on behalf of the victim. Of course, the criminal may not have actually thought of his act as a denial of rights in general. As an empirical matter, such a thought may never have crossed his mind. Nevertheless, the denial of rights may properly be imputed to the intentional wrongdoer for a reason I shall try to explain.

Insofar as I am a free agent, I am capable of making into an object of consciousness my carrying out a particular purpose. For example, in robbing Tom, I as an agent am aware not only of my desire to rob Tom but also that it is I who am desiring and doing this.[54] By virtue of this capacity for ascribing my concrete purposes to myself as a subject, I may be taken to affirm in my intentional act not only the particular, foreground purpose (robbing Tom) that the act accomplishes but also the universal, background end—namely, the self—that my conscious purpose expresses in a certain way. That background end is the principle behind my action, the deeper point my act embodies. Further, if I as a free agent will the underlying principle of my action, I also will the necessary implications of that principle when it is taken seriously as a principle—that is to say, when it is universalized. This is so whether or not I am empirically aware of the deeper implications of my act; for my willing the principle and its logical consequences is something I do simply in virtue of being a subject whose concrete intentional acts express a universal idea that cannot logically be confined to any of its particular expressions. The universal idea behind my willful interference with another's liberty or property is that the isolated self is an absolute end possessing a right to a liberty unlimited by respect for others. The logical implication of this idea is that no one has any real right to the concrete embodiment of liberty in bodily and proprietary sovereignty. Accordingly, in willing the violation of a particular person's right, I will the nonexistence of rights as such.

3.3 Penal Justice as Desert

The fact that crime is distinguished from tort by its challenge to the existence of rights explains how coercion of the criminal is legitimated (as "punishment") within formal right. A common criticism of Hegel's theory of punishment is that it at most explains why it is not unjust to coerce the criminal but offers no positive reason for punishing, and indeed cannot do so without invoking the very consequentialist considerations it wants to exclude.[55] I shall try to state the theory in a way that reveals this criticism as mistaken. We should bear in mind, however, that the following account of punishment presupposes a legal framework that excludes from normative relevance all considerations of the good because it identifies them (mistakenly, as it turns out) with considerations of appetite. It is thus an account of punishment that applies paradigmatically to intentional violations of personality but not (as we shall see) to breaches of statutes directed to a social good.

We saw that the criminal wills a principle—the end-status of the isolated self—that, when universalized, involves the nullity of concrete rights. This means that the criminal also wills the nonexistence of his own rights, so that in punishing him we do nothing that the criminal does not implicitly license. "The action," writes Hegel, "is a law which [the criminal] set up and, in [his] deed, [he has] fully recognized its validity."[56] Thus the criminal, in denying rights, logically forfeits his own; he wills the negation of his own right that his right-denying principle entails. If Hegel's account of punishment stopped there, one could fairly protest that he has shown why it is not unjust to punish but has provided no affirmative reason to do so. If in search of such a reason he were to look to some social good, then he would have committed himself to rethinking his account of criminal wrong, for this account presupposed the legal irrelevance of the good. And if criminal wrong were reconceptualized, how could the theory of punishment based on the initial conception survive?

But Hegel says more.

> The infringement of the right as right is something that happens and has positive existence in the world, though inherently it is nothing at all. The manifestation of its nullity is the appearance, also in the external world, of the annihilation of the infringement. This is the right actualized, the necessity of the right mediating itself with itself by annulling what has infringed it (97).

By this passage I think Hegel means the following. Implicit in the criminal's intentional wrong was a right-claim. In exalting the isolated self as an absolute end, the criminal asserted a right to an unlimited liberty destructive of rights to actual liberty. The universalization of this claim shows it, however, to be absurd. For in denying that persons have rights to respect, the criminal also denied his own right to respect *and so contradicted his original claim to an absolute worth in isolation.* The fact that the criminal contradicts his original right-claim is crucial to Hegel's account of punishment; for it is only through the autonomous disclosure of this contradiction that the intersubjective will is confirmed as the true ground of rights and actualized as the supreme normative principle against its challenger. Now, the act of retribution is precisely the worldly manifestation of the contradiction latent in the criminal's principle. The nullity of his right-claim is outwardly demonstrated by the act that coerces him in return. This act might take the form of the victim's revenge, or it might take the form of punishment meted out by a dispassionate (and therefore more fitting) executive of the intersubjective will. The positive point of punishment within the pure agency paradigm, then, is twofold: first, it manifests the self-destructive implication of the claimed end-status of the isolated will and so too the invalidity of that claim; second and concomitantly, it confirms to rational insight that intersubjectivity is the sole coherent foundation of the person's right to respect. Yet the positive point is not a good that we as empirical individuals promote in punishing; it is not we who affirm a social commitment to rights by expressing our disapproval of acts that deny them. Were this so, punishment could not be justified to the criminal (whose notional assent alone matters), for perhaps his idea of the good differs from ours. Rather, punishment is the process by which the intersubjective will gains proof of its normative authority through the revealed self-contradictoriness of its adversary. Beginning with the singular self as unconditioned end, we see that the logical culmination of this principle is crime, the recoiling of crime in retribution, and therewith the validation of intersubjectivity as the ground of rights. Since this process is an autonomously rational one, its end-result (the confirmation of intersubjectivity to insight) cannot be viewed as a good that we as punishers seek to promote.

To this account of punishment, however, a further objection may be raised. To say that crime is self-contradictory and that punishment manifests this contradiction does not really explain or justify the actual practice of punishment. For if the criminal's act is inherently or conceptually self-nullifying, why do we need to punish him? Whether we punish the criminal or let him alone, the truth of the matter remains unchanged: his right-claim is absurd and so impotent (as Hegel admits) to undermine the intersubjective will as the true ground of rights (97, 99). One might therefore argue that on Hegel's account, the real-world practice of punishment is a mere ceremonial appendage to a conceptual truth complete without it—a symbolic morality play we could either dispense with or else justify by needs of popular education extrinsic to (and so illicit within) the pure agency model. From the standpoint of this model, accordingly, actual punishment appears as a gratuitous piece of violence. For if the act (as distinct from the concept) of retribution is not determined by the criminal's deed, then the sentence is arbitrarily imposed by the judge rather than willed by the wrongdoer.

This objection misses the full force of the claim implied in the criminal act. By intentionally wronging another, the criminal impliedly, as we said, claims that the isolated person is an absolute end. But the criminal does not make this claim in the philosopher's study. He actualizes it in the world by deliberately infringing someone's right. He thereby shows that he is serious about his claim, that he means it to be effective in the world, to have the force of law.[57] His claim is no doubt conceptually absurd. But the logical absurdity of the claim does not by itself rule out its existential validity; for it is possible that the idea of a coherent right is an intellectual construct with no real authority over life. The point of punishment within the pure agency paradigm is to show that this is not the case. Punishment actualizes the intersubjective will *as law* against the law set up by the criminal. It thus demonstrates that rights have force in the world, that the logical absurdity of crime is also its ontological nullity (99). Again, however, it is not we who assert the ineffectuality of crime in order to express our belief in the reality of human rights. Rather, the impotence of crime is disclosed by the criminal act itself. In acting out his dream of supremacy, the criminal willed as law—as having force in the world—a conception of an end that, when universalized as law (having force in the world), leaves his own right vulnerable to real-world infringement.[58] Hence the criminal wills not only the logical downfall of his principle but also his actual punishment.[59]

From this account of criminal wrong and the invalidation thereof we can derive the criteria of penal justice generated by the pure agency paradigm. These are the criteria that distinguish punishment from the original coercion of the criminal or from wrongful violence in general. The first point to observe is that punishment within this framework has the significance of retribution, of the recoiling against the criminal of his own disdain for personality. It is thus not arbitrary force externally imposed on the criminal for another's good but the internal nemesis of the criminal's own act. This means that the ethical justification of punishment as a form of coercion categorically distinguished from the criminal's lies in a past intentional wrong rather than in a desired goal to which punishment is a means. Stated otherwise, penal justice here consists in the inner connection between the principle of the criminal's act and his liability to coercion rather than in the maximization or promotion of good. A good-oriented or instrumentalist punishment is impossible here, because there is as yet no good distinct from subjective preference, hence none qualified to ground a distinction between punishment and arbitrary violence.

The idea that penal justice consists in the conceptual connection between criminality and liability to coercion yields two possible formulations of the criterion of just punishment. One can say that penal justice consists in the deservedness of punishment, where desert is understood stringently as the entailment of the criminal's moral vulnerability by the disrespect for personhood implied in his deed;* or one can say that penal justice consists in the immanence of punishment in the criminal's own will, hence in the congruence of punishment with the agent's autonomy. Punishment is immanent in the criminal's will—that is, assented to—in a dual sense. First, it is immanent in his *actual* will, for it is the application to him of the law set up by his intentional act. Second, punishment is immanent in his *rational* will, for it aggrandizes not another particular will (not even that of a majority) external to the criminal's but the intersubjective will in which his own end-status is confirmed (100). In this dual form of assent to punishment we see the dialogic structure of penal justice within the pure agency paradigm. On the one hand, the intersubjective will submits for confirmation of its authority to the self-contradiction of the criminal will, and its force is just punishment only if authored by the agent through a willful wrong; on the other hand, the agent (ideally) educated through this process submits to the intersubjective will as to the known basis of his solid worth. Because, moreover, his punishment is conceptually authorized by the criminal, it is consistent with personality's absolute right (see Chap. IV, 3.1) within the formalist paradigm against external interferences with liberty or proprietary sovereignty.

3.4 Implications for Doctrine

From the foregoing account of criminal wrong and punishment we can derive the basic elements of criminal culpability recognized by the common law. These are the elements that make coercion of the agent just (deserved) punishment immanent in his will rather than the external violence of another criminal will. Thus the mens rea requirement is the requirement that there be the willful denial of the end-status of personality that entails the nullity of one's own right to liberty as its necessary implication. This requirement is satisfied, as we have seen, when the wrong to another is intended—when one knowingly transgresses the limits reconciling one's liberty with another's. However, the mens rea requirement is not only met by the central case of intention, that is, by desiring the (believed to be possible) product of one's act and acting from that desire;[60] it is met too by any state of mind that signifies disrespect for the equal freedom of another self. Thus mental states one might want to distinguish for the purposes of a philosophical psychology or as marking fine distinctions

---

*This sense of penal desert is stringent because the criminal's forfeiture of his right to respect is entailed by his intentional act quite apart from positive law. Later I contrast a weaker sense of desert according to which someone deserves punishment if the unlawful act is morally attributable to him and regardless of whether doing the act (e.g., possessing a narcotic) would imply one's liability to coercion apart from positive law.

of moral character are treated as equivalents from the standpoint of criminal wrong and the annulment thereof. One manifests disrespect for another's free will when one destroys, uses, or alters the embodiments of his will without his consent whether one desires that very outcome or, knowing that it will certainly or likely result from one's act, is indifferent to whether it does; when one knowingly imposes an asymmetrical degree of risk on another and accidentally injures him; or when one is willfully blind to the circumstances that render one's act a wrong. Conversely, states of mind that fall short of denying the end-status of personality imply no negation of right that could rebound against the wrongdoer; hence they cannot justify the degradation of criminal treatment however compatible with the responsibility of the agent or morally censurable they may be. From the standpoint of the pure agency paradigm, an unwitting imposition of excessive risk can never be a legitimate ground of criminal liability, no matter how far below the standard of care the agent fell and regardless of his capacity to conform to the standard. Though proscribable (as we shall see) by a regulatory statute, such an act is not deserving of criminal punishment in the rigorous sense of desert understood within the pure agency paradigm, for it implies no denial of an obligation to respect liberty and hence no license for the disrespect of one's own. Moreover, if disrespect for his freedom is not licensed by the agent, then it amounts to a forcible use of the individual for the benefit of others, indistinguishable in principle from crime.

The act requirement of criminal liability is likewise intelligible from the standpoint of the pure agency account of criminal wrong. In order that there be a *criminal* wrong, there must first be a wrong in the sense we have explained—an exercise of liberty inconsistent with the equal objectified freedom of another. A wrong against a specific person will obviously satisfy this requirement, so that a tort, if committed intentionally or recklessly (i.e., with advertence to the excessiveness of the risk), becomes an actus reus as well as a tort. However, because a criminal act presupposes the intentionality of wrongdoing, it has a significance different from that of a tort. When coupled with intention, the wrongful act signifies the objective realization—the transition into outward and public reality—of the claimed end-status of the isolated will. Without this external embodiment, the claim to an absolute liberty (and the corollary denial of the right of persons) remains a subjective conceit or fancy; it does not rise to the status of a transindividual principle implicitly claiming the force of law. One may harbor private fantasies of one's domination of others, or communicate one's intention to realize them, or even take steps furthering one's aim; however, until there is action *reflecting* the aim—until there is a deed mirroring in the external world the criminal purpose—the intention is a subjective wish and not a principle claiming objective validity. If, however, the intention claims no objective validity, there is no logical impetus to universalize it, hence no inner determination of punishability. Accordingly, just as (within the pure agency paradigm) a wrongful act becomes an actus reus only when united with intention or its equivalents, so does an evil intention become a mens rea only when united with an act that embodies it. Each element of criminal culpability presupposes the other; hence, as the common law recognizes, only their concurrence produces a criminal wrong justifying punishment.[61]

Now if the significance of the actus reus is that it objectifies the claimed end-status of the isolated will, there is no reason to limit criminal wrongs to intentional torts—to wrongs against specific persons. An act (e.g., of driving) manifesting a reckless indifference toward the life or physical integrity of persons is a crime whether or not it results in injury to a victim. Similarly, an act intended to work one's will with the life, body, or property of another but that fails to realize the agent's purpose may nonetheless amount to an actus reus if it, no less than the completed act, outwardly embodies the criminal intent.[62] Thus attempts are crimes if there is an act that, viewed in all the circumstances, cannot reasonably be interpreted as having other than a criminal purpose; and if this test is met, the fact that it was (factually or legally) impossible to commit the crime or that the accused desisted is irrelevant. Salmond's unequivocality test is thus the appropriate specification of the pure agency paradigm in relation to attempts.[63]

The account of criminal wrong generated by the pure agency paradigm also explains the common-law excuses based on absence of mens rea and indicates solutions to venerable controversies. The mens rea of criminal culpability is not whatever state of mind or level of fault a lawmaker has stipulated for an offense;[64] nor is it the level of moral blameworthiness needed to justify the severest sanctions a legal system administers;[65] nor is it any one of several states of mind that a philosophical psychology tells us is consistent with the idea of a responsible agent.[66] The morally obvious fact that a competent but thoughtless actor is responsible for the reasonably foreseeable consequences of his act does not logically take us to liability to punishment as a criminal as distinct from tort liability, liability to regulatory penalties, or from moral blameworthiness. What alone takes us to criminal punishment is the intentional or (advertently) reckless disdain for the liberty of another self that, when absolutized as a principle, involves the insecurity of one's own liberty as its necessary consequence. Hence the core excuse from criminal liability takes the form "I did not intend (desire, know of, foresee, willfully blind myself to) the infringement of right."

This principle yields the following doctrinal implications. An honest belief in consent should excuse from criminal liability for assault (sexual or otherwise) even if the mistake is unreasonable.[67] The requirement of a reasonable mistake belongs, as we shall see, to the paradigm of welfare. Moreover, if intoxication rendered the accused incapable of forming the requisite intent, then he should be excused whether the intent is "basic" or "specific," though he is guilty of criminal negligence causing the unlawful consequence if he adverted to the hazards of getting drunk and took no precautions. Insanity excuses if it rendered the accused incapable of appreciating the nature of his act or of knowing it exceeded the bounds of mutual respect, for in either case there is lacking the devaluation of personality that alone implies the nugatoriness of one's own rights.[68] Insanity that does not manifest itself in this degree of cognitive impairment is not a proper excuse. For example, there can be no question (outside of a plea of automatism) of an insanity excuse based on irresistible impulse or on an incapacity to conform one's conduct to the law.[69] If the accused had the cognitive capacity to know what he was doing and that it was wrong, then he also had the capacity to refuse an impulse, for self-consciousness *is* that capacity. If such a person is to be excused, then so must everyone who fails to resist an overwhelmingly (for him) powerful urge or temptation even in the absence of circumstances that would support a plea of necessity. But this would deny the postulate of free choice on which the capacity for rights (and hence the possibility of wrong) rests. Thus the M'Naghten rules are the appropriate specification of the pure agency paradigm in relation to insanity.

The excuse of insanity is worth dwelling on, for it is the clearest confirmation of the theory of criminal wrong we are deploying. That theory says that a knowing denial of the intersubjective basis of rights alone constitutes a crime in the sense of a wrong deserving or calling forth punishment. Thus, to be liable to punishment as a criminal, one must both intend the product of one's act and know that one's act is outlawed by the standard of intersubjective reason. This, I submit, is what mens rea in the full sense means. In the normal case, however, the full content of mens rea is not explicitly at issue, for there is a presumption (which is simply a truism) that rational agents know the wrongfulness of unjustified homicide, coercion, takings, and so on. Thus the only part of mens rea normally in question is the intentionality of the deed, not of the wrong: we ask, for example, whether the accused intended to kill the victim, taking for granted that he knew killing another person is wrong. When, however, the presumption of rationality is removed, the full meaning of mens rea is engaged. The insane accused will be exonerated either if he did not understand what he was doing or if he could not know that what he was doing was wrong. Moreover, there is growing common-law support for the position that "wrong" means not only "against positive law" but also "contrary to the standard of reasonable persons."[70] Accordingly, the

M'Naghten rules make explicit an element of culpability—knowledge of a breach of intersubjective reason—that is tacitly present in all the other excuses based on absence of mens rea. These rules let us see what mens rea truly means.

They also help us to understand the rule about ignorance of the law. *Pace* Holmes and Fletcher, that rule is no counterexample to the subjectivist theory of criminality, for (as Hale's explanation makes evident) the rule merely reflects the tautological proposition that rational agents know the inherent unlawfulness of acts inconsistent with the mutual recognition of persons as ends; and every adult person is presumed rational until he demonstrates otherwise. Rational agents know the unlawfulness of acts disrespectful of personality because they know that such acts contradict the only rights that can exist objectively; and because they know that the reality of rights demands the annulment of whatever show of validity these acts make. Accordingly, if the adult accused wishes to claim that he did not know his homicide was unlawful by the standard of intersubjective reason, he must do so within the context of a plea of insanity (the infant is presumed not to know and for that reason excused unless the contrary is proved). If his plea is successful, his ignorance of the law will excuse him from punishment as surely as would any other circumstance negating criminal intent; but he will be subject, if he is still dangerous, to the prophylactic (not punitive) restraints reserved for those who conspicuously lack the capacity for freedom supportive of the full rights of personality. If, however, the accused knew his act was unlawful judged by the standard of mutual respect but did not know that this standard was the true criterion of right and wrong (thinking, perhaps, it was a mere societal convention favoring the timid and weak), he will not be excused, for this kind of ignorance is criminality itself. Thus the rule that ignorance of the law is no excuse is in perfect accord with the subjectivist theory of criminal culpability; for it either reflects a rebuttable presumption of sanity or else restates the insight that a challenge to the intersubjective basis of right is the essence of crime.

All of these doctrinal conclusions flow from the basic norm of the pure agency paradigm. As part of a noninstrumental understanding of punishment, they follow logically from a normative standpoint that takes the choosing self as the sole absolute end, and that therefore recognizes no common goal or value for the sake of which the self could, consistently with its autonomy, be coerced. As we have thus far derived them, the doctrines of the pure agency model of the penal law merely form a coherent system ordered by a certain conception of an unconditioned end. They do not yet have an absolute justification, for the theory of the unconditioned from which they flow is itself a particular and contestable one. Our endorsement of these doctrines has so far merely anticipated what has yet to appear—the normative foundation that justifies within limits a doctrinal paradigm serving no value.

For anyone immersed in this paradigm, of course, there is no such higher justification. The conception of the unconditioned on which the model rests is from this standpoint not simply *a* conception of the unconditioned. It is the unconditioned itself and, as such, forms the horizon of legal thought. For this preskeptical attitude, the mere demonstration of the coherence of a doctrine with the foundational principle will be enough to establish its absolute validity, for it is in the nature of a foundational principle that it cannot itself be further justified; it is self-justifying and everything else is justified (or not) through it. As we shall now see, however, there are phenomena within the pure agency paradigm itself that testify to the incoherence of its principle as a conception of the unconditioned and that drive us to a welfarist principle formative of a new paradigm of penal justice. Once this new framework comes into view, the pure agency paradigm can no longer be self-justifying; one can no longer persuasively argue for the doctrines native to it simply by appealing to its foundational norm, for this norm has now been revealed in its particularity and historical relativity. As a result, the elements of criminal justice that formerly seemed fixed and certain—elements such as the centrality of desert, the subjective standard of fault, and the independent act requirement—are now called radically into question. They may yet turn out to be absolutely justified. However, whether they are will now depend on whether we can vindicate the pure agency paradigm and the defective principle that informs it from the standpoint of a normative foundation beyond and inclusive of that framework.

4. THE EQUIVOCATIONS OF FORMALISM

We have seen that the pure agency paradigm is organized by a conception of the absolute end as the abstract and vacuous self. Because all value is treated as subjective, it is excluded from the unconditioned end that supports valid duties. And because welfare denotes the satisfaction of value, it too must be regarded as without public significance and hence as irrelevant to the notion of wrongdoing.

Yet the instability of this abstract conception of the unconditioned is revealed within the pure agency model itself. As we saw in the chapter on tort, the formalist paradigm recognizes that the self must embody itself to objectify or confirm its status as an end. It recognizes this necessity in treating interferences with the person's self-possession and property as violations *of* personality. Such interferences are not, after all, coercive of the pure will as such. Strictly speaking (as Hegel says), the pure will cannot be coerced, for it is theoretically capable of renouncing its attachment to life, body, and property when the latter are threatened (91). Since it *can* renounce these values, its submission to someone who holds them in his power signifies a choice not to do so; hence if freedom were identified with this purely formal capacity to choose, one would be compelled to say that the person who submits to another's will under threat of death or bodily harm has not been coerced. Of course, the pure agency paradigm does not say this. On the contrary, it is the criminal who, by repudiating the freedom embodied in the mutual recognition of property, privileges abstract over objective freedom and who therefore takes the formalist premise of the pure agency paradigm to its logical and self-destructive conclusion. The incoherence of crime is thus also the incoherence of the abstract conception of the unconditioned on which the pure agency paradigm overtly rests and which it is always covertly denying. In treating interferences with life, physical well-being, and property as wrongfully coercive, the pure agency paradigm acknowledges these objects as aspects of personality indispensable to its freedom, *as values the self is not free to renounce.*[71] But then it is embodied and not abstract freedom that is the unconditioned end supportive of valid duties. And once we acknowledge the necessity to freedom of embodiment, we grant the existence of objects universally valuable for agency and hence too the possibility of being harmed in ways that are juridically cognizable.

The inescapability of value for a coherent conception of agency is also revealed in the way that the pure agency paradigm apportions punishments to crimes. The popular notion that punishment must fit the crime is perhaps an intuitive perception of the inner connection between crime and retribution within the formal agency paradigm. Because, however, this connection is conceptual and abstract rather than empirical or quantitative, it cannot determine how much punishment any particular crime deserves. That coercing the criminal is the logical consequence of the criminal's own principle implies that crime and punishment are conceptually equal in the sense that the rule laid down by the criminal is applied equally to him. But this equality is too abstract to guide us in deciding what crimes deserve what penalties (the "eye for an eye" rule is a possible application of the equality principle but not a necessary one, so that the absurdities to which it leads do not touch the principle itself), nor can any other principle determine this (101).[72] Hence the concrete application of the fitness criterion requires a gradation of crimes according to their "seriousness," to which order a parallel scale of punishments is then roughly fitted. This ranking of crimes cannot occur, however, without comparing the embodiments of freedom in terms of their value for agency (96). Thus minor theft is punished less severely than minor assault, because personality is more integrally connected with the body than with any particular external object; and assault is punished less severely than culpable homicide, because the former interferes with agency while the latter extinguishes it altogether. Accordingly, in concretely applying its principle of equality between crime and punishment, the pure agency paradigm cannot avoid grading wrongs according to the harm they inflict on valuable objects.

The same tacit acknowledgment of the normative relevance of harm can be seen in the significance the criminal law attaches to consequences. An attempt is criminal because it implies the same disrespect for personality as does the accomplished purpose; yet the completed offense is punished more severely than the attempted one. An assault causing death (manslaughter) attracts more punishment than one of equal ferocity from which the victim luckily recovers. Reckless conduct that materializes in death is punished more severely than that which produces "bodily harm," which in turn draws more punishment than the same conduct without harm, even though the significance for equality of all three acts is the same. Thus, while liability to punishment per se flows from a theory of criminal wrong that excludes all mention of harm—from the willful disdain for the free will of another—the *measure* of punishment depends on relative harm to fundamental interests.

The puzzle here is not, as some believe, that fortuities are credited to an agent whose moral blameworthiness or dangerousness is no different from that of someone whose identical act happened to produce harmful consequences. The problem appears in this light only to one who thinks that criminal punishment is justified by its good effects; for no deterrent or reformative purpose is served by imposing different punishments on convicts neither of whom intends the additional consequence (or, in the case of attempt, where both intend the completed offense) and whose degree of depravity is the same. However, the fact that the vicious assailant derives the benefit of his good fortune in not killing his victim poses a different sort of puzzle within the pure agency paradigm; for here criminal liability has nothing to do with one's moral worth or dangerousness (hence the irrelevance of motive, noble or otherwise, to criminal culpability) and everything to do with one's outwardly embodied denial of equal freedom as the basis of rights.[73] From this vantage point, what is striking about the relevance of consequences is that acts having the same juridical significance as denials of equal rights of freedom are differentiated normatively on the basis of a factor—the causing of harm—that plays no role in the account of liability. The welfare considerations that are excluded from normative significance at the level of retributive theory insinuate themselves at the level of punitive practice. This occurs, of course, because the embodiments of freedom matter to freedom, because agents thus have objective in addition to subjective interests, and because they can therefore be harmed in ways that affect the relative gravity of wrongs.

There are, in addition, defenses in the criminal law that further reflect the equivocation of the formalist paradigm with respect to the subjectivity of all values. The overt indifference of this paradigm (for we must now contrast this to a covert attention) to considerations of welfare is exemplified in the normal inaptness of consequentialist reasoning to the issue of criminal culpability. It is, in general, no defense to a willful interference with the embodiments of another's freedom that one thereby produced more good in the world than harm. Thus the surgeon who kills a psychopath and distributes his vital organs among several needy philanthropists will be punished as a murderer. However, the limits of this exclusion of consequentialism are revealed in situations where the essential embodiments of agency—life, bodily integrity, and property—come into conflict. If someone jettisons cargo in the reasonable belief that death from drowning is otherwise imminent, or if someone steals under threat of death or serious bodily harm from another person, he will be exonerated under the law of necessity and duress, respectively.[74] Whether one conceives these defenses as excuses or justifications, one cannot treat them as exculpatory without acknowledging an objective scale of value based on the importance of an object for the expression of freedom. If one sees necessity and duress as excuses negating voluntariness, one will have to admit that the act is involuntary only because the accused is entitled to treat his life or health as inalienable when they conflict with another's property in some particular thing; he would not be entitled to do so if they conflicted with another's life.[75] Hence the judgment that the act is involuntary presupposes a ranking of goods according to their value for agency, which is perhaps why crimes excused by necessity are sometimes said to be "normatively involuntary,"[76]—that is, involuntary not because the will does not choose but because the choice is affected by powerful inclinations that moral theory endorses. If, however, one treats necessity and duress as justifications, one explicitly postulates a hierarchy of goods according to which property must yield to values (life, bodily integrity) more important to the foundational end—personality—through which property is itself justified.

The limits of the formalist paradigm are revealed, finally, in the exceptional relevance to culpability of motive—a consideration that, while inadmissible on the question of liability, is acknowledged in mitigation of sentence. Within the formalist paradigm, motive is irrelevant to criminal culpability, because it is understood as a subjective end of action devoid of public significance—something whose admissibility as an excuse would thus subvert the intersubjective character of right.[77] Thus (outside the stringent limitations of the defenses of necessity and duress) it is no excuse to a crime that one committed it for altruistic reasons—to benefit one's family, humankind, or the victim himself. In *R. v. Dudley and Stephens*,[78] however, two shipwrecked seamen in a lifeboat devoured a cabin boy to avoid imminent starvation. In this situation (as the court held) the defense of necessity is unavailable, for neither the rationale of justification nor that of normative involuntariness applies where the values in conflict (here life) are equal. For the formalist paradigm, indeed, the case is an easy one. The accused seamen are viewed as abstract egos who intentionally asserted their worth as persons at the expense of the cabin boy's. Their reasons for doing so are subjective ends of action having no bearing on their objective culpability. They are thus guilty of murder. Yet their culpability does indeed seem to be affected by their circumstances; for if they killed under pressure of motives to which a person of ordinary fortitude would also have succumbed, then as an empirical matter they have not set themselves above the standard of intersubjective respect. In a noumenal sense they have done so, but empirically they have not. And the fact that they have not done so empirically is thought to bear enough resemblance—to be a sufficiently close simulacrum—to the excuse of unintentional wrong to warrant not only a drastic reduction of sentence but also an exercise of the sovereign power of pardon.[79]

We see the same idea at work in the defense of provocation. Provocation reduces murder to manslaughter if the accused killed in the heat of a passion to which the person of ordinary self-control might also have surrendered.[80] This circumstance is thought to be significant not simply for the purpose of tailoring (within the statutory range decreed by considerations of desert) a sentence to the specific reformative needs of the convict; were this the point of the provocation plea, the objective standard of ordinary self-control would be incoherent, for it would artificially obstruct an empirical inquiry into the propensities of *this* accused. Rather, circumstances of provocation are thought to mitigate *culpability*. The fact that the accused has not departed empirically from the standard of all-too-human conduct is thought to simulate the conceptual basis of excuses (namely, that the accused, through lack of intention, meant no challenge to the intersubjective basis of right) so as to warrant conviction on a less serious charge.[81] Accordingly, in circumstances of provocation as well as in those of a necessity not covered by the defense of necessity, the criminal law practically admits the relevance to culpability of a motive of which the formalist paradigm takes no official account.

5. THE PARADIGM OF WELFARE

5.1 The General Happiness and the Common Good

I have argued that the pure agency paradigm, while explicitly based on a conception of the unconditioned as abstract selfhood, acknowledges *sub silentio* the impossibility of such a conception; and that it implicitly identifies the unconditioned end with freedom embodied in life, physical integrity, and property and recognized by other selves. That is to say, it implicitly recognizes realized rather than formal freedom as a right of the person and so as the basis of valid duty. The self-conscious elevation of this principle to the status of a foundational norm generates the paradigm of welfare.

What are the characteristic features of the welfarist model of the penal law? To begin with, we must distinguish between two senses of welfare. The latter may denote the satisfaction of values relative to individual desire, or it may denote the satisfaction of values derived from the concept of a free agent.[82] Both conceptions have a place within the welfarist paradigm, and each constitutes a subsystem of its own. I shall use the term "general happiness" to designate the system of law based on subjective values and the term "common good" to refer to the system based on values essential to agency. Before deriving the principles of right respectively native to these systems, let us see how the subjective values excluded from relevance under the pure agency paradigm acquire standing under the welfarist model.

The recognition (already implicit in the formal agency model) that personality's worth is real only as outwardly embodied entails a rehabilitation of the subjective goals of the individual as something whose realization is a matter of public importance. Because the choice and pursuit of individual values are the medium through which generic agency expresses itself, the authoritative actualization of the common freedom involves (in addition to enforcing negative rights against torts and crimes) promoting the general happiness understood as the result of some arithmetic operation (e.g., a summing or averaging) performed on the satisfactions of discrete individuals. Whether "promoting" should mean maximizing an impersonal sum or average, equalizing, encouraging Pareto-superior moves, or maximizing the happiness of the least well off will depend on the justification for treating preference satisfaction as a public good—as something a public authority ought to facilitate. The justification that informs the welfarist legal paradigm is action-based. That is to say, it begins not from the brute fact of desire (as does utilitarianism and the economic analysis of law) but from freedom and the requirements of its self-expression. The public authority does not promote happiness because the gratification of preference is in itself a good. As subjectively contingent ends, preferences by themselves have no standing in normative discourse; they generate no duties in others to respect or serve them. Thus a penal restriction of liberty justified by the greater pleasure of others would be arbitrary force. Rather, the public authority promotes happiness because the realization of agency is a universal end and because this process necessarily involves the formation and pursuit of subjective values (121–124).

This justification for promoting the general happiness through penal laws is egalitarian. If my subjective welfare is worth promoting because I am a free agent whose freedom requires concrete expression, then the felicity of all other agents is equally worthy of public concern (125). Accordingly, the agency-based argument for the moral salience of the general happiness rules out any interpretation of this norm that countenances the sacrifice of the satisfactions of some for a greater happiness overall, or that treats certain substantive choices regarding how best to live as inherently less worthy of public support than others.[83] We see here another manifestation of dialogic community as the foundation of valid claims against others. Within the pure agency paradigm, the normative force of mutual recognition appeared as a demand that valid laws reflect mutual respect for spheres of private sovereignty and that the power of intersubjectivity be itself dialogically validated (as punishment) in the self-condemnation of willful wrongdoing. Within the welfarist paradigm, the normative force of dialogic community manifests itself further in the idea that authentic laws must reflect an equal concern of each citizen for the welfare of all; hence that penal laws must (with a limitation I will soon mention) be neutral with respect to preferences respectful of equal liberty, and inequalities of welfare must work to the long-run advantage of everyone whom the laws oblige.[84]

Once we justify the pursuit of happiness by reference to the realization of agency, we see that the promotion of the general happiness cannot exhaust the welfare agenda of a public authority founded on the normativity of the intersubjective will. Viewed from the standpoint of realized freedom, welfare means the satisfaction not only of contingent preferences but also of values indispensable to the coherent self-expression of agency—values whose goodness is thus based on reason rather than subjective desire. In order that the goals one chooses be authentically one's own or self-determined, one must have a minimum degree of life security, physical health, education, and economic wherewithal. One must also be nurtured in an environment of habits and attitudes that fosters a rational sense of one's worth and of one's capacity to be author of what one becomes. And one must be protected from those who would enslave others by procuring their addiction to substances the need for which exerts a tyranny over one's life choices. These are not primary goods in John Rawls's sense, because they are not things every rational agent would want more of to achieve the ends that he has. Rather, they are goods every rational agent would want to a sufficient degree in order that the ends he pursues can be freely chosen rather than chosen under prejudice or constraint. They are thus necessary conditions of authentic freedom rather than of success or happiness; and when pursued within bounds drawn by the requisites of freedom, they are normatively prior to (and so properly constrain the pursuit of) subjective ends, for the latter became morally salient only as expressions of freedom (130).

The conditions of freedom can be produced in part by penal laws protecting the health, safety, and self-respect of citizens. To distinguish these values from those relative to individual desire, let us call them aspects of the common good of autonomy; and let us correspondingly distinguish between penal laws aiming to increase the general happiness taking individual values as given and those aiming to promote the effective autonomy of all. Laws promoting competition in the market or regulating the harvesting of a depletable resource are examples of the former, while laws regulating the sale of food, liquor, and drugs, prohibiting environmental pollution, demanding a certain standard of safety in factories and on highways, and prohibiting the dissemination of hatred toward a racial group are examples of the latter.

We can now delineate the basic features of the welfarist paradigm of the penal law through a contrast with the pure agency model. First, the point of penal sanctions is not retribution for a past denial of the end-status of personality but the deterrence of activity inimical to a fair distribution of satisfactions or harmful to essential goods. Since the rationale for sanctions is goal-oriented or instrumentalist, the concept of desert no longer plays the pivotal role in justifying punishment that it did within the pure agency paradigm. There desert was the *model* of justification; punishment could not be justified otherwise than by a crime. Here the moral force of the goal justifies the sanction; and the requirement of desert is retained only as reinterpreted from the welfarist standpoint—as a constraint on policy that is itself teleologically justified by the goal of individual autonomy. So interpreted, desert is no longer meant stringently as the entailment of the agent's coercibility by his deed, for this sense will in general not be available where punishment is a prospective means to an end (price fixing, for example, does not logically imply a forfeiture of one's right against coercion); rather, desert is now understood in the weaker sense of the moral responsibility of the agent for the actus reus of the statutory offense. In a society ordered to the goal of individual autonomy, instrumentalist punishment is justified only if one's liability to use for the deterrence of others is a fate over which one may exercise control.

Second, the doctrine of mens rea as understood within the pure agency paradigm has no theoretical support within the welfarist model. This is so not because (as is often assumed) the lighter penalties for welfare offenses allow a relaxation or elimination of the fault requirement but because the idea of apportioning punishment to desert is out of place in this context. Recall that in the formal agency paradigm, subjective mens rea was an essential element of criminal desert because it triggered the conceptual circuit between wrongdoing and punishment. The willful infringement of a right to respect implied a denial of personality's worth whose universalization recoiled on the criminal in the nullification of his own right to liberty. In the welfarist paradigm, however, there is no necessary connection between the intentional deed and liability to punishment.[85] Apart from positive law, my catching of undersized lobsters does not entail the nullity of my rights as a necessary implication; nor even does my possession or sale of a narcotic. Here punishment (including the measure thereof) is justified not by the deed but by a goal; and because it is justified by a goal (which might conceivably be attained in other ways), it is contingently justified. Accordingly, the doctrine of mens rea has no role to play in the theoretical account of punishment within the welfarist paradigm; it is not part of an account of the inner logic and deservedness of punishment, because there is here no inner logic or deservedness to comprehend.[86] The requirement of subjective mens rea is thus firmly embedded within the pure agency paradigm and hence within the sphere of crimes infringing negative rights—rights against interference with liberty, bodily integrity, and property. When transplanted to the welfarist paradigm, mens rea becomes a flexible concept referring to any of the responsible states of mind from which a legislature may choose in acknowledging an autonomy-respecting constraint to its pursuit of welfare. Moreover, since a requirement of subjective mens rea (with its defense of unreasonable mistake) would frustrate the purpose of a welfare statute, liability within the welfarist paradigm is standardly based on negligence: only a reasonable mistake of fact or an exercise of "due diligence" will excuse.[87]

5.2 Penal Justice as the Priority of Autonomy

If penal justice within the welfarist framework does not consist in punishing in accordance with desert, in what does it consist? What are the principles of justice applicable to statutes creating welfare offenses? The utilitarian one—that the welfare goal be attained at the least cost in human suffering—is an obvious possibility, but we have already seen that it is ruled out by the agency-based justification for the public promotion of welfare. A happiness (or wealth) maximization principle would not only countenance the infliction of suffering on some for the particular advantage of others; it would also collapse the desire for autonomy-based goods into individual preferences and accept whatever quantum and distribution of these goods a competitive market produced. It would thus operate at the expense of the very freedom that gives preference satisfaction its moral standing.

The principles of penal justice indigenous to the welfare paradigm must be derived from the agency-based justification for the promotion of welfare. That justification supports principles of justice in the form of priority rules—that is, of rules that resolve conflicts between competing ends (e.g., happiness, formal liberty, positive freedom) not by reducing them to some all-embracing good but by establishing a rank order between them.[88] Since the state's promotion of the general happiness was justified with reference to the self-expression of agency, that enterprise must be constrained by respect for rights of equal freedom. As Hegel puts it, "[m]y particularity . . . is only a right at all in so far as I am a free entity. Therefore, it may not make claims for itself in contradiction to this its substantive basis, and an intention to secure my welfare or that of others . . . cannot justify an action which is wrong" (126). That is to say, one cannot infringe the rights established within the pure agency paradigm for the sake of the general happiness, for one cannot coherently pursue happiness at the expense of the free agency through which preference satisfaction first rises to moral and public significance. Accordingly, the principle of penal justice applicable to laws promoting the general happiness is the priority of autonomy over welfare or (in Rawls's formulation) of the right over the good.

What forms of liability does this principle exclude? In general, it forbids the promotion of happiness by means of sanctions that impinge on the agent as an incalculable and unavoidable fate and that, by failing to respect the person as a self-determining agent, one-sidedly reduce him to a means for the deterrence of others. Thus the state cannot enforce the policy behind a welfare statute by penalizing someone innocent of the unlawful act; nor can it do so by imposing absolute liability for lawbreaking;[89] nor can it penalize under the authority of an unpublished, retroactive, or excessively vague law;[90] nor if the accused reasonably relied on an erroneous official statement of the law.[91] Liability is excluded here not because the accused is undeserving of punishment—the idea of desert (strictly understood) has no application in this context—but because the pursuit of happiness must be constrained by respect for the agency that alone gives happiness its moral significance. In this priority rule we have another manifestation of dialogic community as the foundation of valid obligations. The individual can be legitimately coerced for the sake of the general happiness only insofar as the enforcement of the general happiness reciprocally respects the individual agent as an end.

The principle of penal justice applicable to laws promoting the common good is different. Here we cannot speak of the priority of autonomy over welfare (or of the right over the good), because welfare in this context denotes the satisfaction of the conditions of *effective* autonomy, by which rights of formal liberty must be limited if they are to be consistent with the equal end-status of persons (and so coherent as rights). Here, in other words, dialogic community manifests itself as the priority of the common good over formal liberty, since the unlimited exercise of negative rights leaves to chance the satisfaction of the conditions for the equal effective autonomy of all (130). This does not mean that the strictures against an unpredictable liability apply with less force here than in the system ordered to the general happiness. All the substantive and procedural rights against arbitrary coercion secured by the priority of the right over happiness are equally guaranteed by the priority of the good where the good is itself understood as the effective autonomy of the agent. More particularly, they are guaranteed by what I shall call the noncontradiction proviso. This proviso states that the common freedom cannot be enforced by legislative means that gain autonomy for some by denying it to others. This principle too excludes absolute liability for public welfare offenses, for the common good of autonomy cannot coherently be enforced against the individual through a liability over which he has no control.

There is another principle of justice applicable to laws ordered to the common good that is not applicable to laws directed to the general happiness. In the latter context, rights of formal liberty are normatively prior to the exigencies of preference satisfaction, so that rights of free speech or freedom of movement (for example) are absolute constraints on the pursuit of happiness. The public authority may not restrict speech or mobility merely because the subjective welfare of the least happy in society would be enhanced by the suppression of certain opinions or by the confinement of certain individuals. In the present context, by contrast, rights of formal liberty are subordinate to the common good, for the same mutual respect of persons that defines the scope of rights to formal liberty demands that these negative rights be exercised in a manner consistent with the equal effective autonomy of everyone. Subordination, however, does not mean immersion. The rights of formal liberty native to the pure agency paradigm retain an independent normative weight, one resistant to thoroughgoing definition by the common good. This is so because the inward determination of rights by the common good submerges the discrete end-status of the individual agent and so contradicts the essence of the common good, which is the autonomy *of* the individual. Accordingly, the primacy of the good must manifest itself through an override of preestablished rights that retain their force rather than through an internal limitation or definition of rights (129). This desideratum yields the third principle of justice applicable to penal laws ordered to the common good. It is that rights of formal liberty may be abridged by such laws only to the extent necessary to achieve the social purpose. Thus, an abridgment is unjust if there is available an alternative means of achieving the goal that is less restrictive to liberty. This principle is, however, subject to the noncontradiction proviso: the public authority may not adopt means that negate the autonomy of some persons even if no other instrument would effectively achieve its goal, for such means are inherently incompatible with the common good.[92]

6. THE IMPERIALISM OF WELFARE

We have thus far distinguished a pure agency and a welfarist model (itself internally differentiated) of the penal law, each based on a certain conception of an absolute end and each displaying features derived from that conception. Now since the principle underlying each paradigm purports to be the ground of law, it will exhibit an intellectual drive to subdue the whole of the penal law to its exclusive hegemony.[93] If formal liberty is the sole end that grounds valid duty, then coercion of the agent is justified only if that consequence is willed by him. Coercion of oneself is willed, however, only if the boundary of another's rightful liberty has been knowingly or recklessly transgressed, for only conscious wrongdoing affirms a principle subversive of all rights to liberty. But then, it seems, any coercive sanction applied against the individual requires a subjective mens rea, and it makes no difference whether the offense committed is a violation of rights to life, liberty, or property or a breach of a regulatory statute. And if a requirement of subjective mens rea would defeat the prophylactic point of a welfare statute, then (so the argument runs) let the regulatory aim be pursued by nonpenal means.[94]

If, however, the absolute end is effective or realized freedom, then the ground of law is a goal rather than a background condition of conceiving goals. Hence the structure of legal justification is consequentialist rather than retrospective. Penal laws are justified if they serve this goal in ways that are consistent with individual autonomy. Moreover, because the end of law is human welfare in the two senses distinguished above, the aim of penal laws is the prevention of harm, and the point of punishment is the correction and incapacitation of the dangerous as well as the deterrence of others. From this standpoint, the wrongs visible to the formalist paradigm—those against life, liberty, and property—are reinterpreted as harms to basic welfare interests, so that no essential difference is recognized between criminal and regulatory law. The aim of all penal law is the prevention of harm, and it can make no difference whether the harm averted threatens specific individuals or everyone collectively.

We have already seen how the absolutization of the principle of the pure agency model leads to its self-contradiction in crime and punishment, and how this paradigm is thus led into a pattern of dissimulation whereby it covertly acknowledges the normative relevance of factors excluded by its overt principle. The revealed inadequacy of this principle as the ground of law is the argument for the validity of the welfarist norm and of the doctrinal innovations (basically, the due diligence defense to "public welfare" offenses) it generates. However, if it is also true that the absolutization of the welfarist norm at the expense of the formalist one leads to its self-contradiction, then the ground of law will have been revealed as a totality that embraces both principles as subordinate elements. If the principle of each paradigm contradicts itself when pursued to the exclusion of the other, then each requires the other for its own coherence; and this notional continuity of the principles discloses a totality in which both the pure agency and the welfarist paradigms are preserved as mutually complementary normative frameworks.

Let us then consider what follows if we make the effective autonomy of agents the absolute end of the penal law. Since the end of law is now a goal, *all* punishment is justified instrumentally. Hence the strong sense of desert as the entailment of coercibility by crime has no justificatory role to play anywhere in the penal law. Indeed, since the connection to which desert refers has been buried in the instrumentalist relation, talk of desert now seems "mystical" or "mysterious."[95] Concomitantly, the rationale for subjective mens rea disappears. The forward-looking aims of punishment are now constrained only by the requirement that agents have a fair opportunity to avoid liability to sanctions. This requirement is equally met by intentional, reckless, or negligent wrongdoing, so that mens rea is now an empty vessel into which one can pour whatever content accords with the social purpose. Intention and advertent recklessness are disqualified, however, for the availability of excuses of unreasonable mistake, voluntary intoxication, and inadvertence to risk subverts the preventative aims of the law. Hence the "subjectivist orthodoxy" native to the obsolete framework is overthrown in favor of a modified negligence regime that, consistently with autonomy, considers the accused's capacity to conform to the law.[96] Yet one may question whether this regime meets its own commitment to individual autonomy. Since the basis of criminal liability is now negligence, the right to liberty is no longer lost by implication of one's deed. If not implicitly forfeited, then the right has been infringed for the sake of collective security. This is an override of a right to liberty by the common good that must satisfy the welfare model's *own* principles of justice. Yet it violates the noncontradiction proviso, for it promotes the autonomy of some by denying it to others.

The requirement of subjective fault is not the only casualty of welfare's empire. If the point of punishment is the prevention of harm, the retributivist rationale for the act requirement also disappears. The point of this requirement is now to provide evidence of a dangerous character, of someone whose control over aggressive impulses society has reason to distrust. Accordingly, if a prisoner about to be released after serving his term reveals himself through psychological tests as still dangerous, we will not wait for another criminal act to incapacitate him; we will keep him locked up until we are satisfied that it is safe to release him. Likewise, if someone inflicts harm while unconscious, the absence of an act will not preclude state coercion if the unconscious episode itself indicates someone dangerous to others. It will not matter whether the episode manifested clinical insanity or a physiological disorder such as epilepsy, arteriosclerosis, or a brain tumor. If the accused's condition is dangerous, we will call him insane and forcibly confine him.[97] We will also reinterpret the act requirement of attempts. One will now be guilty of an attempt if one has the intent to commit an offense and takes steps indicative of a dangerous resolve whether or not the act can be said to embody or objectify a criminal intent.[98] Thus the act ceases to play an independent role in establishing criminal liability; its sole function is to *evidence* a firm intent (which, if sufficiently proved by other evidence, will relieve the burden on the act) and hence a suitable candidate for restraining and corrective measures. One will be punished for intent alone.

The lesson of these consequences seems to be this: the absolutization of individual autonomy as the ground of penal law negates the autonomy of the agent. In a sphere of wrongdoing where it is conceptually possible to deserve punishment in the strictest sense, the individual is subjected to coercion he does not deserve in that sense. Where (as in the context of regulatory offenses) no intelligible meaning can be ascribed to the notion of desert, punishment for negligence is not undeserved, for punishment can be undeserved only if it is possible to deserve it. Where, however, desert refers to an intelligible connection between deed and retribution, someone who ignores this connection imposes undeserved and hence arbitrary "punishment." Similarly, where crime is intelligible as a specific category of wrong essentially distinguished from tort, the individual who is named a criminal though lacking any of the mental states definitive of that category bears a stigma he does not deserve. Relative to the possibility for the conceptual self-imposition of punishment in the sphere of crimes, the accused who is punished as a criminal for a negligent infringement of rights is subjected to external violence. And the same may be said of someone punished for a criminal intent that does not attain objective embodiment as determined by the test of Salmond, J. in *R. v. Barker*.[99] To the extent, however, that punishment is not self-determined, the agent is used for the aggrandizement of a common good that fails reciprocally to recognize him as an end and that thus reveals itself as neither common nor a good.

7. TOWARD A DIFFERENTIATED STANDARD OF PENAL JUSTICE

The self-contradictoriness as grounds of law of both formal liberty and positive freedom produces the phenomenon of mixture to which interpretive skeptics are fond of pointing as indicative of law's essential incoherence. Thus an accessory may be liable for the consequential offenses of the principal on a foreseeability standard, even though the principal is liable only on a subjective standard.[100] Automatism or an honest mistake of fact excuses from a crime of basic intent unless the mistake or automatism was attributable to the accused's drunkenness.[101] Mental disorder negating intent excuses from murder if the accused is insane but results in a conviction for manslaughter if he is not.[102] To the same point are legal fictions designed to feign a commitment to the subjective standard even as that standard is eroded; thus the rule that intoxication is no defense to a crime of basic intent is supported on the theory that the intention to get drunk supplies the mens rea for the offense charged.[103]

The skeptic's claim that such inconsistencies are endemic to the penal law can be justified only on the premise that the antagonism of the paradigms is a necessary and constant reality. This would be the case if there were indeed a logical imperative to absolutize one or the other principle as the ground of law. Yet the process whereby each fell into contradiction when absolutized in isolation shows us that there is no such imperative. If the elevation as an end of both formal agency and positive freedom leads to their self-contradiction, then neither can alone be the ground of law. That each suffers inversion when pursued at the other's expense shows that each needs the other for its own self-consistency. This should not be surprising. Formal agency was objectively an end only insofar as it manifested itself as such in property and bodily autonomy, so that it already implicitly contained the welfare dimension it purported to exclude. Similarly, both the general happiness and the common good were interpreted in terms of individual autonomy, so that they too implicated the end-status of the individual that their absolutization negates. Because each principle implicitly contains the other within itself, its domination of the other nullifies an element of its own nature and so results in its self-destruction.

The contradiction into which each principle falls when pursued intransigently discloses a conceptual whole wherein each is preserved as a constituent principle informing a distinctive but bounded subsystem of law. The genuine ground of law is neither formal agency nor the common good but the whole of which both are mutually complementary parts. This whole evinces the structure of mutual recognition we have called dialogic community and is indeed the archetype of which the relationships seen earlier are instances. The common good is both authentically common and authentically a good only insofar as it respects the discrete end-status of the individual agent and hence the distinctive legal paradigm ordered by that principle. Conversely, the individual agent is an end only insofar as it recognizes the authority of the common good whose self-inadequacy alone first establishes its end-status as a reality. That this structure of reciprocal deference is the true ground of law was revealed in the self-realization of the pretenders to that title; for it was, as we saw, the subtextual theme of both paradigms. And it was decisively revealed in the process whereby each of these pretenders collapsed when absolutized to the exclusion of the other. Accordingly, the validation of dialogic community as the ground of law is just the process of its manifestation in, and emergence from, paradigms ordered to rival principles; and since the justification of a foundational end must be internal to its notion (or it would not be foundational), these paradigms are, despite their limitations, constituent elements of the foundation (129–130).

If the ground of law is dialogic community, then the principle of each paradigm is normatively resistant to the expansionist claims of the other. Though each principle is deficient insofar as it pretends to be the absolute ground of law, each is nonetheless preserved as an essential component of an adequate conception. The implication is that the penal law is a differentiated totality composed of two principal subsystems of law, each characterized by indigenous principles of justice and standards of fault. There is thus no "general part" of (in the sense of a single set of principles applicable throughout) the penal law; and yet the penal law is a unity, for each special system embodies in a distinctive way the ground of law that connects the systems to each other.[104]

That the penal law is a differentiated whole implies that the principle of each paradigm is valid only within limits consistent with the distinctive existence of the other. Once the whole comes forward as the ground of law, the hegemonic claims of the constituent principles cease to appear logically natural and become indicative instead of conceptual pathology. Conversely, their mutual respect is no longer a compromise of principle but a demand thereof. Neither is there any longer a "choice" between paradigms to undermine ab initio the rationality of legal discourse; for the principle of each model applies only within definite boundaries. The border between the systems is marked by the difference between the private rights of atomistic persons and the public goals of citizens united for the enhancement of their freedom. What judges call true crimes are denials of the end-status of personality as embodied in the exclusive authority it exercises over its body and external possessions and in the reasonable care of "neighbors." Public welfare offenses are breaches of statutes aiming at the general happiness taking individual values as given or protecting the social conditions of effective autonomy.[105]

Because each system is part of a whole, each must be actualized by judges and legislators with a moderation that reflects this constituent status. It is a mistake to extend the principle of either the pure agency or the welfarist paradigm over the whole penal law, for this absolutizes a principle whose validity is inherently relative to a specific context. Hence it is a mistake to make negligence the basis of liability for crimes against personality or to weaken the strict retributivist understanding of desert for such offenses. Subjectivist orthodoxy is appropriate for true crimes. However, it is also a mistake to make subjective fault the standard of blameworthiness for welfare offenses or to assess the justice of penalties for such offenses from the standpoint of desert. Because welfare laws are justified instrumentally, the concept of desert strictly understood has (with one exception I will mention presently) no intelligible application within this sphere.

Even within the sphere of welfare offenses, the principle of penal justice is not monolithic. It varies, as we have seen, depending on the meaning of welfare. Where welfare means the satisfaction of preferences undetermined by the idea of effective autonomy, the appropriate principle of justice is the priority of autonomy over happiness, for the latter becomes normatively significant only through the end-status of personality. Applied to statutory interpretation, this principle rules out offenses of absolute liability (for persons but perhaps not for corporations) and favors defenses of reasonable mistake of fact and of due diligence in seeking to comply with or ascertain the law. At the legislative level, it screens out utilitarian (or other aggregative) justifications for penal laws as well as what Feinberg calls legal moralism, the penalization of activity (e.g., the consumption of alcohol) to advance a relative view of the good life; for these justifications signify the coercion of persons for the benefit of others. Insofar, however, as welfare means the satisfaction of values essential to effective autonomy, the appropriate principles of justice are that rights of formal liberty are validly limited by the common good to the extent necessary to achieve the aims of the law and to the extent that the legislative means do not contradict the end they purport to further. The latter proviso excludes absolute liability offenses in this context as well.

The principles of right applicable to welfare statutes yield a position regarding the legitimacy of imprisonment within this sphere. The priority of autonomy over happiness rules out prison sentences for offenses against nonfundamental values unless the statutory breach is intentional or advertently reckless. Imprisonment is justified for willful breaches, for although the intentional act would not have deserved punishment apart from positive law, the intentional breach of statute posits a principle subversive of law and so also of the lawbreaker's liberty. Thus imprisonment is here justified by desert. Incarceration is also ruled out for inadvertent breaches of laws promoting fundamental values, for the common good of autonomy cannot coherently be furthered through a total deprivation of liberty unwilled by the agent; here the means would contradict the end. We may conclude that the penalty of imprisonment understood as a qualitative deprivation of freedom is justified by desert (i.e., by willful lawbreaking) or not at all.

However, this result need not render welfare laws ineffectual. Where a statute protects interests essential to autonomy, the legitimacy of the means least restrictive to liberty implies that partial or quantitative restrictions of liberty are justified not only by a willful breach but also where monetary penalties sufficiently heavy to deter would be beyond the financial capacity of most lawbreakers. Partial restrictions include probation orders and—at the extreme—confinement for intermittent periods. The latter penalty is justified, however, only if there exists a distinct class of penal institution for the noncriminal offender. Where restrictions on liberty are justified by a goal but not by desert (e.g., in the case of inadvertently dangerous driving), special institutions and administrative leniencies are required to reflect the categorical difference between welfare offenders and criminals. In their absence, confinement even for intermittent periods is wrong as a penalty for regulatory offenses. In general, there should be no implication of depersonalization for the welfare offender; his penalty is the intermittent confinement and nothing else. Further, the maximum overall term should be lower than that of the lowest maximum for crimes; and since the point of the sanction is deterrence rather than retribution for a wrong, the penalty need not vary with the consequences of the conduct.

8. THE CASES REVISITED

Let us now specify our interpretation of the penal law further by applying it to the cases described at the outset.

8.1 R. v. Tutton and Tutton

If, as I have argued, a negligence standard of penal liability has no place in the sphere of crimes, then the Tuttons are innocent of criminal negligence causing death. They are, however, guilty of failing to provide necessaries for someone in their care, a welfare offense in Canada that can be committed through ordinary negligence.[106] Hart's case for a negligence standard is perfectly valid insofar as it assumes a legal paradigm ordered to human welfare; indeed, the theory of excuses on which this case rests—that respect for autonomy requires that the agent have a fair opportunity to obey the laws—belongs essentially to this paradigm. However, when applied to criminal wrongs involving the infringement of common-law rights of liberty, property, and reasonable care, a negligence standard violates the very autonomy constraint on punishment that Hart (and the welfare model) acknowledges; for it obliterates the real connection between punishment and free choice that exists uniquely within this sphere. It is true that subjective foresight of harm is not essential to one's being morally responsible for the harm; but it is also true that moral responsibility for a harm (even a wrongful one) is not a sufficient condition for punishing the harm-doer as a criminal, since agent responsibility is equally consistent with tort and crime. Moreover, the often-heard argument that gross negligence is punishable as a crime because worthy of public condemnation misses the point entirely. Of course, the egregious negligence of a competent agent is culpable in a purely moral sense relevant to the assessment of character and so deservedly attracts the censure of the community. Such conduct may also be penalized for deterrence and educative purposes by regulatory penalties less severe than imprisonment. However, no blameworthy state of mind short of intention, advertent recklessness, or willful blindness has significance as a denial of personality's worth; hence no other culpable disposition exhibits that tight connection with judicial coercion which renders the deprivation of his liberty specifically authorized by the criminal, leaving no room for the instrumentalist manipulation of the person.

8.2 Campbell and Bradley v. Ward

We have seen that an act is required for criminal liability because it signifies the transition of a subjective purpose into outward, public reality. This transition raises what would otherwise be a private wish into a principle claiming objective validity. And it is this claim to validity that justifies visiting the implications of the principle on the wrongdoer. Accordingly, to attract criminal liability, the act must outwardly embody a criminal intention. It will do this, of course, if the criminal purpose is consummated. However, acts falling short of completion may also embody a criminal intent if, when viewed in context, they cannot reasonably be interpreted as having anything but a criminal purpose. And, as we have seen, this is precisely the test for the actus reus of attempts that Salmond, J. proposed.

But what of Glanville Williams's objection that no act short of the completed purpose will unequivocally manifest a specific criminal purpose unless we take into account what we know of intent from extrinsic sources? And what of *Campbell and Bradley v. Ward*, which is generally regarded as the reductio ad absurdum of the unequivocality test?

Williams's objection mistakes the nature of the end that the act must signify. The account of the unequivocality test we have given shows that the act must, to be punishable, manifest criminality unequivocally, not any specific criminal purpose. The identification of the particular purpose is needed only to determine the appropriate *measure* of punishment. Accordingly, once the issue of punishability is settled by the unequivocality test, there can be no objection to using extrinsic evidence of the accused's intent to determine the precise offense attempted. This is what the judge in *Campbell and Bradley* should have done. Judging by their deeds alone, there was no reasonable doubt, as Adams, J. acknowledged, that McCallion and his cohorts were up to crime. Once this was established, their amenability to punishment was proved. The judge could then have resorted to Bradley's confession to determine the specific crime intended, which determination would have yielded the appropriate sentence.

8.3 R. v. Campbell and Mlynarchuk

The idea behind the rule that ignorance of the law is no excuse is that rational agents know the inherent unlawfulness of acts condemned by the standard of mutual respect, and every adult is presumed rational until the contrary is proved. This rationale, however, is specific to wrongs correlative to the negative rights established within the pure agency paradigm—to the rights of liberty, self-possession, property, and security against wrongful harm; for these rights *require* legal enforcement for their effective reality. Negative rights need legal enforcement against those who infringe them to be meaningful as rights; hence in this context to know the wrongfulness of an act is also to know its unlawfulness—its preinstitutional amenability to legal sanctions.[107] By contrast, the welfare goals aimed at by penal statutes can conceivably be achieved by noncoercive means (e.g., by public education), so that there is no inherent necessity that acts proscribed by public welfare statutes attract coercive sanctions. These penal laws are thus inherently positive; their validity is entirely contingent on enactment. Accordingly, there is in this context no basis for the claim that rational agents must know of the legal prohibition. The blanket application of the ignorance rule thus involves an extension of the pure agency paradigm's jurisdiction beyond its rightful borders.

What modifications should the ignorance rule undergo when migrating to the welfarist setting? Our analysis suggests that the applicable principle is the priority of autonomy, which says that a penal law is validly applied against an agent only if he or she had a fair opportunity to avoid its sanctions. Thus it is uncontroversial that ignorance of positive law is an excuse if the law was not published or otherwise knowable at the time the act was committed. However, the unknowability of a law is only one instance of the lack of a fair opportunity to avoid the sanction. Even if the law is knowable, the accused might have taken all reasonable steps to ascertain the law and yet may have unwittingly violated it. For example, he may have assured himself that no regulation outlawed his intended activity, only to learn too late that the regulations had been amended shortly after he consulted them;[108] or a foreigner newly arrived in a jurisdiction might commit an offense unknown in his own country before he could inform himself of domestic laws;[109] or someone might have relied on an erroneous statement of the law by an official charged with applying it.[110] In all these cases, the accused's ignorance should excuse him, for otherwise the law acts on the agent as an incalculable power in which he cannot see respect for his autonomy and which thus appears as another's good. That is to say, the law acts in a way that contradicts its nature as law.[111]

There is, however, another consideration that should inform a welfarist rule concerning ignorance or mistake of law. As Jerome Hall forcefully argued, an excuse of ignorance should apply only to the extent consistent with the idea of a legal order.[112] Thus, in a case of first instance involving the application of a legal standard to novel facts, the accused cannot plead ignorance or mistake of law, for otherwise private opinion will have replaced the court as the arbiter of the legal standard. Nor, for the same reason, is the due diligence standard satisfied by consulting a lawyer: the accused must have received an opinion from the official or body charged with applying the law.[113] These limits on an excuse of ignorance do not, however, compromise the autonomy constraint. For if the accused relied on his own or on a lawyer's opinion regarding the application of a legal standard, he took a calculated risk and lost.

In *R. v. Campbell and Mlynarchuk*, Ms. Campbell violated a law promoting public morals. Let us leave aside the question whether such a law is a valid exercise of the legislative power in view of the (circumscribed) duty of state neutrality toward conceptions of happiness. It is enough to observe that this is a public welfare offense, since it promotes a certain conception of the good rather than protecting a right against interference with liberty, bodily integrity, or property. The accused knew the law prohibited an "immoral show" but was initially uncertain whether the kind of dancing her employer had in mind fell within this standard. She would not have been entitled to rely on her own or on a lawyer's lights in applying the legal standard to her activity, but she did not. She relied on a Supreme Court judge. And since no appellate court had spoken at the time, she could not have exercised any greater degree of diligence. If we regard the judge's statement as true at the time he made it, then Ms. Campbell was tried under a retroactive law. If it was untrue, she reasonably relied on an erroneous official statement of the law. In either case, her plea of ignorance should have been a complete answer to the charge.

CHAPTER VI

Idealism and Fidelity to Law

1. THE DEATH OF LAW?

In the *Philosophy of Right,* Hegel writes,

> The principle of rightness becomes the law when, in its objective existence,
> it is posited, i.e., when thinking makes it determinate for consciousness and
> makes it known as what is right and valid; and in acquiring this determinate
> character, the right becomes positive law in general.[1]

He then remarks that the "inner essence" of positive lawmaking (in which
he includes judicial lawmaking) is the "knowledge of the content of the
law in its determinate universality." By determinate universality Hegel
means a unity or system wherein a single principle—the "principle of
rightness"—is instantiated in diverse laws and applied to particular cases.

In the preceding chapters I have tried to comprehend the main branches
of the common law in their determinate universality. Specifically, I have
tried to interpret the common law as a series of instantiations of dialogic
community, understood as the mutual recognition of distinct selves as
ends. Moreover, I have tried to show that this idea not only unifies the
classical system of formal right based on "possessive individualism"; it also
unifies this system with the modern communitarian or welfarist legal paradigm in a way that keeps both within their proper bounds, preventing
either from devouring the other. The upshot is that the common law is
(inherently, though more or less imperfectly in fact) a unity not only of diverse doctrines but also of diverse doctrinal *systems.* This unity of subunities constitutes the good order and justice of the common law and reveals
injustice as the hypertrophic extension of some constituent principle, such
as formal liberty, the general happiness, or positive freedom. In exhibiting
the common law's inherent unity, I believe I have vindicated the rule of

law against the prevalent view that the common law is inescapably torn by ideological conflict.

The final question we have to consider concerns the status of this interpretation. Does it offer only a particular perspective on the common law, one that can perhaps help us see law from an unfamiliar angle but that cannot lay claim to any superiority over alternative perspectives? Or has it succeeded in revealing the common law's *own* unity and in thus having told the truth about the common law? Moreover, if our interpretation has disclosed law's own unity, what is the normative status of the unity it has revealed? Have we simply described the positive unity of a particular tradition without justifying this unity by a standard of right valid for all traditions? Worse, have we, in describing the common law's internal unity, deferred uncritically to its normative standards, and have we thereby ascribed a false universality to a particular historical formation? Or have we revealed a unity of the common law that is justified by a critical standpoint different from the law's? And if so, how can justification in light of this external standpoint be squared with a claim to have surrendered ourselves to the internal unity of the common law?

I wish to argue that an interpretation of the common law in light of dialogic community both reveals the immanent unity of law and justifies this unity from a critical standpoint different from the law's. That is to say, such an interpretation is immanent without being uncritically deferential and transcendent without being constructionist or artificial. In short, an interpretation in light of dialogic community reconciles critical idealism with fidelity to law. To see better what is at stake in the search for this harmony, let us first see why the unity of idealism and fidelity to law might be a problem for legal interpretation; and let us consider the consequences of their disunity.

I shall begin by defining my terms. By idealism I mean the view of reality for which an object's true nature is given not by its immediate existence prior to the shaping it undergoes in being apprehended by consciousness but by its existence as mediated or formed in accordance with some self-conscious end or idea. In the idealist view of law, for example, law consists not in the mass of often contradictory decisions reached by lawmaking agencies but in the propositions that flow from the best unifying account of this material.[2] So understood, idealism is critical because it distinguishes between the brute "existence" of an object and its "actuality" or full development; or it grasps an intellectual criterion for an object's true nature that may then be deployed to criticize empirical reality, to sort out the mature from the underdeveloped, the stable from the ephemeral, true intuitions from errors, rational traditions from merely positive ones. Our understanding of the common law has been idealist in this sense, for we have grasped a relation of mutual recognition between free and equal selves as the idea of law; and we have applied this idea to the criticism of certain doctrines (e.g., the parol evidence rule, the Learned Hand test of negligence, negligence-based criminal liability) and to the justification of others.

By fidelity to law I mean the virtue of legal understanding that consists in its conforming to the inner unity of the common law considered as a semiautonomous normative order, distinct from political legislation for the common good, from the order constituted by norms of personal virtue, and from the order governed by an ideal of beatitude. The vice corresponding to this virtue is the artificial construction of law in light of a purpose foreign to it, or the imposition on the common law of an end (e.g., wealth maximization or human excellence) derived from normative systems external to it. Of course, the artificial construction of law is a defect of interpretation only if fidelity to law is an attainable ideal, which remains to be shown.

At first sight, idealism and fidelity to law are not in tension. If law's true nature lies in its conformity with an idea—a "principle of rightness"—then an interpretation of a legal tradition in light of this idea will be faithful to the true nature of law. More generally, if the nature of a practice is given by its ideal development, then cognition in light of the ideal yields a true understanding and valuation of the practice. Yet the unity of idealism and fidelity to law is very problematic indeed; and this problem has disquieting consequences for our project, for the rule of law hinges (as we shall now see) on the possibility of such a unity.

The problem may be introduced by asking why an idealist might plausibly be optimistic about his capacity for fidelity to a practice he is in the business of altering. After all, the idealist does not seek to conform thought to a human practice as the latter is immediately given to him in the way that a natural scientist seeks to conform thought to nature.[3] Rather, he understands a practice only as shaped by a purpose that he surmises; and he is not averse to expelling some phenomena from the practice rightly understood on the ground that they do not fit within the unity he has constructed. A physicist whose theory of the atom failed to account for a repeatedly observed phenomenon would never dream of dismissing that phenomenon as a mistake or as "bad nature"; and yet (mutatis mutandis) this is just the sort of judgment an idealist interpreter of the common law might make regarding a legal rule marooned by his theory. But how can theory change a practice and be faithful to it at the same time?

For the optimistic idealist (we shall soon distinguish a skeptical one), a purposive interpretation of a human practice (such as law) can be faithful to its object because it does not impose meaning on something that is alien and indifferent to purposive order; rather, it unifies a practice under a conception of the latter's own end or point. It can do so, the idealist contends, because human practices are intentional structures. Even if the participants regard them as existing independently of human agency (e.g., as immemorial custom or as divinely prescribed laws), they are nonetheless expressions of an idea or realizations of a human project. As such, they do not await philosophic reflection to tell them what they mean. Rather, they are themselves processes of self-interpretation—processes wherein those engaged in a practice try to intuit its point, to purify it of inessential elements, and to develop the practice further. For the idealist, accordingly, reflective interpretation can be true to a practice because it only grasps self-consciously the point of a practice that the participants already understand more dimly; and it thereby achieves a theoretical unification that is already partly accomplished prior to its setting itself to work. Indeed, it is precisely because human practices present themselves to reflective thought as already partially formed through interpretive work that their "actuality" or consummation lies in their explicit conformity with a self-conscious idea.

Law is a good example. When reflective thought confronts a body of law, it does not encounter a mass of disconnected rules and decisions. Rather, it finds something already organized under general categories such as property, contract, tort, and crime; and within these categories, it finds subunities based on such general ideas as possession, consideration, the neighbor principle, negligence, mens rea, and the like. These ideas embody intuitions concerning the scope of valid rights and of legitimate coercion—intuitions that reflection need only clarify and confirm to theoretical insight. In law, moreover, reflection encounters an enterprise that on its own plane aspires to organic unity and coherence—witness Hale's metaphor of "the Argonauts ship" that remains identical throughout successive changes,[4] Lord Mansfield's description of the common law as law "that works itself pure,"[5] and such maxims as "like cases must be treated alike" and "where the reason of the law stops, there also stops the law." Because law is *already* an interpretive practice—already a thoughtful, unifying, self-critical activity—reflection can (says the optimistic idealist) yield a true understanding of law if it provides an integrated account of law's own ideas. Such an integration no doubt alters the material originally presented to thought as a collocation of rules and principles; but this altering is no refraction or distortion, for it is just the fruition of law's own work.[6]

The interpretation of the common law offered in previous chapters proceeded within this general epistemological framework without, however, scrutinizing its capacity to support a true understanding of law. Thus one could describe our project in terms of this framework as an attempt to bring to explicit consciousness the idea of dialogic community that has been intuitively present to common-law jurists, who have themselves been imaginatively engaged in interpreting and specifying their tradition. And we hitherto thought it a good confirmation of our interpretive thesis that it seemed to account for and integrate a significantly large body of well-settled legal doctrine.

We were, however, naive to think that an account of fidelity could rest there. That self-conscious interpretation seems to be in touch not with "facts" but only with prephilosophic interpretations of facts poses a problem for any idealism that wishes to be faithful to law. This is so because the law against which an interpretive idea is to be judged faithful or unfaithful is now itself an interpretation that, according to idealism, inchoately possesses the very idea to be tested. If the jurists' intuitions adduced to test an interpretive thesis did not already anticipate the thesis, then idealism could not defer to them for confirmation and remain idealism; for it would then treat untested opinion rather than reflection as the standard of true law: reason would have surrendered to prejudice or to the brute existence of a legal doctrine. If, however, idealism defers only to intuitions that foreshadow its idea, then it never hears aught but its own voice; it never gets beyond itself to an independent object and so never receives the confirmation it seeks. Accordingly, idealism seems to be faced with the following dilemma: either it exposes its interpretive thesis to falsification by *any* legal phenomenon, in which case it ceases to be idealism; or it submits only to those phenomena that satisfy its idea (and casts out the others as errors), in which case idealism does not *submit* to the object at all but rather manipulates it from outside. It would seem, then, that idealism cannot be faithful to law.[7]

The problem, however, goes deeper than this. To say that idealism cannot be faithful to law might suggest that there is something called "law" to which idealist interpretation can be faithful or unfaithful. However, one may doubt whether this is so and whether the idealist can thus even make sense of the idea of fidelity to law. An interpretation is meaningfully faithful to law only if the thematic unity it claims to see in the law is a unity *of* law or conforms to the structure of law as it exists prior to interpretation. Yet for idealism such a correspondence between theory and an independent object is inconceivable. This is so because the idealist is committed to the view that theory is prior to one's experience of an object or practice; that the selection of phenomena for interpretation already presupposes a theory of what gives unity and meaning to a practice; and that there is thus no sustainable distinction between one's theory of a practice and the practice presented for theorizing.[8] I shall call this feature of idealist understanding (i.e., the identity of theory and object) its self-enclosedness or self-referentiality. That idealism exhibits this feature need not mean that interpretation is without disciplining constraints, since there usually exist common opinions about the boundaries and core elements of a practice to which the interpreter must conform if he wishes to persuade his audience, or within which (according to some) he is inevitably situated. However, this caveat only reinforces the point that the only meaningful sense of fidelity for the idealist is fidelity to the common opinion and not to some independently existing object. On the idealist view, indeed, there is never available an embedded structure or meaning that announces itself without alteration by the interpreting subject and to which a theory might correspond; rather, the only structure available to the interpreter is the one that he, as situated within an interpretive tradition, introduces. For the consistent idealist, therefore, the interpreter who claims to be seeking law's own unity must appear a rather comic figure; for he is like the bungling sleuth who cannot help treading on the footprints he is trying to match to a shoe.

That the law is not available to a theorist except through an interpretation that changes it has the following consequences. First, there is no accessible preinterpretive unity against which an interpretation can be tested for its fidelity to the object; hence the ideas of fidelity and infidelity to law are incoherent. Second, all unity is manufactured by the interpreter and imposed on previous layers of inaccessible (and equally artificial) meaning. No doubt the artificiality of unity would warrant the conclusion that all interpretation must be unfaithful to its object if the preexisting object had any solid reality. For the idealist, however, it does not. Because objects present themselves only as shaped and formed through interpretive construction, their only reality (according to the idealist) lies in their mediated character. But then the unavailable object lacks the ontological standing that would render meaningful a judgment of fidelity or infidelity. Since the preexisting object is a will-o'-the-wisp—an untrue mode of the object's existence—it is of no interest to the idealist interpreter; and there is no point in calling an interpretation unfaithful if fidelity is not a desideratum of understanding. This conclusion casts a new light on our earlier statement that idealism cannot be faithful to law. This is so not because idealism falls short of capturing an existing law-in-itself but because there is no law-in-itself to capture. Or rather, the law itself is the law mediated by interpretation, outside of which there is nothing of significance.[9]

With this conclusion we have reached a thoroughgoing interpretive relativism. Since there is no independent object by which to confirm or disconfirm an interpretation, it follows that interpretation can be neither true nor untrue; it can only provide a perspective that is on a par (as far as truth is concerned) with any other point of view, and there is no limit to the number of possible perspectives. Lacking a criterion of fidelity, we cannot evaluate interpretations as faithful or unfaithful but only as more or less pleasing to our "considered" aesthetic and moral sentiments; and because these sentiments are themselves rooted in a particular interpretive outlook, there is ultimately no standard by which to judge an interpretation other than its service to the interests that drive a perspective. The implications for the rule of law are obvious: if law is, as the idealist holds, whatever accords with the idea that provides the best interpretation of a legal tradition, then law dissolves into the interest of those whose moral sentiments currently dominate the legal "community"; and the ideal of fidelity to law is the myth by which this hegemony is sustained. It would seem that the realization of the idealist conception of law is the collapse of law into masked tyranny.[10]

If idealism consumes the independent object and so makes fidelity to law a nonsensical idea, then an ideal of fidelity must (it would seem) be grounded in a rejection of idealism. One rejects idealism if one holds that the law is given independently of interpretation in light of a purposive idea; that it consists in the meaning of basic concepts (e.g., duty, right, possession) employed in legal discourse, in the well-settled meaning of words written in legal texts, in the intentions (considered as psychological facts) of their authors, and in certain social facts (such as habitual obedience) designating these authors and texts as authoritative sources of law. In short, an ideal of fidelity to law seems possible only within the framework of legal positivism.

Yet the rule of law turns out to be no less an illusion on the ground of positivism than it did on the ground of idealism. For if law is identified by nonnormative facts, then there is a famous analytical disjunction between what the law is and what it ought to be.[11] This means that for anyone whose fidelity to law is built on positivism, moral criticism of the law must renounce fidelity. Such criticism, in other words, cannot claim to be evaluating law in light of its own aspirations but must confess to be judging law against a moral standard external to it. This dichotomy between fidelity and criticism gives rise to conflicting obligations for a judge. Where the law identified by positivist criteria is immoral by the external standard, the judge must choose between his institutional duty of fidelity to law and his moral duty to change it. This is an insoluble dilemma just because each duty captures one essential aspect of a genuinely ethical attitude and yet they are opposed. By an ethical attitude I mean one that distinguishes not only between the "is" and the "ought" but also between the "ought" considered as a public standard with a stable and ascertainable content and the "ought" as a general idea having nothing but private opinion to give it determinate shape.[12] Ethical action seems to require conformity with an "ought" of the former kind, for if the "ought" is specified by private opinion, then its actualization produces a condition indistinguishable from the battle of self-interested forces characteristic of the "is." The ethical attitude shuns the tyranny of moral preference no less than submission to the given.

However, the ethical attitude is impossible for the positivist judge, as a

consideration of his dilemma will show. On the one hand, the judge may
say that he must apply the law as given rather than change it in accordance with his personal moral views. But since the law as given is identified by criteria that abstract from value and purpose, the duty of fidelity
becomes incomprehensible; there can, after all, be no obligation to obey
the law just because it is the law if law is identified by factual criteria.[13] On
the other hand, the judge may abjure an apparently nonsensical fidelity
and change the law to suit morality. But then he judges not according to
law but according to a morality that, just because it is opposed to law *as objective and publicly ascertainable fact,* is a subjective or private morality that
he now tyrannically imposes on others. Thus the choice for a positivist
judge faced with an unjust law is between an immoral legality and an arbitrary moralism. And since each side of this antithesis has one element
(objectivity or normativity) essential to ethical action, the choice is itself
undetermined. A judge will be conservative or reformist according to his
personal inclinations—according to whether he prefers an arrogant moral
conscientiousness or a servile adherence to law. There is no unified obligation to constrain him.[14]

Accordingly, whether we initially stand on the ground of idealism or
positivism, a tension emerges between critical idealism and fidelity to law;
and this tension proves fatal to any normatively significant idea of the rule
of law. On the ground of idealism, fidelity to law becomes an incoherent
notion, and law dissolves into the tyranny of the dominant interpretive
perspective. On the ground of positivism, fidelity and criticism are sev-
ered, and this divorce corrupts both poles. Fidelity to law means an ab-
dication of reason to brute facts: law rules but without normative force.
Moral idealism means a tyranny of moral preference: conscience rules but
without law.[15] Though perennial foes, therefore, idealism and positivism
converge in a common fate, one that Owen Fiss has aptly characterized as
the "death of law."[16] They meet here because each lacks what the other
posits as fundamental. Idealism lacks the "fact itself" against which interpretations could be tested as faithful or adventitious; positivism lacks the
idea of immanent purpose that would harmonize its fidelity to law with
moral criticism. The thought arises as to whether it may be possible to
unify these old antagonists in a single conception of law.

2. DWORKIN'S ATTEMPTED SYNTHESIS

Let us consider a recent attempt by Ronald Dworkin to develop a theory
of law that reconciles critical idealism with fidelity to law. That theory consists of two main parts. One part defends the interpretive approach to law
generally against both legal positivism and moral instrumentalism; the
other part offers a particular interpretive theory of law in light of an idea

Dworkin calls "integrity." By integrity Dworkin means the coherent elaboration of the conceptions of justice and fairness that provide the best interpretive account of a legal tradition, whatever those conceptions might be.[17] I shall concern myself here only with the first part of Dworkin's theory. The entire preceding account of the common law of property, contract, torts, and crime may be taken as an alternative to Dworkin's reading of law in terms of integrity, albeit as one that also aims to exhibit integrity considered as a feature of any theoretical explanation worthy of the name. That account is, I believe, a better alternative, because the idea of integrity is a purely formal one that accounts for no specific legal doctrine or for any substantive goal or value; indeed, it is hospitable to any. Dworkin's defense of the interpretive approach is more interesting to us, for here he tries to reconcile an idealist theory of law with the thesis that disputes about the best interpretation of a legal practice are amenable to rational solution. I will try to show that Dworkin's attempted synthesis fails but that the failure reveals the ground of the possibility of a genuine reconciliation. That ground is dialogic community, which turns out to be neither idealism nor positivism but the synthetic unity of both.

In *Law's Empire*, Dworkin poses a time-honored question in a novel way. In asking "What is law?" Dworkin joins an ancient debate with such thinkers as Aquinas, Austin, Kelsen, Holmes, Hart, and Raz. While the question is familiar, however, its meaning has changed radically in Dworkin's manner of posing it. Traditionally, the questioner asked for a definition of law in terms of genus and specific difference. He wanted a stable criterion for distinguishing law from what is not law—a criterion by which acts claiming the force of law could be tested, or that would identify sources to which judges and lawyers could appeal to justify their decisions or claims. The questioner might find this criterion in social facts that identified a supreme law-giving authority or a rule by which such an authority might be recognized; or he might find it in the moral dictates of human nature. In all cases, however, he sought an essence, a concept, something abstracted from the concrete instances of law and considered self-sufficient as a standard in this abstraction. Because the ground of law was preconceived in this way, the inquiry as to its nature traditionally organized a special discipline alongside the law of property, contracts, torts, crime, and the Constitution—a discipline known as jurisprudence.

Without clearly indicating why this line of inquiry is fruitless, Dworkin abandons it.[18] The question "What is law?" is still central for him, but he no longer invites a reply in the form of a theory about law's abstract essence. Rather, he invites a theory of the meaning immanent in a concrete practice, that is, a theory of the law of property, contracts, torts, crime, and the Constitution. Law, according to Dworkin, consists in the propositions that flow "from the principles of justice, fairness, and procedural due process that provide the best constructive interpretation of the community's legal practice" (*LE,* 225). This hermeneutic conception of law synthesizes two directions of legal thought that Dworkin believes are incapable of capturing what judges do in cases where neither statute nor precedent determines a solution. One, which he calls the plain-fact view, identifies law with the past decisions of bodies that convention specifies as law-giving and regards these decisions as law irrespective of their moral merit; its problem is that it cannot account for the attention judges and lawyers continue to pay to past decisions even when they fail to specify a result (*LE,* 130–131). The other orientation, which Dworkin calls pragmatism, views law as a means to an end justified by a moral reasoning unfettered by any independent (i.e., nonpragmatic) concern for consistency with past decisions; its problem is that it cannot account for the way in which past decisions constrain goal seeking in judicial argument, and so it must discount the latter as dissimulating rhetoric (*LE,* 154–156). In contrast to the plain-fact theorist, Dworkin sees law as mediated by moral theory; in contrast to pragmatism, he views the relevant moral theory as one embedded in past decisions.

At first sight, Dworkin's "interpretive turn" seems to abandon the quest for a universal idea of law that the essentialist inquiry sought. It seems to be a turn toward historicism and cultural relativity—a reorientation with disturbing implications when conjoined with Dworkin's antipositivist stance. In place of the positivist's amoral conception of law, Dworkin offers a theory of law that sees it as expressing an underlying public morality. Yet this theory is apparently hospitable to whatever values inform a particular tradition, so that (for example) Nazi laws may seem on this view to be not only laws but laws with moral force.[19] Further, the interpretive turn seems to abandon the certainty of the metaphysical ground in favor of something far less secure. If there is an essence of law, then disagreements among lawyers about what the law is in a particular case can in principle be resolved by reference to its essence. There is a common standard to which they can appeal and that renders their disagreement meaningful. If, however, there is no such abstract essence—if disagreement is over whether this or that theory of purpose best explains and unifies past decisions— then disputes about what law is seem inherently insoluble. They begin to look less like lawyers' disputes and more like the debates literary critics have when they argue about the most illuminating view of a novel. Since there is apparently no right answer, what passes for a scholastic argument is really a political conflict among incommensurable perspectives.

Dworkin assures us, however, that the interpretive turn entails neither of these outcomes. It does not entail the loss of a standard by which to evaluate opinions, because "the competing interpretations are directed toward the same objects or events of interpretation" (*LE*, 46). Further on he says that "[i]t does not follow . . . that an interpreter can make of a practice or work of art anything he would have wanted it to be . . . [f]or the history or shape of a practice or object constrains the available interpretations of it" (*LE*, 52). Hence a criterion of interpretive fidelity will be the degree to which an interpretation "fits" the object. It need not fit every aspect thereof (for interpretation has a reformist potential), "but it must fit enough for the interpreter to be able to see himself as interpreting that practice, not inventing a new one" (*LE*, 66). Accordingly, disagreements among interpreters are meaningful because they are disagreements about the best way of interpreting the same object. The object is the touchstone for the validity of theory.

However, the deferral of theory to the object raises the first concern we mentioned: that the interpretive turn renders theory incapable of evaluating a practice except by standards internal to it. The rejection of a transcendent essence of law seems to imply, in other words, an uncritical accommodation to the given norms of a tradition. Again, however, Dworkin assures us that this is not the case. The criterion of fit is only one of the standards by which to assess the merits of an interpretation. Another is the extent to which interpretation makes the object "the best possible example of the form or genre to which it is taken to belong" (*LE*, 52). Or again, "all interpretation strives to make an object the best it can be, as an instance of some assumed enterprise" (*LE*, 53). Thus the best interpretation, the right answer to the question "What is law?" is the one that makes the object the best *it* can be. There are two constraints here on the caprice of the interpreter. First, the object's empirical character sets limits on the value that can be ascribed to it; a tyranny (if I may offer my own example) cannot be dressed up as an ideal political order, but it can be interpreted so as to approximate this order to the degree that its tyrannical character allows—say, by reading out as nonintegral with the regime official acts lacking the elementary formal attributes (e.g., generality, prospectivity) of law. Thus interpretation renders a practice the best *possible* example of what it is. But second, the object's ideal nature sets limits on the *kind* of value ascribable to it, or it sets limits on the meaning of "best." The best is the object's own best, given that it is the kind of thing that it is. Thus (again my example) the ideal of the polity is different, presumably, from that of the family, so that the interpretation of a political despotism must be guided by the former ideal rather than by the latter. Accordingly, if the object as found is the touchstone of theory, this involves no mere accommodation to the given, because in turn the truth of the object is its ideal nature, in light of which the interpreter construes the object as a more or less adequate approximation. Moreover, this construal is interpretive rather than arbitrarily constructionist, because it is constrained by the history and shape of the object. Thus interpretation, says Dworkin, "is a matter of interaction between purpose and object" (*LE*, 52).

To read *Law's Empire* is to observe the process by which this initially assumed harmony of idealism and fidelity breaks down, leaving Dworkin's position no different from that of the legal nihilists he seeks to refute. The first hint of trouble occurs when Dworkin begins to describe the stages of the interpretive process. The "preinterpretive stage" is that at which the object to be interpreted, say, the law of property, is identified or defined. This is the object, recall, whose historical shape must constrain interpretation and be capable of validating it as an interpretation rather than an invention. To perform this function, however, the object must be capable of demarcation in a value-free (i.e., noninterpretive) manner, for otherwise the definition of the object will itself be an interpretation in need of validation ad infinitum. But value-free definition is, Dworkin assures us, impossible. The identification of property law will itself be implicitly theory-laden (hence subject to controversy), for "social rules do not carry identifying labels" (*LE*, 66). Presumably, the meaning of this metaphor is that the categories under which rules are subsumed are not their own but are imposed on rules pursuant to some human interest. If so, then the object's demarcation already involves its alteration and hence the creation of a difference between the object as it exists in itself and the object as it exists for interpretation. From now on I shall call the former object—the one that interpretation leaves outside—the differentiated object or simply the "other." The differentiated object—the object that is other than the object mediated by interpretation—has now become the inaccessible object "out there." At various points in his argument, Dworkin acknowledges this object as something (a "noumenal metaphysical fact") the interpreting subject is compelled to think (*LE*, 81). But because he is an idealist, he regards this object as a thing not worth speaking about.[20] It is insignificant. To the extent that Dworkin refers to it at all, he does so with galactic imagery ("what Law whispered to the planets," "transcendental tablets in the sky," or "atmospheric moral quaverings") conveying disdain (*LE*, 4, 80). Accordingly, the object by which interpretation is to be constrained turns out to be undifferentiated from it; it is itself the product of interpretation. Properly speaking, therefore, there is no preinterpretive phase, and Dworkin places the phrase within inverted commas. This means that it is, after all, not the object that is to constrain interpretation but a "consensus" within the interpretive community as to what the object is—a consensus that, Dworkin must admit, may or may not exist (*LE*, 66–68).

Furthermore, the constraint posed by this consensus-defined object translates into a requirement of fit between the interpretation and the practice. The assessment of a good fit, however, requires the interpreter to have a "preinterpretive" sense of the paradigmatic or essential features of the practice, those features that "any plausible interpretation must fit" (*LE,* 72). Because, however, the practice does not autonomously announce its essential features, these too will be a matter of intuition and conviction that are once again interpretive. Thus not only the definition of the object but also the idea of a good fit is implicitly theory-mediated; and for Dworkin theory-mediated being now has the significance of relative being, of being-for-interpretation, since he cannot help thinking about the "fact" that mediation leaves outside, however much he would like to deny its importance. Moreover, as the object dissolves into interpretation, a contingent consensus is invariably introduced as a substitute constraint (*LE,* 67).

If the first criterion of interpretive truth (the historical shape of the object) evaporates in the preinterpretive phase, the second (does the theory make the object the best it can be?) dissolves at the interpretive stage. This is the stage at which the practice previously defined is integrated under a fully self-conscious theory of purpose. This activity, we will recall, was supposed to exhibit the object as the closest possible approximation to its own ideal nature. Since, however, the differentiated object (i.e., the "noumenal metaphysical fact") is assumed to be foreign and indifferent to purpose, any value-laden interpretation is necessarily the imposition on the object of the interpreter's own opinion as to what reveals it in its best light (*LE,* 67, 87). At this level, not even the consensus forged by professional socialization can be expected fully to arbitrate controversy; nor indeed (says Dworkin) would conformity be desirable here, for if there are no natural constraints on value judgments, conventional ones are tyrannical (*LE,* 88). Rather, the only constraint on the interpreter's fancy is the requirement of a good fit between the valued purpose and the paradigmatic features of the practice. For this constraint to operate, however, both the identification of paradigmatic features and one's idea of a good fit must be conceptually independent of the hypothesis as to the point of the practice (*LE,* 67–68). They cannot explicitly presuppose or adjust to the hypothesis, for then they could not constrain. Yet since the selection of paradigmatic features, the assessment of fit, and the formulation of purpose are all interpretive—*since they all fall within the same interpreting mind*—no strong distinction between these operations is possible here (unless we wish to take schizophrenia as the model of the interpretive attitude). Hence Dworkin must fall back on a "psychological" constraint—a voice of intellectual conscience—urging the interpreter to keep separate his judgments about fit and his judgments about what purpose lends most value to the practice (*LE,* 234–235).

This constraint is, however, problematic in two senses. First, because the selection of paradigmatic features is interpretive, it presupposes at some intuitive level a theory of the purpose that animates the practice. This theory cannot be different from the one consciously adopted at the reflective stage of interpretation, for we are dealing here with one interpreting mind. Consequently, there is no clear or ontologically grounded distinction between the stages of interpretation to which scruple can conform, or at least none that Dworkin has revealed; hence any moral compunction the interpreter may feel about manipulating the object to suit his theory, while "phenomenologically genuine," appears within this framework as incoherent and so as merely sentimental (LE, 235). Accordingly, while reminding us of our psychological inhibitions against rigging interpretive outcomes, Dworkin actually gives the strong-minded a reason for shedding them.

Second, the psychological constraint is fragile on its own terms, both for a reason that Dworkin acknowledges and for one he does not. He admits that the standard of fit one adopts, as much as one's theory of purpose, reflects a judgment as to what lends value to a practice; and he admits that trade-offs will occur between one's aesthetic convictions about how much integration is required and one's substantive convictions about which ends most ennoble a practice. However, if I am permitted to relax my standard of fit for the sake of the net gain in subjective value to be won by an ill-fitting ideal, then there is no meaningful sense in which my choice of purpose is constrained. My freedom is not limited in any important respect simply because my taste for a substantive ideal is balanced with my taste for an aesthetic one, for it is in the end *my* tastes that determine the law. Furthermore, the psychological constraint exerts at best a temporary hold, because another imperative of the interpretive attitude overrules it. The order to insulate the intuitive identification of paradigms from the thesis about substantive point is countermanded by the order to revise or at least to test intuitions in light of the thesis, for otherwise unexamined intuitions rather than reflection would be the criterion of law. Thus the supposedly core elements of a practice that were to constrain interpretation may in the end be revealed by interpretation as ephemera. What is phenomenologically genuine in the resultant oscillation between contradictory attitudes is not interpretive constraint but the simulation thereof.

Accordingly, because Dworkin is sure that the object of interpretation evinces no embedded meaning or purpose—that it does not autonomously announce its structure to the interpreting mind—interpretation becomes an artificial projection rather than a witness to an immanent order. As a consequence, the distinction that Dworkin wishes to make between interpretation and invention collapses: there are only inventions. In the face of this result, Dworkin can maintain a belief in the possibility of fidelity (and hence in the possibility of a rational solution to interpretive disputes) only by concealing the collapse. Partly this dissembling consists in substituting a contingent and fragile consensus for the lost object as a constraint on interpretation. More basically, however, it takes the form of a virulent attack against the very relativism Dworkin espouses.

The name he gives to this relativism is "external skepticism" (*LE,* 78).[21] The external skeptic opposes Dworkin's thesis about meaningful disagreement by claiming that value-oriented interpretation is necessarily perspectival because lacking an independent object capable of validating it. As the inaccessible residue of interpretive mediation, the object is unavailable to arbitrate disputes, which are therefore at bottom political conflicts between different worldviews. The skeptic may hold and attempt to defend interpretive hypotheses as passionately as the interpretive realist; he will not, however, defend them as true understandings of the object but rather as projections that are pleasing to the aesthetic and moral sentiments of those he seeks to persuade. Since these sentiments are, however, equally ungrounded in an independent reality, they are as naturally manifold as the interpretive claims that appeal to them. Hence an interpretation may only be popular or unpopular; it can never be right or even better than any other.

Dworkin's response to the skeptic's objection is to accept his epistemological assumptions but to deny their force against the thesis that interpretive disputes are soluble. They have no force against this thesis, argues Dworkin, because he does not claim for the hermeneutic concept of law the "bizarre" kind of objectivity that the skeptic denies (*LE,* 81). The kind of objectivity he claims is rather the subjective conviction of objectivity that accompanies moral statements as distinct from reports about taste. The difference, says Dworkin, between a statement like "slavery is wrong" and one like "rum raisin ice cream is good" is that with the former the speaker intends a proposition he believes to be impersonally valid rather than valid only for individuals with certain kinds of needs or interests. The further claim of objectivity for the moral statement, he argues, adds nothing except emphasis to this belief. It is only objectivity in this philosophically redundant sense, Dworkin now tells us, that he is claiming for the best interpretive theory of law. To this sense of objectivity as emphatic restatement of moral belief he contrasts the objectivity that consists in the matching of an interpretation to "a noumenal metaphysical fact" or in its confirmation by "atmospheric moral quaverings." This metaphysical sense of objectivity Dworkin both ridicules and renounces. In doing so, he thinks he has declawed the external skeptic, whose criticism assumed the relevance of objectivity in the metaphysical sense.

The derisive rhetoric Dworkin uses to characterize the notion of metaphysical objectivity serves a purpose. By dismissing this kind of objectivity as a chimerical and irrelevant standard, Dworkin reinforces the pretense that the *conviction* of interpretive fidelity can pass for the objectivity needed to ground his thesis or to make it interestingly different from the nihilist one, even though everyone might defend conflicting ideas of fit and value with equal moral fervor. That there is a right interpretation of a practice is now reduced to the thesis that interpreters sincerely believe their interpretations are right rather than expressions of their particular interests. Moreover, we have only to inquire whether the belief is true or false to see that even this diluted thesis is an unstable resting point. To be sure, this question would make no sense to Dworkin if it assumed a "noumenal metaphysical fact" against which the belief in rightness could be tested. However, we can pose the question in a way meaningful for Dworkin if we ask whether the belief is true to, or coherent with, the rejection of metaphysical objectivity as a relevant standard for criticizing interpretations. If, as Dworkin believes, no objectivity in the metaphysical sense is available, then the distinction between convictions of impersonal rightness and subjective preferences is ultimately untenable; the former are but self-deceptive versions of the latter, albeit stronger and more widely shared. In the end, therefore, Dworkin is distinguished from the external skeptic only by his failure to follow through intransigently his rejection of metaphysical objectivity.

The pretense of opposition to external skepticism serves not only to conceal Dworkin's nihilism but also to repress the claims of the other that the skeptic in his own way properly asserts. For Dworkin, the skeptic's objection is "silly," "wasteful," "confused," and "to no point" (*LE*, 85–86). It is a second-level argument about the metaphysical status of interpretive claims rather than an argument within the enterprise of interpretation itself. Dworkin would like to convert the external skeptic into an internal one, that is, into one whose denial of the truth of some moral claim (e.g., that slavery is wrong) is not an argument about the epistemological status of such claims but an interpretive hypothesis about the actual practice of morality (*LE*, 83–86). Dworkin welcomes all skeptical challenges on this hermeneutic terrain but resents the use of metaphysical arguments of infidelity as easy substitutes for arduous, interpretive ones. This urge to reduce or to interiorize the skeptic is necessitated by the one-sidedness of Dworkin's hermeneutic standpoint. Since the differentiated object is taken to lie *outside* interpretation, any demands it makes to be respected must also be external (metaphysical) ones that, while entertainable in "a calm philosophical moment," are irrelevant to the actual business of interpretation. These demands can therefore (Dworkin thinks) be ignored by interpretive theorists: only internal skeptics need be listened to.

But are the claims of the other irrelevant? Dworkin himself makes these claims powerful, for his thesis states that interpretations may be criticized as right or wrong, better or worse, that disagreement about the best interpretation of a text or practice is meaningful. In other words, the ideal of fidelity to the object is already implicated in Dworkin's hermeneutic standpoint: the latter claims to reveal the truth about the object, to have the right answer about its meaning. Thus Dworkin's right answer thesis makes relevant the very differentiated object that he must at the same time discredit to preserve the thesis against the skeptic's accusations of infidelity. Yet the disparagement of that which is immanently necessary exacts a price. Since the question as to whether right answers are possible is a "metaphysical" question raised outside interpretation, interpretation itself must assume the existence of a right answer unquestioningly. Hence the only arguments Dworkin accepts as relevant to his thesis are those that cannot challenge the thesis because they take its truth for granted.[22] However, this arbitrary silencing of opponents renders the thesis itself arbitrary and a mask for interest-based interpretation.

We can summarize our critique of Dworkin in the following way. In grounding law in the best interpretation of legal practice, Dworkin empowers against himself the very independent object that the idealist standpoint fails to compass. Because this standpoint holds that law is *truly* apprehended only through interpretation, it already implies an ideal of fidelity to the object or an intelligible distinction between interpretation and invention. Yet in actualizing itself as the ground of law, the idealist standpoint loses the very differentiated object needed to support that distinction. All interpretations are now artificial projections on an alien object. To sustain the distinction (between interpretation and invention) in the face of this loss, the independent object must be devalued, its demands ridiculed, its accusatory voice silenced. However, once the independent object—the criterion of fidelity—is declared to be of no significance for interpretation, there is nothing to distinguish the right answer thesis from the thesis that there are no right or wrong answers, only equally unprivileged perspectives. The gulf that originally separated Dworkin from the interpretive skeptic has narrowed to the vanishing point.

3. BEYOND SKEPTICISM IN INTERPRETATION

The collapse of the idealist standpoint as a foundation of interpretive truth yields a vantage point from which to understand and criticize contemporary skepticism about legal interpretation. That skepticism has now all but conquered the field. The starting point of contemporary theories of legal interpretation—a starting point most consider too well accepted to require a defense—is that truth or fidelity to the object is off the agenda. The debate is now over whether, once it is conceded that there is no independent object by which to test interpretation, the latter is free or significantly constrained by something else. For radical skeptics, the absence of a "text" means that interpretations are freely ideological and should openly declare their political interests rather than mask them with the rhetoric of discovery.[23] For conservative skeptics, legal interpretation is constrained by convention in ways that differentiate it (albeit contingently) from open-ended political advocacy—constrained, for example, by "disciplining rules" accepted as binding by an "interpretive community," by a consensus on values, or by traditional communal preconceptions within which the interpreter is always "already situated."[24] Since I want to dispute the skeptical premise, I will not enter this intramural debate among varieties of skepticism except to remark that the conservative position seems an unstable halfway house between interpretive objectivism and interpretive nihilism. For once we deny the constraint of the object, there is nothing to guarantee the impartiality of the disciplining rule, of the interpretive consensus, or of the communal preconception. It will always be possible to criticize these surrogates for the object as dominant understandings masquerading as shared ones.[25] If there are dissident understandings, then community is attained by ostracizing them; if there is a uniform understanding, this can only be because dissident ones have not yet emerged or have been suppressed. Community is either a facade or living on borrowed time.

It would seem, then, that the rule of an impartial law is theoretically possible only if we can recover the lost object as the touchstone of interpretive truth—only, that is, if we can rehabilitate on the ground of idealism the idea of fidelity to law. To do this we require a critique of skepticism. Such a critique cannot, however, dogmatically reassert the availability of a pristine fact—the plain meaning, the discoverable intention—undistorted by interpretation; such a positivist move would clearly have no persuasive force against our skeptical opponent. Indeed, the idealist's usual defense against criticisms of the self-enclosedness of his interpretive understanding is just that such criticisms betray a positivist hankering for an uninterpreted object, which simply does not exist. Since the idealist identifies the differentiated object with the pregiven fact whose authority he rejects, he is able to admit the circularity or self-referentiality of his understanding and yet deny that these features constitute a defect.[26] He is even able to refuse the names skeptic, subjectivist, or relativist, since he believes that these labels assume the availability of the positivist alternative.[27] Yet the idealist could not so easily deflect a critique of the self-enclosedness of his understanding (or refuse the name skeptic) if this feature were shown to be a defect (because of the availability of a differentiated object) from the standpoint not of positivism *but of a more consistent idealism*—one that revealed the skeptic as a vestigial positivist. This is another way of saying that a critique of skepticism must proceed on skepticism's own ground. Skepticism's ground is idealism, which holds that there is no significant object for consciousness apart from the object mediated by interpretation. A powerful critique of skepticism must show that skepticism is untrue to this—its own—insight.

Dworkin's critique of skepticism failed because skepticism is the nemesis—the logical culmination—of Dworkin's idealist position. Having seen, however, how skepticism emerges from this position, we now have a stronger base from which to criticize it. Skepticism claims to be the truth about interpretation. It claims to be the truth not about interpretation within a specific idealist framework but about interpretation per se. That there can be no such thing as fidelity to the object is held to be an absolute and freestanding truth. Yet this turns out to be an unsupported assertion. Having witnessed (in Dworkin's work) the collapse of the idealist ground of interpretive truth, we can see that skepticism is not an autonomous position but the outcome *of* a particular constructive theory of interpretive understanding. Contemporary skepticism about interpretation is, in Hegel's phrase, a "determinate negation," that is, the negation of a specific conception of the ground of interpretive truth. The truth of skepticism is thus a partial truth relative to that conception; any claims skepticism makes to universal truth are dogmatic, for they involve a logical leap from the failure of the idealist ground to the (undemonstrated) failure of all possible grounds.

Yet this by itself is not an adequate answer to skepticism. Even were it not a freestanding truth, skepticism would nonetheless be the *final* truth if there were no possibility of movement to a new ground of interpretive fidelity—to one that has encompassed the lessons learned through the collapse of the previous one. Yet there is such a possibility, and skepticism (as we shall now see) itself points the way to it.

Let us begin by reexamining the structure of the idealist foundation as it stood prior to its downfall. On that foundation, the fully reflective interpretation of a practice (like the common law) was initially thought capable of being true to the practice, because the latter exists only as already interpreted by the participants' intuitions, which inchoately possess the thematic idea consciously grasped by thought. The test of theory was thus its ability to integrate well-settled intuitions (Dworkin's "paradigms") held with a conviction approximating that produced by insight; and the theory so corroborated could then be used to sift more doubtful intuitions as well as to elaborate the practice in relation to novel problems. For an example of this procedure, consider how one might approach the question concerning the meaning of criminal negligence. In the relatively uncontroversial judicial intuition that criminal liability requires a "guilty mind," one might see a foreknowledge that just punishment must be the logical consequence of the claim of validity implied in the wrongdoer's intentional act; and this theory of mens rea might then be employed to select conscious recklessness rather than egregious negligence as the appropriate standard of fault for criminal negligence.

Observe, then, that the structure of interpretive truth on the idealist foundation is a dialogic one. That is, reflection submits for confirmation of its theory to the participants' intuitions; and this submission of thought is compatible with its preservation as the standard of truth because intuition in turn submits to reflection as its criterion of validity.[28] Thought and intuition are thus mutually complementary. Their complementarity is assured by the fact that both fall within one interpreting mind or self-consciousness; they are internal divisions of a whole. Thus intuition is an unclear mode of thinking, while thinking is a clearer form of intuition—a clarification of intuition's enigmatic insights. For simplicity's sake I shall refer to this whole (the idealist foundation) as "mind," which must in this context be understood with the following determinations. First, as a putative basis for the true nature of objects, mind is here not this or that individual mind but the universal mind of a human community—a cosmos or world that, while self-conscious only insofar as an individual mind comprehends its unity, nevertheless exists independently of any particular individual. Second, mind here denotes not simply thinking but the reflective organization of prior intuitions (embedded in language, customs, laws, etc.) already implicitly imbued with thought. That mind is a concrete totality of intuitions implies that its unity is quite compatible with its particularization in distinct communities possessing diverse languages, cultural traditions, and positive laws and yet recognizing certain ends as common to rational beings as such.

Now let us recall what went wrong with idealism. The dialogic foundation of truth collapsed because of its one-sidedness in relation to the other. Idealism excluded and made alien the very differentiated object whose autoconfirmation interpretation required; and the result was that interpretation became an imposition on the object rather than a truth independently confirmed by it. Further, once the criterion of truth was lost, the interpretive framework of an erstwhile universal mind disintegrated into the finite perspectives of a (theoretically limitless) multiplicity of parochial minds; and truth was then redefined as that which accords (for the time being) with the custom or consensus of the particular community. Accordingly, the idealist foundation collapsed because it was inadequate to its own dialogic structure. While implicitly encompassing the difference between subject and object (in the difference between reflection and intuition), the idealist foundation embraced this difference within an *undifferentiated* unity (since reflection and intuition fall within one mind) that excluded and devalued the truly different object. And with this exclusion, idealism's epistemological optimism turned into skepticism.

Yet insofar as idealism remains skeptical, it persists in the equivocation that characterized its position from the start. On the one hand, idealism claimed that mind is the foundation of all reality—the crucible wherein alone all things exist—and considered everything outside it a nullity; thus, according to the idealist, there is nothing but interpretation, and so the positivist quest for a neutral touchstone is vain. On the other hand, idealism kept within a self-enclosed circle of interpretations only because it equated the other with the positivist's pregiven fact, which thus still maintains its power over the idealist. Idealism, in other words, defined itself *in opposition* to the positivist submission to brute facts. It thus allowed its conception of the foundation to be decisively shaped (as self-enclosed, self-referential) by the very object whose authority it denied. Given its residual dependence on this object, idealism had to admit the existence of an "outside" that rendered interpretation an "imposition." A cleft thus opened between mind's claim to be the sole ground of reality and the fact that its reality was now "for" interpretation and distinguished from objectivity. Idealism then sought to remove this contradiction (to go "beyond relativism") by denying the object's reality; but the result was the dissipation of idealism into interpretive "politics." Throughout this life cycle, idealism was shadowed by the pregiven object from which it recoiled and which its reflexive posture raised to a competing absolute. Because idealism identified the differentiated object with the positivist's object, it had to identify reality with a self-enclosed mind; having done so, it could not vindicate mind as the foundation without annulling objectivity per se and therewith itself as a foundation of *truth*. Idealism, accordingly, betrays a vestigial positivism, for it assumes the existence of an external other, which while in one breath declared to be without significance for human understanding, is in the next allowed to condition this understanding as "finite," "culture-bound," or "historical."

It will help us to see this equivocation as intrinsic to idealist skepticism if we observe it at work in the philosopher who gave this form of skepticism its most intransigent expression. Let us then consider the following passage by Nietzsche, the father of modern perspectivism.

> Every center of force adopts a perspective toward the entire remainder, i.e., its own particular valuation, mode of action, and mode of resistance. The "apparent world," therefore, is reduced to a specific mode of action on the world, emanating from a center.
>
> Now there is no other mode of action whatever; and the "world" is only a word for the totality of these actions. Reality consists precisely in this particular action and reaction of every individual part toward the whole—
>
> No shadow of a right remains to speak here of *appearance*—The specific mode of reacting is the only mode of reacting; we do not know how many and what kinds of other modes there are.
>
> But there is no "other," no "true," no essential being—for this would be the expression of a world *without* action and reaction—
>
> The antithesis of the apparent world and the true world is reduced to the antithesis "world" and "nothing."—[29]

Here Nietzsche denies that the humanly constructed world—the world organized by the ends of action—is an "appearance," since there is no truth or reality outside action. At the same time, he acknowledges the existence of a residual antithesis between "world" and "nothing," an antithesis that conditions "world" as a multiplicity of perspectives. Elsewhere, while vehemently denying the existence of a thing-in-itself, he variously refers to the "arranged and simplified world" as one that is "true for us," or as a "falsifying" and an "overpowering."[30] Thus, while all the sensible properties of the other have been brought within the horizon of consciousness, the bare thought of the other remains to constitute the intrahuman sphere a falsification. For skepticism, the positivist's object retains this power because it is taken to lie *outside* mind as a self-standing other—a competing absolute—upon which mind, pursuant to its own interests, constructs an artificial order. The image is one of an impenetrable curtain separating the humanly interpreted world from the void outside it. But the only reason the "nothing" is taken to lie "outside" is that idealism has privileged as the sole basis of truth a *one-sided* mind. Thus the absolutization of mind empowers a contrary absolute, whose annulment pluralizes mind, whose outcome reveals the persistent force of the annulled.

In the skeptic's shuttling between the poles of "world" and "nothing" we already see the mutual conditioning of opposites that belies the separation assumed by the skeptic. The absolutization of mind conditions the other as "outside"; the outsideness of the other conditions interpretation— the work of mind—as a multitude of opinions. This mutual conditioning suggests a connection or mutual dependence of the polarities. Insofar, however, as this interdependence is not consciously apprehended in a unified conception, it manifests itself subliminally as an endless cycle of violence against various popular representations of the other (nature, the feminine, the foreigner, the Jew, etc.) and as the perspectivism (i.e., cultural or gender relativism) of the crusaders against such violence. That is, the realization of mind as absolute foundation requires the annihilation of the other; but the other's disappearance leads to the fragmentation of mind, which must therefore continually reinstate the other to gain confirmation of its supremacy.[31] However, were we to grasp the interdependence of the poles synthetically in a new conception of the ground of interpretive truth, then we will have transcended skepticism as well as the dreary cycle of violence it engenders. At the same time, we will have fulfilled skepticism's own aspirations, for we will only have followed through intransigently the skeptic's claim that there is nothing (i.e., no powerful reality) outside interpretation.

But what is the "other" whose connection with mind has suggested itself? How is it to be conceived? And how are we to conceive the connection between mind and the other? The argument will proceed best if we

consider the last question first. Having witnessed the collapse of the idealist foundation, we now know that the other is not the separate and independent reality that the skeptic takes it to be. The other became significant only through the negation of mind as the sole ground of reality. That
is to say, the collapse of idealism showed that mind *lacked* the other's at-
testation to its being the structure of truth. And the other became significant only through mind's immanent need for it. This need for the other
implies the enfranchisement of what has hitherto been excluded and devalued—no longer as a wholly autonomous, separate, or competing reality but as a partner in a dialogue; and it means, obversely, the renunciation of mind's claim to be the exclusive ground of truth and its sharing
this ground with the other. Each pole now submits to the other as to that
through whose recognition each is confirmed as an end. Thus the other
(we shall soon see what it is) defers to mind as to that through whose need
it first acquires an essential value; and mind reciprocally defers to the independence of the other, which confirms mind's dialogic structure as the
other's *own* structure, in which mind sees itself reflected. We arrive, then,
at the bedrock reality that guarantees the fidelity of interpretation in terms
of dialogic community: the dialogic structure that characterizes mind also
characterizes the relationship between mind and its other; hence this
structure is indwelling in the independent object itself. Put succinctly, the
other is itself embedded within a dialogic whole. But before we can fully
grasp what is involved in this statement, we must ask the question we have
hitherto postponed, namely, what is the "other"?

4. THE OTHER AS THE SINGULAR SELF

For the skeptic, of course, the other is precisely that which cannot be named
or characterized, for any naming is an interpretation from which the other
must again be distinguished. Thus Nietzsche writes,

> But even supposing there were an in-itself, an unconditioned thing, it would
> for that very reason be unknowable! Something unconditioned cannot be
> known; otherwise it would not be unconditioned! Coming to know, however,
> is always "placing oneself in a conditional relation to something"—one who
> seeks to know the unconditioned desires that it should not concern him,
> and that this same something should be of no concern to anyone. This in-
> volves a contradiction, first, between *wanting* to know and the desire that it
> not concern us (but why know at all then?) and, secondly, because some-
> thing that is no concern to anyone *is* not at all, and thus cannot be known
> at all.[32]

The unknowability of the other thus presupposes that the other is an
unconditioned—that is, a wholly autonomous, self-standing, self-sufficient—
object. We have already seen, however, that this way of looking at things

depends on privileging mind as the sole basis of reality and that the supposed unconditionedness of the other is thus itself something conditioned or created. It is only because idealism withdraws into a self-enclosed mind that the other appears autonomous and "of no concern to anyone." This means that the other is not truly autonomous but is rather the other *of* mind. Because the other is a determinate other—the other of something— there is really no insuperable problem in characterizing it; and indeed Nietzsche, after telling us emphatically that the other is unknowable, proceeds to characterize it in two ways. Let us then derive the conception of the other from the relativist's own mouth.

One of Nietzsche's names for the other we have already heard. He calls it the "nothing." The other is the "nothing" because it is the sheer abstraction from all the possible ways of interpreting objects. It is *not* what mind makes of the world, or more simply, it is the not-world. But we know what this abstraction from all determinateness is. It is the self. The self is precisely the void that we are forced to think when we strip away all the concrete features of the world—all the ways in which sensation and intuition mold objects in preparing them for thought. Accordingly, the other is not an inaccessible and unknowable beyond; nor is it the stars, planets, galactic monsters, non-Western cultures, the female, or the Jew. The other-than-mind is another mind, but an abstract mind, stripped of all determinate perceptions, feelings, and intuitions. If we now put this conclusion together with the one reached at the end of the previous section, we obtain the following result: the ground for the possibility of fidelity in interpretation is not the unity of a self-enclosed mind (as idealism believed) but the dialogic bond between one mind and another.

The second way in which Nietzsche describes the other is as follows:

> Our psychological perspective is determined by the following: 1. that communication is necessary, and that for there to be communication something has to be firm, simplified, capable of precision. . . . The material of the senses adapted by the understanding, reduced to rough outlines, made similar, subsumed under related matters. Thus the fuzziness and chaos of sense impressions are, as it were, logicized. 2. the world of "phenomena" is the adapted world which we feel to be real. The "reality" lies in the continual recurrence of identical, familiar, related things in their logicized character. . . . 3. the antithesis of this phenomenal world is not the "true world," but the formless unformulable world of the chaos of sensations—*another kind* of phenomenal world, a kind "unknowable" for us.[33]

Here Nietzsche formulates the "unformulable world" as a formless world, a chaos. The phenomenal world, the world present to consciousness, is a world of structure in which diverse things are "logicized" or subsumed under universals. If, then, the other is that which escapes reduction to this artificial unity, then it must be conceived as that which is irreducibly singular, atomistic, as well as external and indifferent to other singular entities. It must be conceived, in other words, as formless multiplicity. Moreover, there is a connection between Nietzsche's two ways of conceiving the other. For if one assumes (as one must if one absolutizes a one-sided mind) that the atomistic monad has a self-standing or unconditioned reality, then a problem arises concerning how to understand the monad's unconditionedness. As a singular entity, after all, the monad is conditioned on all sides by other monads outside it. It is vulnerable to their influence, pressure, and impact; it is what it is by virtue of being different from something else, and so on. Any plausible notion of the monad's unconditionedness must therefore abstract from or exclude the particularity and external dependence of the monad. But this means that the monad is plausibly unconditioned only as emptied of all determinate character—only as the blankness of the self.

We arrive at the conclusion that the absent other—the other hitherto evicted from the real world by idealism, the other declared inaccessible, unknowable, and of no human significance—is the atomistic self or "person" of legal thought. This is the self who resists becoming reduced to, situated in, or constituted by, a one-sided communal mind and who instead takes the emptiness of its own freedom as the sole absolute end. Earlier, however, we saw that (contrary to what it thinks) the other does not stand self-sufficiently outside the communal mind; that it becomes salient only through the self-inadequacy of mind as a foundation of truth. And we said that this inherent connectedness between mind and the other pointed to a new ground of interpretive fidelity. Let us now pursue this suggestion further, armed with the understanding that the other is the atomistic self.

5. DIALOGIC COMMUNITY AS THE UNITY OF IDEALISM AND FIDELITY

Once we see the connection between mind and the other, the possibilities of interpretation are freed from the limitations of a one-sided idealism. Because the other is the other-of-mind, the two premises of interpretive skepticism—that the object is unavailable for testing and that it is devoid of an immanent, self-announcing structure—no longer hold. The object is not unavailable; on the contrary, it is that which is nearest and most familiar to us: it is the self of the individual. Nor is the object bereft of an immanent structure. Because the self's value inherently depends on the self-inadequacy of another self, its claim to self-sufficiency as an isolated monad will prove erroneous. The individual will rather experience its solitude as a defect from the standpoint of its own self-aggrandizing aims; and it will thus seek a reflected or received reality, one mediated through another's self-interested submission to its freedom. In particular, it will seek confirmation as an end through another's recognition of its property, through another's promissory submission to its mastery of time, through another's reciprocated care for its welfare, through the vindication of mutual respect as the basis of its worth in compensation for torts and in punishment for crimes. Moreover, because the self wants to *know* itself as an end, it will give an account of this activity in a legal discourse that intuitively apprehends mutual self-abnegation as the basis of individual rights and that specifies this insight in endless detail. In this way, the "other" will evince an autonomous (and self-interpreting) motion toward structures of mutual recognition that reflect the dialogic structure of mind and that thus spontaneously attest to its being the structure of all valid claims to worth.

Once the object of interpretation is seen to possess both an autonomous motion and an embedded structure, interpretation has something to which it can be faithful. A criterion now genuinely exists for distinguishing between interpretation and invention, between true understandings and artificial constructions of law. Legal interpretation need no longer see itself as imposing meanings on an indifferent object; rather, it can submit to the spontaneous movement on the object, passively observing its self-structuring in accordance with the pattern of dialogic community and listening to the discourse through which the self renders this activity self-conscious. Moreover, once the radically differentiated object is seen to be itself embedded within a dialogic whole, the relation between the interpreting mind and its object ceases to be an incestuous one between two operations (reflection and intuition) of the same mind. The object is now sufficiently distinct from mind to be capable of constraining and validating (instead of merely echoing) an interpretation; and yet it is also sufficiently present to mind to yield itself up to interpretation without suffering distortion.

We can now see that the theme of dialogic community by which we have hitherto interpreted the common law is itself the ground for the possibility of this interpretation being true to its object. The ground of interpretation and the theme of interpretation are one and the same. Moreover, the interpretive method we followed itself reflected dialogic community as the ground of valid interpretation. Our method was to hover between, or to adopt simultaneously, two interpretive standpoints—the individualistic one of the common law and the philosophic one, which discerned the relations of mutual respect and concern formed by atomistic selves and certified by common-law judges as sources of right. We adopted this method because it is the one uniquely appropriate to the dialogic foundation of true theoretical claims about the common law's inner structure. Thus the theme of dialogic community is validated as the immanent unity of law insofar as it is spontaneously produced by the atomistic self in search of its own *individual* reality; conversely, the atomistic self is preserved as a thematic principle because the standpoint of community defers to it for the sake of its own confirmation as the foundation of valid rights.

We are now in a position to respond to the series of questions we posed at the outset of this chapter. First, an interpretation of the common law in terms of dialogic community can claim to be more than another "perspective" on law. It can claim to have discerned the common law's own unity, because the structure of dialogic community is, by virtue of the interdependence of mind and its other, immanent in the action of the atomistic self whose realized worth is the common law's end. Because this self's value depends on another self's need for its freedom, it freely enters into relations of mutual respect wherein alone it finds objective confirmation for its claims of final worth; and these relations define the scope of the rights that common-law courts enforce. Interpretation, as Hegel says, merely "looks on" at the spontaneous formation of these relations and self-consciously grasps the intersubjective basis of rights already intuitively apprehended by jurists. In that the object now independently attests to intersubjectivity as the basis of rights, interpretation can, without loss of fidelity, declare as "bad law" those doctrines implying a servile relation between the parties or between the community and the individual. Observe that this account of interpretive fidelity does not contradict the account given earlier by the naive idealist. We still say that an interpretation can be faithful to law because it only makes explicit the thematic principle already implicitly apprehended by the legal imagination; and we still say that our interpretation is well supported if it integrates a wide range of doctrine that in turn commends itself to reflection in light of our "principle of rightness." However, we are now *entitled* to say this, whereas the naive idealist was not. Because dialogic community embraces the full difference between the interpreting mind and its object (instead of collapsing the difference into a single mind), it provides a basis for the idealist's epistemological confidence that was missing within the idealist framework itself.

Second, the submission of thought to the law's internal unity involves neither a morally neutral description of a tradition's coherence nor an uncritical acceptance of the tradition's own norms. It involves no mere positive description of a tradition, because the unifying theme of the common law can plausibly lay claim to a normativity valid for all traditions. It can do so because, as a relation formed by the mutual surrender of free and equal selves, dialogic community is the structure of all nonviolent, nondomineering realizations of final ends, however these ends may be conceived (whether individualistically or communally); hence it is the structure of all valid claims to respect and concern as well as of their corresponding obligations. Nor does thought's submission to the common law involve an uncritical deference to the law's internal norms. The principle of right by which we interpret the common law is not the principle that self-consciously animates it; our principle is rather the *latent* theme of the law, a theme only dimly known to it and which comes to clarity only through the collapse (when separately absolutized) of the principles (formal liberty, positive freedom) by which the law is explicitly ordered. For the law itself, the freedom of the atomistic self is the formative principle; private property, contract, tort, and criminal law are first and foremost realizations of a self that considers itself an end apart from any relation to another. Hence the normative standard by which reflection interprets the common law is different from that which manifestly informs it.

Third, an interpretation of the common law in terms of a normative standpoint different from its own is compatible with fidelity to law, because interpretation does not thematize dialogic community to the exclusion of the principles by which law is self-consciously ordered. It does not reduce the common law to *its* unifying theme; which is to say, it does not regard the law's atomistic standpoint as insignificant, illusory, or simply wrong. To be sure, the atomistic self's claim of self-sufficiency is mistaken; but because its mistake is necessary to mind's self-validation as the structure of right, interpretation does not disparage atomism in the name of a one-sided communitarianism. Rather, it regards the two perspectives as equal partners. Thus, interpretation looks on as its dialogic theme is validated out of the mouth of the very self-related person who has ostensibly repudiated relation with another; and it regards this autoconfirmation of its theme by a principle *other* than itself as the only real and satisfying confirmation. We can say, therefore, that legal interpretation occupies the ground where community and the atomistic self meet. It understands the common law in terms of both principles simultaneously; and this understanding itself reflects dialogic community—the mutual recognition of community and atomistic personality—as the ground of valid interpretation. Accordingly, it is this relation that makes possible a reconciliation of critical idealism and fidelity to law; and this reconciliation in turn secures the rule of law against the tyranny of the dominant perspective.

6. A FINAL OBJECTION

At this point, however, a seemingly powerful objection arises. According to our argument, the very possibility of an idealist fidelity to law depends on a postulate—the interdependence of community and atomistic personality—that seems to imply the greatest infidelity. By our own admission, this postulate is unknown to the participants of the common-law process—to lawyers, judges, and doctrinal scholars. These participants frequently speak of an irreconcilable conflict between individual freedom and the obligations of communal life—a conflict apparently borne out by their incessant struggle to fashion legal "compromises" to mediate it. To these toilers, therefore, the idea of dialogic community will seem fantastic. At best, it will appear as an unsupported object of faith incapable of persuading anyone not already disposed to accept it; at worst, as a mystical unity of opposites by which one conceals from oneself the realities of contradiction in life. As long, however, as our basic principle opposes the viewpoint of the ordinary lawyer, it comes forward as an external perspective by which we manipulate the law in the service of some unspoken interest. Put simply, if fidelity to law means respecting the law's own point of view, how can an interpretation in light of a utopian harmony of community and atomistic selfhood claim to be faithful?

This objection is not as damaging as it may seem. In fact, we have already answered it repeatedly throughout the course of this book. An interpretation of law in terms of dialogic community is confirmed in its fidelity if and when the postulate we assume at the outset of interpretation is spontaneously produced by the law at the end, that is to say, if and when the law has developed to the point where the idea of dialogic community is already implicit in the oscillation and stalemate between communitarian and individualist paradigms of law. In this dynamic tension between rival absolutes there is revealed the mutual complementarity of the poles that dialogic community involves; all that remains is to grasp this complementarity as a relation of mutual recognition between *subsidiary* principles and to thematize this relation as the fundamental principle of law. Accordingly, the idea of dialogic community does not oppose the viewpoint of the ordinary lawyer; insofar as this lawyer speaks of a tension between individualism and community, he or she has already understood the bond between these principles and so has already understood that neither is separately an absolute end. This insight marks the timeliness of an interpretation of the common law in terms of dialogic community. Interpretation can be said to conform to the common law when the common law hands us the theme by which we interpret it.[34]

It seems appropriate to conclude these studies in Hegelian jurisprudence with a word of reconciliation. Our attempt to see the common law's unity has been mainly inspired by the movement called Critical Legal Studies, which denies the existence of such a unity and which thus denies the difference between law and partisan politics. In one sense, therefore, this movement is the principal intellectual adversary of those who seek to recover a viable conception of the rule of law. Yet the remarks in the preceding paragraph suggest that this adversarial relationship might be a superficial appearance. Roberto Unger has affirmed a deep hostility between CLS and mainstream lawyers and legal scholars.[35] In doing so, he has failed to see the extent to which CLS merely gave clear expression to what many in the profession already believed. Indeed, CLS is perhaps best understood as the epitome of the modern common-law consciousness—as the law's highest awareness of the incoherence of all one-sided grounds of law. Viewed in this way, CLS, far from being an adversary to our efforts at reconstruction, is the decisive precondition for whatever success they may achieve. The awareness of the self-contradictoriness in isolation of the poles of individualism and collectivism is just the precondition for our grasping the interconnectedness of the extremes in dialogic community; and so this awareness constitutes the intellectual situation that guarantees the fidelity to law of an interpretation guided by this theme. We are fortunate, then, to be able to conclude a work based on the unity of opposites with a paradox. The distinction between politics and law depends, we saw, on the possibility of a faithful interpretation of the common-law tradition. CLS guarantees the fidelity of an interpretation in light of the only principle that makes fidelity coherent. Hence CLS underwrites the distinction between politics and law.

NOTES

CHAPTER I: THE CRISIS OF THE COMMON LAW

1. See, e.g., Miller v. Jackson, [1977] Q.B. 966 (C.A.); Boomer v. Atlantic Cement Co., 257 N.E.2d 870 (N.Y.S.C. 1970).

2. See *Restatement (Second) of Contracts* (St. Paul: American Law Institute Publishers, 1981), sec. 90; Walton Stores (Interstate) Ltd. v. Maher, 62 A.L.J.R. 110 (H.C. 1988).

3. See, e.g., Greenman v. Yuba Power Products, Inc., 377 P.2d 897 (Cal. S.C. 1963); Escola v. Coca-Cola Bottling Co., 150 P.2d 436 (Cal. S.C. 1944); *Restatement (Second) of Torts* (St. Paul: American Law Institute Publishers, 1965), sec. 402A. This evolution is traced in George Priest, "The Invention of Enterprise Liability: A Critical History of the Intellectual Foundations of Modern Tort Law," 14 *J. Leg. Stud.* 461 (1985); see also William Prosser, "The Assault Upon the Citadel (Strict Liability to the Consumer)," 69 *Yale L. J.* 1099 (1960).

4. R. v. Caldwell, [1981] 1 All E.R. 961 (H.L.).

5. See Richard Posner, *The Economic Analysis of Law*, 4th ed. (Boston: Little, Brown, 1992).

6. For a pioneering example, see Roscoe Pound, "A Survey of Social Interests," 57 *Harv. L. Rev.* 1 (1943).

7. For essays representative of this tendency, see David Kairys, ed., *The Politics of Law: A Progressive Critique*, 2d ed. (New York: Pantheon Books, 1990). Contemporary feminist jurisprudence has been greatly influenced by the psychological research of Carol Gilligan into contrasting male and female moral orientations; see *In a Different Voice: Psychological Theory and Women's Development* (Cambridge: Harvard University Press, 1982); C. Menkel-Meadow, "Portia in a Different Voice: Speculating on Women's Lawyering Process," 1 *Berkeley Women's L. J.* 39 (1987); R. West, "Jurisprudence and Gender," 55 *Univ. Chic. L. Rev.* 1 (1988).

8. Ferdinand Tönnies, *Community and Society*, trans. Charles Loomis (New York: Harper & Row, 1963).

9. 12 Coke's Rep. 63, 64–65; 77 E.R. 1342, 1343.

10. See Bagg's Case, 11 Coke's Rep. 93b, 77 E.R. 1271. For an excellent commentary on the conflict between common-law theory and political sovereignty, see Gerald Postema, *Bentham and the Common Law Tradition* (Oxford: Clarendon Press, 1986). See also J. A. G. Pocock, *The Ancient Constitution and the Feudal Law* (New York: Norton, 1967), 30–69, and Patrick Callaghan, *The Origin and Evolution of Adjudicative Supremacy* (unpublished LL.M. thesis, University of Toronto, 1993).

11. 198 U.S. 45 (1905).

12. See R. Dworkin, *Taking Rights Seriously* (Cambridge: Harvard University Press, 1977), 82–86.

13. The reorientation of the common law toward collective ends is most advanced in the United States, where it has generated a controversial expansion of liability; see Peter Huber, *Liability: The Legal Revolution and Its Consequences* (New York: Basic Books, 1988); Peter Schuck, "Introduction: The Context of the Controversy," in Schuck, ed., *Tort Law and the Public Interest* (New York: Norton, 1991), 17–43.

14. See R. v. City of Sault Ste. Marie, [1978] 2 S.C.R. 1299; Proudman v. Dayman, 67 C.L.R. 536 (Aust. H.C. 1941).

15. See *Restatement (Second) of Contracts,* sec. 90.

16. For a forthright expression of this tendency, see Anne Bottomley and Joanne Conaghan, "Feminist Theory and Legal Strategy," 20 *J. Law and Society* 1 (1993): "[T]he strength of feminist jurisprudence is tested not by claims to internal coherence but rather by an ability to deliver."

17. In an early edition of his major work on the common law, Richard Posner wrote that it is "essential that the defendant be made to pay damages and that they be equal to the plaintiff's loss. But that the damages are paid *to the plaintiff* is, from an economic standpoint, a detail"; *The Economic Analysis of Law,* 2d ed. (Boston: Little, Brown, 1977), 143. Posner explains this "detail" as a bounty paid to the plaintiff to induce him to enforce efficiency-promoting public standards as well as to discourage him from taking wasteful precautions. However, this fails to explain why the plaintiff receives recompense for his loss rather than the amount needed to entice him into public service or the amount needed to make him prefer the loss to the safety expenditure; see Ernest Weinrib, "Understanding Tort Law," 23 *Valparaiso Univ. L. Rev.* 485, 508–509 (1989).

18. See, e.g., Joseph Singer, "The Player and the Cards: Nihilism and Legal Theory," 94 *Yale L. J.* 1, 34–35, 51–52 (1984); Frank Michelman, "Justification (and Justifiability) of Law in a Contradictory World," in J. R. Pennock and J. W. Chapman, eds., *Nomos,* vol. 28: *Justification* (New York: New York University Press, 1986), 82–87. Cf. Richard Rorty, *Consequences of Pragmatism* (Minneapolis: University of Minnesota Press, 1982), 164–165; Richard Bernstein, *Beyond Objectivism and Relativism: Science, Hermeneutics, and Praxis* (Oxford: Blackwell, 1983), 51–79; Thomas Kuhn, *The Structure of Scientific Revolutions,* 2d ed. (Chicago: University of Chicago Press, 1970), 199–200.

19. Bernstein admits that the idea of good arguments in moral conversation presupposes a community based on shared principles of right, and yet this is just what is lacking in periods of paradigm conflict; see *Beyond Objectivism and Relativism,* 157–158, 230.

20. Ronald Dworkin, *Law's Empire* (Cambridge: Belknap Press, 1986); George Fletcher, "Fairness and Utility in Tort Theory," 85 *Harv. L. Rev.* 537 (1972); Richard Posner, *Economic Analysis of Law*, above n. 5; Ernest Weinrib, *The Idea of Private Law* (Cambridge: Harvard University Press, 1995); Ernest Weinrib, "Legal Formalism: On the Immanent Rationality of Law," 97 *Yale L. J.* 949 (1988).

21. Dworkin, *Law's Empire*, 78 ff.

22. Richard Posner, *The Problems of Jurisprudence* (Cambridge: Harvard University Press, 1990), 460.

23. Weinrib, "Legal Formalism," 973.

24. Roberto Unger, *The Critical Legal Studies Movement* (Cambridge: Harvard University Press, 1986), 1.

25. See Duncan Kennedy, "The Structure of Blackstone's Commentaries," 28 *Buffalo L. Rev.* 205, 210 (1979).

26. Unger, *Critical Legal Studies*, 22–27.

27. G. W. F. Hegel, "Differenz des Fichte'schen und Schelling'schen Systems der Philosophie," in Hegel, *Jenaer Kritische Schriften (I)*, ed. Hans Brockard and Hartmut Buchner (Hamburg: Felix Meiner, 1979), 10.

28. Id., 12.

29. Posner dismisses such an account in a sentence; see *Problems of Jurisprudence*, 329: "The ethics of Kant are too abstract, however, to guide the design of legal doctrines." Posner's dogmatism—his inability to criticize an opponent without presupposing the validity of his own perspective—is also revealed in his response to rights theory in general. His strategy is to reduce the idea of a right to some other instrumentalist (e.g., sociobiological) discourse; see id., 331–332.

30. *Hegel's Philosophy of Right*, trans. T. M. Knox (Oxford: Oxford University Press, 1967), par. 211.

31. For a criticism of such approaches, see Weinrib, "Legal Formalism," 955–957.

32. G. W. F. Hegel, *Phänomenologie des Geistes* (Hamburg: Felix Meiner, 1952), 45 (my translation).

33. See Weinrib, "Legal Formalism," 995–999.

34. Id., at 975.

35. See Wayne Sumner, *The Moral Foundations of Rights* (Oxford: Oxford University Press, 1987), 175–198.

36. John Finnis, *Natural Law and Natural Rights* (Oxford: Clarendon Press, 1980), 298–308.

37. The reader will no doubt think here of Bentham's polemic against Blackstone; see Jeremy Bentham, *A Fragment on Government and An Introduction to the Principles of Morals and Legislation* (Oxford: Blackwell, 1967), 3–112.

38. *The Laws of Plato*, trans. T. Pangle (New York: Basic Books, 1980), 865d–867b, 872d–873a.

39. Id., 860d–863a, 870d–871c.

40. See G. W. F. Hegel, *Natural Law*, trans. T. M. Knox (Philadelphia: University of Pennsylvania Press, 1975), 93 ff.

41. Id., at 93.

42. See, e.g., Ernest Weinrib, "Right and Advantage in Private Law," in

D. Cornell, M. Rosenfeld, and D. Carlson, eds., *Hegel and Legal Theory* (New York: Routledge, 1991), 258–284; Peter Benson, "Abstract Right and the Possibility of a Nondistributive Conception of Contract: Hegel and Contemporary Contract Theory," 10 *Cardozo L. Rev.* 1077 (1989).

43. See Alexandre Kojève, *Introduction to the Reading of Hegel*, ed. Allan Bloom (New York: Basic Books, 1969), 19.

44. Here I have tried to describe a generic notion of friendship broad enough to include the three species Aristotle discusses, namely, friendships based on mutual pleasure, mutual advantage, and mutual admiration of excellence; see *Nicomachean Ethics*, VIII, 1155b–1157b.

45. *The Complete Writings of Thucydides: The Peloponnesian War*, trans. R. Crawley (New York: Modern Library, 1934), 104.

46. G. W. F. Hegel, *Phenomenology of Spirit*, trans. A. V. Miller (Oxford: Oxford University Press, 1977), 279–289.

47. My use of this phrase should not be confused with that of Richard Bernstein in *Beyond Objectivism and Relativism*, 159, 230. Bernstein uses the phrase to designate a community with shared ethical norms, one within which meaningful argument can take place regarding the meaning and application of those norms in concrete situations. I use the phrase to designate (a) the relation of mutual recognition between community and the atomistic self and (b) the diverse instantiations of this relation in the bonds of mutual respect and concern between persons that form the matrix of valid rights.

48. Examples are Ernest Weinrib, "Right and Advantage in Private Law"; Peter Benson, "The Priority of Abstract Right and Constructivism in Hegel's Legal Philosophy," in Cornell, Rosenfeld, and Carlson, eds., *Hegel and Legal Theory*, 174–204.

49. Thus, Charles Taylor devotes two pages (428–429) to abstract right in his otherwise excellent *Hegel* (Cambridge: Cambridge University Press, 1975) and does not discuss it at all in *Hegel and Modern Society* (Cambridge: Cambridge University Press, 1979). He reads Hegel as seeking a reconciliation between modern individual autonomy and classical communitarianism, but he then gives an undialectical twist to this harmony when he sees it as rejecting atomism and as constituting a "larger life" in which individuals are "immersed" (*Hegel*, 374). Taylor cannot seem mentally to encompass a harmony of communitarianism and atomism; but this is not surprising, since he regards Hegel's ontology as "near incredible" (*Hegel and Modern Society*, 135). For other examples of a one-sidedly communitarian reading of Hegel, see Allen Wood, *Hegel's Ethical Thought* (Cambridge: Cambridge University Press, 1990), 101–104, 195–208, 258–259; Steven Smith, *Hegel's Critique of Liberalism* (Chicago: University of Chicago Press, 1989), 127–131, 136–145, 232–246; Seyla Benhabib, "Obligation, Contract, and Exchange: On the Significance of Hegel's Abstract Right," in Z. A. Pelczynski, ed., *The State and Civil Society: Studies in Hegel's Political Philosophy* (Cambridge: Cambridge University Press, 1984), 159–177.

50. Domestications of Hegel's philosophy abound in the Anglo-American literature on him. Usually this takes the form of extracting Hegel's statements from the framework of his dialectical logic to make them palatable to a contemporary audi-

ence. An extreme example is offered by Z. A. Pelczynski's introduction to *Hegel's Political Writings*, trans. T. M. Knox (Oxford: Clarendon Press, 1964), where Hegel appears as a thinker whose "theory of the modern state . . . is not radically different in approach, method of argument, and level of theorizing from the political theory of Hobbes, Locke, Montesquieu, or Rousseau" (135). More recently, Mark Tunick has offered us a "rehabilitated" Hegel whose wisdom can be "appropriated" by reading him as a good Rortyan pragmatist who dissolves knowledge into interpretation, for whom "laws of right merely describe the customs and practices we share as an ethical community" and for whom an institution is justified if it "shapes us, becomes a part of ourselves"; see *Hegel's Political Philosophy* (Princeton: Princeton University Press, 1992), 4, 14, 17, 32, 103.

51. Emil Fackenheim, *The Religious Dimension in Hegel's Thought* (Boston: Beacon Press, 1967), 83.

52. Hegel, *Phenomenology*, 48–57.

CHAPTER II: THE UNITY OF PROPERTY LAW

1. Contrast the economic analysis of law, for which "the true grounds of legal decision are concealed rather than illuminated by the characteristic rhetoric of opinions." Richard Posner, *The Economic Analysis of Law*, 4th ed. (Boston: Little, Brown, 1992), 23.

2. The prime, contemporary example of such an approach seeks to unify the common law under the goal of efficient resource allocation; see Posner, *Economic Analysis of Law*. There are, however, other examples. Margaret Radin views property law as a means for realizing a certain vision of human flourishing in community; see "Property and Personhood," 34 *Stan. L. Rev.* 957 (1982); "Market-Inalienability," 100 *Harv. L. Rev.* 1849 (1987); "The Liberal Conception of Property: Cross Currents in the Jurisprudence of Takings," 88 *Col. L. Rev.* 1667, 1687–1696 (1988). Frank Michelman reinterprets aspects of takings jurisprudence from the standpoints of welfare maximization and of Rawlsian distributive justice; see "Property, Utility, and Fairness: Comments on the Ethical Foundations of 'Just Compensation' Law," 80 *Harv. L. Rev.* 1165 (1967).

3. See, e.g., George Priest, "The Common Law Process and the Selection of Efficient Rules," 6 *J. Leg. Stud.* 65 (1977); John Goodman, "An Economic Theory of the Evolution of the Common Law," 7 *J. Leg. Stud.* 393 (1978).

4. Richard Posner, "Utilitarianism, Economics, and Legal Theory," 8 *J. Leg. Stud.* 191 (1980); Richard Posner, "The Ethical and Political Basis of the Efficiency Norm in Common Law Adjudication," 8 *Hofstra L. Rev.* 487 (1979).

5. Joseph Singer, "The Reliance Interest in Property," 40 *Stan. L. Rev.* 611, 623–637 (1988); Duncan Kennedy, "Form and Substance in Private Law Adjudication," 89 *Harv. L. Rev.* 1685, 1728–1731 (1976).

6. This point will no doubt seem overstated to some. One might argue that from the absence of a unified theory of law it does not follow that there is nothing but the clash of undiscussable preference; for even in a world of contradictory principles, judges are obliged publicly to justify their decisions in terms of *some* principle as well as to give reasons for their choice of principle, and to that extent

their decisions will not be simply arbitrary; see Frank Michelman, "Justification (and Justifiability) of Law in a Contradictory World," in J. R. Pennock and J. W. Chapman, eds., *Nomos*, vol. 28: *Justification* (New York: New York University Press, 1986), 85. I wonder, however, whether this refuge from a "contradictory world" might be illusory. Leave aside the point that the principle and reasons appealed to may be saluted by only part of the "community," which part will be unable to persuade those whose allegiance is to the contrary principle. To work, the argument must show that the judge is *obligated* to justify his decision with reference to one of a number of contradictory paradigms and to give reasons for his choice of paradigm. But if the obligation to give reasoned judgments itself belongs to a particular ethical paradigm, then in a world of contradictory paradigms, that obligation cannot be set up as a privileged moral fact somehow above the fray. Rather, it becomes itself something contestable and hence no longer valid as an obligation. Of course, if the judge decides without reasons, his activity will not be recognized as an example of judging by those involved in the practice of law; his decisions will be criticized, showing that there is an internal norm requiring principled decision making. But this phenomenon requires a theoretical account, and it seems that only a unified theory of law offers a satisfactory one, since only such a theory renders the idea of obligation coherent. Once one accepts the premise of inevitable contradiction, the conclusion is inescapable that the practice of criticizing judgments in light of internal norms involves a mass self-delusion—a bad faith flight from the reality of lawless freedom. Is not the comforting assurance that there exists a middle ground between a unified theory and nihilism precisely such a flight?

7. Our approach thus differs from that offered in Ernest Weinrib, "Right and Advantage in Private Law," 10 *Cardozo L. Rev.* 1283 (1989), and in Peter Benson, "Abstract Right and the Possibility of a Nondistributive Conception of Contract: Hegel and Contemporary Contract Theory," 10 *Cardozo L. Rev.* 1077 (1989), both of which seek the unifying principle of private law in an undifferentiated normative foundation, namely, the abstract universality of personhood.

8. Stephen Munzer has recently offered what he too advances as a pluralist theory of property; see *A Theory of Property* (Cambridge: Cambridge University Press, 1990). However, the Hegelian theory I am putting forward is pluralist in a way different from Munzer's. Let us first distinguish between a pluralist and an eclectic theory. A pluralist theory of property integrates different foundational principles within a single structure that coherently limits the scope of each principle and prescribes methods for resolving all conflicts. The constituent principles are in one sense "reduced" in that within the whole they are no longer foundational or absolute; but in another important sense they are not reduced, because they retain within limits an independent jurisdiction; they are not subsumed under a more comprehensive principle (a federalist constitution is a good analogy). An eclectic theory combines different foundational principles in a way that leaves each as foundational, so that conflict resolutions appear as compromises. Since Munzer admits the possibility of insoluble conflicts between his principles, and since he would resolve others by intuition (see id., chap. 11), his theory is ultimately eclectic rather than pluralist. Second, the theory we propose is in a sense more inclusive than Munzer's because it incorporates both distributive and nondistributive

justifications of property, whereas Munzer provides only different criteria for just *distributions*—namely, labor desert, utility, and equality. Because it cannot account for a property right that is independent of distributive justice, Munzer's theory of property, whatever one may think of its prescriptive force, does not square well with common-law practice.

9. See H. L. A. Hart, "Positivism and the Separation of Law and Morals," 71 *Harv. L. Rev.* 593, 594–600 (1958).

10. Ronald Dworkin, *Law's Empire* (Cambridge: Belknap Press, 1986), 68–76; cf. Alasdair MacIntyre, *After Virtue* (Notre Dame: University of Notre Dame Press, 1984), 204–225; Hans-Georg Gadamer, *Truth and Method* (New York: Crossroad, 1985), 245–274.

11. For a sustained argument that normative validity can be ascribed only to contents generated from the self-determination of freedom, see Richard Dien Winfield, *Reason and Justice* (Albany: State University of New York Press, 1988), 118–155.

12. See G. W. F. Hegel, *Phenomenology of Spirit*, trans. A. V. Miller (Oxford: Oxford University Press, 1977), 52–57; see also *The Logic of Hegel*, trans. W. Wallace (Oxford: Oxford University Press, 1892), pars. 79–82.

13. *Hegel's Philosophy of Right*, trans. T. M. Knox (Oxford: Oxford University Press, 1967). Numbers in the text refer to paragraph numbers of this work. The letter "A" after a number refers to the addition to the paragraph consisting of lecture notes taken by Hegel's students and included by Knox in his edition of the *Philosophy of Right*; the letter "R" after a number refers to Hegel's own remark to the paragraph.

14. For a clear statement of this position, see Thomas Holland, *The Elements of Jurisprudence*, 11th ed. (Oxford: Clarendon Press, 1910), 1–13.

15. Rudolf Von Jhering, "In the Heaven of Legal Concepts," in Morris Cohen and Felix Cohen, eds., *Readings in Jurisprudence and Legal Philosophy* (New York: Prentice-Hall, 1951), 678–689.

16. Southern Pacific Co. v. Jensen, 244 U.S. 205, 222 (1917).

17. Holland, *Elements of Jurisprudence*, 80: "Jurisprudence is concerned not so much with the purposes which Law subserves, as the means by which it subserves them." The law's divorce from purpose is also an admitted feature of the formalism recently elaborated by Weinrib. For Weinrib, law consists in the "articulations of a coherent justificatory structure," a structure constituted by one of the forms (corrective or distributive) of justice; see "Legal Formalism: On the Immanent Rationality of Law," 97 *Yale L. J.* 949, 969 (1988). Thus a doctrine (like loss spreading) justified in terms of distributive justice cannot be part of the law enforced in an institutional setting whose intelligibility rests on corrective justice. Since the criterion of law (justificatory coherence) is neutral with respect to substantive justifications in terms of purposes, Weinrib must say that "the only function of the law of torts is to be the law of torts." See "The Insurance Justification and Private Law," 14 *J. Leg. Stud.* 681, 686 (1985).

18. See R. E. Megarry and H. W. R. Wade, *The Law of Real Property*, 5th ed. (Agincourt, Ont.: Carswell, 1984), 67–70. A fee simple embraces all the incidents of ownership (e.g., the right to possess, enjoy, alienate) atemporally. It is thus the

practical equivalent of absolute ownership. A defeasible fee simple is one that can be defeated on the happening of some event specified by the grantor, e.g., Black-acre to John for as long as he remains married to Jane.

19. Heath v. Lewis, 3 De G. M. & G. 954, 956, 43 E.R. 374, 375 (1853), per Knight Bruce, L.J.

20. Thus animals are purposive, but because they standardly do not create in terms of purposes, they are not a source of rationality.

21. The formerly rigid distinction between the concepts of lease and contract (as a result of which a landlord had no duty to mitigate his damages if a tenant abandoned the leased premises and lost all further claims against the tenant if he did mitigate) is another example of this form of conceptualism; see John Hicks, "The Contractual Nature of Real Property Leases," 24 *Baylor L. Rev.* 443 (1972); Douglas Stollery, "The Lease as Contract," 19 *Alberta L. Rev.* 234 (1981).

22. This outcome impels legal thought to distinguish between "law in books" and "law in action"; and it leads to a conception of law as regularities in judicial behavior on the basis of which one may predict the outcome of litigation; see O. W. Holmes, "The Path of the Law," 10 *Harv. L. Rev.* 457 (1897). Inasmuch as its general theory of law as behavioral regularity presupposes the downfall of a spe-cific conception of law as norm, "realistic" jurisprudence lives entirely within the shadow of the formalism it opposes.

23. See Felix Cohen, "Transcendental Nonsense and the Functional Approach," 35 *Col. L. Rev.* 809, 821–834 (1935); Rudolf Von Jhering, *Law as a Means to an End*, trans. Isaac Husik (Boston: Boston Book Co., 1913), 325–347.

24. This is now the conventional wisdom about property; see John Cribbet and Crowin Johnson, *Principles of the Law of Property*, 3d ed. (Westbury, N.Y.: Foundation Press, 1989), 5: "Occasionally in your reading of cases, you will find a court saying, 'We cannot grant the relief requested by the plaintiff because no property interest is involved. . . .' Is not this reasoning in reverse? If the court grants the protection, it has created a species of property. . . . No particular harm is done by the legal for-mula set forth above as long as you realize that property is not a mystical entity es-tablished by some fiat outside the framework of the law." See also Arnold Weinrib, "Information and Property," 38 *Univ. Toronto L. J.* 117, 120–122 (1988); Singer, "The Reliance Interest," 637–641.

25. See Joseph Singer and Jack Beermann, "The Social Origins of Property," 6 *Can. J. Law and Jurisprudence* 217, 241–248 (1993). For the bundle of rights conception of property, see Wesley Hohfeld, "Some Fundamental Legal Concep-tions as Applied in Judicial Reasoning," 23 *Yale L. J.* 16, 24 (1913); see also Felix Cohen, "Dialogue on Private Property," 9 *Rutgers L. Rev.* 357, 373–374 (1954); Tony Honoré, *Making Law Bind: Essays Legal and Philosophical* (Oxford: Clarendon Press, 1987), 165–179; Thomas Grey, "The Disintegration of Property," in J. R. Pennock and J. W. Chapman, eds., *Nomos*, vol. 22: *Property* (New York: New York University Press, 1980), 69–73.

26. Of course, authoritative balancing is less reliable than free market trans-actions, so that efficiency supports "property" when such transactions are feasible. However, this means that property is a variable conclusion of a calculus as to the relative efficiency in the circumstances of market and authoritative reallocations; see Posner, *Economic Analysis of Law*, 49–55.

27. See Grey, "The Disintegration of Property," 69.

28. See Cohen, "Dialogue on Private Property," 380–381.

29. See Susan French, "Toward a Modern Law of Servitudes: Reweaving the Ancient Strands," 55 *S. Cal. L. Rev.* 1261 (1982); Susan French, "Servitudes Reform and the New Restatement of Property: Creation Doctrines and Structural Simplification," 73 *Cornell L. Rev.* 928 (1988); Uriel Reichman, "Toward a Unified Concept of Servitudes," 55 *S. Cal. L. Rev.* 1177 (1982).

30. G. W. F. Hegel, *Vorlesungen über Rechtsphilosophie 1818–1831*, ed. K.-H. Ilting (Stuttgart-Bad Cannstatt: Frommann-Holzboog, 1974), IV, 172.

31. On the principle of logical consistency as a way of moving from right-claims to valid (because mutually recognized) rights, see Alan Gewirth, *Human Rights: Essays on Justification and Applications* (Chicago: University of Chicago Press, 1982), 51–55.

32. Contrast the approaches of Margaret Jane Radin and Jeremy Waldron, on the one hand, and Peter Benson, on the other. Radin begins an account of property from an advanced conception of moral personality as embracing concrete projects, thereby rendering invisible the system of property law based on abstract personality; see "Property and Personhood," 34 *Stan. L. Rev.* 957 (1982). Likewise Waldron interprets Hegel as justifying property "as something everyone needs in order to develop his freedom and individuality," ignoring Hegel's claim that abstract right prescinds from all considerations of welfare; see *Right to Private Property* (Oxford: Clarendon Press, 1988), 351. The idea of a human good for which property might be needed is not introduced until the section on "Morality"; see *Philosophy of Right,* par. 128. Since Waldron conflates the paradigms of abstract right and morality, he has to criticize Hegel for incoherently connecting a human need theory of property with a right to things specifically acquired by acts of possession; see id., 386–389 (how these two theories connect is precisely the burden of this study). If Radin and Waldron fail to see abstract right, Benson sees nothing else. In failing to move beyond the paradigm ruled by abstract personality, Benson suppresses the doctrines of contract law embodying a right of intention; see "Hegel and Contemporary Contract Theory," 1147–1196.

33. See, e.g., R. v. Stewart, [1988] 1 S.C.R. 963; International News Service v. Associated Press, 248 U.S. 215, 248–267 (1918), per Brandeis, J.

34. See INS v. AP, 238, per Pitney, J.; Krouse v. Chrysler Canada Ltd., 25 D.L.R. (3d) 49, 59–62 (Ont. H.C. 1972); Exchange Telegraph Co. Ltd. v. Howard and Manchester Press Agency Ltd., 22 T.L.R. 375 (1906), per Buckley, J.: "The knowledge of a fact which is unknown to many people may be the property of a person in that others will pay the person who knows it for the information as to that fact."

35. An entailed estate passes to the lineal heir automatically; it cannot be freely alienated in a will. Fines and recoveries (their differences are unimportant here) were collusive procedures whereby a tenant in tail, with the acquiescence of the court, offered no defense to a stranger's suit for the land, so that the stranger took the land free of the entail. The stranger then either paid the purchase price or conveyed the land, now unencumbered, back to the tenant. The common-law rule against the remote vesting of interests (also called the rule against perpetuities) declared void any remainder that might vest later than the period of a life-in-being plus twenty-one years. For example, in the grant "on trust to A for life, remainder

to A's firstborn son when he turns thirty," the remainder is void if A's firstborn son is under nine years old at the time of the grant.

36. Duke of Norfolk's Case, 2 Swans. 454, 460 (1681).

37. Id.

38. See, e.g., Re Collier, 60 D.L.R. (2d) 70 (Nfld. S.C. 1966).

39. See Davies v. Davies, 36 Ch.D. 359, 393 (1887), per Bowen, L. J.: "The law of England allows a man to contract for his labour, or allows him to place himself in the service of a master, but it does not allow him to attach to his contract of service any servile incidents,—any elements of servitude as distinguished from service." See also In Re James Sommersett, 20 St. Trials 1 (1771–1772); Archer v. The Society of the Sacred Heart of Jesus, 9 O.L.R. 474 (Ont. C.A. 1905).

40. Guido Calabresi and A. Douglas Melamed, "Property Rules, Liability Rules, and Inalienability: One View of the Cathedral," 85 *Harv. L. Rev.* 1089, 1111–1112 (1972).

41. See Charles Callaghan, *Adverse Possession* (Columbus: Ohio State University Press, 1961), 89–96.

42. Aristotle's justification of private ownership is an example of this type; see *Politics,* 1262b–1265b. So, of course, is Jeremy Bentham's; see "Principles of the Civil Code," in C. K. Ogden, ed., *The Theory of Legislation* (London: Routledge & Kegan Paul, 1931), 158 ff. Contemporary examples are Munzer, *A Theory of Property,* chaps. 4–6; Jeremy Waldron, *Right to Private Property,* chaps. 8–10; Harold Demsetz, "Toward a Theory of Property Rights," 57 *Am. Econ. Rev. Papers and Proceedings* 347 (1967).

43. John Locke, *The Second Treatise of Government,* ed. Thomas Peardon (Indianapolis: Bobbs-Merrill, 1952), pars. 25–51.

44. For critiques of the "mixing" theory, see Waldron, *Right to Private Property,* 184–191; Robert Nozick, *Anarchy, State, and Utopia* (New York: Basic Books, 1974), 174–175; William Lucy and François Barker, "Justifying Property and Justifying Access," 6 *Can. J. Law and Jurisprudence* 287, 299–303; Lawrence Becker, *Property Rights: Philosophic Foundations* (Boston: Routledge & Kegan Paul, 1977), 33–43.

45. For accounts of Hegel's theory of property that adopt this perspective see Peter Stillman, "Hegel's Analysis of Property in the *Philosophy of Right,*" 10 *Cardozo L. Rev.* 1031 (1989); Jeremy Waldron, *Right to Private Property,* chap. 10.

46. Since a "thing" is simply an entity that lacks the capacity for self-consciousness, there is no reason to limit property to tangible things, and the common law never did so (witness incorporeal hereditaments). Accordingly, there is no basis for the view that the modern "dephysicalization" of property is inconsistent with the classical notion of property; see Kenneth Vandevelde, "The New Property of the Nineteenth Century: The Development of the Modern Concept of Property," 29 *Buffalo L. Rev.* 325, 331–340 (1980); Morton Horwitz, *The Transformation of American Law, 1870–1960* (New York: Oxford University Press, 1992), 145. I discuss the conceptual genesis of intangible property below, n. 83. Moreover, since a thing is whatever lacks self-consciousness, there is no reason to limit property to things outside the self. Thus, skills, talents, and time-restricted exercises of labor power may also be the subject matter of property; see Hegel, *Philosophy of Right,* par. 67. Radin criticizes Hegel for basing the distinction between property and

nonproperty on an elusive distinction between what is outside and what is inside the self, a distinction he then supposedly violates in allowing labor power to be alienable property; see "Market-Inalienability," 1891–1898. But this critique rests on a misunderstanding of Hegel's statement that only things "external by nature" can be property (*Philosophy of Right*, par. 65). This does not mean that only things external *to the self* can be property; it means that only things that lack the interiority of self-consciousness and that are thus "external by nature" can be property.

47. Hegel, *Vorlesungen*, III, 187, 197.

48. The law of co-ownership exemplifies rather than contradicts the private nature of common-law property. Joint tenants merge (by virtue of the four unities) into a single person who is considered to hold indivisibly all rights in respect of the object. The single owner is not a transcendent or common personality in whose ownership the several persons have a distributive share; rather, it is quite literally a single person in which the several individuals are obliterated. Thus joint owners in theory own no shares in the object (hence the right of survivorship), and a statute was required to allow one joint tenant to sue another for appropriating more than an equal share; see Megarry and Wade, *Law of Real Property*, 417–433. By contrast, tenants-in-common own shares in the object; yet they do so not as beneficiaries of a common property but as private owners of segments that have not yet been divided.

49. Thus, apart from contract, an obligation to look after someone's property arises only if one has assumed legal possession of the object, for only then is one's obligation a negative one not to interfere with or "take" the bailor's property. Someone who merely licenses the use of his premises for the storage of property assumes no duty of care; see E. L. G. Tyler and N. E. Palmer, eds., *Crossley Vaines' Personal Property*, 5th ed. (London: Butterworth, 1973), 79–82.

50. Epstein affirms the unity of the incidents of ownership but gives no account of this unity; see Richard Epstein, *Takings: Private Property and the Power of Eminent Domain* (Cambridge: Harvard University Press, 1985), 57–62. The argument for unity consists in a series of rhetorical questions disputing the possibility of coherently subtracting any of the incidents from ownership. "Is it sensible," Epstein asks, "to have a notion of ownership without the right of possession?" (id., 60). Someone might reply, however, that this subtraction is precisely the basis of the landlord-tenant relationship, which, if incoherent, is not self-evidently so. Epstein also claims that rights of ownership are of "infinite temporal duration" (id., 60). But how is this consistent with a grant of rights of possession and use for a finite temporal duration? If there is some time during which I do not possess these rights, then I do not possess them for an infinite duration. The correct formulation would seem to be that ownership embraces its incidents conceptually and therefore atemporally.

51. Lawrence Becker summarily dismisses Hegel's argument that first possession confers a right to exclude on the ground that Hegel's statements establish at best a right to appropriate but not to keep; see Becker, *Property Rights*, 29–30. However, Becker misses the normative claim behind appropriation that establishes the right to keep. If my possession makes good the claim that I am the thing's final end, then the thing is "mine" (subject to any superior self-validation by another).

52. Cf. Immanuel Kant, *The Metaphysics of Morals*, trans. M. Gregor (Cambridge: Cambridge University Press, 1991), 68–77.

53. The usual explanation for this rule is instrumentalist. Giving the finder a right subject to the right of the previous occupier prevents free-for-alls while vindicating expectations of secure possession; for a version of this argument, see David Hume, *A Treatise of Human Nature* (Oxford: Clarendon Press, 1888), 505. Yet this rationale fails to determine the rule, since chaos will also be prevented by a rule giving the state custody of lost objects subject to the right of the true owner. Arguments might be advanced for the pragmatic superiority of a finder's right, but their validity would be relative to circumstances. By contrast, the argument from personality determines the rule, for it explains how possession by itself could be thought to confer a right to possess.

54. Keron v. Cashman, 33 A. 1055 (1896).

55. It follows, too, that objects susceptible only to an incomplete reduction to the will are the subject of a qualified property. Thus, a person has an unconditioned property in a tame animal but a qualified one in a wild animal; once the wild animal regains its liberty, it is no longer his. See 2 William Blackstone, *Commentaries on the Laws of England*, 4th ed. (1771), 392–393.

56. This is Posner's view; see *Economic Analysis of Law*, 35–36. In the economic theory of property, rights of exclusive possession emerge when it becomes worthwhile to internalize the costs and benefits of resource use. This occurs when changes in demand make certain resources acutely scarce in relation to human want. At that point property is needed to ensure that investors capture the benefits of their labor (for otherwise the incentive to produce what others want will be lacking) as well as to ensure that the costs of resource utilization are internalized to the user (for otherwise the incentive for efficient utilization will be lacking). See Harold Demsetz, "Toward a Theory of Property Rights," 57 *Am. Econ. Rev. Papers and Proceedings* 347 (1967). According to economic theory, then, property is a policy response to a competition for scarce resources that, if unregulated, would produce inefficient outcomes. Scarcity itself is left unexplained, since human wants are accepted as given. Also unexplained is the goal of efficiency, which is simply assumed as a value. Thus, economic theory explains property as a device for achieving an unexplained goal in the face of an unexplained problem.

57. See Carol Rose, "Possession as the Origin of Property," 52 *Univ. Chic. L. Rev.* 73, 81–82 (1985). It is difficult to see how, short of a statutory recording system, a requirement that possession be notorious eliminates uncertainty of title. As Rose notes, the question as to what constitutes notorious possession remains a fecund source of conflict.

58. See South Staffordshire Water Co. v. Sharman, [1896] 2 Q.B. 44.

59. See D. R. Harris, "The Concept of Possession in English Law," in Anthony Guest, ed., *Oxford Essays in Jurisprudence* (Oxford: Oxford University Press, 1961), 82–84.

60. See Kant, *Metaphysics of Morals*, 83–84; 2 Blackstone, *Commentaries*, 258; Richard Epstein, "Possession as the Root of Title," 13 *Ga. L. Rev.* 1221 (1979); Rose, "Possession as the Origin of Property," above n. 57.

61. O. W. Holmes, *The Common Law*, ed. M. Howe (Cambridge: Belknap Press, 1963), 163–167.

62. This error is responsible for a number of false steps in the common law; see below, n. 67.

63. Armory v. Delamirie, 93 E.R. 664 (1722).

64. That ownership is distinct from best possessory title is shown by the fact that an owner with no right to immediate possession (e.g., a bailor) can sue for damages to his reversionary interest; see Tyler and Palmer, *Personal Property*, 79.

65. Hegel, *Vorlesungen*, IV, 218: "A property without *ususfructus* is only an empty word."

66. The superiority of use to possession as an embodiment of personality (and so as a basis of title) is also reflected in the ancient doctrine of alteration. Someone who wrongfully takes another's grapes and turns them into wine has the best property in the wine; he is liable in damages only for the value of the grapes; see 2 Blackstone, *Commentaries*, 404.

67. See, e.g., Rodgers v. Elliott, 146 Mass. 349, 15 N.E. 768 (1888). Considered as inwardly limited by the requirement of objectivity (and so by the equal right of others), the right to use is prolific of common-law and statutory doctrines. It underlies not only nuisance law but also the tenant's right to quiet enjoyment, the landlord's duty to provide and maintain residential premises fit for habitation, restrictions on tenants' use, the right to lateral and subjacent support, riparian rights, and the law of easements and of restrictive covenants. The tendency to privilege possession at the expense of use as the paradigm of property is responsible for some of the more egregious false steps of the common law. Until recently, for example, the tenant's right to quiet enjoyment was regarded as protecting him only against physical invasions inconsistent with possessory title. Interferences with ordinary use were not per se enjoinable unless associated with the use of the landlord's property or unless construable as an effective eviction. Similarly, public regulation depriving an owner of a reasonable use of his land has sometimes been denied the status of a compensable taking because the owner retains his possession. And a breach of the landlord's duty to provide premises fit for habitation was traditionally viewed as providing no justification for withholding rent because rent was seen as consideration for a possessory right, which the tenant still held. Finally, the rule that economic loss is recoverable in tort only if consequential on physical damage to property seems also to exalt possession from an element of property to a criterion thereof. Yet all of these errors have either been corrected by statute or are in the process of revision by the common law.

68. See Sturges v. Bridgman, 11 Ch.D. 852 (1879).

69. That the right to use is circumscribed by the equal user right of others reveals the limited sense in which it is true to say that property is a conclusion of tort law. This statement is true to the extent that one's claim of right must be objectively validated, and this requirement of objectivity implicates at least one other will; thus one's property in specific uses must be codetermined with that of another person according to an objective and impersonal standard. What begins as an asocial relation between a person and a thing culminates in a social one between persons, and I shall presently say more about the significance of this movement. However, the statement is interpretively dubious if it implies that one's property in uses is flexibly mediated through a criterion of social welfare independent of the priority of the person. The account of property that fits the dominant

common-law discourse is one that reveals property as an objectively valid connection between a thing and an abstract person. The objectivity of this connection makes relevant the abstract persons of others but consigns to irrelevance their welfare. There is thus a formally determined property in uses that is independent of welfarist considerations and whose invasion constitutes a transitive taking. The welfarist conception of property, as Ronald Coase has shown, leads to the result that property does not matter, since bargaining will theoretically produce the optimal welfarist result wherever the entitlement is initially placed; see Ronald Coase, "The Problem of Social Cost," 3 *J. Law and Econ.* 1 (1960). The obsessive preoccupation of courts with what is economically irrelevant must then be explained by the existence of real-world negotiating costs that obstruct movement toward the efficient outcome. This explanation is unsatisfying, however, since it only reaffirms the position that property is irrelevant. If the court awards the entitlement to the party who would, but for transaction costs, have bought it from the other party, it implies that the process of market transfer is of no intrinsic importance, that only the result matters, even though the process (who pays whom) is determined precisely by the locus of the property right. Further, the economic interpretation of nuisance law leads us to expect that, where transaction costs are low, judges would resolve a dispute over conflicting uses randomly (thus saving the expense of hearing legal argument, guessing the optimal assignment, etc.), an expectation disconfirmed by experience. The reply must then be that judges do imperfectly something other than their rhetoric avows. To this we can respond only with an alternative account of judicial practice, one that is validated by its rhetoric rather than isolated by it.

70. See Tulk v. Moxhay, 41 Eng. Rep. 1143 (Ch. 1848).

71. See Cribbet and Johnson, *Principles,* 375–376; French, "Toward a Modern Law of Servitudes," 1289, 1292.

72. See French, "Servitudes Reform," 929–930.

73. See *INS v. AP,* 238, per Pitney, J.; Krouse v. Chrysler Canada Ltd., 25 D.L.R. (3d) 49, 59 (1972); cf. Locke, *Second Treatise,* par. 27.

74. Epstein, "Possession as the Root of Title," 1226.

75. Locke, *Second Treatise,* par. 27.

76. For a discussion of the relation between labor and property in Hegel's theory of property, see Alan Ryan, *Property and Political Theory* (Oxford: Blackwell, 1984), 124 ff.

77. Locke, *Second Treatise,* par. 27; Robert Nozick, *Anarchy, State, and Utopia* (Oxford: Blackwell, 1974), 174–182.

78. How can we reconcile this conclusion with the right of the first occupier? As long as we are on the path toward a full property, each step on the way is self-contradictory, driving us forward. Thus, first occupation confers a property, for it is an incursion of personality in the thing that must be respected if personality is to be respected as an end. However, the unilateral nature of the exclusion means that possession is a defective and hence inchoate property. When we arrive at the culminating condition of property, each of the preceding phases is retrogressively validated. First occupation now confers a coherent property (defeasible by the adverse possessor) because the conditions are now in place which render it consistent with the equal right of others to an unlimited appropriation.

79. See S. von Pufendorf, *De Officio Hominis et Civis Juxta Legem Naturalem Libri Duo*, trans. F. G. Moore (New York: Oceana, 1964), II, 62; Hugo Grotius, *De Jure Belli Ac Pacis Libri Tres*, trans. F. W. Kelsey (New York: Oceana, 1964), II, 189–190.

80. That property in a thing is conceptually fulfilled by the power freely to alienate it explains the special common-law remedies for intentional infringements of property. Trespasses are actionable without proof of physical damage and even if the plaintiff is benefited, for the act's inconsistency with property lies not in the material harm it inflicts but in its failure to respect the free choice of the owner. To protect this choice, courts enjoin takings before they occur, and they may award damages in excess of the market value of something converted if ordinary damages would amount to a sale forced on the plaintiff; see John Fleming, *The Law of Torts*, 8th ed. (Sydney: Law Book Co., 1992), 69. Indeed, if the defendant's gain exceeds the plaintiff's loss, they will allow the plaintiff—through waiver of tort—to capture the gain in order to vindicate his right freely to dispose.

An instrumentalist view of the injunctive remedy sees it as promoting efficient resource allocation in situations where transaction costs are low, since injunctions permit the free expression of the parties' subjective valuations and so ensure that the object will find a home where it is valued most; see Calabresi and Melamed, "Property Rules, Liability Rules, and Inalienability." Thus we do not protect an entitlement with a property remedy in order to reflect its status as property; rather, something is property because we protect it with a "property" remedy, and the decision to do so is driven by the variable exigencies of efficiency. Were it simply a political program for the reorganization of property law under the primacy of economic efficiency, the economic perspective could not be immanently criticized as either true or false, since it would recognize no object by which to test the validity of its ultimate norm. One could criticize it only as a dogmatism that, because it gives equal standing to rival dogmatisms, renders theoretical disputes absurd. Perhaps to avoid this result, the economic perspective presents itself not as an opinion as to how legal remedies ought to be remodeled but as a "view of the cathedral," that is, as an interpretive account of the practice and discourse of property law. Yet once it recognizes this discourse as a touchstone for the truth of its own, it convicts itself of uttering falsehoods, for its account of property transforms the latter into something entirely different from the property understood by the common law. Common-law property refers to an objectively valid connection between an external object and an individual person. It is an individual right of exclusive control. In the economic account, the idea of a valid bond between object and subject is still present, but the subject of this relation is no longer the individual person but the collective one. What the common law calls property is for economic analysis simply an entitlement protected by an injunction, a remedy one will receive only if transaction costs will not distort efficient trading. Thus the only noncontingent property consists in the relation between the object and the collective person whose welfare-maximizing goal determines where entitlements rest and how they are protected. Whatever one may think of this notion as a political proposal, it unquestionably presents a distorting perspective on the cathedral.

81. Thus Seyla Benhabib is not strictly correct in saying that for Hegel the "proprietary rights of the individual are stipulated prior to the act of contract."

See "Obligation, Contract, and Exchange: On the Significance of Hegel's Abstract Right," in Z. A. Pelczynski, ed., *The State and Civil Society: Studies in Hegel's Political Philosophy* (Cambridge: Cambridge University Press, 1984), 163.

82. Fountainebleu Hotel Corp. v. Forty-Five-Twenty-Five, Inc., 114 So.2d 357 (Fla. S.C. 1959); Port v. Griffith, [1938] 1 All E.R. 295.

83. We are now in a position to understand the significance of property in such intangibles as shares, choses in action, trade secrets, endorsing power, and good-will. Once property is fulfilled in exchange, commensurability between diverse objects requires an abstraction from corporeal things to incorporeal value. At this point, one's property is not confined to the sensuous thing one temporarily possesses but extends perdurably to its exchange value vis-à-vis all other objects; that is, one's final property is in a certain extent of control over the material world in its entirety (see *Vorlesungen*, IV, 227). But sensible objects are not the only sources of such control. Legally recognized entitlements to resources (e.g., corporate shares) are too, as are trade secrets and commercial reputation. Thus, once juridical control over the world is established in exchange, that control becomes itself amenable to exchange. It becomes possible for incorporeal value to attach not only to physical objects but to already existing entitlements to objects or to the power to accumulate objects. If we forget the origins of this development, we may arrive at the conclusion that property is any legally protected valuable interest; and then it is a short step to treating property as an idle concept—as any entitlement secreted from the political accommodation of competing interests; see Vandevelde, "The New Property," 329. The fallacy in this reasoning lies in assuming that the logical culmination of a developmental process makes the preceding stages superfluous—an assumption that would make adulthood intelligible without childhood and adolescence. From the fact that property is conceptually fulfilled in a right to exchange value, it does not follow that the concept of property is swallowed up by the idea of a valuable legal interest. One may view all the developmental phases of property as essential to its concept, in which case possession and use confer a property independently of public policy.

84. Cf. Kant, *Metaphysics of Morals*, 218–219. Thus Radin errs when she writes that the framework of right based on abstract personhood logically culminates in universal commodification; see "Market-Inalienability," 1897–1898.

85. See Johnstone v. Johnstone, 12 D.L.R. 537 (Ont. C.A., 1913). Because a valid gift emerges only from a relation (albeit an imperfect one) of mutual recognition between ends, it is vitiated by factors—for example, mistake, fraud, and undue influence—that undermine mutuality. Thus, the donee may recognize the owner's capacity to dispose, but the gift will fail if mistake undercuts the donor's recognition of the donee. Conversely, if the donee overpowers the independent will of the donor, the latter becomes incompetent to establish a property in the donee.

86. See Hegel, *Phenomenology of Spirit*, 290–328.

87. See Morris Cohen, "Property and Sovereignty," 13 *Cornell L. Q.* 8, 11–14 (1927); C. B. MacPherson, "The Meaning of Property," in MacPherson, ed., *Property: Mainstream and Critical Positions* (Toronto: University of Toronto Press, 1978), 12.

88. See Inwards v. Baker, [1965] 2 Q.B. 29 (Eng. C.A.).

89. See Pascoe v. Turner, [1979] 1 W.L.R. 431 (C.A.).

90. See Hurst v. Picture Theatres, Ltd., [1915] 1 K.B. 1 (C.A.); see also Errington v. Errington, [1952] 1 K.B. 290 (C.A.).

91. See Sorochan v. Sorochan, [1986] 2 S.C.R. 38; Pettkus v. Becker, [1980] 2 S.C.R. 834.

92. The exception of public expropriation will be explained below, sec. 7.

93. See Perka v. The Queen, [1984] 2 S.C.R. 233.

94. See Post v. Jones, 60 U.S. (19 How.) 150 (1856).

95. See Woollerton and Wilson Ltd. v. Richard Costain Ltd., [1970] 1 W.L.R. 411.

96. 124 N.W. 221 (1910).

97. Ernest Weinrib, "The Case for a Duty to Rescue," 90 *Yale L. J.* 247, 268–279 (1980).

98. Above n. 33.

99. See Victoria Park Racing and Recreation Grounds Co. Ltd. v. Taylor, 58 C.L.R. 479 (H.C. 1937).

100. Singer, "The Reliance Interest," 633–637.

101. For example, United States v. Bethlehem Steel Corp., 315 U.S. 289, 326 (1942), per Frankfurter, J.: "[I]s there any principle which is more familiar or more firmly embedded in the history of Anglo-American law than the basic doctrine that the courts will not permit themselves to be used as instruments of inequity and injustice? Does any principle in our law have more universal application than the doctrine that courts will not enforce transactions in which the relative positions of the parties are such that one has unconscionably taken advantage of the necessities of the other?" Stockloser v. Johnson, [1954] 1 Q.B. 476, 488–489 (C.A.), per Denning, L.J.: "The claimant invariably relies, like Shylock, on the letter of the contract to support his demand, but the courts decline to give him their aid because they will not assist him in an act of oppression." Lloyd's Bank v. Bundy, [1975] 1 Q.B. 326, 336–337, per Lord Denning, M.R.: "There are cases in our books in which the courts will set aside a contract, or a transfer of property, when the parties have not met on equal terms—when the one is so strong in bargaining power and the other so weak—that, as a matter of common fairness, it is not right that the strong should be allowed to push the weak to the wall." Re Diplock, [1948] Ch. 465, 532 (C.A.), per Lord Greene, M.R.: "[E]quity intervenes not to do what might be thought to be absolute justice to a claimant but to prevent a defendant from acting in an unconscionable manner. Equity will not restrain a defendant from asserting a claim save to the extent that it would be unconscionable to do so. If this limitation on the power of equity results in giving to a plaintiff less than what on some general idea of fairness he might be considered entitled to, that cannot be helped."

102. My conclusion regarding *Vincent v. Lake Erie,* therefore, is that it is either a case of this type or it was wrongly decided (i.e., the plaintiff was entitled to compensation for the expropriation in addition to that for damage to the dock).

103. The good faith purchaser for value exception to the rule that *nemo dat quod non habet* is also explicable in these terms. Here equity protects the projects of

the good faith purchaser against a property law that, in the circumstances, impinges on him in the form of a blind and incalculable fate. Since its effects are beyond the scope of the purchaser's rational foresight and control, property law would, if enforced in these circumstances, contradict the agent's autonomy. The law's enforcement would thus subvert its own universality, for it would be unrecognizable to the rational agent as *his* good, as supporting his self-determination. Once again, therefore, equity revokes the self's estrangement in formal property by canceling the power of property insofar as this power acts externally. The limitations of the exception ensure that it will govern only in circumstances where the enforcement of formal property would subject the purchaser to an incalculable fate rather than to consequences under his rational control. Thus, the purchaser must take in good faith; he must believe the seller has good title. Moreover, his belief must be based on reasonable grounds (e.g., he must have purchased in a "market overt" or must have reasonably relied on the owner's assurance that the transferor had a right to transfer the goods). Finally, he must give value for the goods; that is, he must be innocent of wrongdoing himself, for otherwise the enforcement of property against him is immanent in his rational will (as a vindication of the equal worth of persons) and not external to it. Equity thus cancels property only in order to realize better the end that property itself embodies.

104. Hegel formulates the right operative here in *Philosophy of Right,* par. 107: "The moral standpoint . . . takes shape as the right of the subjective will. In accordance with this right, the will recognizes something and is something, only in so far as the thing is its own and as the will is present to itself there as something subjective." See also *Vorlesungen,* IV, 301.

105. It would be preferable to cease all reference here to an affirmative duty on the part of the person seeking to enforce his or her property. The duty is on the court. The observance of this duty means, of course, that the plaintiff forgoes his or her right. But the court is not enforcing the plaintiff's duty; it is conforming to its own. This is why an equitable right is said to engage the conscience not of the other party but of the court; see George Keeton and L. A. Sheridan, *Equity,* 3d ed. (London: Barry Rose, 1987), 3.

106. Sometimes judges give explicit expression to the idea that equity fulfills a formal right that, if absolutized, contradicts itself. See, e.g., Morehead v. People of State of New York ex rel. Tipaldo, 298 U.S. 587, 627 (1936), per Hughes, C.J.: "We have had frequent occasion to consider the limitations on liberty of contract. While it is highly important to preserve that liberty from arbitrary and capricious interference, it is also necessary to prevent its abuse, as otherwise it could be used to override all public interests and thus in the end destroy the very freedom of opportunity which it is designed to safeguard."

107. See Joseph Sax, "Some Thoughts on the Decline of Private Property," 58 *Wash. L. Rev.* 481, 484 (1983); Posner, *Economic Analysis of Law,* 32-38; Singer, "The Reliance Interest," 650; Horwitz, *Transformation,* 164-167.

108. See Michelman, "Property, Utility, and Fairness," 1214-1224. In Penn Central Transportation Co. v. New York City, 438 U.S. 104 (1978), the U.S. Supreme Court framed the compensation issue in terms having nothing to do with property. Writing for the majority, Justice Brennan said, "[T]his court . . . has been

unable to develop any "set formula" for determining when "justice and fairness" require that *economic injuries* caused by public action be compensated by the government" (124; my emphasis). The majority proceeded to enumerate a number of factors to be weighed in the balance, including the nature of the governmental action (a physical invasion will "more readily" be viewed as requiring compensation than other forms of interference) and the extent of the economic impact on the claimant. Some later decisions of the Court have resiled from the balancing approach of Penn Central toward a property-oriented analysis; see, e.g., Loretto v. Teleprompter Manhattan CATV Corp., 458 U.S. 419 (1982); Lucas v. South Carolina Coastal Council, 112 S.Ct. 2886 (1982); Hodel v. Irving, 481 U.S. 704 (1987). For a critique of this tendency from an instrumentalist perspective, see Singer and Beermann, "The Social Origins of Property."

109. See Charles Reich, "The New Property," 73 *Yale L. J.* 733 (1964).

110. Susan Rose-Ackerman, "Inalienability and the Theory of Property Rights," 85 *Col. L. Rev.* 931, 931–933 (1985); Charles Donahue, "The Future of the Concept of Property Predicted from Its Past," in J. R. Pennock and J. W. Chapman, eds., *Nomos,* vol. 22: *Property,* 28; Grey, "The Disintegration of Property," 69.

111. Jeremy Waldron, "What Is Private Property?" 5 *Oxford J. Leg. Stud.* 313, 336 (1985); Grey, "The Disintegration of Property," 70–73.

112. See Boomer v. Atlantic Cement Co., 257 N.E.2d 870 (N.Y.S.C. 1970); Miller v. Jackson, [1977] 3 All E.R. 338 (C.A.).

113. See Spur Industries v. Del E. Webb Development Co., 494 P.2d 700 (Ariz. S.C. 1972). Another illustration: in deciding whether someone is liable in trespass to the owner of property, a court will have to consider whether the property is so affected by a public interest as to warrant a qualification of the owner's right to exclude; see Amalgamated Clothing Workers of America v. Wonderland Shopping Centre Inc., 122 N.W.2d 785 (Mich. S.C. 1963). See also the dissenting judgment of Laskin, J., in Harrison v. Carswell, 62 D.L.R. (3d) 68, 69–77 (S.C.C. 1975).

114. For this tension in the public takings jurisprudence of the U.S. Supreme Court, see Margaret Radin, "The Liberal Conception of Property: Cross Currents in the Jurisprudence of Takings," 88 *Col. L. Rev.* 1667 (1988).

115. See Kaiser Aetna v. United States, 444 U.S. 164 (1979); Loretto v. Teleprompter Manhattan CATV Corp., 458 U.S. 419 (1982).

116. I mean here *any* actual, nonnuisance use, not *all* economically viable nonnuisance uses. The latter is currently the threshold for compensable regulatory takings set by the United States Supreme Court; see Lucas v. South Carolina Coastal Council, 112 S.Ct. 2886 (1982).

117. See Hodel v. Irving, 481 U.S. 704 (1987).

118. See Armstrong v. United States, 364 U.S. 40, 49 (1960); cf. Pennsylvania Coal Co. v. Mahon, 260 U.S. 393 (1922), per Holmes, J.

119. Drucilla Cornell has drawn attention to the dialogic nature of Hegel's idea of community. See "Dialogic Reciprocity and the Critique of Employment at Will," 10 *Cardozo L. Rev.* 1575 (1989).

120. Hegel, *Natural Law,* trans. T. M. Knox (Philadelphia: University of Pennsylvania Press, 1975), 94–104.

121. Those who identify Hegel's fully developed state with the one-sidedly

"substantial" community come to the conclusion that private property is submerged in Hegel's state. For example, Radin writes ("Property and Personhood," 976–977), "Hegel's theory of the state carries the seeds of destruction of all liberal rights attaching to individuals (because in the state particular arbitrary will passes over into willing the universal). Hence, there is in Hegel's theory a foundation for the communitarian claim that each community is an organic entity in which private property ownership does not make sense. Hegel does not make this claim, perhaps because he is too firmly rooted in his own time." Hegel does not make this claim, because the community that reduces the individual is inadequate to the idea of community (as the common good *of* individuals). The community that fully conforms to its idea recognizes the individual self as an independent end and so contains liberal anticommunitarianism as an enduring moment of its self-development; see Hegel, *Philosophy of Right,* par. 260.

122. The theory of property advanced here thus takes a dim view of much of the public takings jurisprudence of the United States Supreme Court and, in particular, of the position represented by *Penn Central Transportation Co. v. New York City,* above n. 108. It rejects the view that the issue of compensation is properly decided by balancing the costs to the claimant against the benefit to the public; it rejects the view that a regulation of use must deprive the owner of all economically viable use (or otherwise inflict severe economic harm) before it becomes a taking; it rejects the view that the extent of the diminution of the *value* of the property is a relevant consideration (since there is no property in value prior to exchange); and it rejects the view that the frustration of "reasonable investment-backed expectations" is relevant to the takings clause of the Fifth Amendment (since either these expectations are linked to a property interest, in which case they are protected as property and not independently; or they are not, in which case they are protected, if at all, by the due process clause, not by the takings clause).

123. Of course, the individual might be disproportionately burdened even if no taking has occurred. For example, the construction of a superhighway might severely diminish the profitability of a filling station on a country road with no reciprocal advantage to the owner and without infringing possession, ordinary use, or the right to alienate. In this case, any duty to compensate derives not from the right to property (hence neither from the takings clause of the Fifth Amendment nor from the common-law presumption against uncompensated takings) but purely from the requirement to distribute fairly the costs and benefits of social cooperation. Our vindication through dialogic community of the distinction between private and public law (and hence of the division of function between courts and legislatures) explains why the duty arising from distributive justice is in most common-law jurisdictions thought to be unenforceable by courts in the absence of a compensation statute. It follows, moreover, that Justice Holmes's "average reciprocity of advantage" criterion for compensable injuries is inappropriate to a takings jurisprudence; see Pennsylvania Coal Co. v. Mahon, 260 U.S. 393, 415 (1922).

124. Thus legislative interferences with freedom of alienation to protect the real interests of the weaker party (e.g., rent control statutes) require no compensation, but a ban on the sale of eagle feathers acquired prior to the enactment of a

conservation statute does. See Andrus v. Allard 444 U.S. 51 (1979), where the United States Supreme Court held there was no taking in the latter case. For the Court's position on rent control, see Pennell v. City of San Jose, 108 S.Ct. 849 (1988), holding that statutes regulating economic relations between landlords and tenants are not per se takings.

125. These and the following remarks draw their inspiration from Hegel's theory of the corporation; see *Philosophy of Right,* pars. 249–256.

126. Adolf Berle and Gardiner Means, *The Modern Corporation and Private Property* (New York: Harcourt, Brace & World, 1968), 3–10, 78–111, 126–140, 244–252.

127. See Michael Fogarty, *Company and Corporation—One Law?* (London: Chapman, 1965), 60–153; Walter Kolvenbach, *Workers Participation in Europe* (Deventer, The Netherlands: Kleuver, 1977).

128. See Patrick Macklem, "Property, Status, and Workplace Organizing," 40 *Univ. Toronto L. J.* 74 (1990); see also State v. Shack, 277 A.2d 369 (N.J.S.C. 1971).

129. Singer, "The Reliance Interest."

130. Cornell, "Dialogic Reciprocity."

131. Above n. 96.

132. Singer, "The Reliance Interest"; Grey, "The Disintegration of Property," 80; David Beatty, "Industrial Democracy: A Liberal Law of Industrial Relations," 19 *Valparaiso Univ. L. Rev.* 37, 68 (1984); Macklem, "Property, Status, and Workplace Organizing."

CHAPTER III: RECONSTRUCTING CONTRACTS

1. Act V, scene 1.

2. See Roberto Unger, *The Critical Legal Studies Movement* (Cambridge: Harvard University Press, 1986), 58–90. Duncan Kennedy, "Form and Substance in Private Law Adjudication," 89 *Harv. L. Rev.* 1685 (1976); Clare Dalton, "An Essay in the Deconstruction of Contract Doctrine," 94 *Yale L. J.* 997 (1985); Jay Feinman, "Promissory Estoppel and Judicial Method," 97 *Harv. L. Rev.* 678, 708–712 (1984).

3. See Patrick Atiyah, *The Rise and Fall of Freedom of Contract* (Oxford: Clarendon Press, 1979), esp. Pt. II.

4. de Koning v. Boychuk, [1951] 3 D.L.R. 624 (Alta. S.C.).

5. Thornton v. Shoe Lane Parking Ltd., [1971] 2 Q.B. 163 (C.A.).

6. Suisse Atlantique Société D'Armement Maritime S.A. v. N.V. Rotterdamsche Kolen Centrale, [1966] 2 All E.R. 69 (H.L.).

7. See Henningsen v. Bloomfield Motors, 161 A.2d 69 (N.J.S.C. 1960).

8. See Grant Gilmore, *The Death of Contract* (Columbus: Ohio State University Press, 1974); Patrick Atiyah, *Consideration in Contracts: A Fundamental Restatement* (Canberra: Australian National University Press, 1971); see also H. Collins, *The Law of Contract* (London: Weidenfeld, 1986), 8–21.

9. S. M. Waddams, *The Law of Contracts,* 2d ed. (Toronto: Canada Law Book, 1984), 326.

10. Duncan Kennedy, "Distributive and Paternalist Motives in Contract and

Tort Law, with Special Reference to Compulsory Terms and Unequal Bargaining Power," 41 *Maryland L. Rev.* 563, 580–584, (1982); see also Kennedy, "Form and Substance," 1717–1722, 1731–1737.

11. See E. J. Weinrib, "Legal Formalism: On the Immanent Rationality of Law," 97 *Yale L. J.* 949 (1988).

12. Kennedy, "Form and Substance," 1774–1776.

13. This idea is developed more fully below (see under sec. 8).

14. Numbers in the text refer to paragraphs in *Hegel's Philosophy of Right*, trans. T. M. Knox (Oxford: Oxford University Press, 1967).

15. See E. J. Weinrib, "Right and Advantage in Private Law," 10 *Cardozo L. Rev.* 1283, 1291–1293 (1989).

16. *Hegel's Phenomenology of Spirit*, trans. A. V. Miller (Oxford: Oxford University Press, 1967), 109–119 (henceforward referred to in the text as *PhS*). Michel Rosenfeld has also sought to explain contract by tracing its genesis from the relation of master and slave; see "Hegel and the Dialectics of Contract," in D. Cornell, M. Rosenfeld, and D. Carlson, eds., *Hegel and Legal Theory* (New York: Routledge, 1991), 236–250.

17. See J. M. Bernstein, "From Self-consciousness to Community: Act and Recognition in the Master-Slave Relationship," in Z. A. Pelczynski, ed., *The State and Civil Society: Studies in Hegel's Political Philosophy* (Cambridge: Cambridge University Press, 1984), 15.

18. See *The Logic of Hegel*, trans. W. Wallace (Oxford: Oxford University Press, 1892), par. 187.

19. The relevant tradition is not coextensive with contract theory in general. Contract can be illuminated in different ways by relating it to different contexts. Economics sees contract as a vehicle for allocating scarce resources among competing wants and may prescribe regulatory measures to ensure that this mechanism produces optimal outcomes; see A. Kronman and R. Posner, eds., *The Economics of Contract Law* (Boston: Little, Brown, 1979). Sociology views contract as a form of social cohesion distinguished from forms based on status and hierarchy and may identify evolving forms of contractual relations that legislation should facilitate; see Ian MacNeil, *The New Social Contract: An Inquiry into Modern Contractual Relations* (New Haven: Yale University Press, 1980). A jurisprudence of contract (such as ours) sees contract as a type of obligation, seeks to explain the specific difference of contractual obligation, and elaborates the criteria of enforceability and excuse implicit in its theory. Because our theory of contract is a theory of contractual obligation, it views contract in abstraction from its undoubted connection to the market and to civil society; for the basic elements of these institutions—empirical wants, needs, group interests, etc.—are irrelevant from the standpoint of a moral theory of obligation. A comprehensive theory of contract would integrate all these contexts into an all-embracing one giving each special context its due; see Michael Oakeshott, "The Concept of a Philosophical Jurisprudence," *Politica*, December 1938, p. 352. In this chapter, however, I offer only a jurisprudence of contract, and the relevant field consists of theories of contractual obligation.

20. See Charles Fried, *Contract as Promise* (Cambridge: Harvard University Press, 1981), 9: "What is a promise, that by my words I should make wrong what before was morally indifferent?"

21. Hume, for example, discusses contractual obligation under the heading "Of the Obligation of Promises"; see David Hume, *A Treatise of Human Nature* (Oxford: Clarendon Press, 1888), 516–525; see also John Finnis, *Natural Law and Natural Rights* (Oxford: Clarendon Press, 1980), 298–308; Fried, *Contract as Promise.*

22. Immanuel Kant, *Foundations of the Metaphysics of Morals*, trans. L. W. Beck (Indianapolis: Bobbs-Merrill, 1959), 40.

23. In Lon Fuller's terms, promissory obligation belongs to the morality of aspiration rather than to the morality of duty; see *The Morality of Law* (New Haven: Yale University Press, 1969), 5–9.

24. See L. Fuller and W. Perdue, Jr., "The Reliance Interest in Contract Damages," 46 *Yale L. J.* 52 (1936); Atiyah, *Consideration in Contracts*, 45–61. For an early critique of the reliance theory, see M. Cohen, "The Basis of Contract," 46 *Harv. L. Rev.* 553, 578–580 (1933).

25. See, e.g., Patrick Atiyah, *Essays on Contract* (Oxford: Clarendon Press, 1986), 19–21.

26. Fried, *Contract as Promise.*

27. Id., 16–17.

28. Id., 20–21.

29. This criticism of Fried is also made by Peter Benson, "Abstract Right and the Possibility of a Nondistributive Conception of Contract: Hegel and Contemporary Contract Theory," 10 *Cardozo L. Rev.* 1077, 1116 (1989).

30. G. W. F. Hegel, *Vorlesungen über Rechtsphilosophie 1818–1831*, ed. K.-H. Ilting (Stuttgart-Bad Cannstatt: Frommann-Holzboog, 1974), IV, 249–250.

31. Fibrosa Spolka Akcyjna v. Fairbairn Lawson Combe Barbour Ltd., [1943] A.C. 32 (H.L.).

32. Norwich Union Fire Insurance Society v. Price, [1934] A.C. 455, 461–462 (P.C.).

33. Craven-Ellis v. Canons, Ltd., [1936] 2 K.B. 403, 412 (C.A.).

34. By the same principle, if A confers a benefit on B in circumstances where forcing B to reciprocate would unilaterally subordinate him to the will of A, then A has no right to recover; he is a mere volunteer. See In re Rhodes, Rhodes v. Rhodes, L.R. 44 Ch.D. 94 (1890).

35. See *Vorlesungen*, IV, 257–258. Since we have understood the wholly executory exchange as the best embodiment of personality, we have also understood the judicial treatment of this form as the paradigm case of contract—as the standard for determining the remedy in the partly executed contract. However, since we have also understood the concrete exchange of benefits as a determinate instance of dialogic community, our theory leaves room for a distinctive law of quasi-contract to deal with transfers of benefits involving no promises. There is thus no need to assimilate the exchange of benefits to the executory model by imputing fictitious promises.

36. Fuller and Perdue, "The Reliance Interest in Contract Damages," 57–66.

37. Richard Posner, *The Economic Analysis of Law*, 4th ed. (Boston: Little, Brown, 1992), 119.

38. A powerful objection to the efficiency account of the expectation measure is raised by Ian MacNeil. MacNeil argues that, assuming zero transaction costs, efficiency would be served as well by a remedy of specific performance requiring the

party wishing to breach to buy out the other party. The superior efficiency of the expectation measure would then depend on whether the costs involved in such transactions would exceed those involved in litigating or settling damage claims— a question that can be answered only by empirical inquiry. See "Efficient Breach of Contract: Circles in the Sky," 68 *Virginia L. Rev.* 947 (1982).

39. O. W. Holmes, *The Common Law*, ed. M. Howe (Cambridge: Belknap Press, 1963), 235–236.

40. Payzu Ltd. v. Saunders, [1919] 2 K.B. 581 (C.A.). Normally, the date at which the promisee is required to mitigate is the date of breach, but the breach date rule is modified where the property is subject to wide fluctuations in value; see Asamera Oil Corp. Ltd. v. Sea Oil & General Corp., [1979] 1 S.C.R. 633; Miliangos v. Geo. Frank (Textiles) Ltd., [1976] A.C. 443 (H.L.).

41. The expectation measure of damages is also limited by the rule in Hadley v. Baxendale, 156 E.R. 245 (1854), regarding consequential losses too remote for recovery. Although the promisee's right is to be put in the position he would have been in had the promise been performed, this right extends only to compensation for losses that were reasonably in the contemplation of both parties at the time of the agreement. The test of reasonable foreseeability appears to some as empty and manipulable, since the court will (it is said) regard as reasonably foreseeable those consequences that it thinks the defaulting promisor should pay for. The test is thus thought to conceal other grounds of decision such as the relative cheapness with which the parties can insure against the risk of loss; see Waddams, *Law of Contracts*, 557–563. Such skepticism about the rule in *Hadley v. Baxendale* ignores the latent rationality it embodies. A closer examination reveals the rule as an imprint of dialogic community.

The point of the rule is to limit the promisee's right to the value of his expectancy in accordance with the intersubjective relation within which the right is first established. The promisee's right to the value of his expectancy is the objective confirmation of his status as an end. Because this right depends on the parties' mutual deference, it cannot be determined independently of the mind of the promisor. To make the promisee's expectations alone determinative would require the promisor to insure the promisee against risks without an opportunity to extract compensation, and so would imply a one-sided subordination of the promisor to the promisee's interests. But neither can the promisee's damages be determined by the subjective foresight of the promisor, for this would place the promisee at the mercy of the promisor's idiosyncratic capabilities. The expectation to which the promisee has an objective right is one that is codetermined in accordance with a common will that mediates between the isolated subjectivities of the parties, and to which each can thus defer without self-loss. Translated into the language of *Hadley v. Baxendale*, this means that the defaulting party is liable only for those consequential losses that were reasonably in the contemplation of *both* parties. However, the common will is not detached from the actual minds of the parties. The measure of reasonableness is not a disembodied mind that determines what consequences are probable in abstraction from the limited horizons of the contracting persons; for the totality that grounds contractual rights is formed by the interaction of individuated, not homogenized, selves. The standard of reasonableness is thus intersubjective rather than wholly external. The test is whether a particular consequence would have been foreseeable by both parties given their embeddedness in a particular situation and their knowledge of unusual circumstances. The formula in *Hadley v. Baxendale* thus embodies dialogic community as the foundation of contractual rights. The skeptics are right, of course, to deny the power of this test rigidly to determine any particular result, but this hardly means that the rule is empty. Though not determinative of uniquely correct solutions, the test ensures that any solution consistent with it is just.

42. *Chitty on Contracts,* ed. A. G. Guest (London: Sweet & Maxwell, 1989), 52.

43. See Balfour v. Balfour, [1919] 2 K.B. 571 (C.A.).

44. See Smith v. Hughes, L.R. 6 Q.B. 597, 607 (1871); Hobbs v. Esquimalt & Nanaimo Railway Co., 29 S.C.R. 450 (1899); Staiman Steel Ltd. v. Commercial & Home Builders Ltd., 71 D.L.R. (3d) 17, 22 (Ont. H.C.J. 1976).

45. See Hurley v. Eddingfield, 59 N.E. 1058 (Ind. S.C. 1901).

46. See Holmes, *Common Law,* 204; Lon Fuller, "Consideration and Form," 41 *Col. L. Rev.* 799 (1941); John Swan, "Consideration and the Reasons for Enforcing Contracts," in Barry Reiter and John Swan, eds., *Studies in Contract Law* (Toronto: Butterworths, 1980), 29.

47. Atiyah, *Consideration in Contracts,* 60-61.

48. See Holmes, *Common Law,* 199 ff.

49. Holmes seems to have acknowledged this; see *Common Law,* 214: "A covenant or contract under seal was no longer a promise well proved; it was a promise of a distinct nature, for which a distinct form of action came to be provided."

50. See J. B. Ames, *Lectures on Legal History and Miscellaneous Legal Essays* (Cambridge: Harvard University Press, 1913), 150: "[a] simple contract debt, as well as a debt by specialty, was originally conceived of, not as a contract, in the modern sense, that is, as a promise, but as a grant."

51. Atiyah, *Consideration in Contracts,* 9.

52. See Pao On v. Lau Yiu, [1979] 3 All E.R. 65, 76 (P.C.). This is not to say that the bargain may not be avoided for other reasons—for example, unconscionability or the court's refusal to lend its aid to a transaction (such as a promise to pay a policeman for performing no more than his duty) tending to corrupt the administration of justice.

53. See Stilk v. Myrick, 170 E.R. 1168 (1809); Gilbert Steel Ltd. v. University Construction Ltd., 67 D.L.R. (3d) 606 (Ont. C.A. 1973).

54. See, e.g., Barry Reiter, "Courts, Consideration, and Common Sense," 27 *Univ. Toronto L. J.* 439 (1977); Swan, "Consideration and the Reasons," 30-33; Waddams, *Law of Contracts,* 102 ff. See also *Restatement (Second) of Contracts* (St. Paul: American Law Institute Publishers, 1981), sec. 89(a).

55. See, e.g., Atiyah, *Consideration in Contracts,* 12: "It is in fact quite plain on the authorities that the presence of a benefit or a detriment is neither a *sufficient* nor a *necessary* condition for the enforcement of a promise, and that therefore a *definition* of consideration in terms of benefit or detriment is simply inaccurate." (Emphasis in original.) See also Waddams, *Law of Contracts,* 90.

56. Westman v. Macdonald, [1941] 4 D.L.R. 793 (B.C.S.C.).

57. Hamer v. Sidway, 27 N.E. 256 (N.Y.C.A. 1891).

58. The situation changes, however, if during the performance of the contract facts come to light that would entitle the party seeking modification of the agreement to rescission under the equitable doctrine of common mistake; see Linz v. Schuck, 67 A. 286 (Md. C.A. 1907). Under these circumstances, equity regards the initial price as inadequate consideration for performance, hence treats the first agreement as rescinded and the modification as creating a new agreement.

59. Consider, however, the case of forgiving a debt. A creditor promises to forgo his right to the full debt in return for prompt payment of a part. Here again part payment is not good consideration for the promise because there is a preexisting contractual duty to the creditor; see Foakes v. Beer, 9 App. Cas. 605 (H.L. 1884). However, while formal right will not enforce the creditor's unbargained-for promise, equity will prevent him from reasserting his full legal rights if his doing so would subject the debtor to his caprice (and so reduce formal right to an instrument of oppression)—that is, if the debtor has changed his position in reasonable reliance on the waiver; I try to reconcile these principles in the discussion of promissory estoppel (sec. 7.1). The situation changes, of course, if the debtor refuses to pay any part of the debt unless the creditor agrees to take a part in satisfaction of the whole. Here formal right will not enforce the creditor's promise for want of consideration, nor (even assuming debtor's reliance) is there any equitable ground for preventing the creditor from reasserting his full rights, since the debtor is the one exploiting a dependency.

60. Here we are interpreting the significance of mistake and fraud as negating the relation of will to will rather than consent. This seems more consistent with the paradigm of formal right, for which consent consists in formal voluntariness and is therefore negated only by nonvolitional behavior or by coercion. Although it is common to regard mistake as negating consent, there is support for the view presented here; see J. Gordley, *The Philosophical Origins of Modern Contract Doctrine* (Oxford: Clarendon Press, 1991), 190–192.

61. Kennedy v. Panama Royal Mail Co., L.R. 2 Q.B. 580, 587 (1867), per Blackburn, J.

62. *Smith v. Hughes,* above n. 44.

63. See Rosenfeld, "Hegel and the Dialectics of Contract," 247–249.

64. See L'Estrange v. Graucob, [1934] 2 K.B. 394.

65. See Goss v. Lord Nugent, 110 E.R. 713 (1833); Hawrish v. Bank of Montreal, [1969] S.C.R. 515.

66. Prenn v. Simmonds, [1971] 3 All E.R. 237 (H.L.).

67. Atiyah, *Consideration in Contracts,* 12–18.

68. See *Chitty on Contracts,* 114, and cases cited therein.

69. See Gordley, *Modern Contract Doctrine,* 201–208. For a discussion of formal right's requirement of equivalence in exchange, see Benson, "Hegel and Contemporary Contract Theory," 1187–1196.

70. See Schnell v. Nell, 17 Ind. 29 (1861).

71. Here we must note that Hegel himself apparently did not draw this conclusion from formal right. In par. 77 of the *Philosophy of Right,* he refers approvingly to the Roman law doctrine of *laesio enormis,* according to which a contract was void if the price agreed to was less than one-half of the commodity's market value. Hegel

says that this doctrine reflects the principle that a valid contract is an exchange of equivalent values. If this is indeed the rationale for laesio enormis, it is difficult to see how the doctrine can be reconciled with the abstract foundations of formal right. The latter rests on the premise that the free will alone has normative force. By contrast, the doctrine of laesio enormis (as interpreted by Hegel) implies that the will's choices are constrained by the utility schedule of a universal subject that has internalized and rendered commensurable the preferences of discrete individuals. But if the free will need not defer to the preferences of any concrete individual, why should it bow to those of a superindividual? The normative authority of market value conflicts with the abstract foundations of formal right. Moreover, if Hegel is right about laesio enormis, then that rule has little to do with the modern, common-law doctrine of unconscionability, which (as we shall see) focuses on the improvidence of a bargain rather than on lack of equivalence. Thus, suppose I buy a sandwich on a train for more than twice the price it costs in the city. On Hegel's reading of laesio enormis, the latter would presumably invalidate this contract, but the common law probably would not (if one objects that the train is the relevant market, then the response is that there is then no reason not to narrow the market further to any particular transaction, in which case the external standard of market value collapses). By contrast, if an elderly widow without independent advice and without appreciation of the consequences promised every penny of her fortune for a delivery (for consumption purposes) of bubble gum at market price, the modern law of unconscionability will likely permit her to avoid the contract, whereas the Roman doctrine would not.

Having said all this, we must now question Hegel's interpretation of laesio enormis. The latter means "excessive damage" and the doctrine seems to have applied only to sales of land. Moreover, a laesio enormis rendered a contract voidable rather than void ab initio. All this suggests that the doctrine was a forerunner of the modern law of unconscionability in its concern for improvident rather than uneven bargains.

For an account of Hegel's theory of exchange value substantially in agreement with the one given here (but which ignores the problem of laesio enormis), see Richard Dien Winfield, *The Just Economy* (New York: Routledge, 1988), 109–110.

72. See Richard Epstein, "Unconscionability: A Critical Reappraisal," 18 *J. Law and Econ.* 293, 294–295 (1975). For a discussion of the conceptual problems involved in the idea of substantive unfairness as nonequivalence of values, see M. J. Trebilcock, "The Doctrine of Inequality of Bargaining Power: Post-Benthamite Economics in the House of Lords," 26 *Univ. Toronto L. J.* 359, 376–381 (1976).

73. See Smith v. Hughes, L.R. 6 Q.B. 597 (1871).

74. Couturier v. Hastie, 10 E.R. 1065 (1856); Cooper v. Phibbs, L.R. 2 H.L. 149 (1867).

75. See Bell v. Lever Bros. Ltd., [1932] A.C. 161 (H.L.).

76. See U.S.A. v. Motor Trucks, Ltd., [1924] A.C. 196 (P.C.).

77. Bourgeois v. Smith, 58 D.L.R. 15 (N.B.S.C. 1921); see also Paget v. Marshall, 28 Ch.D 255 (1884).

78. See Tilden Rent-a-Car Co. v. Clendenning, 83 D.L.R. (3d) 400 (Ont. C.A. 1978).

79. [1947] K.B. 130.

80. Id., 134.

81. [1951] 1 All E.R. 767 (C.A.).

82. Id., 769; see also Hughes v. Metropolitan Railway Co., 2 App. Cas. 439, 448 (1877), per Lord Cairns.

83. *Combe v. Combe*, 770.

84. See Post v. Jones, 60 U.S. (19 How.) 150 (1856). Does the involuntariness of the drowning man's (A's) promise mean that he could also avoid a bargain in which he promised the rope salesman (B) market price for a rope? Technically, he could successfully defend against a suit for breach of contract but not against a suit for restitution. Since formal right views any agreement formed in this situation as involuntary, it would allow A to bypass contract and take B's rope, but B would have a valid restitutionary claim. The result cannot be different simply because A bargained rather than took.

85. See Archer v. The Society of the Sacred Heart of Jesus, 9 O.L.R. 474 (Ont. C.A. 1905).

86. The reason for nonenforcement in all these examples is that the person cannot consistently with the end-status that is the source of its rights treat as optional an interest essential to that status, so that its assent is involuntary in the eyes of the law. This principle cuts across threats ("sign if you value your life"), offers (the drowning man example), and cases unspecifiable as either threats or offers apart from a prior theory of entitlements (e.g., duress of goods); hence it reveals the inadequacy of the threat-offer distinction as a criterion of coercion. For views of coercion resting on this distinction, see Alan Wertheimer, *Coercion* (Princeton: Princeton University Press, 1987), 204–221; Fried, *Contract as Promise*, 96–99. For an approach that (strangely) makes a finding of coercion depend on considerations of economic efficiency and institutional competence, see Michael Trebilcock, *The Limits of Freedom of Contract* (Cambridge: Harvard University Press, 1993), chap. 4.

87. [1975] 1 Q.B. 326 (C.A.).

88. It is no accident, therefore, that the earliest examples of equitable relief for unconscionability are cases involving forfeitures of land on a debtor's default; see Howard v. Harris, 23 E.R. 406 (1683).

89. This account of the unconscionability doctrine is not meant to describe the actual reasons given by Lord Denning in *Lloyd's Bank v. Bundy* but rather to suggest a rational basis for the doctrine. Lord Denning sometimes delivers himself of formulations suggestive of our account, but in the main he seems to regard an unconscionable transaction as one in which unequal bargaining power has produced an exchange of unequal values.

90. See, e.g., Hart v. O'Connor, [1985] A.C. 1000, 1024 (P.C.); Mundinger v. Mundinger, 3 D.L.R. (3d) 338 (Ont. C.A. 1969); Marshall v. Canada Permanent Trust Co., 69 D.L.R. (2d) 260 (Alta. S.C. 1968).

91. See U.S. Uniform Commercial Code, art. 2-302 (Official Comment): "The principle [of unconscionability] is one of prevention of oppression and undue surprise and not of disturbance of risks because of superior bargaining power."

92. See Sherwood v. Walker, 33 N.W. 919 (Mich. S.C. 1887); see also Solle v.

Butcher, [1950] 1 K.B. 671 (C.A.); Magee v. Pennine Ins. Co., [1969] 2 W.L.R. 1278 (C.A.).

93. Simmons v. Evans, S.W.2d 295 (Tenn. S.C. 1947).

94. Krell v. Henry, [1903] 2 K.B. 740 (C.A.).

95. Since the standard of equivalence is the concurrence of the parties' wills in their particular transaction, there is no lack of equivalence simply because one party knows of the other's ignorance of conditions affecting or likely to affect the market price of the product. Thus, in Laidlaw v. Organ, 15 U.S. 178 (1817), Organ bought tobacco from Laidlaw without informing him of a change in market conditions (the lifting of the British blockade of New Orleans) likely to drive up the price. The Supreme Court rightly held that, absent fraudulent misrepresentation, the contract was enforceable against Laidlaw.

96. This is the position of the *Restatement (Second) of Contracts*, sec. 90. See also Walton Stores (Interstate) Ltd. v. Maher, 62 A.L.J.R. 110 (H.C. 1988).

97. Above n. 96.

98. See *Walton Stores v. Maher*, above n. 96, at 115, 134. Brennan, J. saw promissory estoppel as a method of protecting the promisee's reliance; see *Walton Stores*, above n. 96, p. 126. In The Commonwealth v. Verwayen, [1990] 64 A.J.L.R. 540, a majority of the Court (including Mason, C.J.) emphasized that promissory estoppel works not to enforce promises but to avoid detriment to the promisee.

99. Above n. 79.

100. See A. Kronman, "Contract Law and Distributive Justice," 89 *Yale L. J.* 472 (1980).

101. Id., 495–497.

102. See A. Kronman, "Paternalism and the Law of Contracts," 92 *Yale L. J.* 763, 773 (1983).

103. Kennedy, "Distributive and Paternalist Motives," 624–649.

104. This is the argument of E. J. Weinrib; see "Legal Formalism," 970–971.

105. Compare Michael Sandel, *Liberalism and the Limits of Justice* (Cambridge: Cambridge University Press, 1982), 105–109.

106. But legislatures may also actualize the right of intention by confining freedom of contract within welfare constraints (e.g., factory safety standards) for the benefit of those who, because of extreme need, are likely to acquiesce in harmful bargains.

CHAPTER IV: THE CASE FOR TORT LAW

1. 3 William Blackstone, *Commentaries on the Laws of England,* 4th ed. (1771), 208.

2. See Richard Posner, *The Economic Analysis of Law,* 4th ed. (Boston: Little, Brown, 1992), 163–167. The standard historical explanations for the rise of negligence are that it favored enterprise generally or that it amounted to a judicial subsidy to infant industry; see, e.g., O. W. Holmes, *The Common Law,* ed. M. Howe (Cambridge: Belknap Press, 1963), 77; Charles Gregory, "Trespass to Negligence to Absolute Liability," 37 *Virginia L. Rev.* 359, 365 (1951); John Fleming, *The Law of Torts,* 8th ed. (Sydney: Law Book Co., 1992), 101–102; Morton Horwitz, *The*

Transformation of American Law, 1780–1860 (Cambridge: Harvard University Press, 1977), 85–108.

3. U.S. v. Carroll Towing, 159 F.2d 169 (1947); for Justice Hand, a defendant was negligent if the costs of the accident discounted by the probability of its occurring exceeded the costs of avoiding the accident.

4. For a historical account, see George Priest, "The Invention of Enterprise Liability: A Critical History of the Intellectual Foundations of Modern Tort Law," 14 *J. Leg. Stud.* 461 (1985).

5. See, e.g., Zeppa v. Coca-Cola, [1955] 5 D.L.R. 187 (Ont. C.A.); Roe v. Minister of Health and Another, [1954] 2 Q.B. 66.

6. Gold v. Essex C.C., [1942] 2 K.B. 293; Yepremian v. Scarborough Hospital, 110 D.L.R. 3d 513 (Ont. C.A. 1980); Ormrod v. Crossville Motor, [1953] 1 W.L.R. 1120 (C.A.).

7. Nettleship v. Weston, [1971] 3 All E.R. 581 (C.A.). Some claim that liability insurance has also affected the magnitude of damages awarded in personal injury cases; see Patrick Atiyah, *Accidents, Compensation, and the Law* (London: Weidenfeld & Nicolson, 1970), 262.

8. Fleming James, Jr., "Accident Liability Reconsidered: The Impact of Liability Insurance," 57 *Yale L. J.* 549–550 (1948).

9. Greenman v. Yuba Power Products, Inc., 377 P.2d 897 (Cal. S.C. 1963); a forerunner of this development is Justice Traynor's concurring opinion in Escola v. Coca-Cola Bottling Co., 150 P.2d 436, 440 (Cal. S.C. 1944).

10. See *Restatement (Second) of Torts* (St. Paul: American Law Institute Publishers, 1965), sec. 402A.

11. See generally Guido Calabresi, *The Costs of Accidents: A Legal and Economic Analysis* (New Haven: Yale University Press, 1970).

12. James, "Accident Liability Reconsidered," 569.

13. See the discussion and citation of various studies by Atiyah, *Accidents, Compensation, and the Law,* 299–304.

14. See Woodhouse Report, Royal Commission of Inquiry, *Compensation for Personal Injury in New Zealand* (1967).

15. Richard Epstein, "A Theory of Strict Liability," 2 *J. Leg. Stud.* 151 (1973); "Defenses and Subsequent Pleas in a System of Strict Liability," 3 *J. Leg. Stud.* 165 (1974).

16. George Fletcher, "Fairness and Utility in Tort Theory," 85 *Harv. L. Rev.* 537 (1972).

17. Ernest Weinrib, *The Idea of Private Law* (Cambridge: Harvard University Press, 1995); "Toward a Moral Theory of Negligence Law," 2 *Law and Phil.* 37 (1983); "Causation and Wrongdoing," 63 *Chicago-Kent L. Rev.* 407 (1987); "Understanding Tort Law," 23 *Valparaiso Univ. L. Rev.* 485 (1989).

18. Above n. 16.

19. For criticisms of this part of Fletcher's theory, see Ernest Weinrib, "The Special Morality of Tort Law," 34 *McGill L. J.* 403, 404–406 (1989); Izhak Englard, "The System Builders: A Critical Appraisal of Modern American Tort Theory," 9 *J. Leg. Stud.* 27, 65–66 (1980).

20. The alternative was seen this way by James Barr Ames, "Law and Morals,"

22 *Harv. L. Rev.* 97, 99 (1908). See also Holmes's utilitarian argument for fault in *Common Law,* 77.

21. Fletcher, "Fairness and Utility," 564–569.

22. The loss spreading achieved by enterprise liability can be justified on utilitarian grounds if one accepts the postulate of the diminishing marginal utility of money (see Calabresi, *Costs of Accidents,* 39 ff.). The argument is that a $1 loss suffered by 100 people is less burdensome overall than a $100 loss suffered by one person because the disutility of each dollar lost increases the less one has. However, this reasoning could justify shifting accident costs to a small group of the very wealthy as easily as it justifies loss spreading over the entire community and so provides no specific rationale for the latter. Loss spreading is better understood as serving the aim of the welfare state generally: that of guaranteeing to all agents the basic material conditions of an autonomous life. This goal requires loss spreading rather than a search for the deep pocket, since the latter (imposing as it does a burden disproportionate to one's obligations under distributive justice) is forced philanthropy and so inconsistent with autonomy.

23. Fletcher's only response to this development is a note saying that it confuses corrective with distributive justice; see "Fairness and Utility," 547, n. 40. But there is no confusion. Enterprise liability *ignores* corrective justice in the same way that the reciprocity paradigm ignores distributive justice. The argument thus assumes what must be demonstrated—that some part of accident law must be concerned with correcting wrongs.

24. Fletcher's particular formulation of the nonreciprocal risk principle has exposed him to criticisms that do not touch the principle itself. Fletcher seems to determine whether risk is nonreciprocal by focusing on the specific roles that plaintiff and defendant perform in their transaction. Thus, a dynamite blaster imposes a nonreciprocal risk on an adjacent cattle farmer and is therefore strictly liable for injuries caused. But then, it may be objected, a car driver always imposes a nonreciprocal risk on a pedestrian and so should, on Fletcher's theory, also be strictly liable for injury even if the pedestrian was negligent; see Jules Coleman, "Moral Theories of Torts: Their Scope and Limits, Part I," in Michael Bayles and Bruce Chapman, eds., *Justice, Rights, and Tort Law* (Dordrecht: Reidel, 1983), 62. Such problems are avoided, however, if we view plaintiff and defendant not as particular role players but as moral agents for whom any role is theoretically possible (so the car driver of today may be the pedestrian of tomorrow and vice versa). Now we must judge whether risk is nonreciprocal by measuring it against a social background of ordinary risk—that is, by asking whether the defendant imposed on the plaintiff a risk greater than that ordinarily adjunct (and to which he is thus reciprocally exposed) to social interaction at a given stage of urban and technological development. This is the version of the nonreciprocity principle that I will later endorse.

25. In a subsequent article, Fletcher criticized his risk analysis of tort liability for failing to capture the notion of trespass, which involves a focus on the defendant's actual intrusion on the plaintiff; see "Synthesis in Tort Theory," in Bayles and Chapman, eds., *Justice, Rights, and Tort Law,* 120: "Risk analysis has powerful synthetic power, but it cannot serve to reduce the currently conflicted ex ante and

ex post modes of tort analysis to a single framework for analyzing liability." I mean to show that the two sorts of analysis—corresponding roughly to negligence and trespass—are not conflicted.

26. The reaction against monistic theories produces "mixed" theories that sacrifice unity to multiplicity; see, e.g., Peter Cane, "Justice and Justifications for Tort Liability," 2 *Oxford J. Leg. Stud.* 30 (1982).

27. Richard Epstein, "Strict Liability," 151, 153–154.

28. Morriss v. Marsden, [1952] 1 All E.R. 925; *Restatement (Second) of Torts* (1965), sec. 283B.

29. Epstein, "Strict Liability," 158–160.

30. For criticisms of Epstein's theory, see Weinrib, "Causation and Wrongdoing," 420–424; Coleman, "Moral Theories of Torts, Part I," 52–57; Stephen Perry, "The Impossibility of General Strict Liability," 1 *Can. J. Law and Jurisprudence* 147 (1988).

31. Epstein, "Strict Liability," 159.

32. Id., at 164.

33. Id., at 179.

34. Id., at 172.

35. Epstein acknowledges this in "Nuisance Law: Corrective Justice and Its Utilitarian Constraints," 8 *J. Leg. Stud.* 49, 50–51 (1979).

36. Richard Epstein, "Causation and Corrective Justice: A Reply to Two Critics," 8 *J. Leg. Stud.* 477, 499–501 (1979).

37. See Richard Epstein, *Takings: Private Property and the Power of Eminent Domain* (Cambridge: Harvard University Press, 1985), 74.

38. Cf. Weinrib, "Causation and Wrongdoing," 424. An intentional destruction of another's property would, however, amount to an usurpation of proprietary sovereignty, and so such an act is, as Epstein has argued, morally indistinguishable from a taking; see *Takings*, 38.

39. Epstein thinks that strict liability achieves a reconciliation between the right to act and the right to security, inasmuch as everyone is free to act without taking account of others as long as he does not cause harm; see "Strict Liability," 203–204. However, this amounts to saying that the agent has a right to create risk for others as long as the risk does not materialize. It is difficult to see what a right to create risk would mean if it did not confer on the agent an immunity from responsibility for at least some materializations of risk.

40. An argument that loss and gain are not correlative in this situation has been put forward by Jules Coleman. The gain to the actor, he argues, equals the savings realized by foregoing precautions, and this gain would accrue whether or not anyone suffered a loss; see Jules Coleman, "Corrective Justice and Wrongful Gain," 11 *J. Leg. Stud.* 421, 424–427 (1982); cf. Stephen Perry, "The Moral Foundations of Tort Law," 77 *Iowa L. Rev.* 449, 457–461. Coleman has lately modified his views somewhat; see "The Mixed Conception of Corrective Justice," 77 *Iowa L. Rev.* 427 (1992).

41. "Toward a Moral Theory of Negligence Law," above n. 17; "Causation and Wrongdoing," above n. 17; "Right and Advantage in Private Law," 10 *Cardozo L. Rev.* 1283 (1989); "Understanding Tort Law," above n. 17; "The Special Morality of Tort Law," above n. 19; *The Idea of Private Law*, above n. 17.

42. Weinrib, "Right and Advantage," above n. 41.

43. The attempt to invoke both Kant and Hegel to support his theory leads Weinrib into difficulties from which he has yet to extricate himself. In particular, it leads him to affirm that the foundation productive of exclusively negative rights is an absolute foundation of right (Kant) but that there are nonetheless positive rights derived from principles external to formal right (Hegel); see "Right and Advantage," 1308–1309.

44. See Immanuel Kant, *Critique of Practical Reason*, trans. L. W. Beck (Indianapolis: Bobbs-Merrill, 1956), 65–66; for a lucid commentary on this Kantian principle, see Michael Sandel, *Liberalism and the Limits of Justice* (Cambridge: Cambridge University Press, 1982), 1–14.

45. Weinrib observes this without criticism. "Abstract right," he says, "is the normative structure that corresponds to the most fundamental condition of the will's freedom: the capacity to abstract from any particular object of choice" ("Right and Advantage," 1288).

46. Weinrib, "Right and Advantage," 1288.

47. Id., at 1289.

48. "In abstract right, advantages are valued not for their own sake but only inasmuch as they represent embodiments of an abstractly free will. Instead of being conceived as the particular benefits enjoyed by particular persons, the rights of private law are seen as expressions of the universal nature of the will's freedom" ("Right and Advantage," 1286).

Stephen Perry has criticized Weinrib's formalist theory of tort for its inability to account for tort law's concern for human welfare both at the stage of wrongdoing and at the stage of reparation; see "Moral Foundations," 481–488. Perry's critique, while partly correct, is too one-sided; it misses the dialectical tension in formal right. He is right to say that the principle of formal right excludes welfarist concerns and so renders much of tort law mysterious. However, he does not see that this principle contains an impetus for self-embodiment, hence makes certain universal interests relevant to tort law, and so contains more than formal right's emphasis on pure agency allows it to accommodate. The problem with formal right is not that it is indifferent to welfare; its problem is that it is avowedly indifferent but actually and inevitably concerned. Formal right has within it the elements of agency and welfare, but because it identifies law's foundation with pure agency, it does not, qua formal right, know how to grasp the elements as a whole. To grasp them as a whole is to surpass formal right. Furthermore, the abstractness of formal right's foundations is not simply a problem for Weinrib's theory of tort law, as Perry believes; rather, it is the problem of classical tort law itself, whose internal contradictions Weinrib has faithfully reproduced.

49. Weinrib, "Understanding Tort Law," above n. 17.

50. This was, in fact, the gist of Fleming James's response to Charles Gregory's critique of his views on contribution among tortfeasors; see Charles Gregory, "Contribution Among Tortfeasors: A Defense," 54 *Harv. L. Rev.* 1170 (1941). For James, contribution was regressive because he thought it would mean shifting losses from superior to inferior loss spreaders; see "Contribution Among Tortfeasors: A Pragmatic Criticism," 54 *Harv. L. Rev.* 1156, 1165 (1941). Gregory sympathized with the goal of loss distribution, agreed that the fault system was outmoded, but

thought that in the absence of administrative compensation it was better to perfect the fault system than to bend it to goals it could achieve only imperfectly. James replied that to prefer a more coherent fault system to a partial realization of social insurance was to "sacrifice good sense to a syllogism—and an outworn syllogism at that." Fleming James, "Replication," 54 *Harv. L. Rev.* 1178, 1183 (1941).

51. 3 Blackstone, *Commentaries,* 116.

52. Fowler Harper, Fleming James, Jr., and Oscar Gray, *The Law of Torts* III (Boston: Little, Brown, 1986), 113–114, 131; Holmes, *Common Law,* 77–78.

53. Charles Gregory, "Trespass to Negligence to Absolute Liability," 37 *Virginia L. Rev.* 359, 365 (1951); Horwitz, *Transformation,* 97–101.

54. See G. W. F. Hegel, *Vorlesungen über Rechtsphilosophie 1818–1831,* ed. K.-H. Ilting (Stuttgart-Bad Cannstatt: Frommann-Holzboog, 1974), IV, 174.

55. 114 So.2d 357 (Fla. S.C. 1959).

56. Id., at 359.

57. The independence of wrongdoing from harming is also reflected in the tort defense of *volenti non fit injuria.* If disrespect for the freedom of personality is a wrong regardless of the benefit conferred, respect for freedom absolves from wrongdoing regardless of the magnitude of harm inflicted. Suppose A accidentally and nonnegligently kills B in a highly risky surgical operation to which B has consented. A has committed no wrong, for though he has undoubtedly dealt a devastating blow to B's interests, he has shown no disrespect for the freedom of personality. Moreover, since freedom is here defined in utter abstraction from the particular knowledge of the individual, the consent that absolves from wrongdoing is formal consent; in a formal right unmodified by any requirements derived from a more concrete understanding of right, it is irrelevant that the victim was ignorant of the risks associated with the act and that the defendant knew this. Provided the defendant has not deceived the victim, the uncoerced consent of someone with legal capacity is sufficient to negate the wrong even if the consent is uninformed. Thus in Hegarty v. Shine, 4 L.R. Ir. 288, 294 (1878), recovery was denied a woman who sued her lover for assault claiming he withheld information that he was infected with a venereal disease. See also R. v. Clarence, 22 Q.B.D. 23 (1888).

58. See Yania v. Bigan, 155 A.2d 343 (Penn. S.C. 1959). The "exceptions" to this rule are cases in which plaintiff and defendant stand in a special relationship giving rise to a duty of affirmative action. The special relationships, however, are ones of induced dependence or ones where the defendant has created the danger, so that the failure to help in an emergency is really an imposition of risk indistinguishable from misfeasance. In this sense, the exceptions are really applications of the general rule to special circumstances. See, e.g., Moch Co. v. Rensselaer Water Co., 159 N.E. 896 (N.Y.C.A. 1928); for a discussion of "pseudononfeasance," see Ernest Weinrib, "The Case for a Duty to Rescue," 90 *Yale L. J.* 247, 254–258 (1980).

59. Epstein argues that the misfeasance/nonfeasance distinction reflects the principle of strict liability that causation is necessary and sufficient for wrongdoing. Thus, misfeasance is a causing of harm, whereas nonfeasance is not; see "Strict Liability," 190–191. This seems questionable, however, since there is nothing in the concept of causation (or at least nothing that Epstein reveals) that prevents one from saying that an egregious omission was the cause of a harm; see H. L. A.

Hart and T. Honoré, *Causation in the Law,* 2d ed. (Oxford: Clarendon Press, 1985), 37–38. It is probably better to say that the distinction between misfeasance and nonfeasance rests on the irrelevance of welfare in formal tort law. If there is no wrong in harming, then a fortiori there can be no wrong in failing to benefit.

60. Hegel, *Philosophy of Right,* par. 155; see also Arthur Jacobson, "Hegel's Legal Plenum," 10 *Cardozo L. Rev.* 877, 901–906 (1989).

61. Interestingly, the action for damages seems to have been superimposed on an earlier action for novel disseisin, in which the remedy for dispossession of land was the restoration of seisin but not damages. The early cases in which damages are awarded draw a clear distinction between seisin and damages; see George Woodbine, "The Origins of the Action for Trespass," 33 *Yale L. J.* 799, 807–808 (1924).

62. Here we sidestep the debate over whether the action on the case issued from Westminster II in the thirteenth century or from an independent evolution of the common law in the fourteenth. See E. J. Dix, "The Origins of the Action of Trespass on the Case," 46 *Yale L. J.* 1142 (1937).

63. See, e.g., Leame v. Bray, 102 Eng. Rep. 724 (1803); Reynolds v. Clarke, 92 Eng. Rep. 410 (1726).

64. Mouse's Case, 12 Coke's Rep. 63 (1608); Ploof v. Putnam, 71 A. 188 (Vt. S.C. 1908).

65. 111 N.W. 1 (Minn. S.C. 1907).

66. See London Borough of Southwark v. Williams, [1971] 2 All E.R. 175 (C.A.). For a discussion of the controversy over the juridical significance of necessity, see Alan Brudner, "A Theory of Necessity," 7 *Oxford J. Leg. Stud.* 339 (1987).

67. See Richard Dien Winfield, *Reason and Justice* (Albany: State University of New York Press, 1988), 171–172.

68. This leaves open the possibility that the right to self-possession is subordinate to the state's authority to conscript citizens for military service in order to preserve the legal order. That the state's authority to punish criminals does not contradict the absolute right to self-possession is shown in the next chapter.

69. Hegel, *Philosophy of Right,* par. 48.

70. Weaver v. Ward, 80 E.R. 284 (1616).

71. See Gregory, "From Trespass to Negligence," 361–376; Fleming, *The Law of Torts,* 16–19; Fowler v. Lanning, [1959] 1 Q.B. 426; Letang v. Cooper, [1965] 1 Q.B. 232, 239–240, per Denning, M.R. For a contrary view substantially in accord with mine, see Cane, "Justice and Justifications," 35–36.

72. That there was ever a shift from a clear strict liability regime to a clear negligence regime is disputed by several writers; see, e.g., Gary Schwartz, "Tort Law and the Economy in Nineteenth-Century America: A Reinterpretation," 90 *Yale L. J.* 1717 (1981); R. Rabin, "The Historical Development of the Fault Principle: A Reinterpretation," 15 *Ga. L. Rev.* 925 (1981).

73. See The Case of Thorns, Year Book, 6 Ed. IV, 7, pl. 18 (1466) (as reported in Bessey v. Olliott & Lambert, T. Raym. 467; 83 E.R. 244 [1681]). Here, however, we must remind ourselves that the same extraformalist intuition that produced the negligence-based action on the case for nontrespassory harms may also have insinuated itself into the action for trespassory harms. In fact, there is evidence that by the seventeenth century, a trespassory infliction of harm created only a prima facie

case of liability *for the harm,* one rebuttable by the defendant's showing a lack of fault; see *Weaver v. Ward,* above n. 70, where it was said that "no man shall be excused of a trespass . . . except it may be judged utterly without his fault." Here "without his fault" was understood to include not only cases of involuntary conduct but also cases where "the defendant had committed no negligence to give occasion to the hurt."

74. Stanley v. Powell, [1891] 1 Q.B. 86; Brown v. Kendall, 60 Mass. 292 (S.C. 1850).

75. To see this, consider again the (admittedly unlikely) situation in which A takes unwelcome sexual liberties with B reasonably believing that B is consenting. Were it feasible for B to seek an injunction against the unwanted contact, can there be any doubt that she would be successful? Moreover, the law is clear that an action for nominal damages will lie for a faultless trespass to land. It would be odd if a landowner could recover nominal damages for a trespass to land but a person could not receive nominal compensation for unwanted intimacies with her body.

76. The Tubantia, [1924] All E.R. Rep. 615.

77. Hegel, *Philosophy of Right,* par. 40. In this context belongs Blackstone's famous definition of property as "that sole and despotic dominion which one man claims and exercises over the external things of the world, in total exclusion of the right of any other individual in the universe." 2 Blackstone, *Commentaries,* 2.

78. 3 Blackstone *Commentaries,* 209: "For the right of *meum* and *tuum,* or property, in lands being once established, it follows as a necessary consequence, that this right must be exclusive; that is, that the owner may retain to himself the sole use and occupation of his soil: every entry therefore thereon without the owner's leave, and especially if contrary to his express order, is a trespass or transgression."

79. Basely v. Clarkson, 3 Lev. 37 (1681).

80. The foregoing account of strict liability is in disagreement with the conventional view in yet another respect. The standard view is that strict liability belongs to a communal or preindividualist conception of rights whereas fault is individualistic because it allows more scope to individual liberty and correspondingly affords less security to common human interests; see Harper, James, and Gray, *The Law of Tort,* III, 113. However, this view involves an anachronistic reading of ancient strict liability in the light of modern strict liability. Modern strict liability with its emphasis on loss distribution is indeed connected to a social conception of rights, but ancient strict liability is radically individualistic and fault is social in relation to it. Ancient strict liability is individualistic because it is the liability regime correlative to a conception of property rights that sees them as established prior to any social interaction and hence as unmediated by any deference to the liberty of the defendant. Fault is social because the plaintiff's right to security is not absolute but is mediated by the defendant's right to freedom of action.

81. The point is illustrated in Rodgers v. Elliott, 15 N.E. 768 (Mass. S.C. 1888).

82. Colls v. Home and Colonial Stores Limited, [1904] A.C. 179, at 185.

83. See Bamford v. Turnley, 122 E.R. 27 (1862); Losee v. Buchanan, 51 N.Y. 476 (1873). Why does a usufructuary right and not a possessory one require another's deference and hence a reciprocating accommodation to his liberty? The reason seems to be that A's possessory right over Blackacre cannot conflict with B's

possessory right over Whiteacre; and so neither needs any self-abnegation from the other. However, given the possibility of incompatible uses, A's property in use requires B's self-denial and hence (since no right can emerge from a servile relationship) a return recognition of B's liberty to interfere with A's use up to a limit (ordinary use) compatible with A's equal user rights. Of course, A's possessory right might extend over the whole planet and so be incompatible with any possessory right of B. But in formal right, there is only a negative right to exclude others from things already reduced to the will; there is no positive right to property.

84. Sturges v. Bridgman, 11 Ch.D. 852 (C.A. 1879); M. J. Horwitz sees the move from the priority rule to the reasonable user rule as a judicial aid to newer and more efficient uses of land; see Horwitz, *Transformation*, 33–34. From our point of view, the help to industry is incidental; the legal development is intelligible on its own terms as one to a superior (because more intersubjective) conception of property.

85. Karl Marx, *Capital: A Critique of Political Economy*, ed. F. Engels (New York: Modern Library, 1906), 81–96.

86. L.R. 3 H.L. 330 (1868).

87. *Restatement (Second) of Torts* (St. Paul: American Law Institute Publishers, 1977), sec. 519–520. The ratio in *Rylands* has been extended to such activities as blasting, crop dusting, and the storing of flammable liquids; see, e.g., IHB v. American Cyanamid 662 F. Supp. 635 (1987). However, the modern extensions of *Rylands* (especially the *Restatement of Torts*, sec. 519) have transcended *Rylands's* narrow nuisance theory of liability. Liability in *Rylands* is based on an interference with *use* caused by an extraordinary use of defendant's land (see for confirmation of this point Rickards v. Lothian, [1913] A.C. 263 [P.C.], per Lord Moulton). The extensions of *Rylands* have grounded liability on the causing of *harm* by activities that are ultrahazardous; whether the activity is within the normal use of the locality is only one factor to be considered in determining whether the activity is ultrahazardous. It has become customary to view such liability as strict, but it is really a form of negligence liability. Negligence consists in the imposition of socially abnormal risk on someone to whom one owes a duty of care. The crucial feature of ultrahazardous activities (including the keeping of dangerous animals) is that, if carried on in populated areas, no practicable precautionary steps can bring the risk down to the socially normal. Thus, neither *Rylands* itself nor the ultrahazardous activities rubric is exceptional.

88. Hegel, it must be said, chose to emphasize the misfeasance aspect of breach at the expense of its nonfeasance side; see *Vorlesungen*, IV, 176–177. His argument is that breach of contract infringes a property already established by the "stipulation" or exchange of words. This is true, but recall that the stipulation itself involved one party's self-renunciation for the sake of another's realized freedom. Each party's property came into being through the other's positive act.

89. Hegel, *Philosophy of Right*, pars. 75, 81.

90. Gregory, "Trespass to Negligence," 364.

91. *Brown v. Kendall*, above n. 74; *Stanley v. Powell*, above n. 74. The sole relevance of intention in torts is that it imposes a probability of harm approaching one and so subjects the victim to a degree of risk exceeding the socially normal.

The intentionality of the harm makes unnecessary the usual tests for determining whether the risk was unreasonable. Because intention is significant only as a place-holder for the unreasonableness of the risk, it follows that the intention of a tort (unlike that of a crime) relates only to the causing of harm, not to the wrongful-ness of the harm; see Morriss v. Marsden, [1952] 1 All E.R. 925.

92. Holmes, *Common Law,* 63.

93. 152 E.R. 402 (Exch. 1842).

94. Id., at 405.

95. Donoghue v. Stevenson, [1932] A.C. 562, 580 (H.L.), per Lord Atkin. Cf. Heaven v. Pender, 11 Q.B.D. 503, 509 (1882), per Lord Brett; Mcpherson v. Buick, 111 N.E. 1050 (N.Y.C.A. 1916).

96. Justice Cardozo put it well in *Mcpherson v. Buick,* 1053: "We have put aside the notion that the duty to safeguard life and limb, when the consequences of neg-ligence may be foreseen, grows out of contract and nothing else. We have put the source of the obligation where it ought to be. We have put its source in the law."

97. These phrases are, of course, Ronald Dworkin's; see *Taking Rights Seriously* (Cambridge: Harvard University Press, 1977), 272–273.

98. 132 E.R. 490 (1837).

99. Id., at 492.

100. How are we to explain the fact that the common law adjusts the objective standard to the capacities of children and the physically disabled unless the child is engaged in an adult activity or the disabled person is doing something an ordi-narily prudent person with his disability would not do? See McHale v. Watson, 115 C.L.R. 199 (Aust. H.C. 1966); *Restatement (Second) of Torts* (1965), sec. 283A. We will understand this phenomenon if we recall that negligence consists in the fail-ure to avoid a socially extraordinary or nonreciprocal risk. Part of the everyday risks we run are those of being exposed to the naturally lower capacities for risk appreciation and risk avoidance of children and the disabled when they perform activities that are considerably less risky than those performed by people with aver-age capacities. Thus, adjusting the objective standard to the capacities of the or-dinarily prudent child, blind person, etc., within the sphere of comparatively in-nocuous activities is consistent with an intersubjective right to care: the child still has a duty to avoid a risk (e.g., riding a tricycle in motor traffic) judged unreason-able not by him or even by the average child but by an ideal person who measures the risk against those that children at play ordinarily pose. When, however, the child performs an activity of normal risk (e.g., driving a car), his abnormally low capacity turns this risk into an abnormal one (an ultrahazardous activity, as it were), and so a right to care implies that he must be held legally accountable for any harm he causes even though the average person of his age would not have been able to avert the accident.

101. Above n. 3.

102. [1951] A.C. 850 (H.L.).

103. [1966] 2 All E.R. 709 (P.C.).

104. 162 N.E. 99 (N.Y.C.A. 1928).

105. Id., at 99.

106. Id., at 103.

107. The neighbor principle is sometimes said to give rise to a prima facie duty

of care, subject to limitation by "policy" where liability would otherwise be too onerous; see Anns v. London Borough of Merton, [1977] 2 All E.R. 496 (H.L.). One such supposed limitation occurs with negligently spoken words. One will be liable for negligent misstatement only if one encouraged the plaintiff to rely on one's words and if he did in fact rely; see Hedley Byrne & Co. v. Heller and Partners Ltd., [1964] A.C. 465 (H.L.). However, there is no need to regard the rule in Hedley Byrne as a compromise of negligence principles. The risk of being misled by another's mistaken utterances is surely as normal in the conditions of modern life as the risk of being jostled in a public thoroughfare. For the image of crowded public places one has only to substitute that of far-flung connections made possible by modern communications technology. To take the risk imposed by the defendant out of the socially normal and reciprocal, therefore, he must have encouraged the plaintiff to rely on his words (e.g., by giving advice in the knowledge that the plaintiff would rely on it) and the plaintiff must in fact have been at risk, that is, he must have relied. Indeed, the contrast between reciprocal and nonreciprocal risk underlay Lord Reid's reasoning in *Hedley Byrne.* "The most obvious difference between words and acts," he wrote (at 482–483), "is this. Quite careful people often express definite opinions on social or informal occasions even when they see that others are likely to be influenced by them; and they often do that without taking that care which they would take if asked for their opinion professionally or in a business connection. . . . But it is at least unusual casually to put into circulation negligently made articles which are dangerous."

108. William Prosser, "Palsgraf Revisited," 52 *Mich. L. Rev.* 1, 20 (1953).

109. [1921] 3 K.B. 560 (C.A.).

110. [1961] A.C. 388 (P.C.).

111. Weinrib, "Causation and Wrongdoing," 414–416.

112. For a judicial suggestion to this effect, see Rivtow Marine Ltd. v. Washington Iron Works, 40 D.L.R. (3d) 530, 552–553 (S.C.C.), per Laskin, J.

113. Judith Jarvis Thompson, *Rights, Restitution, and Risk* (Cambridge: Harvard University Press, 1986), 199–202.

114. See also Aristotle's image of the divided line in *Nicomachean Ethics,* V, 1132a–b.

115. See J. Coleman, "Moral Theories of Torts: Their Scope and Limits, Part II" in M. Bayles and B. Chapman, eds., *Justice, Rights, and Tort Law* (Dordrecht: Reidel, 1983), 95–96.

116. It might be thought that liability insurance is inconsistent with the requirement that the plaintiff's remedy move from the defendant and that, since the defendant normally does not pay, there is no reason to insist on fault; see Atiyah, *Accidents, Compensation, and the Law,* 262–274. However, there is no inconsistency here. After all, the defendant contracts with the insurance company to insure *his* liability. The fact of liability insurance does not undercut the corrective nexus between plaintiff and defendant; on the contrary, it presupposes that nexus; see E. Weinrib, "The Insurance Justification and Private Law," 14 *J. Leg. Stud.* 681 (1985). Liability insurance becomes problematic for tort law only if one assumes that a central aim of tort law is to punish the wrongdoer. But tort law does not punish; it merely restores the balance between plaintiff and defendant.

117. See, e.g., Blackstock v. Foster, [1958] S.R. (N.S.W.) 341 (S.C.). Our

understanding of the factual cause requirement as an expression of the correlativity of wronging and being wronged is indebted to E. Weinrib, "Causation and Wrongdoing," above n. 17.

118. For recovery for emotional distress, see Hambrook v. Stokes Brothers, [1925] 1 K.B. 141 (C.A.); Dillon v. Legg, 441 P.2d 912 (Cal. 1968). For recovery for "pure economic loss," see *Hedley Byrne & Co. v. Heller and Partners Ltd.*, above n. 107; Caltex Oil (Australia) Pty. Ltd. v. The Dredge "Willemstad," 136 C.L.R. 529 (H.C. 1976); Union Oil Co. v. Oppen, 501 F.2d 558 (9th Cir. 1974); Canadian National Railway Co. v. Norsk Pacific Steamship Co., [1992] 1 S.C.R. 1021. Sometimes awards for economic loss go too far, as when recovery is allowed not only for setbacks to economic well-being but also to make good an expectation of gain despite the absence of privity of contract; see *Anns v. London Borough of Merton*, above n. 107. Overreaction to *Anns* has resulted in a recent setback for pure economic loss recovery in England; see Murphy v. Brentwood District Council, [1991] 1 A.C. 398 (H.L.).

119. By social insurance I mean not any particular scheme for dealing with accident losses but any scheme whose aim is the redistribution of the costs of accidents so as to maintain individuals at a humanly decent standard of living. By this definition, American products liability law is as much an example of social insurance as Workers' Compensation statutes; see Harper, James, and Gray, *The Law of Torts*, III, 132, n. 7. As I am using the term, moreover, social insurance embraces both social security measures that guarantee a basic welfare floor and compensation plans that guarantee a level of welfare approximating the one enjoyed by the victim at the time of the accident.

120. Henningsen v. Bloomfield Motors, Inc., 161 A.2d 69 (N.J.S.C. 1960).

121. See Priest, above n. 4; P. W. Huber, *Liability: The Legal Revolution and Its Consequences* (New York: Basic Books, 1988), 36-44.

122. See Harper, James, and Gray, *The Law of Torts*, III, 103-126; Atiyah, *Accidents, Compensation, and the Law*, 449-477; Stephen Sugarman, *Doing Away with Personal Injury Law* (New York: Quorum Books, 1989), 3-72.

123. T. Ison, *The Forensic Lottery* (London: Stapless Press, 1967).

124. Atiyah, *Accidents, Compensation, and the Law*, 449-450, 453-460.

125. See Weinrib, "Understanding Tort Law," 502-503; Englard, "The System-Builders," 57-59; S. Smith, "The Critics and the 'Crisis': A Reassessment of Current Conceptions of Tort Law," 72 *Cornell L. Rev.* 765, 778-785 (1987).

126. One aspect of the social insurance critique of tort law can, however, be dismissed. It is often argued that tort law is inadequate when measured against *its own* objectives, for it wants to condemn moral wrongdoing and yet the objective fault standard takes no account of personal capacities that may negate the actor's blameworthiness (see Harper, James, and Gray, *The Law of Torts*, III, 115-117); or it is argued that the penalties tort law imposes are often wholly disproportionate to the blame. We have seen, however, that the condemnation of moral failure forms no part of the internal rationality of tort law. The latter vindicates individual rights against external acts inconsistent with them; it does not penalize immorality except as incidentally concomitant with that purpose.

127. The milestones on the road to strict liability are *Escola v. Coca-Cola Bottling Co.*, above n. 9 (where the idea appeared in a concurring opinion by Justice Tray-

nor), *Henningsen v. Bloomfield Motors,* above n. 120 (which imposed liability on the theory of breach of warranty but which waived the privity requirement and invalidated a clause excluding liability), *Greenman v. Yuba Power Prods., Inc.,* above n. 9 (which explicitly put liability on the foundation of tort rather than contract), and sec. 402A of *Restatement (Second) of Torts* (1965). The logical culmination of this process must, as George Priest has argued, be absolute liability for injuries resulting from the use of products; see Priest, "Enterprise Liability," 527. Products liability law retains a vestige of fault in the requirement that the injury be caused by a defect in manufacture or design. In particular, negligence ideas have been reintroduced in the idea of a design defect, which must be defined in relation to ordinary consumer expectations of safety or to alternative designs whose benefits outweigh their costs; see Barker v. Lull Engineering Co., 573 P.2d 443 (Cal. S.C. 1978). The logical momentum of products liability law is toward elimination of the requirement of a product defect. Moreover, the loss-spreading rationale of no-fault liability also implies the elimination of defenses of contributory negligence and voluntary assumption of risk.

128. For a discussion of the problems inherent in allocating costs to their sources, see M. Trebilcock, "The Social Insurance–Deterrence Dilemma of Modern North American Tort Law: A Canadian Perspective on the Liability Insurance Crisis," 24 *San Diego L. Rev.* 929, 987–980 (1987); see also the discussion by Perry, "Moral Foundations," 461–467.

129. See Guido Calabresi, "Concerning Cause and the Law of Torts: An Essay for Harry Kalven, Jr.," 43 *Univ. Chic. L. Rev.* 69, 84–87 (1975); John Fleming, "Probabilistic Causation in Tort Law," 68 *Can. Bar Rev.* 661, 667–669 (1989).

130. Cook v. Lewis, [1951] S.C.R. 830; Summers v. Tice, 199 P.2d 1 (Cal. S.C. 1948).

131. Sindell v. Abbott Laboratories, 607 P.2d 924 (Cal. S.C. 1980).

132. Allen v. U.S., 588 F. Supp. 247 (1984); In re "Agent Orange" Product Liability Litigation, 597 F. Supp. 740 (1984).

133. The irrelevance of causation is finally admitted in Hymowitz v. Eli Lilly, 539 N.E.2d 1069 (N.Y.C.A. 1989), where liability was apportioned according to the percentage of the total risk created to the public, and the defendant could not avoid liability by showing it did not cause the injury.

134. S. Sugarman, "Doing Away with Tort Law," 73 *Cal. L. Rev.* 555 (1985).

135. At least three broad types of mixed scheme are possible. One uses the tort system as a backup to the insurance scheme (modified no-fault); another uses insurance as a backup to the tort system (add-on scheme); and a third allows everyone a choice between alternative regimes (elective scheme). Under the first model, insurance benefits are generous and the tort system is retained only to allow victims to sue their faulty injurers for the difference between social insurance benefits and full compensation; victims suffering losses below a threshold are barred from seeking vindication of their private rights in court. Under the second, accident victims immediately receive benefits (typically less generous than under modified no-fault) with no prejudice to their right to sue in tort. Unsuccessful plaintiffs continue receiving insurance benefits, while successful plaintiffs reimburse the fund or have collateral benefits deducted from the damage award. Under the third type, each individual elects either to receive guaranteed compensation for

pecuniary loss or to take his chances for full recovery in court; for a specific proposal exemplifying the third model, see J. O'Connell, "Statute—A Draft Bill to
Allow Choice Between No-Fault and Fault-Based Auto Insurance," 27 *Harv. J. Legis.*
143 (1990).

136. It has been argued that a dual system best achieves loss-spreading and deterrence goals by obviating the need to compromise either in a single system.
Deterrence is achieved by a system that allocates liability according to fault without
regard to loss spreading, while the best spreading of losses is achieved through social insurance funded from general revenue; see S. Stoljar, "Accidents, Costs and
Legal Responsibility," 36 *Modern L. Rev.* 233 (1973); cf. W. Blum and H. Kalven,
Jr., "The Empty Cabinet of Dr. Calabresi," 34 *Univ. Chic. L. Rev.* 239, 270 (1967).

137. Thus, of the three mixed models outlined in n. 135, only the add-on
model and the elective model are consistent with the justifying theory presented
here. The modified no-fault model is an unjustifiable infringement of rights. The
choice between the two permissible models can be determined by considerations
of cost, deterrence, and the like.

Most North American auto plans (e.g., those of New York, Massachusetts,
Michigan, Florida, Ontario) are modified no-fault schemes. Inasmuch as they abolish the right to sue in tort for less serious injuries, they are inadequate to the ideal
dual system my argument points to. It is easy to think of a tort action as an expen-
sive frill if the victim is already nearly compensated by the fund, particularly since
very few individuals in this situation are likely to exercise their right to sue.
However, this sort of thinking betrays the one-sidedly communitarian mind-set that
sees tort law as another compensation mechanism rather than as an institution for
identifying and correcting wrongs against the person. Given a contest between the
right to vindicate personality's worth and guaranteed levels of welfare above the
minimum compatible with human autonomy, it would not be eccentric to suggest
that the latter rather than the former is the luxury.

138. See Huber, *Liability,* 3–5.

139. Id., 202.

140. Add-on auto schemes (see n. 135) are in place in Delaware, Maryland,
Oregon, Arkansas, Texas, South Carolina, Washington, and Saskatchewan. New
Jersey and Pennsylvania have adopted elective schemes.

CHAPTER V: AGENCY AND WELFARE IN THE PENAL LAW

1. Joel Feinberg, *The Moral Limits of the Criminal Law,* vol. 1, *Harm to Others*
(New York: Oxford University Press, 1984), 11.

2. Id.

3. Feinberg would also allow offense to others as a criterion of permissible
criminalization; see Feinberg, *The Moral Limits of the Criminal Law,* vol. 2, *Offence to
Others* (New York: Oxford University Press, 1985).

4. Feinberg, *Harm to Others,* 37.

5. Id., 112.

6. *Restatement (Second) of the Law of Torts* (St. Paul: American Law Institute Publishers, 1965), chap. 1, sec. 7.

7. Id.

8. Feinberg, *Harm to Others,* 113, 206–214.

9. The defense of necessity has sometimes been interpreted as a counterexample to this principle, but I have elsewhere offered an interpretation that coheres with it; see Alan Brudner, "A Theory of Necessity," 7 *Oxford J. Leg. Stud.* 339 (1987). Moreover, the utilitarian theory of necessity has been rejected by the Supreme Court of Canada; see Perka v. The Queen, [1984] 2 S.C.R. 232.

10. See Sherras v. De Rutzen, [1895] 1 Q.B. 918; R. v. Ewart, 25 N.Z.L.R. 709 (1905); Proudman v. Dayman 67 C.L.R. 536 (Aust. H.C. 1941); Morissette v. United States, 342 U.S. 246 (1952); R. v. City of Sault Ste. Marie, [1978] 2 S.C.R. 1299.

11. Jerome Hall, "Negligent Behavior Should Be Excluded from Penal Liability," 63 *Col. L. Rev.* 632 (1963).

12. Oliver Wendell Holmes, *The Common Law,* ed. M. Howe (Cambridge: Belknap Press, 1963), 42–62.

13. See Reference Re Section 94(2) of the Motor Vehicle Act, [1985] 2 S.C.R. 486, 514, per Lamer, C.J.

14. See H. L. A. Hart, *Punishment and Responsibility* (Oxford: Clarendon Press, 1968), 22–24, 44–53, 180–185. The drive to enforce a single principle of penal justice heedless of boundaries is evident in the following statement by Holmes, *Common Law,* 39: "Again, a *malum prohibitum* is just as much a crime as a *malum in se.* If there is any general ground of punishment, it must apply to one case as much as to the other."

15. See David Nelken, "Critical Criminal Law," in Peter Fitzpatrick and Alan Hunt, eds., *Critical Legal Studies* (Oxford: Blackwell, 1987), 112–115; Mark Kelman, "Interpretive Construction in the Substantive Criminal Law," 33 *Stan. L. Rev.* 591 (1981).

16. [1989] 1 S.C.R. 1392.

17. R.S.C., 1985, Chap. C-46, sec. 219.

18. See R. v. Caldwell, [1981] 1 All E.R. 961 (H.L.).

19. See Hart, *Punishment and Responsibility,* 152–157.

20. This is the view of the American Law Institute (ALI), *Model Penal Code* (Official Draft, 1962), sec. 2.02 (2)(c); see also O'Grady v. Sparling, [1960] S.C.R. 804.

21. Hart, *Punishment and Responsibility,* 136–157; a similar argument has been advanced by George Fletcher, "The Theory of Criminal Negligence: A Comparative Analysis," 119 *Univ. Pa. L. Rev.* 401 (1971).

22. J. W. C. Turner, "The Mental Element in Crimes at Common Law," 6 *Cambridge L. J.* 31 (1936).

23. Hart, *Punishment and Responsibility,* 149–150.

24. Id., 152.

25. Id., 180–183.

26. Id., 8–10.

27. [1955] N.Z.L.R. 471 (S.C.).

28. [1924] N.Z.L.R. 865 (N.Z.C.A.); cf. People v. Bowen, 158 N.W.2d 794 (Mich. 1968).

29. Salmond, J.'s precise formulation was (above n. 28, at 875): "That a man's unfulfilled criminal purposes should be punishable they must be manifested not by his words merely, or by acts which are in themselves of innocent or ambiguous

significance, but by overt acts which are sufficient in themselves to declare and proclaim the guilty purpose with which they are done." See also J. W. C. Turner, "Attempts to Commit Crimes," 5 *Cambridge L. J.* 230, 237–238 (1934).

30. Above n. 27, at 477.

31. See *New Zealand Crimes Act* (1961), sec. 72(3).

32. Glanville Williams, *Criminal Law: The General Part,* 2d ed. (London: Stevens, 1961), 630.

33. See ALI, *Model Penal Code* (Official Draft, 1962), sec. 5.01; Deutsch v. The Queen, [1986] 2 S.C.R. 2.

34. See Commonwealth v. Skipper, 294 A.2d 780 (Pa. 1972).

35. R. v. Sorrell and Bondett, 41 C.C.C. (2d) 9 (Ont. C.A. 1978).

36. 10 C.C.C. (2d) 26 (Alberta District Court 1972).

37. R.S.C. 1985, Chap. C-46, sec. 19.

38. Above n. 36, at 31; see also Holmes, *Common Law,* 41.

39. For an analogous American case, see State v. Striggles, 210 N.W. 137 (Iowa 1926).

40. Sir Matthew Hale, *The History of the Pleas of the Crown* (London: Professional Books, 1971), I, 42.

41. See Liparota v. United States, 471 U.S. 419 (1985); Lambert v. California, 355 U.S. 225 (1957); Long v. State, 65 A.2d 489 (Del. 1949).

42. See, e.g., Molis v. The Queen, [1980] 2 S.C.R. 356.

43. Holmes, *Common Law,* 41–43.

44. Fletcher, "The Theory of Criminal Negligence," 422.

45. G. W. F. Hegel, *Philosophy of Right,* trans. T. M. Knox (Oxford: Oxford University Press, 1967), pars. 90–104. Numbers in the text refer to paragraphs of this work. I will also refer occasionally to G. W. F. Hegel, *Vorlesungen über Rechtsphilosophie 1818–1831,* ed. K.-H. Ilting (Stuttgart-Bad Cannstatt: Frommann-Holzboog, 1974).

46. Immanuel Kant, *Foundations of the Metaphysics of Morals,* trans. L. W. Beck (Indianapolis: Bobbs-Merrill, 1959), 43–47.

47. See, e.g., Plato, *Laws,* 642b–645c; Gorgias, 472d–479d.

48. The common-law view of the status of values is classically articulated by Thomas Hobbes, *Leviathan* (Oxford: Blackwell, 1957), 32: "But whatsoever is the object of any man's appetite or desire, that is it which he for his part calls *good*; and the object of his hate and aversion, *evil*; and of his contempt, *vile* and *inconsiderable.* For these words of good, evil, and contemptible are ever used with relation to the person that uses them, there being nothing simply and absolutely so, nor any common rule of good and evil to be taken from the nature of the objects themselves." (Emphasis in original.)

49. See also *Hegel's Phenomenology of Spirit,* trans. A. V. Miller (Oxford: Oxford University Press, 1977), 109–111.

50. See Bamford v. Turnley, 122 E.R. 27, 33 (1862), per Bramwell, B.

51. Bolton v. Stone, [1951] A.C. 850 (H.L.).

52. Hegel identifies three ways, putting fraud midway between tort and crime as involving intentional wrongdoing but with a pretense of respect for the victim's consent; see *Philosophy of Right,* pars. 87–89. Since fraud's oblique tribute to rights has implications for sentencing but not (as far as I know) for substantive doctrine,

I will treat fraud as a species of crime. For a discussion of the difference between tort and crime along Hegelian lines, see Bruce Chapman, "A Theory of Criminal Law Excuses," 1 *Can. J. Law and Jurisprudence* 75, 81–84 (1988).

53. For a lucid account of Hegel's theory of crime, see Peter Nicholson, "Hegel on Crime," 3 *History of Political Thought* 103 (1982).

54. See Robert Pippin, *Hegel's Idealism: The Satisfactions of Self-Consciousness* (Cambridge: Cambridge University Press, 1989), 19–24.

55. See Allen Wood, *Hegel's Ethical Thought* (Cambridge: Cambridge University Press, 1990), 116–117; Mark Thornton, "Against Retributivism," in Wesley Cragg, ed., *Retributivism and Its Critics* (Stuttgart: Steiner, 1992), 83–84.

56. G. W. F. Hegel, *The Philosophical Propaedeutic*, trans. A. V. Miller, eds. Michael George and Andrew Vincent (Oxford: Blackwell, 1986), 31.

57. I take this to be the meaning of Hegel's statement that "[t]he infringement of right as right is something that happens and has positive existence in the external world" (*Philosophy of Right*, par. 97).

58. No doubt the criminal's law leaves *everyone's* right vulnerable, and one might ask why the criminal is singled out to bear the force of a principle that logically applies to all. Why does not crime call forth universal destruction as its punishment, as in the story of the Flood? The answer is that crime's claim to validity has an existence solely in the criminal's will; the challenge to the validity of rights exists only in the person who actively denied their validity, and so it is sufficient to defeat this challenge to visit the self-contradictory implications of crime on the criminal. Moreover, the intersubjective will can apply no more force than is necessary to defeat the challenge to its normative validity, or else it is another wrong. See *Vorlesungen*, IV, 284.

59. Allen Wood has recently directed a number of criticisms against Hegel's theory of punishment; see *Hegel's Ethical Thought*, 115–124. In addition to making the points answered in the text of this chapter, he argues that Hegel (a) assumes that those punished see themselves as persons and thus gives no guidance for the treatment of people who, because of extreme poverty, do not see themselves as persons and who can therefore assert no law in their actions; (b) shows why it is permissible to punish but does not show that punishment is demanded; (c) has no account of punishment for *mala prohibita*, the penalization of which would be unjust on his theory (since the lawbreaker violates no abstract right of another and so does not will his own punishment).

(a) The sense of personality underlying Hegel's theory of punishment is very thin. One need only have a sense of oneself as formally free (i.e., not an automaton) in order to qualify as someone to whom principled action may be imputed. There is no reason to think that poverty vitiates this minimal sense of self, and it degrades the poor to think that it does.

(b) It is true that Hegel's theory does not tell us why the state *must* punish, but this is a virtue of the theory, since it explicitly leaves room for the power of pardon (see *Philosophy of Right*, par. 282). A theory of punishment that (like Kant's) left no such room would be deficient.

(c) It is true that Hegel has no explicit account of punishment for mala prohibita, but such an account may be elaborated from his theory of welfare and of the good, and this is what I try to do. Hegel's retributive theory of punishment does not rule out or render unintelligible penalties for negligently committed public welfare offenses, because the theory applies specifically and narrowly to *crimes,* i.e., paradigmatically to intentional infringements of abstract right and by analogy to intentional violations of positive law. It thus leaves open the possibility of a different theory of punishment for public welfare offenses. Hegel no doubt sometimes refers to offenses such as counterfeiting as crimes (suggesting to Wood that he meant retributive theory to apply across the board). But this is because he sees crime as any intentional violation of the framework of rights (see *Vorlesungen,* IV, 273); and an intentional violation of positive law is indeed punishable under the same retributive theory as an intentional infringement of abstract right. In both cases the wrongdoer denies the validity of the legal order that makes rights possible and so contradicts his own right-claim to absolute liberty. There remain, however, the many regulatory offenses that may be committed through negligence or through no fault at all, and nothing Hegel says suggests he thought that retributive theory applied to these.

60. See R. A. Duff, *Intention, Agency and Criminal Liability: Philosophy of Action and the Criminal Law* (Oxford: Blackwell, 1990), 58–63.

61. The fact that in exceptional cases omissions suffice for the actus reus does not contradict this account of the act requirement. Sometimes omissions are culpable because they are best seen as part of a larger act; see Fagan v. Commissioner of Metropolitan Police, [1969] 1 Q.B. 439. At other times they are culpable because they are part of a context in which the accused has actively created a danger to property or life; see R. v. Miller, [1983] 1 All E.R. 978 (H.L.).

62. The mens rea for attempts is properly determined not by semantic considerations (which might lead one to conclude that there is no "attempt" without an intention to produce a state of affairs) but by the role of mens rea in the justification of punishment. Since the requirement of an explicit denial of the intersubjective basis of rights is satisfied by a reckless disdain for the end-status of another no less than by an intentional one, there is no reason to limit the mens rea for attempts to intention. For a case in agreement with this view, see People v. Castro, 657 P.2d 932 (Colo. 1983); to the contrary are People v. Harris, 377 N.E.2d 28 (Ill. 1978) and R. v. Ancio, [1984] 1 S.C.R. 225.

63. Although the impossibility (whether due to factual circumstances alone or to the interplay between fact and law) of completing the intended offense should be irrelevant to culpability once the unequivocality test is satisfied, impossibility *may* affect a court's judgment as to whether the act unequivocally manifests a criminal intent. Suppose, for example, D, believing he is selling a fake Picasso, actually sells a genuine one. Here (assuming otherwise ordinary circumstances), the impossibility of committing a fraud renders D's act easily amenable to an innocent interpretation. Though not itself a defense, impossibility here goes to the question of remoteness. Conversely, suppose D, believing he is selling a large shipment of heroin, completes a transaction under very incriminating circumstances (in a secluded place in the dead of night, each party backed up by armed guards, a suitcase full of money, etc.). It turns out, however, that the merchandise is milk powder. Here the impossibility of completing the offense has little bearing on how we interpret the act.

In Anderton v. Ryan, [1985] 2 All E.R. 355, the House of Lords followed the approach suggested here; however, it overruled itself in R. v. Shivpuri, [1986] 2 All E.R. 334, on the ground that, because all acts short of the completed criminal purpose are by definition "objectively innocent," the essence of a criminal attempt lies in the intent alone—a principle that will anomalously (as the Court conceded) convict the seller of the genuine Picasso as well as someone who "steals" his own umbrella. However, the reasoning in *Shivpuri* fails to do justice to the Court's own intuition in *Anderton*. The unequivocality test does not require that we consider whether incomplete acts are guilty or innocent "objectively" or independently of intent; on the contrary, it holds that an attempt is criminal only if it embodies a criminal intent. But to determine whether it does so, we must look at the act in its context and ignore evidence *aliunde* of intent. In this way alone is the traditional principle that a crime requires *both* a guilty intent *and* a guilty act preserved without compromise in the context of attempts.

64. See Sir James F. Stephen, *A History of the Criminal Law of England*, vol. 2 (London: Macmillan, 1883), 94–95.

65. This is currently the view of a majority of the Supreme Court of Canada; see R. v. Martineau, [1990] 2 S.C.R. 633.

66. Hart, *Punishment and Responsibility*, 149–157; Brenda Baker, "Mens Rea, Negligence, and Criminal Law Reform," 6 *Law and Phil.* 53, 79–86 (1987).

67. As the House of Lords held in D.P.P. v. Morgan, [1975] 2 All E.R. 347; and as the Supreme Court of Canada held in R. v. Pappajohn, [1980] 2 S.C.R. 120. By contrast, few American courts allow an unreasonable mistake regarding consent to excuse from rape, and some reject even an excuse of reasonable mistake; see Susan Estrich, "Rape," 95 *Yale L. J.* 1087, 1097–1099 (1986). Although an honest mistake as to consent should excuse from the *crime* of sexual assault, anyone acquitted on this ground could be guilty of a less serious public welfare offense if his mistake was negligent or rooted in sexist assumptions.

68. *Incapacity* to know the act's wrongfulness is crucial here, for every criminal impliedly asserts a right to do the wrong and in that sense is ignorant of the wrongfulness of his act. What distinguishes the legally insane actor from the criminal is that the latter knowingly exalts his claim of right above the intersubjective will (or the standard of reasonable persons), while the legally insane person (much like the tortfeasor) believes that his act conforms to that standard. Since the incapacity distinguishes innocent from culpable ignorance of wrongfulness, proposals to abolish the insanity defense in favor of a straightforward inquiry into mens rea are, in my view, misguided; see J. Goldstein and J. Katz, "Abolish the Insanity Defense—Why Not?" 72 *Yale L. J.* 853 (1963).

69. The American Law Institute's *Model Penal Code* adds this defense to the traditional M'Naghten test of culpability; see sec. 4.01(1). See also United States v. Brawner, 471 F.2d 969 (D.C. 1972), which follows the ALI. The irresistible impulse defense has been rejected in Canada; see R. v. Borg, [1969] S.C.R. 551.

70. Thus, someone may be excused who, while knowing that his deed was against the law, acted under the delusion of necessity or of self-defense; see R. v. Chaulk, [1989] 1 S.C.R. 369; People v. Skinner, 704 P.2d 752 (Cal. 1985); Stapleton v. The Queen, 86 C.L.R. 358 (Aust. H.C. 1952).

71. Hegel, *Vorlesungen*, IV, 270–271.

72. See David Cooper, "Hegel's Theory of Punishment," in Z. A. Pelczynski,

ed., *Hegel's Political Philosophy: Problems and Perspectives* (Cambridge: Cambridge University Press, 1971), 157–158.

73. For a contrary view, see Michael Moore, "The Moral and Metaphysical Sources of the Criminal Law," in J. R. Pennock and J. W. Chapman, eds., *Nomos*, vol. 27: *Criminal Justice* (New York: New York University Press, 1985), 14.

74. Mouse's Case, 12 Coke's Rep. 63 (1608); Reg. v. Gill, [1963] 1 W.L.R. 841.

75. See R. v. Dudley and Stephens, 14 Q.B.D. 273 (1884); R. v. Howe, [1987] 1 All E.R. 771 (H.L.).

76. See George Fletcher, *Rethinking Criminal Law* (Boston: Little, Brown, 1978), 802–804; see also Perka v. The Queen, [1984] 2 S.C.R. 233.

77. For the irrelevance of motive to culpability, see United States v. Pomponio, 429 U.S. 10 (1976); Lewis v. The Queen, [1979] 2 S.C.R. 821.

78. Above n. 75.

79. In *Dudley and Stephens,* the convicts' death sentences were commuted by the Crown to imprisonment for six months. In a similar American case, where the occupants of a lifeboat threw some of their number overboard to prevent the boat from sinking, the accused was sentenced to six months hard labor and a fine of $20; see United States v. Holmes, 26 Fed. Cas. 360 (1842).

80. See ALI, *Model Penal Code* (1962), sec. 210.3(b); D.P.P. v. Camplin, [1978] 2 All E.R. 168 (H.L.); R. v. Hill, [1986] 1 S.C.R. 313.

81. Jeremy Horder has recently offered a different understanding of provocation. On his view, a wrong committed in the heat of passion may, according to the logic (which he contests) of the defense, be justified if the accused acted in accordance with the mean appropriate to the virtues connected with anger; or it may be excused to some extent if the accused exceeded the mean by some small degree given the nature of the provocation; see Jeremy Horder, *Provocation and Responsibility* (Oxford: Clarendon Press, 1992), 134–136. The difficulty with this view is that it confuses the circumstances of legal justification, excuse, and mitigation with those relevant to moral praise or blame. Apart from circumstances of self-defense, a person's rights are consciously violated by a killing in anger even if (if such a thing were possible) the killer acted virtuously. Otherwise, one's rights would be at the disposal of the man of virtue. The considerations Horder adduces are relevant to the exercise of sentencing discretion, not to the determination of *legal* culpability. A similar problem arises with the theory of excuse put forward by George Fletcher in "The Individualization of Excusing Conditions," 47 *S. Cal. L. Rev.* 1269 (1974). Here Fletcher elevates the peripheral relevance of motive in necessity (of the *Dudley and Stephens* type) and provocation into a general theory of excuse based on the illicitness of an inference from act to moral character. However, this move illustrates the dangers of raising subordinate principles into ruling ones. If the breakdown of the inference from act to moral character excuses from criminal liability, then someone who intentionally commits wrongs from worthy motives should be acquitted, and so once again the private moral conscience is above the law.

82. There are no doubt other conceptions of welfare (e.g., as the fulfillment of human nature or of humanity's supernatural end), but we can ignore them in a work on the common law as being interpretively unilluminating.

83. These elements of the paradigm have, of course, been thoroughly worked

out by John Rawls and Ronald Dworkin; see especially John Rawls, *A Theory of Justice* (Cambridge: Belknap Press, 1971), 150–192; Ronald Dworkin, *Taking Rights Seriously* (Cambridge: Harvard University Press, 1977), 184–205, 266–278. We shall presently see that there are rational limits to the requirement of state neutrality toward preferences.

84. A rule enjoining the equalization of happiness or permitting only those increases that make no one worse off in the short run would also conform to the egalitarian requirements of the agency-based justification. However, the "maximin" principle (enjoining us to maximize the long-run advantage of the least well off) allows greater levels of preference satisfaction within the egalitarian constraint. Since the agency-based justification bids us to conceive projects and to pursue them enthusiastically for the sake of freedom, it prefers the rule that allows the greatest scope for this activity.

85. I am speaking here of the situation anterior to the enactment of a statute. Once a welfare statute is in place, punishment can be deserved, since an intentional breach of positive law also implies an elevation of self above the legal order that, when universalized, negates rights. However, because the rationale for the penal sanction is in the first place a goal, desert (in the strong sense) will not here be a necessary condition of penalization.

86. This, I believe, is the underlying rationale for the doctrine in *Sherras v. De Rutzen,* above n. 10 (cf. *Morissette v. United States,* above n. 10), that mens rea is not required for convictions for public welfare offenses.

87. See *Proudman v. Dayman,* above n. 10; R. v. City of Sault Ste. Marie, [1978] 2 S.C.R. 1299.

88. See Rawls, *A Theory of Justice,* 40–45.

89. Absolute liability (i.e., liability in the absence even of negligence) has been ruled unconstitutional in Canada if the accused faces the possibility of a prison sentence; see Reference Re Section 94(2) of the Motor Vehicle Act, [1985] 2 S.C.R. 486; see also ALI, *Model Penal Code,* sec. 2.05. Moreover, in Canada and Australia, a court will construe a public welfare statute as allowing a defense of due diligence unless the statute explicitly dispenses with fault; see *R. v. City of Sault Ste. Marie,* above n. 87; *Proudman v. Dayman,* above n. 10. For the contrary position, see State v. Stepniewski, 314 N.W.2d 98 (Wis. 1982).

90. The Supreme Courts of both the United States and Canada have held that excessively vague penal laws violate constitutional guarantees of "due process" or "fundamental justice"; see United States v. Harriss, 347 U.S. 612, 617 (1954); R. v. Nova Scotia Pharmaceutical Society, [1992] 2 S.C.R. 606. For a famous violation of the fair notice principle, see Shaw v. D.P.P., [1962] A.C. 220 (H.L.).

91. ALI, *Model Penal Code* (1962), sec. 2.04(3)(b); R. v. MacDougall, 60 C.C.C. (2d) 137 (Nova Scotia C.A. 1981).

92. The four principles of justice indigenous to the welfare paradigm (the priority of autonomy over happiness and of the good over formal liberty, the noncontradiction proviso, and the requirement of the least restrictive means) are embodied (albeit confusedly) in the test devised by the Supreme Court of Canada to determine whether statutory infringements of constitutionally entrenched rights are "reasonable limits" in a "free and democratic society"; see R. v. Oakes, [1986]

1 S.C.R. 103. Limitations of rights are justified, first of all, only if the goal served by the impugned statute is "pressing and substantial." This test intuitively grasps the distinction between goals relative to contingent desire, which cannot override fundamental rights, and goals relevant to the common good of autonomy, which can. However, the common good can limit rights only to the extent necessary to achieve the goal; hence the proportionality test in *Oakes* demands that the means be rationally related to the end and that they limit rights as little as possible. The third aspect of the *Oakes* proportionality test—that the deleterious effects of the statute must not outweigh the expected benefits—appears to be part of a utilitarian model, but it can also be understood as screening out self-contradictory attempts to promote the effective autonomy of all by denying it to some.

93. The figures who best personify these opposing tendencies are Jerome Hall and H. L. A. Hart.

94. See Jerome Hall, *General Principles of Criminal Law,* 2d ed. (Indianapolis: Bobbs-Merrill, 1947), 351–359.

95. See Holmes, *Common Law,* 37; Ted Honderich, "Culpability and Mystery," in Antony Duff and Nigel Simmonds, eds., *Philosophy and the Criminal Law* (Wiesbaden: Steiner, 1984), 71.

96. Hart, *Punishment and Responsibility,* 136–157; Don Stuart, *Canadian Criminal Law: A Treatise,* 2d ed. (Toronto: Carswell, 1987), 194–195; *R. v. Tutton and Tutton,* above n. 16, per Lamer, C.J. Under a negligence regime one is punishable for "murder" if one causes death by an act whose fatal consequences one ought to have foreseen; see D.P.P. v. Smith, [1961] A.C. 290 (H.L.). One is liable for manslaughter if one negligently breaches a legal duty of care and death results; see R. v. Lawrence, [1982] A.C. 510 (H.L.). One is guilty of sexual assault if one has nonconsensual intercourse with a person in the unreasonable (though honest) belief that she consented; see *Criminal Code of Canada,* R.S.C. 1985, Chap. C-46, sec. 273.2. One is punishable for any offense committed as a result of negligently becoming intoxicated; see D.P.P. v. Majewski, 62 Cr. App. R. 262 (1976).

97. Bratty v. A-G Northern Ireland, [1963] A.C. 386 (H.L.); Rabey v. The Queen, [1980] 2 S.C.R. 513.

98. See ALI, *Model Penal Code* (1962), sec. 5.01, which defines a "substantial step" as one "strongly corroborative of the actor's criminal purpose"; cf. R. v. Shivpuri, [1986] 2 All E.R. 334 (H.L.); R. v. Sorrell and Bondett, 41 C.C.C. (2d) 9 (Ont. C.A. 1978); Deutsch v. The Queen, [1986] 2 S.C.R. 2.

99. Above n. 28.

100. People v. Kessler, 315 N.E.2d 29 (Ill. 1974); R.S.C., 1985, Chap. C-46, sec. 21(2).

101. *Bratty v. A-G Northern Ireland,* above n. 97, per Lord Denning.

102. *The Homicide Act,* 1957 (U.K.), c. 11, sec. 2; see also State v. McVey, 376 N.W.2d 585 (Iowa 1985); R. v. Wright, 48 C.C.C. (2d) 334 (Alta. S.C. 1979).

103. *D.P.P. v. Majewski,* above n. 96.

104. George Fletcher has also argued that the criminal law is a unity of different paradigms; see *Rethinking Criminal Law* (Boston: Little, Brown, 1978), 388–390. However, for Fletcher, the three patterns of criminality (manifest criminality, subjective criminality, and harmful consequences) have no immanent connection;

they are alternative and equally plausible theories of criminality that could singly order the whole of the criminal law. Hence the unifying general part does not embrace the patterns as parts of a whole; it merely states general propositions or defines concepts that happen to cut across all three. Despite the general part, the criminal law remains "polycentric." In the view presented here, by contrast, the penal law is a differentiated whole; one pulse beats in all divisions.

105. The distinction we have drawn between criminal law (vindicating private rights) and public welfare offenses (promoting happiness and the common good) does not correspond to the old distinction between *mala in se* and *mala prohibita*. All true crimes are mala in se, but not all mala in se are true crimes. For example, offenses against public morals (e.g., sodomy) were traditionally viewed as mala in se (or "crimes against nature"), but for us these are not crimes unless involving coercion or deception (nor are they for the *Model Penal Code*; see sec. 213.2). Moreover, laws promoting the general happiness outlaw mala prohibita, but those promoting the common good might with good reason be viewed as outlawing mala in se.

106. R.S.C. 1985, Chap. C-46, sec. 215. The offense is punishable by up to two years in jail—too severe, according to our argument, for a negligence offense.

107. This is presumably why the codification of true crimes is thought to be optional, whereas the legislative promulgation of public welfare offenses is considered a requirement of due process.

That wrongfulness in the context of true crimes implies illegality (so that rational agents cannot be ignorant of such law) applies even where a criminal wrong is perversely permitted or authorized by positive law. Thus a ship's captain who maliciously shot the captain of a nonenemy vessel on the high seas, unaware that the high seas exemption from English penal laws had been repealed in his absence, was properly convicted; see R. v. Bailey, 168 E.R. 651 (1800). And so, on this principle, were Nazi war criminals.

108. See Molis v. The Queen, [1980] 2 S.C.R. 356.

109. R. v. Esop, 173 E.R. 203 (1836).

110. State v. O'Neil, 126 N.W. 454 (Iowa 1910).

111. See Hegel, *Philosophy of Right,* par. 215: "If laws are to have binding force, it follows that, in view of the right of self-consciousness . . . they must be made universally known."

112. Hall, *General Principles,* 351–364.

113. See R. ex. rel. Irwin v. Dalley, 118 C.C.C. 116 (Ont. C.A. 1957); to the contrary is *Long v. State,* above n. 41.

CHAPTER VI: IDEALISM AND FIDELITY TO LAW

1. Par. 211.

2. Ronald Dworkin, *Taking Rights Seriously* (Cambridge: Harvard University Press, 1978), 66: "[A] principle is a principle of law if it figures in the soundest theory of law that can be provided as a justification for the explicit substantive and institutional rules of the jurisdiction in question." See also Lon Fuller, *The Law in Quest of Itself* (Boston: Beacon Press, 1940), 9–10.

3. Of course, this distinction between the methods of the human and the natural sciences has become controversial since the appearance of Thomas Kuhn's highly influential *The Structure of Scientific Revolutions*, 2d ed. (Chicago: University of Chicago Press, 1970). Still, even Kuhn would probably admit that, faced with a discrepancy between a theoretical paradigm and an observed natural phenomenon, a scientist could not in the last resort sensibly regard the theory as right and the fact as wrong. Yet this is what a legal theorist routinely does with regard to rules isolated by his theory.

4. Sir Matthew Hale, *A History of the Common Law*, ed. C. M. Gray (Chicago: University of Chicago Press, 1971), 40.

5. Omychund v. Barker, 26 Eng. Rep. 15, 22–23 (Ch. 1744).

6. Ernest Weinrib's work proceeds within the framework of this form of idealism. See "Legal Formalism: On the Immanent Rationality of Law," 97 *Yale L. J.* 949, 962 (1988): "For the formalist, law is *constituted* by thought: Its content is made up of the concepts (e.g., cause, remoteness, duty, consideration, offer and acceptance) that inform juridical relationships. Law is identical to the ideas of which it is comprised, and the intelligibility of law lies in grasping the order and connection of these ideas. Because law is . . . essentially conceptual, it does not present itself as alien to the enquirer's efforts to comprehend it. Thus the formalist assumption is that law is, however inchoately, an exhibition of intelligence. . . . [I]n the formalist view there is in law an integration of the activity of the understanding with the matter to be understood. Since law is assumed to be intelligible from within, the content of law is regarded as being homogeneous with, and therefore accessible to, thought." Cf. Michael Oakeshott, *On Human Conduct* (Oxford: Clarendon Press, 1975), 13–15.

7. The problem can be seen in Ernest Weinrib's proposed method for understanding tort law. In "The Special Morality of Tort Law," 34 *McGill L. J.* 404, 406 (1989), Weinrib writes, "What, then, do we mean by tort law? Without prejudging the moral issue, we must identify our subject matter in a way that remains true to our juristic experience. I propose that we take as minimal a view as possible by concentrating on aspects of tort law that are indispensable to its intelligibility as a distinctive mode of legal ordering. Among the mass of doctrines, holdings, principles, and institutional arrangements that we associate with tort law are features that are constitutive of our conception of tort law. The systemic absence of these features would preclude our identifying what remained as tort law at all. . . ." "For example, causation is one such feature."

Weinrib here claims to be identifying tort law without prejudging the moral issue. We identify it by consulting our "juristic experience" for those elements that are "constitutive of our conception of tort law." Yet our juristic experience is confused; it contains many diverse features that may be incompatible. Indeed, that is why we need an understanding of tort law that goes beyond our immediate juristic experience. In that experience, we find causation as an ordering concept; yet we also find judicial holdings that make causation irrelevant to tort liability. They may be rare and eccentric, but their paucity provides no reason for disqualifying them: the dissenter, after all, may be right. Accordingly, one cannot decide that causation is a constitutive feature of tort law simply by consulting experience; one must presuppose in some inchoate manner the moral issue, that is, the principle of understanding. What, then, will confirm this principle as the principle *of* tort law? The phenomena singled out as "constitutive of tort law" cannot confirm it, for they already presuppose it. For Weinrib, the principle is confirmed if it exhibits tort law as a coherent unity of doctrinal and institutional elements, for the common law itself strives for such "justificatory coherence"; see "Formalism and Its Canadian Critics," in Ken Cooper-Stephenson and Elaine Gibson, eds., *Tort Theory* (North York, Ont.: Captus Press, 1993), 19–20. But on Weinrib's account of the relation between tort law and the theory of tort law (according to which they are "homogeneous" aspects of the same unity; see n. 6 above), the judicial striving for coherence is the very same idealizing activity as that undertaken by the tort theorist; they are continuous activities of the same understanding. How, then, if these activities are not in any strong sense distinct from one another, can one confirm the other? Why are not *both* artificial constructions of legal materials?

8. See Stanley Fish, *Is There a Text in this Class: The Authority of Interpretive Communities* (Cambridge: Harvard University Press, 1980), 330–332, 338–339. See also Hans-Georg Gadamer, *Truth and Method* (New York: Crossroads, 1985), 251–253; Michael Oakeshott, "The Concept of a Philosophical Jurisprudence," *Politica*, September 1938, 204.

9. This implication of idealism has been worked out with great virtuosity by Stanley Fish; see "Working on the Chain Gang: Interpretation in Law and Literature," 60 *Texas L. Rev.* 551 (1982); "Wrong Again," 62 *Texas L. Rev.* 229 (1983). See also Gadamer, *Truth and Method*, 258–274.

10. Stanley Rosen describes this inversion thus: "It is not we who are assimilated into textuality; to the contrary, the text is assimilated into us. The result is . . . a disappearance of distinctions, hence not *différance* but identity. By a dialectical inversion, Heraclitean flux is indistinguishable from Parmenidean monism." *Hermeneutics as Politics* (New York: Oxford University Press, 1987), 144.

11. John Austin, *The Province of Jurisprudence Determined and The Uses of the Study of Jurisprudence* (London: Weidenfeld, 1954), 184.

12. See Hegel, *Philosophy of Right,* pars. 137–139.

13. See Joseph Raz, *The Authority of Law: Essays on Law and Morality* (Oxford: Clarendon Press, 1979), 233–249.

14. This dilemma arises not only in extraordinary situations involving unjust laws but also in the more typical case of first impression—where no preexisting rule covers the facts of the case. Here the judge is torn between his moral duty to do good (according to his conception of the good) and his legal duty to decide in favor of the defendant. When we consider as well the problem of open-textured rules, we begin to see how pervasive is the positivist's ethical dilemma. When it is ambiguous whether the facts of a case come under a particular rule or standard, the judge may with equal justification (and equal guilt) apply his personal morality or seek clues to the lawmaker's desire.

David Dyzenhaus has argued that the positivist is committed to resolving dissonance in favor of upholding unjust laws, because positivism makes sense only within a Hobbesian framework that sees submission to fact as the only alternative to anarchy; see *Hard Cases in Wicked Legal Systems: South African Law in the Perspective of Legal Philosophy* (Oxford: Oxford University Press, 1991). However, there is no reason to equate the argument for positivism with Hobbes's particular version of the argument. The appeal of positivism is enduringly assured by idealism's failure to support a viable conception of the rule of law and hence of legal obligation. If we view positivism as a quest for a stable ground of legal obligation rather than for an empirical condition of peace, then we will understand why it cannot find rest at either pole of the antithesis it faces.

In contrast to Dyzenhaus, some contemporary positivists argue that *nothing* pulls the positivist judge toward submission to law as fact; see, e.g., H. L. A. Hart, *Essays in Jurisprudence and Philosophy* (Oxford: Clarendon Press, 1983), 72–78; Raz, *Authority of Law,* 233–249. But why then are these same positivists so anxious to find a normative dimension in law? See H. L. A. Hart, *The Concept of Law* (Oxford: Clarendon Press, 1961), 79–88; Raz, *Authority of Law,* 155.

15. One may think to have resolved this dilemma by adopting Bentham's advice "to obey punctually [and] to censure freely." See Jeremy Bentham, *A Fragment on Government* (Oxford: Blackwell, 1967), 10. However, this resolution is a merely verbal one. Why obey punctually (i.e., without independent moral reflection) if there is no obligation to obey the law? And if there is an independent obligation to obey the law, then censure from an external moral standpoint is beside the point.

16. For Fiss, the antipodes that shared this fate were the law and economics movement and Critical Legal Studies; see Owen Fiss, "The Death of Law?" 72 *Cornell L. Rev.* 1 (1986).

17. R. Dworkin, *Law's Empire* (Cambridge: Belknap Press, 1986), 225. Henceforward this book is abbreviated in the text as *LE,* and numbers in parentheses refer to page numbers of this book.

18. Dworkin's argument against essentialist theories is that they fail to account for the existence of theoretical disagreement about law; see *LE,* 31–44. However, this is an external critique, because essentialist theories, not being interpretive, do not submit themselves for verification to existing practice.

19. For a critique of Dworkin along these lines, see Catherine Valcke, "Hercules Revisited: An Evolutionary Model of Judicial Reasoning," 59 *Mississippi L. J.* 1, 54–57 (1989).

20. Ronald Dworkin, "My Reply to Stanley Fish (and Walter Benn Michaels): Please Don't Talk About Objectivity Anymore," in W. Mitchell, ed., *The Politics of Interpretation* (Chicago: University of Chicago Press, 1983), 287.

21. Dworkin contrasts the external skeptic, who denies the objectivity of interpretation, to the internal skeptic, who denies the coherence of the practice. The former is an epistemological claim, the latter an interpretive one.

22. The internal skeptic may deny that one substantive hypothesis fits better than any other, but he does not deny that his skeptical interpretation is the right answer. He assumes without question that it is. Yet the arguments of the internal skeptic are the only skeptical ones Dworkin will countenance; see *LE,* 86: "The only skepticism worth anything is skepticism of the internal kind."

23. See Allan Hutchinson, "From Cultural Construction to Historical Deconstruction" (Book Review), 94 *Yale L. J.* 209 (1984).

24. See Owen Fiss, "Objectivity and Interpretation," 34 *Stan. L. Rev.* 739 (1982); Richard Rorty, *Objectivity, Relativism, and Truth* (Cambridge: Cambridge University

Press, 1991), 21–34; Stanley Fish, "Fish v. Fiss," 36 *Stan. L. Rev.* 1325 (1984); Gadamer, *Truth and Method,* 258–267.

25. See Gary Peller, "The Metaphysics of American Law," 73 *Cal. L. Rev.* 1151, 1181 (1985). Charles Taylor has let us see what the validation of an interpretation to a dissenter must mean within a hermeneutic framework that has renounced the independent object; see "Interpretation and the Sciences of Man," in Charles Taylor, *Philosophy and the Human Sciences: Philosophical Papers* 2 (Cambridge: Cambridge University Press, 1985), 54: "[I]n the sciences of man insofar as they are hermeneutical there can be a valid response to 'I don't understand' which takes the form, not only 'develop your intuitions,' but more radically 'change yourself.' This puts an end to any aspiration to a value-free or 'ideology-free' science of man." In view of this outcome, it is ironic that Richard Bernstein, who endorses the movement "beyond objectivism," laments the fragmentation of modern political life, wonders how it came about, and searches for ways to recover the *phronesis* of the polis (which, of course, was based on a belief in an objective human good); see *Beyond Objectivism and Relativism: Science, Hermeneutics, and Praxis* (Oxford: Blackwell, 1983), 157–159.

26. See Taylor, "Interpretation and the Sciences of Man," 52–57.

27. See Bernstein, *Beyond Objectivism and Relativism,* 166–167.

28. John Rawls's notion of "reflective equilibrium" captures the dialogic structure of valid interpretive claims; see *A Theory of Justice* (Cambridge: Belknap Press, 1971), 20–22.

29. Friedrich Nietzsche, *The Will to Power,* ed. W. Kaufmann (New York: Vintage, 1968), 305–306.

30. Id., 306–307. See also Friedrich Nietzsche, *Beyond Good and Evil,* in Walter Kaufmann, ed., *Basic Writings of Nietzsche* (New York: Modern Library, 1968), 209, 213–214, 219.

31. See Rosen, *Hermeneutics as Politics,* 177. The interdependence of these poles is the central insight of Jacques Derrida; see *Of Grammatology,* trans. G. Spivak (Baltimore: Johns Hopkins University Press, 1974), 61, 158–159.

32. Nietzsche, *Will to Power,* 301.

33. Id., 306–307.

34. For a lawyer's intuition of "complementarity" see Izhak England, *The Philosophy of Tort Law* (Aldershot: Dartmouth, 1993), 85–92.

35. Roberto Unger, *The Critical Legal Studies Movement* (Cambridge: Harvard University Press, 1986), 5–11.

INDEX

Designer:	U.C. Press Staff
Compositor:	Prestige Typography
Text:	10/12 Baskerville
Display:	Baskerville
Printer:	Thomson-Shore, Inc.
Binder:	Thomson-Shore, Inc.